Virginia Satir

Virginia Satir

Her Life and Circle of Influence

**edited by Mel Suhd,
Laura Dodson, and Maria Gomori**

Science & Behavior Books
PALO ALTO, CALIFORNIA

Printed in the United States of America.

Library of Congress Card Number 99 075618

ISBN 8314-0087-0

Cover design by Jim Marin/Marin Graphic Services

Manuscript editing, interior design by Rain Blockley

Printing by Banta

Contents

Preface

The structure of this book attempts to show the organic relevance of Virginia Satir, who helped pioneer the field of family therapy. It contains the first published biography of her, followed by biographies and autobiographies of people whose work and lives she affected greatly. Mel Suhd, the original series editor who came up with this new "bioanthology" format for relating history, compared this to talking about the whole tree: the central trunk as well as its many branches.

Otherwise, in almost every field, we often learn about just part of the tree. Theory and methods appear in isolation from the context of development—the roots, sprouting, growth, evolution, and off-shoots—of the individuals who creatively forged them. Likewise, we often learn about gre at people in isolation from the stories of their colleagues, mentors, friends, and family.

That stands in sharp contrast to the style of Virginia Satir, who taught that if we do not live what we teach, "we become liars." She believed that all levels of human interaction need congruent communication, in which intentions align with verbal and nonverbal messages. She believed people could teach and learn congruence (1988a, p. 371):

> My thesis is both simple and logical. If we bring up chil-
> dren in a peaceful context in which adult leaders model
> congruence, the children will become peaceful adults
> who, in turn, will create a peaceful world.

Realizing that "what heals the family heals the world," she became increasingly aware of the challenge of our time: to foster what she called "peace within, peace between [persons], and peace among [nations]." Until her death in 1988, she strove to heal community and cultural systems by drawing on her remarkable grasp of systems theory on the family level.

She spoke of wanting to train "movers and shakers" all around the planet. Each could be a hub in a larger network, part of an international community. To an extent not generally recognized, she did succeed. Wanting people to experience and learn how to develop community, she inspired hundreds of thousands across the country and then around the globe.

Her books, particularly *Peoplemaking*, reached millions. She demonstrated her methods before large groups, not only at universities but for the public at large. Particularly at her extensive residential trainings, she also shared her vulnerability. Attending those workshops was vital to appreciating her fully, and a certain kinship exists among those who were so privileged.

One thing common to Virginia and almost all the authors who so generously contributed chapters to this book was a process she called Family Reconstruction. In this powerful psychodrama, one person (the "star") recreates scenes from several generations of his or her family history, choosing many co-participants to portray various relatives. Virginia focused on the rich interplay of human beings and how they experience each other. She was profoundly aware that humans are always growing: not toward perfection, but *within* the process of developing.

"It is not what happens to us that concerns me," she often said. "It is what we do with it." In other words, while we cannot change past events, we can choose what impact they have on us now, depending on whether we use our experiences for learning. The past can either contaminate or illuminate the present and the future. This is our choice.

She also asked each star to make what she called a Circle of Influence: a map showing the people who were important in his or her life. These people are role models, and we develop our inner resources (parts) according to experiences we have with them. The circle's graphic representation allows us to see our involvement with each other, much as this book attempts to do. It shows Virginia through the accounts of people who studied or worked closely with her and so became like an extended family for her as well as each other. To some extent, we hope, this book creates a kaleidoscopic picture of how Virginia led her life and touched our hearts.

—*Laura Dodson*
Maria Gomori

Virginia Satir

1

Virginia Satir

by Barbara Jo Brothers

In many ways, Virginia Satir was a mystery even to those who knew her best. She also seemed to create different versions of herself when the fancy struck her.

James Hillman's (1995) "Pseudologia Fantastica: A Curious Need to Falsify, Disguise or Destroy the Story of Your Life" may throw light on the discrepancies in Virginia's various accounts of herself. Wittingly or unwittingly, she was "creating her own myth." Hillman notes that a number of highly creative people have believed that a "left-brained, linear" ferreting through their pasts for "the facts" would miss the point of their lives. Highly resistant to being put in such a box, some invented their own stories, others burned their papers. Hillman (p. 97) spoke in terms of there being more than one story for such people: "the genius is the enemy of rational accounts that *ipso facto* explain it away. The great disguiser is the *daimon*."* The angel's fable is more accurate than the literal record (p. 99).

---

* The word *daimon,* not to be confused with *demon,* refers to a kind of alter ego, a source of inspiration. Webster defines it as a subordinate deity, as the genius of a place or a man's attendant spirit.

There was such an angel in Virginia Satir. Sometimes they wrestled; sometimes they anguished. Mostly, they soared. The angel prevailed. Virginia's genius lifted family therapy beyond the walls of therapy offices and into the realms of spirituality. Virginia championed that route (Satir, 1986b):

> All my work and writings are toward this one aim: becoming more fully human. . . . I make no apologies for moving in totally different ways and I hope to move those ways on a mass level.

Lying quietly in this statement is a remarkable credo. Alluding to "mass level" meant she consciously intended to effect change in the human race as a whole. By "moving in totally different ways," she was offering the chalice of reconciliation, cooperation, and partnership. She worked to replace the centuries-old, strife-ridden competitive model based on "who's the biggest guy on the block." Her radically different model was based not on overpowering, but on *em*powering. Virginia wanted to release a floodgate of new energy that could sweep all of humanity toward the higher reaches of its potential.

She was obviously able to do so on a family-by-family basis. Why not bring the gift to the entire family of humanity? Toward this end, Virginia not only traveled the world, she also welcomed large participant-audiences. They usually numbered in the hundreds, sometimes the thousands.

I believe Virginia contributed significantly to the world's store of wisdom by weaving the two concepts together: congruence and Life Force. She spoke often of her reverence for the process of life itself, both biologically (1987b, tape 7)—as in cells and seeds—and spiritually (Satir et al., 1991, p. 19):

> We are all part of the same life force, according to Satir, and we activate rather than create life. She believed people have an internal drive to become more fully human. This intrinsically positive energy, also called the life force, exerts wholesome pulls and pushes on us—physically, emotionally, and spiritually—throughout life.

She demonstrated how congruence (in speech, thought, and behavior) could be seen as the human extension of the much larger growth force behind all of life. Congruence could be both cause (more accurately: point of entry) and effect of this powerful force. She created exercises in which participants *experienced* the weave, leaving the rest of us to do the writing about the results.

Virginia had found human experience holy. With virtually everybody she encountered, she brought about such a quality of interaction. She had come to understand the enormous power residing in the coherence of authenticity—in congruence of body, heart, mind, and speech.

The power of this congruence lies in its relationship to the Life Force which, Virginia had noted, moves in all living beings. She had great reverence for what she often called "a manifestation of life": the unique person. Tuning into this singularity—the richness of a given human being—was, as far as she was concerned, a kind of focusing activity involving mind, heart, and senses. This tuning in was, simultaneously, a teachable skill and spiritual event. She would deliberately pull together her own essential self and reach toward the essential self of the other. This action released the energy of the Life Force, the same energy packed into an acorn or kernel of corn. It is seed force, this truth of soul and self, which can channel through congruence of body–heart–mind–speech. It is all the same entity—a manifestation of the same mighty force we see when we find great boulders heaved aside by growing trees (Satir, 1987, tape 2). This is the same vital drive that re-knits broken bones or closes the open wound.

Virginia longed to show her trainees, clients, and colleagues the healing power she had witnessed residing in authenticity: the congruence of body–mind–heart–soul unified, expressing the same coherent message of self. This union within the one is a cornerstone for communion among the many. Virginia and her angel were aligned with the Life Force (Morgan, 1996, p. 9):

It was for her not so much helping persons fix their problems, but a
reality much deeper than that. Her words have stuck in my mind:
"It's a question of life reaching out to life!" Herein lay the secret of
what was often called the "magic" of Virginia Satir!

The seed-of-life–bearing angel in Virginia Satir knew and
wanted to show us how to mobilize and ride on the crest of that
power rather than to be smashed against the boulders of the tragic
ignorance that has afflicted humanity since Eve and Adam exited
Eden. The first "family of origin" may have eaten of fruit from the
Tree of Knowledge, but they surely did not digest it. Heartache has
prevailed among us since time immemorial, born of century piled
on century of ignorance about how to respect and nurture children,
self, and neighbor.

Virginia and her angel contended it need not be that way. It
could be different. Virginia set about to elevate humankind. A
daunting thought, perhaps, to go about seriously trying to change
the world. But Virginia also had her daimon, which ran beside her,
ran before her. As a result, Virginia's energy was as enormous as
her cause. The schedule she kept—even when she described herself as "cutting back"—was more than enough to keep at least two
people at the point of exhaustion.

Her mode was to set hope in motion. Hope was one of the
grandest gifts in her basket; reframing, one of her major tools. "We
can do it," she said. We can change the way we relate to each other.
Throughout her 50 years of professional work, she held an
unwaveringly hopeful view of the human race.

Today, countless women practice family therapy. In the beginning—in the 1950s, well before it was fashionable to be a
professional woman working in a sea of men, there was only one:
Virginia Satir. She plunged right ahead, re-inventing psychotherapy
with each plunge. When she began private practice in 1951,
therapists had only psychoanalytic thought and method, the pure

method: lie on the couch out of eye contact with the analyst, and free associate. A variation permitted therapist and patient to be upright in chairs, but it was strictly one patient at a time, and the therapist was supposed to think of him- or herself as merely a blank screen. What is now deemed good therapeutic practice—the inclusion of the entire family—was then considered heretical.

Enter Virginia Satir, a very large bundle of immensely creative energy. Nearly six feet tall and having attained that height by the age of 11, she had long been used to standing out in a crowd. Within her profession, that metaphor took larger shape as her busy, highly productive life unfolded. Concurrently with Don Jackson and Murray Bowen, she pioneered working with the whole family in therapy.

In itself, this represented considerable innovation. There was more. Far from being a blank screen, she was responsive and vivid, a wise and compassionate mirror. Utterly convinced that no evil people exist, she was passionately devoted to showing how the "evil"—the destructiveness—lay, instead, in the process between people. This conviction was a major force in her success as a therapist: it drew forth the essential personhood in the other. Essence rose to the surface in the person like cream rises through milk. The soul, however battered and broken, would flutter forth and shimmer there, bathed in the presence of Virginia's own soul. Once a person had this moment of truth, there was no going back. They would carry, forever, this glimpse into their own potential. "All" Virginia had done was to beam in on the person's uniqueness.

Her contribution goes beyond being the founding mother of a new discipline. Her work is loaded with implications for the future of psychotherapy. This became clear to me within a few years of my first contact with her, nearly 30 years ago. I would arrive at a workshop and size up the other participants, noting whose company I wanted to keep and whose I did not. By day three, invariably, the obnoxious people lost their abrasive qualities and turned into people who no longer annoyed me. The dull and boring ones had all begun to sparkle. Within a very short period, the "finest self" was forefront in each participant (Satir, 1988a, pp. 340–341):

> It was as though I saw through to the inner core of each being, seeing the shining light of the spirit trapped in a thick black cylinder of limitation and self-rejection. My effort was to enable the person to see what I saw; then, together, we could turn the dark cylinder into a large, lighted screen and build new possibilities.

Bringing into full view the higher self of each person and enabling this higher self to be plainly seen by the other was her first step. With this deeper, clearer view of each other, people naturally made harmonious connections. After three days with Virginia, we all began to see those inner cores.

As the years since her death have drifted by, I have become increasingly aware of the significance of her contribution to the healing of the woundedness of the whole family of humanity. Virginia's work provides a template for world peace. To all who would listen, she taught the basic, universal patterns and principles she had discovered that could make peace happen—peace within the person, peace between family members, peace among members of the larger family of humankind. Using the systems model, Virginia expanded the principles she had observed in microcosm—in family interactions—for application to the macrocosm.

I am among those who count the gain of having known her worth the loss of having her leave this physical plane. In a letter to her brother Russell, she wrote (Satir, 1988d): "If I should go tomorrow, I would like you and the rest of my family to meet and have a party, being more glad that I lived than sorry that I died."

I appreciate her friends and family members for talking with me and helping me know her even more deeply in the course of writing this chapter.

Ginny Pagenkopf

*Virginia Satir was known to her family of origin
as "Ginny." This was her name as a child.*

This account of Virginia's life begins with a story that occurred
nearly 50 years before her birth—one that may well be a significant thread in the tapestry of her rich and complex personality. As
a therapist, her style included creating what she called the Family
Map and the Family Life Chronology (Satir et al., 1991, pp. 206–
209). Asking clients or the client family to recount their history,
she would go back several generations to capture key stories, which
had helped shape the life of the person(s) with whom she was
working.* To an extent, I use her own model to explore her life: the
beginning stories are those of her forebears (Jahr, *n.d.*).

Maternal Roots

A 12-year-old boy sits on the front porch, holding his 18-month-
old half-sister on his lap. He doesn't know what to do; the rest of
1866, and a great cholera epidemic is sweeping this city clean of

---

*Virginia developed the Family Map to facilitate gathering social histories. Al-
though social workers had always taken notes about such history and hidden
them away in charts, she openly constructed the Family Map and the Family
Life Chronology on a blackboard or large piece of paper. Her innovative interviews made the process an integral part of initial therapy sessions, permitting
much fuller client participation.

The map used a circle to represent each family member and diagrammed
relationships among them. As well as the dates and order of births, it also showed
dates of such family events such as marriages, deaths, and miscarriages. This
in-full-view process meant that family members could follow the unfolding drama
of their own stories.

the family are lying dead inside. Along comes the man whose job it is to drive a wagon around, picking up corpses. This is Germany in in 1866, and a great cholera epidemic is sweeping this city clean of its citizens. The driver's family now being immune, he is not afraid of catching the illness. He tells the boy he cannot take him, but he will take his little sister.

Fate spared that little girl, Henrietta Simon. She is destined to become Virginia Pagenkopf Satir's maternal grandmother. Her story, which later affected Virginia on many levels, is one of orphanage, abandonment, longing, and loss. At 18, in the course of their separate emigrations, Henrietta lost contact with older brother Carl—a loss she mourned all her life. She never learned where he had gone until a year after his death.

Henrietta sailed to the New World at the request of her foster parents, the Sangbusches, who had left Germany without letting her know they were going. Now they had arranged her marriage to Carl (Charles) Philip Wilke, reportedly to settle a debt with him. One version of the story concludes with a note that they gave him a cow as well as Henrietta (Hardel, 1992).

Although Henrietta's family of origin had not been poor, her foster parents sent her out to work when she was 14. The awareness that she had originally come from a family of means set Henrietta up for the Cinderella script later echoed by Virginia as she described her role in the family to Fred Duhl (1974):

FD: The theories you've been able to abstract are so related to your own experiences in growing up. The issue of being different has been important all your life. The issue of self-esteem has been important for you in a personal way. Are there any other pieces you put together as you look back? . . . Part of it is self-esteem, the other part is uniqueness—?

VS: That has to do with paradox. There was a very strong message in my family that I was supposed to be the queen—but how in the hell can the queen also be the scullery maid? You see—

FD: Cinderella—

VS: Yes, that was one of the ways I did it. One of my early fantasies of how I
      would get out of all this was, literally a knight would come on a white horse
      and take me away. . . .

It is easy to wonder if this poignant bit of family history—the lost
child Henrietta—also reaches down the years to set up Virginia's
own wandering pothos,[1] the yearning never quite requited, the
seeking and never quite finding. Perhaps it also set up her move
from one side of the continent to the other, always intending to
eventually settle in one spot and never quite making it happen.
Fritz Perls (1969, *n.p.*) referred to her as a gypsy:

> Virginia, you have my love and my unstinted admiration. In many
> respects we are alike. Restless Gypsy . . .. You are a big woman with
> a big heart . . .
>   You have projected your need for an understanding family, and,
> correspondingly, are family-phobic yourself. Your dreams to settle
> down remain dreams.

If this gypsyness did drift through Virginia's family script,[2] her
personal response to that part of her heritage was to catch its wind
and sail on to a transpersonal level. Her work, for which she wan-
dered, was deeply meaningful to her; she quite consciously intended
to take it to all corners of the world. Her itinerant teacher mode
certainly served family therapists around the globe and carried
seeds that, in germinating, would benefit all humanity.

  Meanwhile, the other half of her family history also holds a
significant portion of what patterned this gifted therapist.

---

[1] Pothos is a classical Greek work meaning "an insatiable longing to do good;
longing, wish, or desire."

[2] In the Transactional Analysis theory developed by Claude Steiner (1974), a
given theme can be seen to flow down through the generations of a family.

Paternal Roots

Another young man in Germany falls in love with a young woman. Her people are of noble birth, including high-ranking military men. This young man is a miller. He gets her pregnant and, since it is Germany circa 1872, they marry. Three years of hostility from in-laws follow. Disowned by the woman's family, the couple decides to get out of the situation entirely. They leave for America with their first-born,* sailing from a port somewhere on the Baltic Sea, across the Atlantic, and through the St. Lawrence Seaway. Eventually, they land in Green Bay, Wisconsin—having put an ocean between them and their disapproving relatives.

These two people are Virginia's grandparents on her father's side: Ferdinand Pagenkopf and Wilhemine Hoppe Pagenkopf. After making their way to the Neillsville, Wisconsin area, they build a log cabin and later become known as pioneers homesteading in that region. (Family legend is that, en route, they buy and sell what is now O'Hare Airport: it was not good farming land.) However, this grandfather is known to Virginia as the person responsible for her earliest traumatic memory (Satir & Banmen, 1983, pp. 407–408):

> I had a recurring dream that was horrible. I was in a mental hospital because I'd killed somebody, and I'd buried them and couldn't remember where. The dream went on and on, until I did my [Family] Reconstruction. And I knew, for instance, that my mother and father lived with my grandparents, that was something I knew because my grandmother lived with us when I was born. And I knew my mother had twins when I was eighteen months old. . . . When I put the Reconstruction together, this is what I found: when my twin brothers were nine months old—I was two and a half—my mother was nursing my two brothers; my [paternal] grandfather and grandmother were

---

*This "first-born" may have been twins—the first of three sets of twins born in this Pagenkopf family.

living there [in the house with us]. I also knew that my grandfather was put in the mental hospital because he was paranoid.

So here is the picture that I put together. I'm two and a half, my mother is nursing the twins one at a time, and my grandmother is there with my grandfather chasing her [grandmother] around with a butcher knife wanting to kill her. And my mother, grabbing me . . . and I begin to feel this . . . grabbing me at this point, so hard, my twin brothers crying, my grandmother screaming, and my mother helpless to do anything about it.

Until I got to that point, I couldn't put this into anything [that made sense]. And when I did the whole thing [recurrent nightmare] evaporated because it all became clear . . . it all became clear. As these things take a meaning, it [the puzzle] then vanishes when you get it clear.

Life was not particularly gentle with Ferdinand Pagenkopf, whatever his personality structure. Along with hardships of hacking out a farm in a new country, he simultaneously contended with being a miller married lifelong to the daughter of a highborn German army officer from Stettin, Germany. (Once part of the eastern Pommern area of Prussia, this city is now part of western Poland.) Ferdinand had a reputation in the family as being tough: to display his marksmanship, he would sit in his log cabin and fire his gun through knotholes in the floor. On the other hand, it is a well-known story in the family that he felt beneath his wife despite his rough, I-can-handle-anything exterior.

Also, the family endured at least one obvious and major tragedy over which Ferdinand had no control. Lightning plunged down the log cabin's chimney one stormy night, killing three of his children who were asleep by the fireplace.

The sudden death of these siblings (one of whom may have been a 14-year-old twin) could help explain the surviving twin, Virginia's "outlaw" Uncle Emil, whose name she often used to illustrate her stories (1972b):

> wherever I go with any group of people of more than twelve, I assume
> my family is going to show up at one point or another. Uncle Emil
> shows up the most; he was in jail [as] a horse thief for a long time!
> [*Audience laughter*]

This example of Virginia's use of humor is not necessarily to be
taken literally. Uncle Emil existed, but I have come across no evidence that he spent time in jail. For Virginia, poking fun at her
own relatives served to universalize "shameful" family skeletons
in a constructive way, cutting away that which would contribute to
further diminishment of self-esteem among family members.

On occasion, she also spoke of her paternal grandparents.
While Grandfather Pagenkopf was, according to Virginia, "ambi-
tious, cruel, mean" and a potential murderer, she described his
highborn wife as "queenly and competent—of royal lineage." In
the 1974 interview conducted by Fred Duhl, she spoke of Grandmother Pagenkopf's importance in her life:

VS: The females in my family, especially on my father's mother's [Hoppe] side,
were part of the royal family of Germany—literally. And the men were all
low-caste group. That image of the queen was held up. No one ever said
exactly that but I heard it a lot. And then I always heard I looked like my
grandmother and there was all that kind of stuff so there was that message.

FD: The grandmother who married the commoner is very central in your images?

VS: Very central; and she was also the one I was close to. Interestingly enough,
the one my mother was also close to, and my father. So there had to be a
queen.

FD: That was where the warmth was.

VS: Exactly. So that was what happened to me.

She speaks clearly about Grandmother Pagenkopf as representing
"the hearth" as well as the inspiration in this family. If not for this
grandmother's presence, it would seem that the extremely warm,
nurturing person we knew in Virginia virtually would have had to
make that personality style herself out of whole cloth. Interviews

with cousins and other relatives suggest that there may have been a very high degree of emotional distancing throughout her entire family, existing, paradoxically, alongside a pressure to stay nearby, physically and geographically. Aunt Helen—the other maternal relative said to be closest, emotionally, to Virginia—cannot, to this day, simply say the words, "I love you" (Counsell & Counsell, 1992). Virginia learned well the bitter price paid for such diffidence. Apparently, she saw and—with her own keen mind—was able to make sense of the damage done.

Out of the great, puzzling mixtures of pain and possibility, she was able either to make sense of the confusing family dynamics, or to transcend them, or both. Partly from her experience in her own family—added to the thousands of families with whom she later worked—she evolved her foundational theories about communication in families: how communication between the self and the other affects self-esteem and, conversely, how self-esteem affects communication.

Virginia's own words for her mother, Minnie Wilke, were "powerful" and "courageous." Other family members describe Minnie in ways that suggest she may have been considered willful for a woman of her day. One cousin said: "Minnie would say what she thought," suggesting that Minnie took after her own father (Carl Wilke), who was said to be a stubborn man.*

This same cousin describes Henrietta as a "gentle person who never complained," which contrasts sharply with other descriptions of this grandmother, including Virginia's. Virginia (1974) spoke of Henrietta as "small, nasty, 'meddly,' bitter, and scared of sex."

At a presentation on differentiation and integration in families (a meeting that also featured Murray Bowen), Virginia demonstrated

---

*This information is hearsay that transcends generations. The cousin who told me this part of the family story was not even born until several years after Carl Wilke's death.

her thinking about her family of origin, using her own model of sculpting the various members. She went on to say that she would like to be able to meet her maternal grandmother today [1974], nearly 30 years after she knew Henrietta, who had tended the children when their parents went out to dances. Pondering possible positive aspects of the grandmother she had not liked in childhood (Satir, 1974), Virginia would have liked to look with adult eyes at this woman.

Virginia had spoken of "splits" in her mother's family of origin that her mother hoped not to have repeated in her own family. Such splits could certainly be one way to explain such apparent contradictions in descriptions of personalities of the Wilke women. The face Henrietta showed most often in Virginia's household may have reflected her relationship with her daughter, the "willful" Minnie. Henrietta had her own rules about how "children" ought to behave in response to parents. Virginia's youngest brother, Ray Pagenkopf (1992), recalls accompanying his mother, Minnie, to visit his grandmother: "We would not be there more than a couple of hours before they would be in a fight and we would leave." Being a child, he "would always wonder why they had to leave when they had just gotten there."

Minnie had married in defiance of Henrietta, who already had another man picked out for her. In Henrietta's day—and certainly in her personal experience—the woman was not a key participant in the decision about whom she married. Minnie may have had her way on October 15, 1915, the day she married Reinhold Pagenkopf, but the man she married may never have come up to the Wilke standard.

Alfred Reinhold Oscar Pagenkopf was stormy old Ferdinand's youngest son—the youngest, in fact, of thirteen, which included three sets of twins. Some had been wiped out by the lightning before Reinhold was born, but nine were alive after he arrived. Minnie, on the other hand, was the second daughter of seven children, with one of the younger siblings being a boy six years her junior. One could speculate that Minnie was used to being in charge even in relation to males. She was three years older than Reinhold, whom many family members describe as being tall and silent or "never having much to say." Virginia referred to him as "sometimes uncertain"—noting that he stuttered (Laign, 1988, p. 29)—while using those words "powerful" and "courage" to describe her mother (Satir, 1974).

In spite of the plans of her small, "meddly" mother Henrietta, Minnie Augusta Marie Wilke insisted on marrying the tall and handsome Reinhold—even though he came from a "rougher" family than the Wilkes. After all, they were carrying on a tradition established in each of their families: one of the women "marrying down." Besides, as noted, Minnie was known for having a mind of her own. Her sisters were not impressed with Reinhold (an assessment that did not change over time).

A week or two past nine months after the wedding, Virginia Mildred ("Ginny") Pagenkopf was born. It was June 26, 1916. Earlier that year, on January 3, Carl Wilke had died. The 25-year-old Minnie must have been still missing him acutely during this, her first year of marriage and her first pregnancy. He died just two and a half months after her wedding and not quite six months before she gave birth to Ginny.

Carl and his daughter had been close. According to Virginia (1974), Minnie had been Carl's "favorite field hand; he would take her out to work with him in the fields."* The loss must have been immense for this newlywed mother. Thus, little Ginny was born

---

*This is the kind of detail that Virginia would have been quick to note, had she been gathering family history in a session. She might have stopped at this point and asked for role players to recreate scenes from the first months of this marriage.

into a situation already burdened, if you will, simply by the timing of her entry into the world.

At this point, Minnie and Reinhold lived on the family farm that belonged to Ferdinand, who was still there with Wilhemine. Old man Pagenkopf had begun to slip into some kind of psychosis, and at some point, the family put him into an institution. (But not before he engaged in the scene that so frightened little Ginny that she dreamt about it for the next 40 years or so.) He died the day before Halloween of the year when Ginny was two.By that time, Ginny already had a set of identical twin brothers, Russell and Roger. They had been born when she was 18 months old. A photograph, taken when the twins were about nine months, shows a very serious little Ginny towering over the baby boys. She could not have been much more than two herself. She has that resolute look in her eye, as if she has already assessed this situation and understands determination and perseverance will be the order of the day.

Virginia with her twin
brothers:
Russell and Roger

In one training session, while illustrating the Family Map, Virginia (1972c) gave a poignant view into her own early childhood:

> I'm in this slot right here [gesturing toward a circle representing the first-born]. Then came two twins—these are males—then comes another female, then comes another male. There is seven years' difference between here and here [pointing at the first-born circle and last-born circle]; my mother had five kids in seven years. These two [the twins] came into the world—one three pounds and one four pounds—and there was a death thing around them, a death fear that lasted almost three years . . ..
>
> . . . For twenty years, these two people [her parents] I was estranged from because of *terrible* messages that I had to take charge, which I couldn't do. . . .
>
> When my mother was dying, I flew every two weeks to her bedside from wherever I was and I had a chance [to ask]—because at that time I was able at least to ask the question that I also had in my head when I was a little kid. And I could get to her personhood.
>
> I could understand, for instance, why it was that these two [the twins]—I was only 18 months when they came—[were so much the center of attention]. I didn't know there were all those death fears around them. I [also found out later] it was at the same time that my father's father was living with us and was psychotic and periodically would chase his wife around the table with a butcher knife while my mother was nursing these two and trying to keep me out of trouble. *[Plaintively and wistfully spoken:]* All I remember is being pushed away. And so, very early, there was the feeling that my mother hated me and that my father was weak and ineffectual and I was supposed to be Queen Mary—to carry the honor of the family somehow.

In addition to the considerable tension Virginia described in her immediate family, work was also always an issue. Some cousins suggest that Minnie was always working and Reinhold was always at the tavern. Ginny stayed with her favorite Aunt Helen awhile, perhaps as a refuge—there being nothing substantial available at home, emotionally speaking.

Virginia said (1972c) her father "always provided for the family." However, she also said (Satir & Banmen, 1983) that her father did not like farm work and "didn't always know when to come home," leaving her mother to do a lot of the work.* When the family first moved to Milwaukee, he got a job as truck driver, which might have meant he would have been away from home for long periods even if he were working. It is possible that Reinhold *did* work— and Minnie worked harder, at least in the eyes of her side of the family.

What is clear is that these were the Depression years and the family was poor—"poor, frugal, and industrious" (Hardel, 1992). A great deal of work was necessary to make ends merely meet. Virginia's younger sister Edith once mused that Virginia "was mad at me because I got all the candy. But there wasn't any candy." Edith was trying to make sense out of why Virginia developed such an aversion to her. As far as Edith was concerned, the aversion was without explanation and happened suddenly, right after Virginia moved to California in 1959.

Time after time, relatives say that the family members "each went their own way," or "We all worked all the time and they [Virginia's family and Minnie's sisters' families] all worked all the time." Very little candy, either literal or metaphorical.

Virginia certainly did not collect the great pool of warmth for which she was to become famous from her parents' relationship with each other. Three weeks after her father's death on February 19, 1972, she reflected (1972c):

> My father was alcoholic for a number of years. He always provided,
> but his beautiful self never *really* got manifest. The scene that I saw

---

*Each family member has a different view. For example, although Virginia stated her father was an alcoholic, neither Ray nor Edith would describe him in those terms.

[the day before] my mother went into the hospital [seven years before my father's death]:

[Before leaving for the hospital, she asked] to come out [from her bed to where] my father [was sitting in the living room]; what she said to him was, *"I'd rather die than go home and live with you."* He moved not a muscle. [She asked then for me to take her back to bed.] I looked at him and the *pain* that came to me. That two people that I knew for years hadn't really connected with one another. And I knew that there was great hope in the beginning. Anyway, she went to the hospital and she died [on March 29, 1964].

The following Thanksgiving I was with my father and my brother and my father who has had psoriasis for thirty years showed me his leg and it was crystal clean. I said to him, "When did this happen?" And he said, "The day of your mother's funeral it started to go away." Now came the death of my mother and my father going through paranoia, leukemia—he got well from both of them—and looked like he was coming into a space in his life he had never been.

In her interview with Fred Duhl (1974), she talked about her struggle to make sense out of her parents' relationship:

VS: . . . at that point [after her parents' deaths], I understood the pieces; it wasn't like it was when I was a child. Because I could make sense that [their relationship] had turned to this kind of way—these two people who were so disappointed in one another. I shudder to think of that scene if *I* hadn't been where I was. You know, I estranged myself from my father for twenty years. I told him when I was age twelve, "I'm leaving when I'm through with college," and the day after graduation from college I left, and I didn't go back for twenty years.

FD: He was the labeled problem in the family?

VS: Yes—"if he had been different . . .." I came, of course, to change [that attitude]. And I was in contact with my mother. But I graduated with my first degree on Friday noon; on Saturday I left. Like that.

She once described having run away from home when she was 12. As she told the story, her family did not find her for a month. When they did, she was a hundred miles away from home and had a job cleaning houses (Satir, 1986a). She related this vignette in session with a family who had experienced having an adolescent who ran away. It may have been only a part of her way of making a connection with the family rather than a factual, literal description of an event that took place in just that way. However factual or fictional, the account may well reflect an inner truth of how she *felt* at 12. At that age, she "did not believe her father had a heart" (Satir, 1974).

Although cousins speak to the contrary, her description of her maternal Grandmother Wilke as a little, dried-up, sour woman remains to be considered. This was the unfortunate Henrietta, sitting in her brother's lap on that porch in Germany, then riding away from him on the cart carrying her parents' bodies. No candy there, for sure.

Aside from the influence of Grandmother Pagenkopf, where did Virginia get all the warmth for which she was so famous? Some of her relatives in the Midwest might contest that "warmth." They read in the paper, years ago, that she would be speaking at a university in the city and went to see her. She was surprised to find them in the audience. They were hurt. She had not even contacted them to say she would be in town; if they had not read it in the paper, they would not have known. They didn't understand why she distanced herself so. Children were born, grew up, married; Virginia missed it all.

She did come when her brother Roger (one of the twins) killed himself in June 1979. Yes, she came. Spent a week and was very good. She had also come when her younger brother Ray's wife died suddenly; Virginia stayed and helped with the children. To that Midwestern part of the family, she was always busy, always working, always trying to get somewhere she wasn't. But not with them.

I believe Virginia was under both the burden and the blessing of a mind of a whole different order than even the average very bright person. Tall—so much bigger than the other children that they didn't think of her as another child—she was not like the rest of them. They had little, if any, idea of what she was about. Whom did she talk to in those days? Her Aunt Helen Wilke Counsell, only ten years her senior? Probably; Virginia very soon would have reached the intellectual level of her aunt. Well before puberty, she would have had the intellectual capacity of an adult.

Perhaps Aunt Helen sustained her in her adolescence as Grandmother Pagenkopf had sustained her in her childhood. According to Aunt Helen's youngest child, David Counsell (1992), Virginia had lived with Aunt Helen for a while. He had presumed she might have been going to college but thought it likely that she simply found his parents' home more pleasant. "Virginia's mother was always working, and her father always at the tavern." But the family rule about not displaying affection publicly also must have prevailed in this household; it is Aunt Helen whom her son and daughter-in-law characterize as still being unable to say, "I love you."

Virginia could. She turned to me as we were exiting an elevator at a seminar she was giving in Miami in March 1988. "Do you know that I love you? I helped birth you, you know."

I remembered. Seventeen years previously, in 1971, this "birthing" had been part of a month-long workshop I had taken with her. Now, for some reason, this particular exchange with her, standing there in the hotel corridor, went straight to my center without bouncing off my usual defenses. Flooded with the memory and the intensity of her suddenly bringing this reality into my awareness, I couldn't think of anything appropriate to say that would acknowledge the depth of my appreciation in that moment. I did want her to know, yes, I know you love me. I turned and hugged her.

I wondered at how wooden she felt in response. I felt a little embarrassed for having suddenly turned and embraced her. Knowing my own tendencies toward holding myself back from engagement with others, I did not even consider trying to sort out what was in her and what might be my own projection. I consoled myself that one could hardly hold oneself guilty for perpetrating hugs—and the message in her face had come through with that crystal-blue clarity that her eyes could carry. Ultimately, it did not matter anyway; I loved her, and I did know she loved me.

The following story—another version of the scene of violence between her grandparents—throws light on that subtle distancing quality in an otherwise extraordinarily warm and nurturing woman and on the puzzling incongruity I had encountered. In an Avanta Process Community program at Crested Butte, Virginia was preparing the group for training in Family Reconstruction. Using herself as example, she repeated the recurring dream generated by her paternal grandfather's psychosis, adding (Satir & Banmen, 1983):

> Everything is registered. . . . I go on the principle that everything that ever happens to us is registered in our consciousness somewhere and available for accessing under certain kinds of conditions. . . . So what I want to put before you is that you have soaked up, I have soaked up, all kinds of stuff and it's registered. What we have to do in our lives is to be able to sort it out and make sense.
>
> . . . That terror [the violent scene between her paternal grandparents] translated itself to me, and once I got all that out, all the nightmares in relation to that disappeared, because I was able now to put whole sense to something that was only frightening [before].
>
> Now, if I expand on that a little bit, the terror to my body and the inability to do anything was not a conscious thing; it was that my body was in that state. Then I was able to see; I know that crazy people act like that. I know they pull out knives, and I know what it is like for a woman to have a young child at her breast and to be frightened and not to want to leave the child, what her hands and arms must have felt like to me in holding me like this. She was holding me out of both wanting to take care of me and out of her fear [of] what would happen to my body. *I couldn't stand for people to touch me for years.* And all that was some part of this.

All right. When I got this all clear, really all clear, what happened then is my body could begin to act differently. Because all that stuff that was registered now came in for some conscious kind of way of understanding this, because it all makes sense. But it doesn't make sense until I could do that [conscious processing] . . .. [*Emphasis added*]

If this experience does not explain when and how Virginia learned to give, it does shed light on why it was so much harder for her to receive for herself.

Life in her family of origin may have had the moments of inspiration she described in her presentations and interviews in her later years. It also held considerable challenge on many different fronts. The scene between her grandparents may have been the beginning of life-threatening events in little Ginny's life, but she also remembered a direct threat to her own life when, at five and a half, she almost died of appendicitis.

Virginia and her mother, Minnie Augusta Marie Wilke

Ginny's mother, Minnie, had been a Christian Scientist since age nine, when her own mother Henrietta had endured what the family at the time perceived as a serious illness. A brother-in-law had met Mary Baker Eddy and suggested they try the Christian Science route since everything else had failed. Henrietta recovered and Christian Science was embraced.

Thus, when little Ginny became ill, Minnie would not allow her to be taken to a doctor. The argument between her parents about taking her for medical care continued for three weeks. Eventually—and, no doubt, in desperation—Reinhold scooped her up and took her to the hospital in Marshfield against Minnie's wishes. When he got there, according to the story Virginia related in the summer of 1988 (King, 1989, p. 17):

> I was nearly dead. Peritonitis had set in by the time my father took me to the hospital, and they said I was dead anyway so why try, but he said, "She can't be dead; she has got to live!" They got somebody to do surgery, but I was in the hospital a long time—several months.

The story is that Reinhold burned Minnie's religious books after Ginny returned from the hospital. In retaliation, Minnie cut off her beautiful, wavy red hair.

This whole incident took place right around the birth of Ginny's younger sister Edith on December 15, 1921. Minnie was either about to deliver or was nursing Edith when it occurred. The new presence of a baby sister in the middle of five-and-a-half-year-old Ginny's life-and-death struggle might not have endeared the new sister to her. Any sick child wants and needs her mother—Virginia understood that this life-threatening illness had been pivotal in her early childhood decisions about how to relate to people.* It

---

*She considered this "early childhood decision" to be an example of the pattern described by her longtime friends Bob and Mary Goulding in *Changing Lives Through Redecision Therapy.*

was at this point that she made a decision to focus her life around working hard instead of engaging emotionally with her parents. Feeling a strong tug to protect both of them against the other, she emotionally disengaged herself and put up an internal barrier that would create problems for her for years to come—problems manifest in her resistance to relating closely. This is paradoxical. Although she was masterful at relating closely in the process of working with any given family, Virginia never quite mastered that level of relating in her personal/social life. She believed this incident—and the decision she made around it at five and a half—set her up for her terminal illness, the pancreatic cancer that later took her life (Satir, 1988c).

In and around the struggles to survive in those early years, life on the farm went on. Like her relatives, Ginny lived on a farm on which most of what they grew went to feed themselves. These farmers all hoped to sell enough extra cream from the cows to pay with money for whatever necessities they could not make or raise. Farm families work hard, and they work every day. Cows need milking twice a day, no matter what the day is like or who is in Congress at the moment. While little Ginny lay so ill, somebody still had to be feeding hogs and chickens and pitching hay for cows and horses.

Ginny Pagenkopf attended a one-room school three miles from their farm. The children usually walked there. When the weather was extremely cold, Reinhold made the rounds of other farmhouses and took the children to school by sled. In the old-fashioned schoolhouse, all grades met in one room at the same time. This enabled Ginny to learn very quickly what was taught in all the grades. Virginia said she taught herself to read at age three, with the only four books her family owned. She didn't know how she did it; she just remembered wanting to know what the books said. In various accounts (Weeks, 1974; Duhl, 1974), she said:

> First of all I took the Sears, Roebuck catalog—that was my wishing
> book, the *Aesop's Fables,* a cookbook, and the Bible. Those were my
> four books and I used to run my mother crazy with all that.
>   ... I taught myself to read at age three. By the time I was nine, I'd
> read 900 volumes—the whole [school] library—including the 24 vol-
> umes of the book of knowledge.

She had also read most of the books in the public library (King,
1989, p. 17). About her grammar school experience, she said:
"There were only 18 kids. I listened to all the kids, you see, so at
seven, I'm running around quoting 'Thanatopsis' and knowing all
that stuff" (Weeks, 1974). Partly as the result of having this advantage of the education in the small country school and partly
because of her own intellectual gifts, she entered high school at
age 12.

Meanwhile, on brighter days and very occasional Sundays,
relatives would come for dinner out on the farm. Minnie was known
to be an excellent cook. As various relatives (1992) remember these
scenes, Ginny is not out swinging with the rest of the children. By
then, she was 11 or 12 and probably was helping in the kitchen. In
any case, cousins and siblings do not remember her being outside
with them. "She was so much bigger than we were," they say, and
"We twins played with each other, Edith played with Ray, and Virginia was by herself" (Pagenkopf, 1994).

Having no complaints about her sister and looking back over
their mutual childhood, Edith's attitude seems to be characterized
by more by wistfulness than anything else as she muses (Hardel,
1992):

> "Solace." I will never forget the word solace. I had a theme due for
> English class and Virginia was helping me with it. She told me to
> change whatever word I had used—I can't even remember now—and
> use solace instead. She was, of course, always so good in school.

Would not the word *solace*—solace on deep levels—characterize
much of Virginia's interaction with her world-scattered clientele?

Curiously, regardless of Virginia's feeling of alienation from her sister, Edith's stated memories are of help with homework, being included in fun activities, and thinking that Ginny was beautiful. Whatever went on between them in their childhood, Edith seems to have been left with the feeling of having been well treated by her big sister.

Ginny's siblings remember going down to the creek to meet the Native American children who lived on the other side of it, probably of the Winnebago tribe that lived in that area. The creek was as far as either group was allowed to play, so they would meet there. (One wonders if Virginia's motivation for Tiyospaye—her extensive project with the Sioux to help heal the scars left by Wounded Knee in South Dakota—had a root or two on the shores of that creek.)

All the same, little Ginny faced considerable stress in her childhood. Her father was often absent, and at some point her mother began taking to her bed for most of the afternoon. Virginia spoke of Minnie becoming depressed after the birth of the fifth child, Ray, and remaining so for some eight to ten years. One relative used the term *nervous breakdown* to describe Minnie's depression; another thought it was a physical condition.

Russell Pagenkopf (1994) remembers Minnie being physically ill during the year that he and Roger were freshmen in high school. The twins would come home from school in the middle of the day to give their mother lunch.

He also remembers that, after he and Roger had graduated and left home, Minnie went through what he describes as a "breakdown." He presents the episode as being emotional in nature; his impression was that it was due to "exhaustion from raising five kids." To recover, Minnie went back to Neillsville and spent two or three months with her sister Hattie.

Ginny was not in the house during either of these periods. At the time of the illness described by Russell, she would have been

16 and a freshman at Milwaukee State Teachers College. This is presumably the period when her cousin spoke of Virginia living with her Aunt Helen. Otherwise, her studying time would have been consumed by nursing Minnie, doing housework, and taking care of 11-year-old Edith and nine-year-old Ray.

It is easy for a family therapist to speculate about Minnie's reported illness coinciding with her daughter's entry into the adult world. Ginny had left the family nest, and it may be that the absence of her able assistance helped precipitate Minnie's physical collapse. Even though Minnie strongly supported education for her children, Ginny's departure would have been a notable loss. Minnie had relied on her help for years. Now Ginny was working and taking 21 hours of college course work during her freshman year. Household duties would not have fit into that schedule.

Wherever Reinhold may have been during these times, he was apparently not a resource for Minnie's physical care. And however powerful she may have been (to use Virginia's word), the record shows that in Minnie's case, power may have been laced strongly with physical weakness. As she was a Christian Scientist, she consulted no doctors; so no medical evaluation ever weighed physical versus emotional etiology of Minnie's illness.

At any rate, as the eldest child—and an extremely bright, capable one at that—Ginny had grown up shouldering responsibilities inappropriate for her age and developmental level. At age seven, for instance, she took on far more responsibility for the care of her baby brother than she otherwise might have done (Satir, 1974). In a family with rules against talking about "negative" things or expressing anger, the toxic quality of such rules left lots of room for disappointment and little room for expressing that pain (Satir, 1971; Satir & Banmen, 1983; King, 1989).

One relative said that Christmases were always difficult for the children because Reinhold would stop off and drink before coming home. Admitting to coming from a family that included alcoholism, Virginia preferred to reframe it considerably in one interview (Laign, 1988):

FOCUS: In recent years, we've seen a proliferation of self-help groups. What do you think of the adult children's movement?

SATIR: There's a problem I have with it. The adult child of an alcoholic is supposed to have all kinds of things in common with other ACoAs. But that is not how it goes. I'm glad we're saying that what goes on in the family affects people. But it seems like there's so much hurrah about the ACoAs that they are the only ones who ever got affected by anything, and that's not true. What has happened is that a new nomenclature has developed, just as it did in psychiatry, and that gives people a license to stop growing. I don't go in for those labels, Literally, I'm an ACoA, but I don't regard myself as such.

FOCUS: How was your family affected by alcoholism?

SATIR: My father drank too much and I think he was an alcoholic—but that was only part of him.

FOCUS: His drinking caused no problem for you?

SATIR: That's right. It wasn't my fault. See, I knew that my father drank because he didn't feel good about himself. Oh, sure, I knew that as a child. I grew up with the fact that my father stuttered; he was the last of thirteen children; he had real difficulties with his parents, and all kinds of things. So I knew that his drinking was a reaction. I never considered it anything against me. I was sad because my father wasn't available to me sometimes. I felt sorry for my father. I couldn't admire him. But he would give his last penny to buy me books. He worked against great odds, and he always took care of his family.

Obviously, this statement does not quite square with comments by other family members, particularly in regard to Reinhold's work patterns. There were many splits both within the Wilke family as well as between the Wilkes and Reinhold Pagenkopf; the viewpoints of one faction could be generated and colored by feelings as well as facts. One branch believed that it was Minnie who was holding that family together.

Virginia's statement reflects her tremendous respect for human beings and her ability to look at the bigger picture. She knew about her father's problems with his parents; she understood. That was her brand of family therapy—that deep empathy with *each* member of the family, whatever the individual's surface shortcomings.

Sixteen to eighteen years had passed between her previous statements about her difficulty in dealing with her parents' toxic relationship with each other and the 1988 statement about her father. True to her beliefs, she had continued in her own quest to see those parents as *persons* (Minnie and Reinhold) rather than roles (mother and father).

This goal—putting person before role—was also a significant part of her teachings about the therapist's use of self (Satir, 1987a). It also exemplifies how her personal philosophy and professional philosophy were the same. In her work with families and in training sessions, she made a point of referring to all family members by their given names rather than their roles. Her purpose was to highlight each as *person* in the eyes of other family members, to cut through the hierarchy that comes with roles.

The new tone of the 1988 interview reflected Virginia's evolving perspective on her own family as well as her positive beliefs about people. Having found the psychoanalytic perspective so limited and corrosive to self-esteem, she evolved a theory of human dynamics that heartily encouraged a positive view of human nature. She held that motivating psychological/emotional growth required firm convictions about people's innate goodness. Thus, this interview is as much a statement of her personal and professional philosophy as it is a statement about her relationship with her father. Virginia believed deeply in *living* her work. In the time between making these two statements about her father in 1972 and 1988, she formed a clearer image of Reinhold the person—a much fuller picture than that of the father of her childhood.

Part of the household picture, according to her sister Edith, was that neither of their parents could read or write English. Her mother allegedly could not read at all, and her father read only German. In spite of this, he would bring home a copy of the *Milwaukee Journal* every day, sit down, and hold it up as if he were reading it. He would then casually turn to the twins and ask one of them to read him a section here and there, never admitting aloud that he could not read.

During the long afternoon periods of Minnie's resting, Edith says she and Ray would come home from school, climb on the bed with their mother, and teach her to read. Eventually, after ten years of the depression or illness, Minnie had become literate (Hardel, 1992).*

In 1929, the family lost the farm. This had something to do with Reinhold's father having left a will bequeathing money that he did not have in cash. Fulfilling the will had thus required mortgaging the farm in 1919. Now came foreclosure—the fate of many a family farm in the year 1929.

The enormous change brought mixed feelings: grief at leaving, on the one hand, and hopes about providing for the children's higher education, on the other. The latter was very important to her mother, according to Virginia; Minnie had intended all along to

---

*Ray Pagenkopf (1992) does not remember his mother as being unable to read or write. Nor does he remember the story his sister tells of the two of them teaching her. He does recall once receiving a letter from Minnie. Although he too was unaware that his father could not read English, he learned sometime after graduating college that this was the case.

Edith reports that her mother went to school briefly but was frustrated by attempts to make her write with her right hand. Ray says Minnie went until the eighth grade. Reports from all quarters are that Minnie was very bright, so in regard to her not being able to read, the question arises about whether she may have had a learning disorder.

move them to the city when it came time for high school (King, 1989; Duhl, 1974).

The United States was sliding into the Great Depression at the time. This hard-working family was destined to continue to work as much and as diligently as they had on the farm, and maybe more. Reinhold got a job driving a truck. Minnie went to work for a seamstress. A few years after the move, the twins built bicycles for themselves and worked in truck gardens on the outskirts of town on the weekends. The job allowed them to bring food with them when they pedaled back home.

Meanwhile, Ginny scrubbed floors on her hands and knees, earning money for school. She worked so hard she developed what was probably Osgood-Schlatter's Syndrome: a breaking down, under trauma, of the bone at the front of the knee. This condition can develop in young people who subject their growing bones to undue stress (Baldwin, 1992). Her sister has memories of Virginia being in extreme pain from this condition but slipping past her mother and hobbling to school anyway. That is how badly Virginia wanted to learn, and that is how hard she was willing to work.

The whole family's hard work enabled them to move from the poor neighborhood on South Thirtieth, where they had first lived after leaving the farm, to Seventh Street off Center. Minnie enrolled in vocational school to learn tailoring, taking her skill with needle and thread to another level. Edith reports that Ginny, who had graduated from college the same year Minnie completed her tailoring course, learned sewing from her mother during her visits home on weekends after her out-of-town teaching job.

High creativity and productivity ran alongside the family pain and limitations. Once a means to survival, Minnie's work rose almost to the status of art form, winning state-fair awards for tailoring. Having mastered the basic principles, she constructed fine articles of clothing. This quality—taking very little and transforming it into something much more valuable—may represent a paradigm for Virginia's passion about liberating the most challenging clients from their restricted lives into fullness and abundance. Thus, she may have learned more than sewing from her mother.

Creativity, determination, and diligence were among Virginia's life-long characteristics. Although the image of Ginny scrubbing floors is that of a young woman whose adolescence spanned the Great Depression, it is also a still frame of her life. She never stopped working that hard. As she lay dying, she was still so deeply involved that she told those who were conducting workshops for her to call and keep her posted. From her sickbed, she also viewed videotapes of these Avanta trainers giving the seminar she would have led. Ardently committed to her vision, she yearned for that work to continue (Dodson, 1991b).

She had a vision of freedom for all of humanity: freedom from the psychological burden we all carry from misinformation about our basic nature, and freedom from the distortions we gather through childhood. Virginia called these *old learnings*. She believed that all people are doing the best they know how for their children with the information available to them at the moment. Our parents only pass on lessons learned from their own parents and from their own childhoods, as well as what they learned about parenting from their own parents. "As parenting goes, so goes husbanding and wifing," said Virginia in 1971, during a month-long seminar in Glenwood Springs, Colorado. Or, as she said more specifically at a two-week seminar on Aruba the following March (1972c): "Mothering goes as goes husbanding and wifing; [your] husbanding and wifing goes as went [your] mothering and fathering."

Virginia's goal was to educate people—by example as well as instruction—to both the possibility and the benefits of cooperative behavior. She wanted to liberate us from the unnecessary misery of old learnings and to show us all that we are shining suns. She said (Starr, 1992, pp. 8–9):

The first thing is doing everything I can do and be [so as] to shed light, to help somebody else open up, develop the kind of consciousness that makes it possible to *join*, to *cooperate*. That is number one and if we don't do that, nothing else matters. Now on one level that is a big job. . . . That is such an alien idea to us, to be cooperative, so alien that it takes a lot to deal with it. I would predict that if we were able . . . to consciously handle ourselves *in such a way as to reflect the light that we have in our being* and in our dealings with people, that [alien idea would move, and cooperation would come into place]. [*Emphases added*]

The concept and, more importantly, the activity of *being* was critical in Virginia's framework. She considered the vital point in her work to be this meeting of each other at the essence point, at the very base of our being.

Ginny Pagenkopf ⟹ Peggy Pagenkopf ⟹ Peggy Rogers

In her young adulthood, Virginia went through a series of nicknames corresponding roughly to her development from a girl into a woman.

Milwaukee's South Division High School yearbook prophetically said: "'Ginger' wants to be a traveling teacher; but, with her love of dramatics and stage make-up, she may end up as a famous screen actress." With her enormous intellectual capability, she could have become whatever she wanted to become; it was her very big heart that drew her in the direction she eventually went.

Motivated in part by the Depression, she carried extra credits to move through school faster. Virginia Pagenkopf graduated from South Division High School in Milwaukee in 1932. A few weeks before her 16th birthday, she went to see the registrar of admissions at Milwaukee State Teachers College. Showing him her diploma (and the three dollars in her pocket), she said she wanted to register as a college student. Apparently, her potential and credibility were obvious even at age 15. The registrar enrolled her—although he did put in a call to her mother when she left, wondering where the rest of the money would come from. Her mother advised him that Virginia would do what she said she would do. Minnie had, after all, watched her daughter almost cripple herself in the process of working to get an education.

Virginia worked at Gimbel's Department Store and for the Work Projects Administration, and took care of children on weekends. Carrying extra credits, she graduated with a Bachelor of Education in 1936, a few weeks before turning 20. A photograph shows her in a graduation gown with her two parents. From left to right are her six-foot-four father, managing to look as silent as he is described as being; her much shorter mother, chin jutting out in a pose of triumph; and a beaming Virginia. She graduated third in her class, which assured her of a job on graduation. Less than ten percent of her fellow graduates found work.

Her first teaching job was in a consolidated school in Williams Bay, Wisconsin. On weekends she took a bus home, or sometimes the twins would drive out to get her. She next took a job teaching for two years at Lake Geneva, Wisconsin; then, in September 1938, at Jones School in Ann Arbor.

During this period, she became "Miss Peggy." As she told it (Duhl, 1974), "The kids couldn't pronounce [Pagenkopf] so started with 'Miss Peggy.' Another piece to that was my mother's favorite sister-in-law was also Peggy—Aunt Peg; she was also my father's favorite sister."

After teaching in Ann Arbor, Peggy Pagenkopf taught for a year (1939–1940) at a private school in Shreveport, Louisiana.

Being an excellent horsewoman, she gave jumping lessons in her spare time. Her sister Edith has a picture from that time, showing Peggy in a riding habit. Their aunt Helen rode horses (and kept riding into her 80s), so this was apparently another interest Virginia shared with this aunt.

Virginia told me of delightful excursions to New Orleans during those days. She would take the train from Shreveport, stay at the Monteleone Hotel, and have dinner at Galatoire's. She came to meet a certain man. She never said who he was, but her eyes glowed when she told the story.

Perhaps a complete discussion of Virginia's romantic relationships is not relevant for this short biography. However, anyone who encountered her even briefly came away with a sense of her earthiness and her lively interest in men. In her seminars, she gave attraction and sexual energy the attention they warranted as integral factors in human relations. She often used the topic of sex to engage her audiences, taking a certain amount of pleasure in the mild shock value of her frankness. She very definitely had a sense of humor and a highly developed sense of play.

Her old friend Vince Sweeney observed that Virginia's career always seemed to take precedence over her romances. On more than one occasion, he had seen her "leaving her current boyfriend standing in the wings with his hat in his hand" (Sweeney, 1992). According to Virginia, this career-first attitude had its roots in her childhood: it was her "earliest wish to become a children's detective on parents that led [her] into teaching" (Brothers, 1983, p. 48). In turn, teaching led her into social work and toward family therapy.

Wanting to know the children she taught, she would go home with a different child every day after school, unless a teachers' meeting took priority. Her pupils did well in school, which she felt was due in large part to her being so close to their families.

Virginia told of the particular incident that pushed her into social work (Brothers, 1983, pp. 48–49):

> A little kid about ten years old came to school one morning and he looked so awful I said, "What happened to you?"
>
> He said, "I was locked out last night; my father came home drunk and I was locked out."
>
> That night I went home with him and I talked to his father. I wasn't "psychiatrically alert" [i.e., she was not being more preoccupied with diagnosing than relating] at the time so I didn't have any trouble talking to the father. Because I got to know the families so intimately I saw all these problems. So I thought, there's got to be more I need to learn about all this. That's when I decided to go on for an advanced degree to help me understand about all these problems, and all I knew about was social work.
>
> That was in 1936; 1937 is when I started my first summer school at Northwestern University because I wanted answers . . . I was always looking for information for how things could be better for people. I wanted to understand what was going on. I never went into social work to become "a social worker." I went into social work to find information to help me understand people. . . . I used any information I got to help me understand more about people, how to help people, and, of course, part of that was understanding myself. Then I got into social work school and went summers while teaching the rest of the year. I would be applying the stuff that I learned and so it just evolved that way. Every time I learned something, something else opened up.

The graduate school at Northwestern University closed within the next few years, ending the part-time approach toward the advanced degree that "Miss Peggy" had been fitting into her summers while she taught in the Ann Arbor area. In those days, it was not uncommon to work part-time for several years toward an advanced degree. However, at a certain point in any social work program, it is necessary to complete a field-work experience. When Peggy enrolled in another school for this purpose, it was at the University of Chicago, in 1941. She was 25 years old.

She met with resistance from her field supervisor and got a "C" in field work her first semester. This is a failing grade in graduate schools of social work. Supervisors have sole discretion over field-work grades, but Peggy knew her supervisor was psychotic. (Two years later, that person committed suicide, jumping off the 44th floor of a building in New York City.) Peggy protested to university authorities. Unfortunately if not unexpectedly, a school official treated her the way such people too often treat students. Paying no attention to her assessment of the situation, the person encouraged her to leave (Brothers, 1983, p. 50). For a young woman whose energy was so dedicated to learning about human dynamics, this episode must have been a frustrating and stressful event.

It was 1941 and wartime. By the end of that fall semester, Peggy had married Gordon Rogers. Leaving school did not seem like such a bad idea. She postponed her academic pursuits for the time being.

Marriage was in the air that year for the Pagenkopf siblings. Edith married Rubin Hardel on August 30. Peggy was not only in the wedding, she and a Japanese friend catered the whole thing. According to Edith, the food was marvelous because Peggy was a wonderful cook who loved the process.

On November 8, Roger (one of the twins) married Enid, who lived across the street from his Aunt Clara. And then, on her way home for the Thanksgiving holidays, Peggy met Gordon Rogers (King, 1989, pp. 36–37). Virginia recounted the story in her interview with Laurel King:

> You see, in 1941 there was such anxiety in the air because we were mobilizing troops and we hadn't declared war, but you saw soldiers everywhere. Most of us, on some level, knew that there would be war coming—terrible things. So among the younger people there were all kinds of anxieties; women wanted husbands, and the men wanted to

have somebody at home because it was kind of like having a link. I hadn't dated that many men, although I had done enough.

So I was taking the train home for Thanksgiving and needed to leave my bag with someone at the station while I went to the washroom. There was this very handsome fellow sitting there in uniform, and I asked if he would watch my bags. Well, it turned out that his mother had just died and he had come home on a furlough for her funeral. He was kind of down, so we talked, and it turned out that he was at an air force base outside of St. Louis. I invited him to dinner because I was taught that you offered hospitality to these men.

Well, he was twenty-two and I was twenty-five, and within a short time we decided that we would get married because he was going overseas. And we did. We got married at midnight and I will never forget it. I wore a black dress.

Two of her younger siblings had married recently, and Japanese forces had just bombed Pearl Harbor on December 6. Add those factors to her unfamiliar situation with school going badly, and it begins to seem not quite as strange that 25-year old Peggy Pagenkopf would decide to marry a man she had known for less than a month.

Contrary to what Virginia said later, her relationship with Gordon endured about eight years. She spent considerable time with him on various bases until the end of the war. So vivid was his presence in Edith's mind and memory that she did not even remember him as having gone overseas at all during the war. Ray says Gordon *was* overseas for a while, in England, as the master sergeant in a ground crew of the Eighth U.S. Air Force.

Prior to that, Peggy Rogers had followed Gordon to his bases in Delaware and Miami, where she taught school. A picture of the couple in Florida shows palm trees in the background. When he was posted to Texas, she worked at a social agency to find foster homes for children. From 1941 to 1948, she and Gordon also socialized with Edith and her husband Rubin. For holidays, the Rogers would leave the military base and get together with the Hardels.

After her initial bad experience with the University of Chicago and during the early days of her marriage to Gordon, Peggy had continued to work at the Chicago Home for Girls, a residential facility for difficult adolescents. It had started as her field placement—not a particularly good one. But Peggy and the new director, Ruth Topping, ultimately transformed the place into one of the outstanding treatment institutions in the country.

During the metamorphosis, the same university person who had counseled Peggy out of graduate school joined the home's board, ironically. After that, Peggy was able to write her own ticket in terms of social work education.

Meanwhile, at some point during her employment at Chicago Home for Girls, she took a particular interest in one of the young residents. Between 1942 and 1944,* a 13-year-old girl, Mary, moved into the home. Edith thinks either Mary or her sister Ruth arrived during a big Thanksgiving dinner that Peggy had cooked. Edith was also there; she used to help Peggy with these events, setting the table and doing other such tasks.

The police had called to say they were bringing some girls to stay at the home and advised Peggy that she needed to be careful, as these children were "wild" and would fight the staff. In fact, Edith recalls, one girl refused to participate in the Thanksgiving meal; she spent the afternoon locked in a bedroom.

Whenever they actually arrived, Mary and Ruth came from an extremely abusive family situation in another part of the state. Edith thinks Virginia later visited the family and confirmed this. Ruth (now Ruth Turpin) suggests that, in the home's rather rough environment, Peggy felt protective of the young Mary. Ruth was in a different group home (Turpin, 1994).

---

* This time frame is from both Virginia (in King, 1989) and Edith Hardel (1992).

In June 1943, Peggy became seriously ill with an ectopic pregnancy.* A doctor told her she would be unable to have children. It was her understanding that this pregnancy and infertility had some connection with the ruptured appendix she had survived at age five. In any case, this was very bad news to Peggy, who until then had envisioned home and children as part of her future.

Subsequent to her work at the Home for Girls, the university placed Peggy at the Institute for Juvenile Research, one of their best available field sites (Duhl, 1974). After completing her thesis, she graduated in September 1948 as Virginia Mildred Rogers. She now had her master's degree in social work from the University of Chicago School of Social Service Administration.

The same year, Gordon and Peggy moved to Dallas, where Gordon had family. They took the young Mary with them. She was then about 17—too old for the Girls Home but too young to be out on her own. Edith and Rubin helped pack and drove down to Texas with them, staying a week to help them get settled. Edith has a picture of herself and Peggy taken at 1319 Idaho Street in Dallas. By January 2, 1949, Peggy was working at the Child Guidance Clinic in Dallas.

Chronicling Gordon and Peggy accurately is difficult due to Virginia's later reticence about the marriage. She did not feel inclined to be clear about this particular relationship, leaving the impression that Gordon had left immediately after the wedding and that she had hardly seen him between the time they married and the time she divorced him. However, Ruth Turpin and relatives fill in the story to some extent.

After a few months in Texas, Mary asked Peggy to allow her sister Ruth to join them in Dallas. Eleven months younger than

---

*Satir (in King, 1989, p. 37) gives the time frame as "within two months of the marriage." However, notes in Virginia's own handwriting suggest the ectopic pregnancy occurred in June 1943 in Texas (Satir Archives).

Mary, Ruth was then facing the same dilemma of having outgrown her own Forest Grove Children's Home. Peggy and Gordon consented and, although Ruth had been very happy in her group home, she describes the next two years in Dallas as idyllic. Not only did she live in a nice house and a room of her own, she finally had two responsible, caring parents.

Well organized in the domestic department, Peggy had refinished some furniture for their rooms and had sewn bedspreads and curtains. The girls went to school regularly, and in the evenings Peggy had delicious meals available.

The girls loved "Daddy Rogers," so the only fly in this otherwise honeyed ointment was Peggy's schedule. She made sure those meals were ready, but her work at the office meant she was rarely at the table herself. Over time, the girls and Gordon became a cohesive family unit, having bonded in Peggy's absence. In fact, she began to feel left out—a theme that had begun in her family of origin and continued throughout her life.

Additional stress arose when 18-year-old Mary, who had an afternoon job as a carhop, got pregnant. Between this and other strains, the home they had all entered with such enthusiasm and high hopes crumbled, along with the marriage. Edith's version of the breakup includes a memory of Peggy and Gordon having a terrible fight at the Nine Mile Inn on the way back from some holiday at the farm (probably Thanksgiving 1949).

On December 7, 1949, Peggy sent a letter asking the Child Guidance Center to accept her resignation as of January 31, 1950. Lewis Lefkowitz (1950), the attorney to whom she addressed the letter, replied:

> It shall be my reluctant duty to recommend [your resignation's] acceptance with regret.
>
> In the course of your work here we have recognized your great value and your real competence. We trust that you will go on in your

work, continuing to serve effectively, and that at some date we shall have the privilege of further association with you.

As to my personal regrets for your departure, I think you well know the cordial relations that have existed and which I regret to see now terminated.

By age 33, in her first job as a fully degreed professional social worker, Peggy obviously had made quite an impression.

After filing for divorce, she took Mary and Ruth back to Chicago. Ruth was heartbroken at leaving Daddy Rogers, but she could see how there was no way he could have kept them: "He was too bruised by the divorce" (Turpin, 1994), which was finalized on July 17, 1950. Within a few months of their return to Chicago, the two young women—both past their 18th birthdays by now—went back to their old home town.

Pagenkopf family members all liked Gordon very much and were sorry to see the split occur. "They were really meant for each other." Edith reports, however, that Gordon did not like Peggy's focus on work rather than on their relationship. For her part, Peggy apparently felt bitter about the end of the marriage.

Virginia later spoke about her identity in those years as her marriage was ending and before her career began taking on clear shape and brilliance (Duhl, 1974):

FD: Once upon a time you were known as "Peggy Rogers." I didn't even know that. I didn't even know who Peggy Rogers was.

VS: "Peggy Rogers" is really quite a different person from Virginia Satir, and that set me to thinking: how many people we house in our skin from time to time—and yet how there is a theme between all these people.

FD: When your skin was named Peggy Rogers, where were you?

VS: I was in transition, I was married. I was going, I think from a little girl to the outer trappings of a woman but not really knowing much what it was about. I found some old pictures of myself not long ago; there is some resemblance, physical resemblance. How naive I was at that time, terribly idealistic—without any awareness of any feeling of my impact on anybody else. 'Cause I never expected there would be any impact for me, 'cause I

was too busy trying to figure out about having a place. Still something I
don't know a whole lot about. I know *something* about that now.

As this interview continued, Duhl commented on Virginia's surprise at being called sexy by Duhl and Frank Pittman at a meeting
of the *Family Process* board in Venezuela in 1972. She explained
her surprise as parallel with her response when somebody asked
her how it felt to be famous: "I don't know how to answer that
'cause I don't feel that way. It's the same kind of thing."

Duhl pursued this apparent lack of clarity of identity on her
part by asking if she was "scrambling to find a place in her family
back in Wisconsin."

She said, on the contrary, "In those days I was very secure in
the boundaries I had. . . . I had no question about who I was. . . . I
was a tall, fat girl who was bright and had to serve people. There
was no question about that." She had begun her married life, her
young adulthood, as Peggy Rogers. During those years, she had a
sense of security while not knowing what was missing. The "scrambling" began when she was about 30 and "began to see there was
something different," began to see the world beyond the param-
eters set by her family of origin.

This evolution started when she "began to feel uncomfortable
in her relationship with her husband." At that point in the interview, she also talked about her very painful experience with her
own psychoanalysis, which took place in Chicago with an analyst
from Chicago's psychoanalytic institute. She said: "I suffered a very
serious setback because then I got into the psychoanalytic stuff
and then I *couldn't* find out [who I was]. All those lovely ideals
went down the drain, all the ways I was going to serve my husband
and all that." She added, "Another thing, too. I was very curious
and looked at everything that came along. I had no prohibitions
about reading anything. And, like anybody else, when I have seen

something, then I can't *not* look." She had found out that there could be more to life than serving a husband.

Virginia agreed with Duhl when he observed, "Something was not going right and analysis changed the way you could act," but she pointed out that the change had been quite adverse: "It limited [the way I could act] tremendously. I'm certain that experience [analysis]—which came at a time when I was really hurting—set new boundaries, but they were negative boundaries."

Duhl wanted to know more about the pain to which she was referring. She told him of the terrible impact of the ectopic pregnancy very early in her marriage. "That shot all kinds of things for me. What followed that was a very serious period of psychological depression and physical problems, you know. But it was also a period, as I look back on it now, to give up what I had set out for myself—to be mother, wife, and all this kind of stuff."

The analytic situation seemed only to have added another kind of pain. She described how "the new boundaries that came out of the psychoanalytic thing were very negative . . . because all my feelings got into negative space. Like that poem: I couldn't be angry, I would have to be hostile; I couldn't be loving, I would have to be seductive; I couldn't be ignorant, I would have to be stupid. All these kinds of things."

Virginia took on the labeling that was inherent in the psychoanalytic process (Duhl, 1974):

> Oh, yes, I bought that for a long time because, don't forget, I had a long history in learning how to accept from somebody else on the surface what I was supposed to be. . . . Except I didn't buy it really and that's what kept me going, I think. But, officially, that made a lot of negative kinds of things. What it did for me was to give me new boundaries and new boundaries are always helpful, but what they bind is something else again.

She noted that the label-makers "incidentally, were all men." Duhl assumed that there was a connection between the analysis and the end of the marriage. She allowed the assumption to stand.

Virginia was an intensely sensitive human being; in regard to empathy, her giftedness included a very deep experience of any given emotion. In most discussions of her two marriages, she minimized the nearly ten years she spent with Gordon. This may have been not because they "did not see each other," as she often said, but because the experience of their relationship and divorce was so emotionally painful for her that she chose to edit the story. Her statement would be quite true, metaphorically speaking. Engaged in being Peggy Rogers, she did not experience herself as being well known in those days—not to herself, let alone others.

Virginia's youngest brother, Ray, reflects on what he knows of her during those years. He speaks with some feeling about having written her for help during that eventful year, 1949; he needed some money for food as he was trying to finish college. She did not even answer his letter. He says it "did not take much of that to make him feel like she was not interested in contact." After that, he said they all began to be busy with families and children, and that was another reason for little contact (Pagenkopf, 1992).

Ray says that Virginia had told Russell, Edith, and him that the family "had kicked her out." They replied that was not true and that it was *she* who had isolated herself from them. Poignancy is thick in the stories of this sister and brother both at critical points in their own lives: her state of mind in 1949 when she did not answer Ray's letter; his hurt and disappointment at having such an urgent request ignored. In a sense, Peggy Rogers was engaged in her own battle for survival. This was the time of the "very serious period of psychological depression" that she mentions in the Duhl interview.

The year 1949 was also when she began her estrangement from Gordon, among the most painful events in her life. With the moves back and forth between Chicago and Dallas, she may not have even received the letter. In any case, Ray's attempt at communication could hardly have come at a worse time. Big sister Peggy, emotionally depleted from her engagement in her own internal struggle, would have had very few inner resources available to attend to little brother's request, however valid. My impression is that the two had never resolved this specific event and probably never discussed it in the years that followed.

This is a telling illustration of Virginia's (1968) statement about the pathos of family relationships: "Too often families are strangers, burdens, or enemies to one another."

Not until 40 years later, in 1986 at Ray's retreat in Alaska, did the two of them have the opportunity to spend quality time together. Ray also had become a social worker. He served as head of Alaska's Department of Public Welfare until his early retirement in 1977, when he decided to stop and simply enjoy life. Ray and Virginia had a lot in common, Ray also being very bright and having a deep interest in improving the lot of humankind.

Why had they not spent more time together? Full schedules and the distance to Alaska are the obvious and superficial answers. And, as Ray points out, the sibling order/age difference had affected how close they were as children: "A 20-year-old and a 12-year-old don't 'chat,' you know" (Pagenkopf, 1992).

He thought her lack of reply to his rather urgent plea for help in 1949 was a good example of how her own behavior served to isolate her from her family. To dip, for a moment, into speculation on her point of view: if she did receive his letter, it probably would not have occurred to Peggy Rogers to make her baby brother a confidante during her emotional trials in the late 1940s. She was too imbued with the idea of taking care of others to allow herself the emotional vulnerability of telling him what was really going on in her life. Ironically, it was this very candor that she taught so eloquently in her therapy and training sessions. Being able to allow herself that same emotional availability was another matter. The tragedy of human alienation is built across such gaps in communication.

Thus, her apparent lack of interest in contact could have had much more to do with her having stayed locked into her big-sister, caretaker-of-others role. Those who worked closely with her in later years experienced this paradoxical reticence alongside her great warmth and sensitivity to others. One colleague who had worked around the world with her for years was not aware until five years after Virginia's death that her surgery in December 1982 had been prompted by a uterine malignancy. Genius therapist though she was, and in direct contrast to what she taught, Virginia never learned how to get enough emotional support from others. She almost always kept to herself that which was most important to her.*

In her conversation with Fred Duhl, her image is of a very vulnerable—if gifted—young woman picking her way through her own personal pain and through the rubble and remains of the life of Peggy Rogers. In the late 1940s, her life as Virginia Satir was just a glow on her horizon.

My interview with her some eight years after the Duhl interview focused less on her personal life and more on the roots of her career. She also said she entered analysis at some point after her graduation(Brothers, 1983, pp. 49–50):

BJB: What kind of personal therapy did you get?
VS: I went through a full psychoanalysis and actually the main things never got touched. That was another thing, I had a good analyst from an analytic point of view but the things that were really basic to me, really troubling me,

---

* For example, having coincidentally called her office the day before Virginia was scheduled for that surgery, I sensed something was very wrong as I spoke with her worried staff. I asked and, too congruent to hide the situation effectively, they decided to tell me. When I then called Virginia, she confirmed that she did not want the information repeated.

never got touched because psychoanalysis is limited in its ability to handle things. When I was through with it I said to myself, "There's gotta be more than this." Because, actually, I see the whole thing of psychoanalysis as a rather pessimistic thing about the hopefulness in people. While I have a great deal of respect for Freud as someone who opened the barriers, I don't consider that Freud and psychoanalysis have that much in common, because he was somebody who was always moving ahead and psychoanalysis got frozen in time by his followers.

I went into analysis, after I had already finished the school of social work in the late 1940s, because I was having some rather serious physical problems. The physicians told me, "This is not a physical problem; it's a psychological problem." So the only thing I knew to do, being in a city and in work that was so psychiatrically oriented, was to get psychoanalyzed; so that's what I did. It helped the physical things, but it didn't really remove the basic things behind them. So I felt even more freedom then to look to see what else there was. I didn't see anything else, so I started looking at me.

Peggy's depression certainly did not slow her down. Within three years, she shifted into high gear.

Virginia Satir—Chicago Years

Virginia's life soon compressed several major events into a short time. She had obtained her master's in 1948 and separated from Gordon Rogers in late 1949. Now she began undergoing psychoanalysis, opened a private practice in Chicago, conducted her first family therapy session, and entered her second marriage in 1951. A telegram to her parents, now in Edith's possession, reads:

September 1, 1951

Mr. and Mrs. R. Pagenkopf
Box 605, Carmichael, California

Norman and I married today. Wish you could be here. Reception today. Very happy. Tell Rus and Jane.

Love, Virginia

Norman Satir seems to have sprung from nowhere into Virginia's life. None of her long-time friends and Avanta colleagues have any idea how she met him. Nor have her siblings or her adopted daughter Ruth heard any stories about how the two got together.

Although some members of the family liked Gordon Rogers better than Norman Satir, all agree that Norman was a decent enough fellow—"he was interested in photography, always had a camera with him" (Pagenkopf, 1994). According to Virginia's brother Russell, he was a lithographer and a union representative. Ruth and Mary, meeting him for the first time, found him "cold." He did not like children, and he did not like the two sisters (Turpin, 1994).

Virginia volunteered little information and invited no questions about this marriage. In many ways, she was a very private person. Jane Gerber (1993), one of her longest-term colleagues and friends, recalls being at a party at Virginia's apartment while the couple still lived in Chicago. Norman was there, but Jane never crossed the room to meet him.

Norman was Jewish, and Virginia was enamored of Judaism. Her first cousin David Counsell quotes Norman as having said, "Virginia is more Jewish than I am." After she and Norman moved to California in 1958, she stopped her tradition of sending her Aunt Helen a Christmas card. Instead, she pointedly waited until well after that holiday to mail a "season's greetings" card.

Meanwhile, along with beginning a new marriage, Virginia began her part in the inventive creation of a new mode of psychotherapy: including the whole family in simultaneous treatment. She called this *conjoint family therapy.*

While she created this new modality partially as a result of the experimental attitude that characterized all her work, she was also on a conscious quest to improve on psychoanalysis, which was the only kind of therapy in practice then. She had found it wanting. Her own analysis had failed to help her identify or address vital issues, and she was disillusioned about the derogatory attitude inherent in the analytic mode. These were motivating factors for her creation of a comprehensive, growth-based model.

Inventing family therapy meant venturing into the whole system from which a person emerges. By asking the entire family to attend sessions, Virginia could observe people's whole context and intervene in any aspect of it. She could actually watch (rather than just hear about) the family dynamics: how the behavior of one family member affected the rest. All in all, through working with the entire family, she found herself able to promote the emerging personhood of parent and child alike.

Her insights into what would be therapeutically useful were by no means always the result of a series of happy accidents, as she would sometimes present it. They were the product of her relentless search for knowledge—for salient information on human behavior—and of her remarkable genius for synthesis.

By 1951 she had seen her first family (Brothers, 1983, p. 59):

> I went into private practice in 1951, and, in 1951 in Chicago, of course, everything was completely psychoanalytic. I got the people that nobody else wanted. I knew the psychoanalytic method wasn't going to work so I was [starting] from scratch. Of course, you can't always be from scratch because you're influenced by things, but one thing I didn't do was that I never followed the dictates of the psychoanalytic idea that you had to be aloof from your patients. I really violated a great many things in that regard. I was still looking for something more. There had to be something more and so that's kind of how that all started. And then it just evolved from there. I'm still looking.

One of those "violations" was seeing the client's family. In those heavily psychoanalytic days, this was considered a serious breach of good therapy. This "transgression," now a well-known psychotherapeutic discipline, was the beginning of her work with families. Today, of course, the mental health field actively prescribes what it once forbade—after the pioneering work done by Virginia Satir, Murray Bowen, and Don Jackson.

This was the first year of Virginia's private practice, when even having more than one "patient" in one's office at a time was unheard of. She described this seminal incident (Satir, in Brothers, 1983, p. 51):

> In an accidental way, I had stumbled on to working with a family. . . . Very briefly: A woman of about twenty-six had come in and things began to change very much. Her diagnosis—one we used to give at that time—was called ambulatory schizophrenia—whatever that is. Anyway, things were going very well, [then] after six months her mother called me and threatened to sue me for alienation of affection. Whatever happened to me that day I don't know, but I heard her plea—the words were a threat but her voice was a plea—and so I asked her to come in and she did. She wasn't supposed to but she did. We were back at square one with her daughter—as I had seen her the first time. So I began to take a look. What's going on here? So I worked with it. Some changes came about and one day I thought to myself, "I bet that girl has a father and that the woman maybe has a husband." Sure enough, So I asked, "Why doesn't he come in?" So he came in and then both of the others went back to square one [regressed]. What I was beginning to see were the roots of what is now called communication, incongruent messages of affect and the verbal, and then I began to see the beginnings of a family system. Well, I said to myself, maybe they've got some more kids. Sure enough. So it took me about a year and a half to do this, but each time I learned something there I would do it with others. And I got the people who were hopeless, I don't know how they found out about me. Gradually I brought the whole family together. The son who came was perfect—the perfect son and the crazy daughter. You see that many times. Well, at that time I was learning about family structures, family process, and family communication. By the time 1955 came around I had seen about 400 families.

Her willingness to depart from the norm paved the way for Virginia's brilliant insights into the critical relationship between self-esteem and communication. With two clients in the consulting room, the therapist can observe interaction as well as participate. Virginia's work thus assumed that all human experience is relational. Individual dynamics could almost be said to be an illusion, as no human being ever functions as utterly separate from other human beings. Our young do not scramble alone to the sea like young turtles. Even the monk in contemplation in the desert still carries internalized dialogue from his own family of origin. Any psychological theory explaining the human animal must take into account the intense interactional factor. Virginia, whose mind was never limited by practices currently in vogue, understood this.

By this time, the quality of her work was beginning to become known. She had already distinguished herself in institutional treatment during her work with Ruth Topping at the Chicago Home for Girls. The psychiatric consultant with whom the two worked, Henry Von Witzleben, had encouraged Virginia to start a private practice and offered her the use of his office. She was then part of a movement to improve training for psychiatric residents and to improve Illinois' state hospital system (which ranked about 33rd in the nation at that point). Spearheaded by the Mental Health Association, the movement was led by R. Novick and Jerry Horab, both "very good psychiatrists who cared about people" (Satir, in Brothers, 1983, p. 51).

They engendered the Illinois State Psychiatric Institute, a training facility scheduled to open in 1955. The program would begin at the Chicago State Hospital and transfer once the new institute was ready. Dr. Kalmen Gyarfas, then head of the Chicago State Hospital, called Virginia in January 1955 and asked, "Will you come teach family dynamics?"

She was astounded. She did not know that people in the mental health field knew about her work with families. She accepted the invitation (Brothers, 1983, p. 52).

> The residents [physicians in training] saw me before they saw any-
> body else; Kalmen was very family oriented and he knew it would
> really work. His name has never been associated with the real roots
> of family therapy in this country but he's very much there. We had
> planned that the residents would not see any patients, they would see
> only the families of the patients; and so I was the one who taught
> them about families.

Among those residents was Ivan Boszormenyi-Nagy, who later for-
mulated the Contextual Family Therapy approach.

Immersed in the psychiatric residency training, she read all
the psychotherapy literature, including Don Jackson's "Toward a
Theory of Schizophrenia." One day in 1956, she found a reference
to Murray Bowen, who was hospitalizing whole families. She felt
good to learn she had company. Until her discovery of Bowen's
concurrent work, she said she had experienced herself as being
"totally alone." They were the first two people to take that pioneering leap of working with the whole system rather than with one
identified patient in a family. She contacted him and responded to
his invitation to come visit him at the National Institute of Mental
Health.

By that time, the life she and Norman shared in Chicago had
become very hectic. She soon had a full practice (Satir, in Brothers, p. 52):

> I had two full offices then, one on 30 North Michigan and one out in
> Hyde Park. I was also consulting to a school [Franklin Park Public
> Schools] and building up a guidance program on a guidance prin-
> ciple rather than a crisis one. I was working with industry and heaven
> knows what—all kinds of stuff.

Her career had taken off and was running pell-mell ahead of her
personal life.

☆   ☆

☆

Virginia Satir—California Years

*Even though the name change—from Peggy
Rogers to Virginia Satir—occurred in Chicago,
the dramatic future that the world came to
know as Virginia Satir emerged in California.*

Moving to California became a critical turning point for Virginia. On the personal level, it was almost as if she had "left town and changed her name." Her sister Edith marks the move as the beginning of the rift between the two of them. Virginia seemed to be consciously leaving her old life behind in Chicago and taking on a new identity in California. Murray Bowen might have said she was in the process of individuating.

David Counsell remembers when Virginia and Norman decided to move across the country to California. They made the rounds first, visiting all the Wisconsin relatives they would be leaving. He remembers their having said to his mother (Virginia's Aunt Helen): "She and Norman had to get away from Chicago. It [the pace] was getting too much for them; life was just too crazy there. They were going to California; they were going to just start anew" (Counsell, 1992).

A long-time friend and associate of Virginia, Jane Gerber (1993) says Virginia made the move in an attempt to save her marriage. Norman's children by a former marriage were in California, and he was very depressed about the distance between them and him.

This decision about the "new start" stemmed from the conflict beginning between the hours in Virginia's work day and the requirements of a personal life. Perhaps we could say "again," as this echoes impressions some of her family members had about her marriage with Gordon, when she was doing child welfare work and going out at midnight in response to calls from police. Virginia, always one who learned from her experiences, tried to cut back to a more normal schedule: "Then, when I got out to California in October of 1958, I had decided that I was working 80 hours a week [in Chicago], what I should do is to be like ordinary people and try for a 40 hour week. So when I went to California I had a chance to do it [professional life] all over again" (in Brothers, 1983, p. 52).

But it did not go as she and Norman had hoped it would. "I didn't do anything for a couple of months and I got depressed—or I was depressed when I got out there," she said later (in Brothers, 1983, p. 52). Her energy level was such that doing nothing for a couple of months and finding the "idleness" depressing could simply refer to the normal gap between terminating one brimming practice in Chicago and establishing another in Palo Alto. In fact, she seemed to make the transition with unusual alacrity: within weeks, she made good professional connections in California.

A couple of years before, she had read that article by Don Jackson: "I don't know who he is [at the time]—and it is called 'Toward a Theory of Schizophrenia.' I read it and lo and behold he's writing about what I've been observing and I say to myself, `At least there's somebody else in the world, besides Murray and me, who is doing this.' . . . So, I file it away in my mind" (Brothers, 1983, p. 52).

Now, soon after her move to California, she remembered this article. Also remembering that Jackson worked in Palo Alto, she called him. In the middle of her explaining who she was and what she was about, Don Jackson invited her to come to the ethnology group at a nearby Veteran's Administration hospital, chaired by Gregory Bateson. Others in the group were William Fry, John Weakland, and Jay Haley.

Jackson also soon asked Virginia to help him start the Mental Research Institute, which has since become a major institution in the family therapy movement. Thus, she was one of the founders of MRI.

She contacted Murray Bowen about the same time, she recalled, and later met Nathan Ackerman. Murray Bowen remembers meeting Virginia in 1958. She was then a social worker at Chicago State Hospital, and he was conducting an all-day panel in New York at the annual meeting of the American Orthopsychiatry Association. They began corresponding, and she began visits with him at the National Institute of Health.

Aware that Bowen planned to attend the Ortho meeting in San Francisco in March 1959, Virginia called before leaving Chicago and offered to meet him at the conference and drive him around. She told him she and her husband were moving to the San Francisco area. Bowen recalls a depressed Virginia arriving in her Volkswagen bug, and the two of them spending all afternoon walking amid the redwood trees in Muir Woods. As Bowen presents it, he wanted to help relieve her depression by getting her connected with people working with families in the area. After their walk, he suggested riding down to Palo Alto to see Don Jackson. Jackson was not there at the time, but they did see some of his colleagues.*
Bowen (1989) also had this to say about Virginia:

> Virginia was a special "doing" person in the early days of the family movement. She was a kind of Pied Piper of "the family" who used her energy to demonstrate and sell the family idea to the masses. I was more inclined to develop a new theory that would sell itself. My contacts with her were less frequent the last few years. . . . My relationship with her covered a period of about thirty years, but I did not know the qualities that made her into an important therapist.

---

*Murray Bowen leaves the impression that he had introduced Don Jackson and Virginia to each other. Virginia said this was not so; she had made contact with Jackson on her own. One therapist who was well acquainted with both Virginia and Bowen says that, in Virginia's version of the meeting in Muir Woods, it was Bowen who was depressed and being looked after by Virginia.

Bowen's last lines make a telling statement: unfortunately, the giants in the field seemed rarely to study in depth with each other. Virginia's work is so multidimensional and process-focused that understanding it almost requires participating in a fairly long seminar on her model.

She emphasized process and *quality* of process as the major factors in her philosophy of treatment. This emphasis is most evident in a interview videotaped during an annual meeting of the Association for Humanistic Psychology (Basch, 1980). Virginia had just been elected president of that organization. In the interview, she quite deliberately blurs the edges of a meditation from which she and the interviewer had both just emerged. This lets her slide into the interview with the energy from the meditation still permeating her consciousness.

Richard Vennard Basch, the interviewer, no doubt thinking this woman was not behaving as if she were entering a videotaped interview, said: "The cameras are rolling."

But Virginia knew exactly what she was doing; she was making a point. She wanted to convey her philosophy about centering oneself and the correlating impact of such careful, honest, respectful attention to one's own inner experience relative to interaction. The relationship between self-esteem and congruence in communication was the cornerstone of her work.

She is at her playful, rich, and resonant best on this tape, relating to Basch in the fullest way appropriate to the context. The point was to show definitively what she meant by *use of self* in interaction with another, to demonstrate the congruence she believed to be basic to honest human relationship.

This use of self, her therapeutic style, was a way of being in the world—no mere compartmentalized technique for handling clients. Relating to the general population in the same way she would relate to her clients contrasts with the approaches of other family systems thinkers who emerged at the time. They were much more heavily focused in the cognitive realm and paid far more attention to what they thought than what their own behavior communicated within the context of client–therapist interaction.

Virginia's training addressed the total person, with the full intent of bringing each trainee into physical and emotional awareness, along with providing a cognitive framework. She saw the affective domain and its corresponding manifestation in the physical realm—a person's body—as a rich, untapped mine of resources hardly explored by psychotherapy at a time when the field's major focus was from the neck up.

Rather than remaining at the intellectual level, or even at the intellectual and emotional levels, she brought in six other areas. She had determined these to be essential for the formation and functioning of any given "self." She trained people to pay attention to:

- whatever is going on in the body at any point in time
- information coming in through the senses
- the interaction between two selves
- the difference made by food taken into the body
- the greater context in which all interaction is taking place
- the spiritual aspect of making contact between the essence of two selves

As she demonstrated in the Basch interview, Virginia paid conscious attention to this wide range of variables. Ever awake to the idea that life is process, she focused on the process between human beings, not only on the content. Her overriding distinction from her colleagues was her conscious intent to encompass, to take into account, the whole range of human experience. This is a major divergence from the linear thinking, problem-oriented mode—and certainly from the psychoanalytic one-therapist-to-one-patient method which even deliberately excluded eye contact.

Virginia's move to California may have represented a troubled period in her personal history. Depressed or not, however, she was letting no grass grow under her feet. Virginia was a ball of continual, moving energy. If anything, her personal problems enhanced her personal creativity as she sought for the most comprehensive explanations for human pain (Brothers, 1983, p. 53).

> So, anyway, I had [a] private practice in California immediately [spring of 1959], but I started at MRI in March [1959]. We wanted to take a look at the relationship between the health and illness of individuals and its relationship to the total family interaction . . . and [that] was a very bold thing to do. . . .
>
> In May I went to a conference in San Francisco where I was program chairman. Somebody called out my name during that meeting. I turned around and it was a man from Camarillo State Hospital who asked me if I was Virginia Satir. I said, "Yes," and he said, "Will you come down to Camarillo and help show us something about families?" Before very long I was involved in all the state hospitals [and] a lot of other places all over California.

Perhaps due in part to the limited scope of that meticulous observation of just one family, she was not interested in doing research at MRI. It lacked enough action to match her high energy level. In those early days, she was the only woman standing in a male-dominated field with all its attending publishing-versus-popularizing discriminations. Useful as it was from the scientific point of view, MRI's focus on a product—this in-depth, rigorous study of one family—limited the context too much for the boundless Virginia. It was very important to her for the world to know and be able to make immediate practical application of all useful information about families.

So while clinicians such as Murray Bowen and Don Jackson were working in their offices in a fashion suited to their styles, she was out making hundreds of clinical observations of families all around the world. By 1955, four years before she helped create the Mental Research Institute, she had already seen 400 families (Brothers, 1983, p. 51). While others studied one family at MRI, Virginia was free of the constraints imposed by formal research and was in an unusually good position for gathering information. As she continued her work into the '60s, '70s, and '80s, she persisted in amassing many more clinical observations and expanding her increasingly more informed inquiry. The sheer volume of her contact in a nearly impossible schedule put her in a position to gather more information than most colleagues. Unlike Virginia, they had spouses, children, houses, and institutions to whom they were also accountable for their time.

Out of this enormous mass of experience, Virginia discovered a critical fact that became the foundation and heart of her theory.* She could divide all human communication into two categories: incongruent or congruent. Incongruencies served to keep up walls between family members (and others, as well). *Incongruent communication* consists of shifting among four specific forms: placating, blaming, distracting, or being super-reasonable.

Congruent communication, on the other hand, builds bridges between family members—or any other two people engaged in interaction—in a process of direct, balanced, heartfelt connection. *Congruence* refers to words, facial expressions, bodily gestures, and emotion as all delivering the same message—such as tears do with sadness, frowns with anger, or smiles with joy. No mixed messages, in other words. It sounds so simple as to be obvious, but

---

*I use the word *theory* with misgiving. Virginia once asked me to remove the same word from an article (Brothers, 1987a), pointing out that these human communication styles were behaviors she had witnessed, not something she had invented (Satir, 1987c).

Virginia noted that people seemed to communicate congruently only about five percent of the time.*

Both congruent and incongruent communication are stimulated and affected by internal feelings of self-worth and self-appreciation. Making communication congruent improves self-esteem; improving self-esteem makes communication shift toward congruence. Two people who understand each other on their respective inner levels are far more likely to treat each other with due respect. As they do, they each reinforce self-respect.

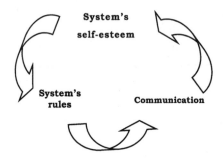

Diminished self-esteem clouds communication; incongruent communication erodes self-esteem. Virginia saw all human behavior in these terms. She also noted that the four incongruent stances could be associated with particular physical illnesses or conditions (Satir et al., 1991, pp. 40–51; Brothers, 1987a, pp. 10–23; Brothers, 1989a, pp. 227–241; Brothers, 1989b, pp. 47–62). However, she

---

*This is the source of the statement John Bradshaw attributes to Virginia: "Ninety-five percent of families are dysfunctional." However, she was more inclined to frame the statement positively, without labeling and without overtones of judgment. Her position was that people were invariably doing the best they could with the information available to them at the time, and in most situations some variation of incongruence would prevail.

did not gather empirical data or write very extensively about the physical consequences she observed. (When I once expressed interest, she referred me to the work of James Lynch [1977, 1985], who had measured the effects of emotions on cardiac functions. His studies were a good start in the direction of exploring the psychobiological nature of communication.)

Virginia took her clinical observations seriously, and she duly respected the need for hard data. She hoped someone else would do future research on the relationship between incongruent communication and physical illness. Meanwhile, her genius lay in making observations and brilliant mental leaps to her conclusions.

Since she did not enjoy the MRI research, Don Jackson put her in charge of a training program for therapists interested in family work. MRI obtained a small grant, then a large National Institute of Mental Health grant, and began the training program in the fall of 1959 with 12 therapist-participants. Sharing what she had learned about making families work was a burning passion with Virginia; training was more to her taste than formal research. And in 1964, she brought out her first book—*Conjoint Family Therapy*—with Don Jackson's fledgling publishing company, Science and Behavior Books. She wrote the book from her lecture notes for teaching (five years before) at the Family Dynamics Residency Training program of the Illinois State Psychiatric Institute.

After about 1966 or 1967, while she was spending much of her energy at the Esalen Institute, she asked one of her trainees, Frederick Ford, to take over most of the MRI training. However, she continued to do workshops and consultations when she was in town.

As I conducted the 1982 interview (Brothers, 1983), I noted that I had seen her interview a family in New Orleans in 1965, then seen her interview another family in 1968. Those two interviews had been dramatically different. It was obvious to me—even then, in 1968, when I was only a few years out of graduate school—that something had made a tremendous impact on her work with families. Now, in 1982, I wondered aloud: what had happened in those three years to account for the difference?

She responded that her involvement with Esalen between 1965 and 1968 accounted for this. Her basic philosophy was to remain open to possibility and, when she found something new, to add whatever fit. Through her experience at Esalen, she "got into what we called the affective domain; I was bringing another whole growth dimension into my work. That was the beginning of a lot of new things." These included associating with people such as Fritz Perls, Ida Rolf, Jim Simkin, and others who were part of the early Esalen era.* She had also begun working in Cleveland at the Gestalt Institute, where Ervin and Miriam Polster were then. Virginia described those years as a time of great integration. This was her first opportunity to move beyond the confines of the cognitive focus and into "the whole affective domain."

Virginia, who credited her sources more often than she herself was usually credited, also noted that she had a lot of association with Eric Berne, who founded Transactional Analysis. A friend of his, she said she "picked up a lot of stuff from him." From her earliest days as a young school teacher, she was open to any and all ideas that seemed to hold promise for furthering human growth.

Officially, she was director of training at Esalen, but—perhaps more importantly—she seemed to have used the place fully as a kind of salon: a place to exchange ideas with other intensely creative therapists of that period. When I asked her about Fritz Perls and their influence on each other, she said (Brothers, 1983, p. 55):

---

* Ida Rolf developed a body-work technique, structural muscular integration, which became known as *rolfing*. Jim Simkin was an early student of Fritz Perls and became a leading Gestalt therapist in his own right and with his own unique style.

"Fritz and I were good friends. . . . Fritz was not somebody who spent a lot of time talking but he respected me; I respected him."

In an interview with Jack Gaines (1979, pp. 267–269), she reflected on the reasons for the mutuality of respect between Perls and herself:

> We touched frequently in our personal relationship, and one of the reasons we had such a strong feeling for each other was that he knew I didn't want anything from him and I knew that he didn't want anything from me, so we could just be together. I respected him and he respected me. We had a very definitely delineated relationship—we were colleagues. I learned much from him and I know he learned some things from me. . . . I want to tell you, it was very hard to be around Fritz when he was Fritzing and not feel totally devastated. If people didn't have a real good sense of their own self-worth, he could be really something, let me tell you. Those were times when he was lonely and he felt that nobody cared. In all my contacts with him, we'd just hug and I'd pat him a little. . . .
>
> He let himself be poignant with me. We were going to build a house at Esalen. He did build one and it finally worked out that I didn't. But, anyway, it was around that time that he and I sat down to talk about some things. He started to tell me about his longings, how he'd always wanted a house that faced the ocean and somehow that got him into talking about his disappointment with Freud. He couldn't understand that he wouldn't be listened to. How could Freud have done such a thing was his feeling, more than just rejection. "I had been reading Freud's stuff and saw there were things Freud hadn't answered. I went to see him—I had an appointment," he told me, "but Freud got very domineering and ordered me out of the house."
>
> . . . He told me how he had hoped to bring this thing to the world through Freud and it didn't work. He had hoped that Freud would understand what he had to say, but Freud didn't want to hear it. Freud treated Fritz like a naughty boy, and Fritz was very hurt by the dismissal. His eyes were misty as he looked at me, and his voice was sad. I remember the pathos and longing I got from his voice and the way he looked. That always stuck with me.

She told me (Brothers, 1983, p. 55):

> I studied, I read the books, and was with him in some of his seminars.
> I thought he was a genius. When he was Fritzing he was terrible.
> When he was gestalting he was magnificent. So I learned to tell the
> difference between these two things, because I think his gestalting—
> really gestalting—was a gentle, loving thing; but when he was Fritzing
> he was terrible.
>
> I learned a lot from him. Fritz would come in and sit in on my
> seminars till I had to throw him out because he was so nasty. But that
> was all right; he didn't mind that. I never went for any formal train-
> ing, but I learned a lot about Gestalt from him. What it really is: a
> way of creating harmony from dualities.

She and Fritz seemed to understand each other deeply. In his autobiography, Fritz's brief sketch reveals his insight into the person
she was—the person behind the therapist. His assessment of her
personal issues alludes to that yearning in her. It echoes the yearning in her orphaned, immigrant maternal grandmother (Perls, 1969,
n.p.): "Restless gypsy . . . you wanted a house, bigger than mine, at
Esalen. An unrealized dream . . .."

He speaks of their similarities in terms of greediness for success and recognition and not being willing to "settle for mediocrity."
He speaks of her "eagerness to learn" and "fantasy for things to
come." Recognizing her "greatest asset is that you make people
listen," he goes on to say that he believed she suffered, like him,
from "intellectual systemititis." He saw her unrealized dreams and
was in tune with her yearnings, as perhaps she was with his.

After hearing about Perls, I wanted Virginia to elaborate on
her own internal experience of her pre- and post-Esalen work. In
1968, she had seemed a lot freer, expanded. In the 1965 interview
sponsored by the Family Service Society at Kingsley House in New
Orleans, she had worn a beige suit as she conducted the interview;
everybody sat in chairs; and all her interventions were verbal. In

1968, she was wearing a bright-colored long dress. She engaged the family—who were part of the audience except for their time on stage—in sculpting, demonstrations using ropes, and a variety of other forms. The difference was more than merely obvious; it was striking.

In response to my query, Virginia reiterated her commitment to remaining dynamic rather than static. She intended the expansion I had seen to be part of a continual process of evolving. Her example in 1982 was that she had now "plugged in the whole spiritual thing." She had also developed her "eight levels of things I look and work at now"—referring to what she called the *Self Mandala*: universal inner resources that are part of any self. These are the physical, intellectual, emotional, sensual, interactional, nutritional, contextual, and spiritual aspects of experience. She contended that most therapies did not take into account all eight aspects, focusing more on the intellectual or the intellectual and emotional (Satir et al., 1991, pp. 275–283).

Since 1968, she had learned much more about systems, the integration of right- and left-brain learning, and "about how we take in things." In places where she had previously relied on intuition, she now had cognitive handles. She was free to make clear and more open use of the information. She added that she was sure she had grown in her feeling of comfort about what she was doing, reminding me that for years she had been the only woman in family therapy. It was a field filled mostly with male physicians, in those days. Almost as if reminding herself, she said, "I have seen more families than anybody else practicing in the field. And I know that. Which I never thought about, but I had" (Brothers, 1983, p. 55).

She was out there for 50 years, the first 30 of which had not yet heard of a women's movement. She entered the world of psychotherapy when it was dominated almost entirely by male psychiatrists using psychoanalysis or the analytic model. In this context, she went on to mention the conclusions about information channels and psycholinguistics that Richard Bandler and John Grinder had, in the early 1970s, "extracted from my work—with my permission at the beginning." They based a great deal of their theory, Neurolinguistic Programming (NLP), on observations of her work as well as that of Milton Erickson and Fritz Perls. NLP subsequently mushroomed into a very popular training program for a variety of professionals in human services and organizational development.

In essence, the developers of NLP had found a way to bypass a client's conscious mind and influence the unconscious mind—with or without the client's informed consent. Virginia told me that she knew she "develops everything intuitively" and that her "right brain is always ahead of her left brain." She added, in passing, that she had considered studying mathematics, as she was always good in math. However, she knew she had a highly developed kinesthetic channel, was able to tune in finely to people, and would "get a lot of images about what is going on."

Bandler, thinking he was seeing miracles, had asked to study her as she worked. She granted permission; he scrutinized all her films and tapes. He met Grinder, who was a linguist, and they began putting together what they had seen. How did master therapists effect change in people? They extracted essential similarities among Virginia, Fritz Perls, and Milton Erickson. Virginia said (Brothers, 1983, p. 54):

> I was excited when that first happened, very excited, because I like to know new things and now I had a great left-brain explanation of what I had been doing. I loved it. But then, what got me is that [my work] was taken, without heart and soul, and then it was used as a manipulation thing as Richard and John got more into that—I think that is changing now—but the arrogance and all the rest that went with it made my stomach hurt.

I prayed that there would be people who would take it and add the spirit and the soul and heart to it, because otherwise it's dangerous stuff. Anything that's potent for change can be used negatively or positively. So I was not very happy about that part of it at all.

I know there are plenty of people in the field who want instant stuff and are so left-brain that the soul doesn't mean anything, and they go about in their logical left-brain ways. So I had alternating feelings of feeling embarrassed about this and feeling angry about it. It was like taking my baby and making a farce out of it as far as I was concerned.

The first part had been very exciting for me, but I didn't count on the internal parts of Richard, particularly in his need to get where he got. So I think that it offers a lot to understand things, a left-brain picture. . . . I found nothing wrong with it when I wrote *Changing with Families* with Richard and John. It's fine. It fits the whole general semantics, linguistics, and all the rest of that, and I knew that it could [all fit together well]. I know it was also a good thing to find out. I just feel bad about how it got used.

Making decisions for the client rather than facilitating decision-making processes *in* the client was in diametric opposition to her philosophy of treatment. Manipulation of the client, "benign" or otherwise, was anathema to her.

Virginia as a young woman

The Vision

Virginia's world view and vision set her apart from her contemporaries, who concentrated on only the smaller field of a given family unit. Her broader focus may have had some roots in her social work training. The discipline of social work has traditionally looked at the context of the client in her or his community. In Virginia's inimitable way, she extended this basic concept of "community" to include the entire universe. She saw people in the context of their relatedness to each other, across artificial political boundaries, and in relation to their spiritual connections with the whole cosmos.

Her vision was multidirectional: broad, deep, and penetrating in a singularly nonintrusive way. It was broad when she looked at the larger patterns visible to her and saw the possibilities for humankind; deep when she looked into the soul of the specific human being at any given moment; and penetrating in that she could perceive what was real when two human beings interacted. She put all this together to make her conclusions about patterns of communication, which those who studied with her have described at length (e.g., Brothers, 1989a, 1990; Englander-Golden, 1990; Satir & Baldwin, 1983; Satir et al., 1991; Loeschen, 1991). She developed her ideas and vehicles for training out of the truth she discovered in her quest for what is good for the specific human being and for humanity as a whole.

Her vision stretched around the globe to include the whole human race in the kind of harmony that she both evoked and taught whenever she worked with a given family. She carried a running count in her head about the exponential number of the world's population she had touched with her work. Her count included seminars that had also been given by people she had trained (Satir, 1973). The same principles would change the world as would change the family; it was simply a matter of increasing the numbers. *Making connections* was her basic theme as well as her mode. In this regard, she gave tribute to Gregory Bateson for having had an important influence on her work. Her vision regarding "The Pattern That Connects" (Bateson, 1979, p. 8) was probably reinforced in her early work at the Mental Research Institute.

Reconciling people with their own inner experience, and then with each other, was her major goal at least as early as 1968, when I met her. She used *reconciling* in its root sense of "weaving back together unraveled threads." In her experience, people could connect with each other if they could first connect with themselves.

In 1961, she did her first seminar abroad: a presentation in Vienna at the first meeting of the International Association of Social Psychiatry (which later made her an honorary member). Over the following 27 years, she covered most of the continents, responding to invitations to train people in Germany, Israel, England, Canada, France, the Scandinavian countries, China, Hong Kong, Eastern Europe, Venezuela, and Central America. She abandoned herself to the road to such an extent that, for a six-year period in the late 1960s and early '70s, she owned neither an apartment nor a car. She stored some belongings in the Palo Alto home of Joan Herrick (who recalls that one closet seemed filled with Virginia's shoes).

Then, in 1971, she bought a house in Columbia, Maryland. At that point, because of a conversation with Joel Elkes at the National Institute of Mental Health (Baldwin, 1996), she expected to do more work with the Johns Hopkins School of Medicine in Baltimore. (Elkes also chaired that school's Department of Psychiatry.) That dream did not materialize in the breadth and depth that she had hoped, however. Within a year, she moved her base back to California.

In the early 1970s, she went to Israel to arrange a seminar. She wanted to create a "laboratory" situation in which both Israelis and Palestinians could experience the similarities innate in human beings. Although the Palestinian turnout was not as large as she wanted, her work with the participants inspired some of the Israelis to proceed with trying to implement similar programs.

In the mid 1980s, Virginia spent time in Eastern Europe. Having been made an honorary member of the Czechoslovakian Medical Society in 1986, she was president of the first Family Therapy Symposium in Prague.* An extended seminar, it lasted several weeks. This symposium may even have been influential in major political shifts that soon followed in Czechoslovakia, according to one pre–fall-of-the-wall Berlin participant, who told me that a number of political people attended that seminar. Virginia reportedly worked with these folks with great care, aware of the potential danger to them, given their positions.

Gerd Mueller notes Virginia's work in Germany was a major influence on family therapy in that country in the 1970s (Mueller & Moskau, 1995. Along with Gaby Moskau, Mueller is a director of the Munich Family College, Institute for Family Therapy, Systems Supervision, and Systems Counselling.) In Germany, Virginia led month-long seminars in 1979 and 1986, as well as ten-day Family Reconstruction seminars in 1983, 1985, and 1987. Her model is reportedly a principal family therapy approach in Berlin, where therapists are said to debate among themselves about whose work most closely follows the Satir model (Scharwiess, 1994).

---

* In attendance was Ivan Urlic, M.D., Ph.D., a Croatian psychiatrist who later worked extensively with both Serbs and Croats—individuals, groups, and communities—to heal the emotional wounds from the Bosnian conflict in the 1990s. After becoming president of the Group Analytic Institute (in Split, Croatia), he spoke at the annual meeting of the American Group Psychotherapy Association (February 26, 1999, in Houston, Texas). As part of a panel on "Living with One's Enemies," he referred to Virginia during his remarks about teaching forgiveness to both sides. Later, he told me he had been at the Prague conference and was very impressed with her work.

Among her final international trips were Central America and what was then the Soviet Union. When I last saw her work, at a several-day seminar in Miami in March 1988, she had just returned from El Salvador. A Spanish grammar book lay on her bedside table. She said, "I have to go back there." So moved had she been by her contact with the people of that violence-racked part of the world, she was already preparing to return.

It is important to remember that Virginia's vision is a living thing with discernible and identifiable aspects rather than pieces we can call elements. What follows is a description of sorts, showing what went on in her work as her vision emerged—manifest in the more "wholed" and healed reality of those fortunate enough to have her interact with them. The evidence of her work was the personal growth that occurred in those with whom she worked.

Virginia *did* peace-weaving—learning, respecting, person-processing. This is why peace and the freedom to experience truth grew from her seeding efforts. She also sought mightily to live what she taught; it was an integral part of her view of what it meant to be congruent.

Peace-weaving

Virginia believed that peace for the world is a real and viable possibility. It could happen. Understanding quite clearly that peace is far more than the simple absence of war, she said (1987b) at the last Process Community she led, in the summer of 1987:

> I am always looking for ways that the wonderful being which we call a *human* being can, through self's eyes and in relation to others, find ways to unlock the wonderful secrets that lead us to love and growth and connectedness. Oftentimes, when I am with people who say they want to have peace, what they really mean is to be against war. I am for that, too, but that is not really where it is. How do we find what

human beings have not found for millennia on any kind of real group basis: How to love and how to connect and how to use each other's energies and such to make the grand things we [as "more fully human" beings] can do.

In her mind, training for effective living within the family was the same as training for effective living within the world family. Family therapy training—using her philosophy—and working for world peace were one and the same.

She saw training as a process of enlightenment. Only secondarily was it a place to develop skills and tools. (This was why Esalen had had such appeal for her: at last, the culture at large had seemed to be moving with her toward nurturing and developing human potential.)

She was as much philosopher as therapist. Echoing Teilhard de Chardin, who wrote (1962): "Peace is not the opposite of war," she said (1984a): "Peace is not the absence of war." Virginia understood that the hope of the world, the hope for peace, lay in the welfare of the individuals who make up the world. This is part of what lay behind her passion for respecting each person; she knew that such respect was the healing force required to keep us from blowing up the planet.

Person-Processing

To effect peace in families or peace among nations, requires more than simply refraining from fighting or calling truces. People also need to take positive action. Virginia had not only the philosophy but the blueprint to build that reality. She was able to breathe life into the concept, which caused it to rise from lecture halls and seminar tables and walk out into the world, no longer only a concept but an alive, functioning *process.*

She both led and taught the individual trainee how to enter into "peace within" that creates the fertile field for growing "peace between" a given pair, which ultimately would lead to "peace among" groups of people. String together enough people who know how to respect themselves as well as others, and you eventually get the necessary critical mass.

Somewhere between Virginia's teaching psychiatric residents in Chicago in the 1950s and doing marathon weekends in California in the 1960s, her Family Reconstruction process began emerging. Looking for ways to "externalize internal processes," she developed her particular style of using role-playing. In it, "a person relives formative experiences that were influenced by three or more generations of his or her family" (Satir et al., 1991, p. 121).

> [T]he first thing around when the reconstruction is done is called the star . . .. We're all stars of our own life. And I call myself the guide, and in a funny way I think . . . it is . . . that I am guiding the star to real stardom, to their health. That's what I feel that it is. And what I feel is—when we reach stardom—it is because we have learned to love, appreciate and know ourselves in a loving way.

Notice that the emphasis is on the *person,* not the performance of the therapist and not the therapist's intervention.

Virginia consistently focused on the people and the "health" of the process inherent in a given interaction. (She was careful about using a word such as *health* without a qualifying statement. She did not believe it useful to focus on pathology and illness.) During this same period, she developed other interventions—what she called "vehicles for change"—that would engage the whole person in the therapeutic process.

Sheldon Starr (1993) recalls, from his early days as an associate at the Mental Research Institute, a step in the evolutionary process of the Family Reconstruction. In the spring or summer of 1968, he participated in a scene reenacted from his childhood. He played himself at age 11, and others in the training workshop played his family members. Virginia served as therapist to the thus "reconstructed" nuclear family.

These workshops were after her formal departure from MRI. According to Starr, she continued to do three-day workshops with the family therapy teachers, holding marathon sessions and working with each of the teachers in this way.

Confined to the participant's nuclear family, this vehicle differed from the expanded psychoeducational model of Family Reconstruction that came later. Eventually, Virginia would take the "star" of the reconstruction back three or four generations. Still, according to Starr, she validated in their later conversations that the work she had done with him and his colleagues at MRI was an embryonic form of the Family Reconstruction she subsequently developed.

In 1969 she conducted her first month-long residential training session for therapists. This seminar was the first of a series which eventually blossomed into the Process Communities she held each summer (beginning in 1981). These were ingredients in her dream of creating what she called The University For Becoming Human (Satir, 1981).

In organizing therapists she had trained and (in 1977) creating the Avanta Network, she made it possible to answer more of the requests from around the world for her style of training. She conducted trainings whenever she could; people who had studied with her extensively handled the rest of the requests. Many of those same people now continue her work.

In 1970, I was present at the first meeting of what became the International Human Learning Resources Network (IHLRN). Launched at the Hacienda Vista Hermosa outside Cuernavaca, Mexico, she called it the meeting of "One Hundred Beautiful People." It was a group of individuals she knew, loved, and respected, and whom she decided to introduce to each other. What might seem, on the surface, to be a giant "house party" thus turned into a vibrant conference, with many workshops evolving during the course of the meeting. This process model for a psychotherapy conference was a novel configuration and was characteristic of Virginia's style of being.

This kind of attentive focus on process in all facets of human experience reflects Virginia's unique attitude toward learning and training. Other master therapists of the time may have been experimenting with different forms for training and supervision, but nobody else was inventing new ways to hold entire conferences. That first meeting in 1970 was unique as a professional meeting: she deliberately let the agenda and content arise ad hoc rather than planning them in advance.

Many important figures passed through the IHLRN conferences, including Betty Friedan, the Lama Govinda, and the founders of Findhorn. Virginia was always seeking information about "how people work"—the ingredients of human-beingness—and she was continually interested in bringing such people together so that they might learn from each other.

It is interesting to note evidence that Virginia was no less interested in learning from the not-yet-famous. Lamas, mystics, mechanics—their station in life was irrelevant; she was equally interested in anybody's information "about people." Among the books in her personal library was a work about assertiveness training with American Indians. Tucked in the pages was a rather formal little note from its author, a doctoral student in Oklahoma, which began, "Here is the dissertation you requested."

Virginia's highly original way of organizing IHLRN reflected her energy and involvement in moving systems—individual, familial, and political—toward *wholeness*. Hope and wholeness were the two factors that she saw as very important. As revealed in the following excerpt from our 1982 interview, she understood that to assist in shifting external systems toward wholeness, the therapist must first attend to her or his own internal system (Brothers, 1983, p. 55).

BJB: What do you feel has been your major contribution to the field of psycho-therapy?

VS: I was thinking about that yesterday. I think the main thing—there are two—is hope, and that *the therapist needs to be a person, a whole, full person in carrying it on.* Those are the two main things. Then, of course, I can make it light, because people often comment on my sense of humor—so it doesn't have to be so tragic. My hunch is that those are the three most important things. The ideas and the ways that I choreograph stuff excite people, and they see new possibilities. That is based, of course, on the idea that as long as something remains in an abstract form, it doesn't have any life; when I make body pictures and things of that sort, then it contains life.

Putting life back into people and process was a large part of Virginia's *raison d'être*. She held that the *self* was the therapist's—and the client's—most important resource, and that clients changed by interacting with the self of the therapist. Affective learning is inseparable from cognitive learning: feelings are an integral part of selfhood.

This foundational idea and others were a bridge to a new paradigm for training and psychotherapy: the *use of self* as change agent. Rather than designing workshops geared to help people collect facts and techniques, she emphasized that the process of teaching was not only as important as the content, it *was* the content. Corresponding to Erich Fromm's (1976) ideas in *To Have or To Be*, she transcended materialism and the obsession with "collecting" education as if it were simply another thing to be possessed. Instead, she plunged her trainees into the *experience* of connecting with each other.

Providing a whole experience, in her model, also meant en-suring each participant's cognitive, affective, sensory, and bodily involvement. Virginia's bubbling pot of creativity consistently served up soups of highly condensed, rich morsels of experiences, thoughts, and humor that satisfied more than intellectual hunger. They went soul deep and into the heart.

Her goal was to bring participants into awareness of their utter uniqueness, which was prerequisite to appreciating the uniqueness of another person. To Virginia, authentically being with another fellow mortal was a spiritual event; she spoke in terms of the "meeting of two manifestations of Life" as being a cause for celebration. How that attitude differs from the plumber/carpenter approach of "find out what's wrong, pull out a psychotherapy technique, and fix it." Virginia did not speak of classification and quantification; she spoke to souls and hearts (Brothers, 1992a).

The 1980 Basch interview exemplifies how she lived this philosophy. She kept the focus on the experience between the interviewer and herself, rather than talking "about" her life, her ideas, and so on. In her absolute commitment to focus on the experience with the other, we see another aspect of what distinguished her work from that of other family therapists of her day. She did not use the occasion to pontificate or even to explicate; rather, she chose to demonstrate what she was about.

She also wove into her work the Gestalt therapy concepts of here-and-now and field versus background. For her, this approach was as least as much a spiritual exchange as a psychotherapy technique. Taoism is evident in her emphasis on flow, balance, and centeredness.* It also appears in a 1977 letter (Satir, 1977a) inviting participation in realizing her dreams about the University for Becoming More Fully Human:

---

*Partly out of the Taoist Buddhist sector of her spiritual and philosophic systems, cremation was part of Virginia's funeral process. Her longtime friend Bob Shapiro personally conducted the private ceremony of placing her body into the crematory fire, according to Taoist custom. See also Brothers, 1996a and b.

> I would like . . . from you: . . . Your willingness to bring your physical
> presence at times and places convenient to you, fitting your Tao (your
> river of life). In no way do I want any of this to be a burden to you, but
> only a joy, an opportunity, and a stimulus to yeasting . . .

Virginia understood life and the cosmos to be one shimmering
network of interconnection, the quest for balance and harmony being
the dynamic common to all parts of this Great System (Brothers,
1996b). She taught that the point was human connection, life
reaching out to life. As she said to Richard Simon (Satir & Simon,
1989, p. 39):

> When I am completely harmonious with myself, it is like one light
> reaching out to another. At the outset [of a psychotherapy session], it
> is not a question of "I will help you." It is simply a question of life
> reaching out to life. All life talks to life when it is in a harmonious
> state.

Large Groups

Constantly pushing to the creative edge, Virginia explored ways to
work with very large systems—at one point even conducting a seminar with 20,000 participants in a stadium in Minneapolis (Baldwin,
1996). Working with whole systems was part of her plan of massive
public education.

In the early 1970s, Wray Pascoe, director of social services in
Thunder Bay, Ontario, invited Virginia to present a workshop. At
the time, Virginia was also a professor of social work at the University of Alberta in Calgary. At the workshop, Wray introduced her to
Maria Gomori, who was then head of social services at St. Boniface
Hospital and who held an appointed seat on Manitoba's health commission (Pascoe, 1997).

From that meeting grew an extensive project. At the request of over 50 organizations—including the provincial department of health and social development, and the school's faculty of medicine—the University of Manitoba invited Virginia to serve as a visiting professor. Her objectives were "working to improve interdisciplinary communication in the health and social development delivery systems, and teaching family therapy orientation and skills in Manitoba" (*Winnipeg Tribune*, 1972a).

Her Manitoba sojourn was planned by a "committee made up of members of government agencies, hospital staffs, social science organizations, and community workers. The committee was chaired by Dr. Arnold Naimark, dean of medicine at the University of Manitoba" (*Winnipeg Tribune*, 1972b).

Maria Gomori actively helped organize this project. Virginia stayed with Maria and also became very good friends with Paul, Maria's husband. Later, Virginia very often spoke of Paul Gomori as having served a very nurturing role in her life.

The entire Manitoba Health Services was among the organizations attending extended seminars led by Virginia. In addition to the seminars, which extended over a three-month period while Virginia was in Winnipeg, she also initiated one of her experiments in working with large groups. In late October 1972, she led nine "Family Theatre" programs in five different Manitoba towns.

With instruction from Virginia, volunteers from the audiences formed mock families and took on the communication stances that make up what she called the *stress ballet* (Satir et al., 1991). Following this role-playing, Virginia invited a real family to come up on the stage. Each member silently lined up behind the role-player who was enacting the stance that the family member usually used during family squabbles. This large-scale public education about the relationship among communication stances, self-esteem, and system rules manifested Virginia's dream of providing this kind of information to ordinary people everywhere.

Respecting

While in Utah to make one of the videotapes that she hoped would help teach this process to the world, Virginia's respect for people was in evidence. Her old friend Vincent Sweeney observed her being as consistently attentive and warm to the camera crew as to the live families with whom she would be filmed. When he commented about this, she replied, almost with wonder that he would question it, "Vince, I wouldn't know how to do it any other way!" (Sweeney, 1992). Of course, she also got the crew's very best performance in the process, but that goal was not primary with her. With her, the *person*—his world, her welfare—came first.

Respect is a key word in understanding what was behind Virginia's work. Respect engenders honoring of the other person; harsh judging atrophies in such an environment. Virginia was deeply respectful of all human beings. In her view, *becoming more fully human* meant increasing access to "the place where you keep the treasure known by your name" (Satir, 1988, p. 339). Within each human spirit is a sacred place of inner resources, and she wanted to help people explore their inner treasure as well as their access to it. In her awareness of process as paramount, she made no distinction between the goal and the route.

Valuing

Virginia understood personal growth to be as inherently natural as the growth of prairie grasses and garden flowers. Intentional cultivation augments the instinct to grow; optimum maturation requires a certain level of nurturing. One does not grow roses by beating on them. One grows roses through a process of appreciating them sufficiently to water and fertilize them, by removing such obstacles as weeds. The human being is somewhat more complex, but the process of appreciating and valuing is parallel—and crucial (Satir, 1987a, pp. 24–25).

> Human beings must evolve a new consciousness that places a high value on being human, that leads toward cooperation, that enables positive conflict resolution and that recognizes our spiritual foundations. Can we accept as a given that the self of the therapist is an essential factor in the therapeutic process? If this turns out to be true, it will alter our way of teaching therapists as well as treating patients.

She saw the benefits of psychotherapy as being too rich to limit to people who assumed a patient/client posture and defined themselves as sick. *All* people had the right to develop "a better state of their own consciousness, a better appreciation of themselves, and a feel of the psychology which psychiatry, social work . . . and the whole of all learning comes from" (Satir, 1985b). She opened her seminars to anybody interested in coming, and she became very distressed if an organizer of any seminar wanted to limit access to professionals only.

She had no interest in adding one more brick to the ivory towers already constructed in the name of therapy. Her position was: "What we know, everybody else needs to know. It's the same way that mathematicians don't have to keep the multiplication tables to themselves" (in Brothers, 1991b, p. 12).

The California Task Force to Promote Self-Esteem and Social and Personal Responsibility (initiated by her friend John Vasconcellos, a state Assembly member) was born of her conviction that the public has this right. Signed into law in October 1986, Vasconcellos's bill implemented the task force soon after. The idea of the importance of self-esteem, pioneered by Virginia Satir, now seems to be seeping into the nation's collective consciousness.

Learning

Virginia's model for psychotherapy was clearly a growth model, not a medical or psychoanalytic model. Neither preoccupied with pathology nor restrained by Freud's drive theory, she linked dysfunction with self-esteem early on (Satir, 1967, pp. 69–70).

> I do not postulate sex as the basic drive of man. From what I have observed, the sex drive is continually subordinated to and used for the purpose of enhancing self-esteem and defending against threats to self-esteem.

Her attitude was that *new* learning—replacing outmoded "old learnings" from earlier days dating back to childhood—is a means for growth with the potential for such change relating directly to the person's level of self-esteem. One sees her train of thought in *Conjoint Family Therapy* (Satir, 1967, p. 130):

> At the same time, the therapist will show the patient how to check on invalid assumptions that are used as fact. He knows that members of dysfunctional families are afraid to question each other to find out what each really means. . . . The therapist uses various questions to ferret out these invalid assumptions . . .. Like any good teacher, the therapist will try to be crystal-clear.

Her attitude about therapy as education becomes even clearer in her next book, *Peoplemaking* (1972). Written for the public as well as therapists, it reflects her belief that learning (on emotional and sensual levels as well as intellectual) is equivalent to therapy. She had very much hoped, as she was writing, that *Peoplemaking* would become a bestseller, but not from a wish to "see her name in lights." Rather, she wanted the general public to have access to this information about the way families work. She purposely constructed the book with the utmost simplicity and clarity, hoping for families to use its contents with their children.

After *Peoplemaking,* she also published (through Celestial Arts) *Self-Esteem, Making Contact,* and *Your Many Faces.* (In 1988 she published a revision, *The New Peoplemaking.*) For therapists, she coauthored *Satir Step by Step* with Michele Baldwin (1983), as she had coauthored *Helping Families To Change* with J. Stachowiak and H. Taschman; and *Changing with Families* with Richard Bandler and John Grinder.* Michele Baldwin and Virginia were guest editors for the Haworth Press *Journal of Psychotherapy and the Family,* Volume 3, Number 1, which was also published as a hardback monograph called *The Use of Self in Therapy.*

The difference between *Step by Step* and the others is it was first book Virginia wrote with a student who had become a colleague. The book's first section is an annotated verbatim transcript of a videotaped family interview. In the book, we see Virginia's underlying belief about the intrinsic value of the human being. In the second part, describing Virginia's beliefs and thinking, Baldwin says (p. 160):

> To Virginia, the world is a place of infinite splendor, evolution, and transformation. Since they are of this world, human beings partake in those qualities. They are creatures of wonder in their physical aspects . . .. Then, of course, people have minds and souls. For years, the "science" of psychotherapy disregarded the soul, which it considered to be the realm of organized religion. This ignored the fact that when people forget their spiritual dimensions, they feel lost because they have no connection with the life force or universal mind.

---

*In the summer of 1994, I happened upon a non–English-speaking Russian social worker in Veronez, Russia—some 300 kilometers south of Moscow—whose office bookshelf held a Russian translation of this book. The young woman was delighted to meet people who had known Virginia personally.

Virginia's notes include the title to the book she would write next: *Third Birth*. That was her term for that time when an individual lays claim to full personhood. Virginia often said she believed we have four births: the first at the moment of conception, the second "when we pop out of the womb," the third when we become our own decision makers, and the fourth "when we join all consciousness." These concepts reflect Virginia's bird's-eye view of human life as a process linking body, mind, and spirit.

After her death, Science and Behavior Books published two more books coauthored by Virginia: *Say It Straight: From Compulsions to Choices (*1990), which she had coauthored with Paula Englander-Golden; and *The Satir Model: Family Therapy and Beyond* (1991), which Virginia had coauthored with John Banmen, Jane Gerber, and Maria Gomori. Haworth Press also published two hardback monographs dedicated to her work: *Virginia Satir: Foundational Ideas* (Brothers, 1991a) and *Couples and the Tao of Congruence* (Brothers, 1996).

Knowing the printed page could never capture her work, Virginia put much of her energy into making videotapes. The Peoplemaking Series, produced by the company Peoplemaking (Paradise, California), and the videocassettes produced by Golden Triad Films (Kansas, Missouri) are in the Satir Archives in Davison Library of the University of California at Santa Barbara. The Golden Triad Films videocassettes include: *Blended Family with a Troubled Boy, Rocks and Flowers, A Family at the Point of Growth, A Step Along the Way,* and *The Essence of Change.* Virginia's intent for the Peoplemaking Series was to cover all of her major tenets in this format, which allows viewers to watch and hear the action.

Virginia used audiotapes and videotapes extensively, as a means to study her own work as well as an adjunct in her training programs. She released her first formally made videotape through Science and Behavior Books. It shows her 1972 presentation at the

University of Manitoba. The company's owner, Bob Spitzer, also videotaped her work in the Soviet Union in May 1988.

Research

In spite of her claim about not being particularly interested in research activity at the Mental Research Institute when she worked with them in the early 1960s, Virginia was actually quite agreeable to participating in such study. She appreciated those who wanted to look at her work from an enlightened but "hard research" perspective. At the height of the human potential movement in the 1960s and 1970s, when the pendulum swung toward getting in touch with feelings, Virginia wanted people to know she was not willing to "lose her head."

She willingly took part in the Virginia Project, which she described in the third edition of *Conjoint Family Therapy* (1983, p. 261):

> Through the Family Institute of Virginia (under the direction of Joan Winter, M.S.W.), the Department of Corrections in the Commonwealth of Virginia undertook an extensive project to study the effectiveness of family therapy in treating juvenile delinquency. They chose three outstanding family therapists [Virginia Satir, Murray Bowen, and Jay Haley] who represented different schools of family therapy. Each of us was to design a program of treatment, enlist therapists we had trained, and supervise the implementation of our respective programs. There were sixty families in each of these three programs, and there also was a control group.

In characteristic fashion, Virginia was delighted with this opportunity to obtain a larger perspective on her work. These three master therapists would supervise the work rather than function as therapists. For the therapy sessions, Virginia chose six people from her Avanta Network: Ken Block, Catherine Bond, Jack Dennis, William Nerin, Anne Robertson, and Margarita Suarez. In addition to those six, Virginia chose three others to serve on the team in various capacities: Jonathan Stolzenberg, Jean Pickering (later McLendon), and Vernon Sparks.

She chose Jonathan because he is a pediatrician. Believing that "the body often says what the mouth cannot say," Virginia (1983, p. 263) wanted a medical consultant versed in family therapy to help "ascertain whether there was a link between delinquent behavior and health, and whether the health of the family members improved as communication within the family improved" (p. 263).

Jean Pickering had an interest in organizational development and served as liaison between Virginia and Joan Winter, the project's director. Vernon Sparks took charge of logistics, such as coordinating the videotaping.

IHLRN

Linking one human being with another was an integral part of Virginia's goal of education. She saw herself as a connecting point (Satir, 1977b):

> I was, and am, in no way interested in empire building, but I was, and still am, vitally concerned with multiplying the yeasting effect of linking one human being to another, and making links with other yeasting centers. Yeasting, for me, is in no sense a "Pollyanna" or "crusader" approach, but it is a way people can be creative with themselves and each other, building with and for one another to make the world a better place for all of us.

In 1969, she decided to create formal structure for this linking process (Satir, 1977b):

> I remember well the day at Esalen . . . when three long-distance phone calls from widely different places in the world came within a

two-hour time span asking for workshops. On that same day, ten letters came from people who shared with me some very special learnings
which they credited my helping them to find. . . .

Then I remembered the many times people had asked me for
names of other people to fill certain jobs, to make contacts in new
places when they moved, to have referral sources for therapy, or to
find consultants. I realized that I had become a combination of Johnny
Appleseed and Paul Revere.

I felt I was the center of a gigantic switchboard, receiving all
kinds of energy, love, and information from people I loved who loved
me. It was a powerful yeasting force. . . .

What would happen, I asked myself, if I could find a way to put
these people in touch with each other? Thus, the Network of the "Beautiful People" was formed. That name has now been translated into the
International Human Learning Resources Network [IHLRN, pro-
nounced "I learn"].

The "One Hundred Beautiful People Conference" was subsequently
formalized as IHLRN. Beyond creating a mixing bowl for people in
the field, Virginia (1977b) saw the possibility that those "Beautiful
People" would act as starter dough in their own communities.

> If all these people could have first-hand contact with each other, what
> even more fantastic yeasting could take place, not only with each
> other, but with themselves as yeasting centers in their own back-
> yards. People would be coming together because of their interest in
> themselves, in each other, in me, and in what could happen as a
> result of this meeting, not because of any organizational requirements,
> academic needs, or prestige hopes.
>
> I was then, as now, acutely aware of the loneliness and isolation
> that exist in the world, much of it because people do not have chan-
> nels through which to flow and connect with other people. I hoped to
> provide some of these channels. The outcome of that day eight years
> ago was a letter from me to five hundred people explaining my idea.
> Almost everyone responded.
>
> Bob Shapiro lent his energies and financial resources to help get
> the Network started. Without him, it probably could not have gotten
> off the ground. The group first met in 1970 In Vista Hermosa, Mexico,
> and has met yearly since that time, with a number of the same people
> attending every year.

IHLRN continues to meet annually and is attended by people from around the world who were in the workshops that Virginia gave in their respective countries.

Peoplemaking, Inc.

Meanwhile, in 1972, Virginia agreed to form another new organization: Peoplemaking, Inc. Her long-time supporter Dr. Bud Baldwin urged her to start a nonprofit organization to disseminate her films, tapes, and other materials on holistic health. His encouragement and backing came along with that of many others: his wife, Michelle; Lorraine Bouffard, Elaine Knutsen, Ruth and Hal Kramer, Bob Lee, Sandy Nye, Art Pines, Jean and Bob Shapiro, and Becky and Bob Spitzer. The organization secured nonprofit status in Nevada (Satir, 1977b).

Peoplemaking, Inc. eventually outlived its original objectives and usefulness. Virginia had hoped "to extend Peoplemaking so that it includes a foundation for making international links." After the rise of IHLRN and Avanta, those two organizations began addressing the same goals, and Peoplemaking faded away.

University for Becoming More Fully Human

Virginia's idea of a University for Becoming More Fully Human evolved from her work in the 1970s, particularly her long Process Community seminars. They usually resulted in life-altering changes in her trainees. One of her fondest dreams was to establish a university for training the deep self (Satir, 1981):

I think I now know how to develop a three-month experience, tentatively called the University for Being More Fully Human, which is aimed simply at one objective: to develop the humanness in the individual, and to prepare that person for more wholeness in the self and a more effective nurturing use of that self in professional life. This, in turn, leads to greater competence and efficient use of self in whatever professional way the person chooses. Next summer [1982] in Utah, I will be initiating this work.

She very much wanted to lift the unnecessary burdens of human existence, such as acting from false premises. The ensuing summary of her ideas for this university (Satir, 1981) highlights this liberating and dynamic conviction: learning is therapy, and therapy is learning.

I have noticed that, particularly in the people-helping professions, there is little direct emphasis on helping the individual teacher, student or practitioner to discover his/her own personhood. Universities, for example, do not yet have any departments which focus exclusively on developing humanness. It is almost always incidental, and exclusively subordinated to the content. For me, personhood is basic to mental and physical health, and to creative use of the self in the practice of one's profession.

. . . The first premise [to be examined and changed] is that all relationships need to be hierarchical, with leaders exercising total and continuing authority over the led, instead of relationships that shift and change, with no one person ever having a fixed power position over another.

The second premise is that the value of the self is based on conformity, namely, that there is one prevailing right way to be, and all persons must judge themselves by how they are like or unlike that one model. Instead each person, being unique, needs to develop uniqueness, so that personal development is in relation to one's own inner core, and not subject solely to an outside prescription.

The third premise [that leads people to unnecessary hardship] has to do with linear thinking, a simplistic way of analyzing cause and effect (A causes B), instead of recognizing that all outcomes are the result of several factors all essential to each other, or a gestalt.

By equating psychotherapy with learning, her aim for this university—as well as for family therapy—was to clear up the erroneous information people received as they grew up. She wanted them to learn that each person has inherent value as a unique human being (Satir, 1981):

> For me, hierarchical management, conforming behaviors, and linear thinking make real human development difficult and skewed.
>
> I would like to substitute equality of relationship (joining two or more wholes), uniqueness of individuals (featuring variations), and gestalt thinking (considering many parts which are essential to each other), in which hierarchy, conformity, and linear thinking are applied only when they fit.
>
> The human usefulness of current concepts (Transactional Analysis, gestalt, psychoanalysis, etc.) ideas, and techniques relating to human education and the therapy professions have vastly different outcomes, depending upon whether the person using them operates under the hierarchical-conforming-linear model or whether it is the equality–uniqueness–gestalt model.
>
> I believe the first model inhibits and often destroy[s] human growth, while the second model expands and nurtures human beings. I am gearing the University to understanding the first model, making the transition and transformation to the second model, and then learning how to live and use that model in conjunction with the first, thus creating a wider base of choice.

Conceiving of such a university exemplifies what Bunny Duhl (1988) meant when she said: "Some have accused Virginia of 'deserting the field' of family therapy. I would reframe that. The field Virginia helped create could not contain her."

Virginia (1987b) emphasized the importance of recognizing three kinds of information: cognitive, emotional, and sensual. This is her understanding of wholeness: use of the *whole* self instead of the intellect only. She believed in not leaving out any of the integral pieces in the teaching/learning interaction; to her, the body was an important part of the information matrix.

In the Western world we have given most of our attention to cognitive information. We read it in a book, we see the words, and the words make the images, but reading it in a book doesn't show how the person is feeling or thinking or how they are gesturing or how they are breathing . . . so it is a totally different thing when we put it into a human context.

I want to give you just enough so that we get a good context for this. If you will remember, when I use information, it is on *all* levels. . . . It is not about just giving words. [Satir, 1987b]

By equating psychotherapy with learning, her image of family therapy aimed to clear up the erroneous information people received in the growing up process. She wanted them to learn that each person has inherent value as a unique human being.

Through the universal human need to "make sense" of experiences, people often come out of their respective childhoods with skewed ideas. They have deduced these ideas the best way they could—given the limitations of a child's mind—just to achieve a sense of closure on life's puzzles. Virginia understood that a human being has an inherent need to solve such puzzles for emotional and intellectual resolution. She pointed out that the nature of the growth process is to push toward completion. So strong is the instinct to grow that trees will push rocks apart as they "muscle" their way toward their entelechy.

On October 21, 1976, Virginia explained her plan in a letter to her potential faculty of 50 carefully selected people (Satir, 1977a).

After having given over nine, month-long seminars, I now see a way of extending this kind of training into a three-month period. Over the past nine years many of the people who have attended these month-longs were students as well as practitioners in various fields relating to therapy and human relations training. . . . Since I am also a roving professor attached to many different universities on the North American continent, and since it was obvious that none of the universities was offering opportunities for the personal development of the individual professional, it seemed both logical and possible for me to find some way to extend this training I had already begun in the month-longs.

I now have conceived of a three-month period which could take place in almost any part of the world. . . . My idea is that there will be three persons who will work together to offer this training to a group of ninety people. I envision it to be self-supporting, and I also envision that the universities will give full credit to those who undergo the training.

I plan to develop a three-person training model which will be made up of people who can work individually, in pairs, and in triads. I further envision training about 200 people who can work well with any two of the other 199 they choose, so that they can design the most appropriate kind of training on the spot. I want these 200 people to represent a wide variation of all the beautiful human flowers in the human garden. That means people of different racial, ethnic, religious, nationality, age, sex, and professional groups so that the "faculty" will represent a world family. . . .

Virginia may have been given to dreaming, but not to the idle variety. The letter presents her carefully considered intention to put her dream in motion. That included the following job description for the faculty.

As both a starting place and a goal, I want people who are already on their way to the six C's: Commitment, Congruence, Competence, Compatibility, Cooperation, and Consciousness. By *commitment* I mean holding a philosophy that human beings and the total welfare of human beings are a priority. By *congruence* I mean having emotional, verbal and behavioral honesty. I see congruence manifested in the living of the five freedoms, which I will explain later. By *competence* I mean that the person has and respects his/her skills and resources and is not limited to any particular body of knowledge or orthodoxy, and is therefore able to continue developing. This includes a respect and feeling of well-being about the competence of the self and others. By *compatibility* I mean the development of the ability to have a human relationship based on dignity, honesty and clarity with everyone with whom one comes into contact. I don't mean that everybody has to love everybody. By *cooperation* I mean that individual efforts are in the direction of building and not competing. By *consciousness* I mean an awareness of the relatedness of all life force. That means a feeling of connectedness with higher intelligence and with things spiritual.

On his copy of this letter, Vince Sweeney added a seventh C: *compassion.* Virginia proceeded with her profile of the faculty:

> All this requires a positive attitude toward one's self and all other people, an ability to stand alone when it is necessary, an ability to be real and straight, and an ability to engage deeply with another human being. This means an appreciation of the uniqueness and the difference in all human beings and respect for that, a sound knowledge of the operation of the individual within him/herself, and a sound knowledge of how a system operates. It means spiral thinking rather than linear, and it means thinking in terms of equality rather than hierarchy. It means further that none of us has fully arrived but are in the process of continuing to grow and develop, feeling a high sense of self worth and infinite possibilities for ourselves and other human beings. This means an ability to design on the spot whatever is necessary, and the freedom to feel good and to have fun wherever one goes. Seriousness is not to be confused with grimness. . . .
>
> . . . The 6 C's add up to one as Human Congruence. I believe the most important thing we have to offer as leaders is our own modeling of our congruence. I do not want to confuse this with proselytizing.

In Virginia's first training seminar for the university's International Faculty, her 50 or so invitees met in Forest Knolls, California from March 6 through 26, 1977. People from that group ultimately helped create Avanta, the Virginia Satir Network, which has continued over the past 20 years and remains a viable organization.

Response to the Vision

Virginia tugged at edges. With every pair, every family, every group, she tugged people's ragged edges toward each other to reweave the unity she somehow saw. With that expanded vision, that gift of being able to sense the greater pattern, she pulled us all toward wholeness.

Therapists given to linear thinking and focus on technique could lose sight of Virginia as she extrapolated from family—nuclear or extended—to family of humanity. Watching her knit together a family in full view was one thing; following her great strides toward the edges of the bigger picture was another.

She dedicated her life to looking for the headwaters from whence might flow peace. Her initial motivation stemmed from yearning for peace in her own family of origin. She expressed this in her anguish at the deep pain she perceived in her parents' marriage. Her yearning also rose out of the chaos that jarred her own very early years, in which she shared the house with her psychotic grandfather. In addition, Virginia would have been keenly aware of the "splits" in her mother's family as well as the tension between her mother and her grandmother Henrietta.

With this longing for the kind of peace she knew was possible, Virginia therefore went out and created new extended families for herself among her colleagues across this continent. Ultimately, she created such colleague families on continents across the oceans, as well. To her, it would seem a natural next step that all these families around the world would join in harmony. As she said (Laign, 1988, p. 20): "The family is a microcosm. By knowing how to heal the family, I know how to heal the world."

Professional training groups in the Satir model have sprung up as tangible results of her belief in that seeding and joining process. They now exist in the Middle East, the Orient, Western and Eastern Europe, and Russia. The Institute for International Connections, Avanta Network, and the International Human Learning Resources Network are concrete examples of the logical progressions: peace within, peace between, peace among. This is Virginia's practical plan in motion, teaching people how to connect with one another and then extend the connections.

These institutes for professional training include:

International	United States
Associacion Venezolana de Orientacion Familiar (Venezuela)	Black Hills Institute (South Dakota)
Taiwan Satir Center	Midwest Satir Institute (Chicago)
Satir Centre of Australia	Satir Institute of the Southeast
Satir Learning Center of Ontario	(North Carolina)
SODI of Manitoba	Southern Star Satir Training Institute (Texas)
Institute for International Connections (U.S. and Eastern Europe)	

Virginia's work in other countries included live demonstrations of pieces of Family Reconstruction with volunteers from her usually large audiences. She wanted to highlight basic similarities among human beings regardless of ethnic origin. She taught that the relationship between self-esteem and communication was the major route to the empowerment of individuals. Quite consciously, she was proceeding around the world with the goal of sufficiently liberating enough of the world's population from self-imposed limitations. She wanted them to have the courage to take the necessary steps "in their own behalf"—and the planet's—to cultivate lasting peace beyond simply "the absence of war."

Her bottomless bucket of mercy for humankind came from her conviction that there are no bad people, only bad processes. In her words (1987b), "So often we mistakenly think that what is bad and wrong is inside and are not aware this is a behavioral description, not an identity."

With this conviction, she could reasonably hold an image of world peace in her mind. Massive education and growth related to making changes in those corrosive processes could stem the tide of destructiveness that has continued to wash the world in blood. With the focus off the viciously circular pursuit of "punishing bad people," an enlightened world would be free to devote more energy and resources to activities that would bring out the humanity in human beings.

Her goals were hardly modest ones. Anyone who spent even a little time with her knew that she seriously intended to make changes in the way the world works. She did not in any way see this as an unreasonable challenge—which is another mark of genius. As John Briggs (1988, p. 83) wrote:

> It is evident that the creator's task is very large. It is nothing less than the re-creation of the universe or, more precisely, finding or constructing a whole, integrated microcosm in order to reflect the whole macrocosm. To do this requires the creator's conviction . . . that a microcosm of the whole can be made to reveal itself in some part.
>
> . . . Great creators are different in the sense that they feel compelled to show the world that their themata in fact point to a hidden reality that people pursuing the consensual themata of the moment have failed to notice.

In Virginia's case, the themata were a burning drive to show the world that growth-enhancing communication is a teachable, learnable skill; and that a vibrant, living peace among human beings is a realizable dream. Teaching the nuts and bolts of what goes into making viable connections between persons was the task to which she gave her life.

Like other important thinkers, philosophers, and geniuses, she anguished over her vision. To her, the frequent bitterness of life seemed utterly unnecessary—because she knew the antidote: making strong, growth-enhancing connections with human beings. This entails being congruent within oneself as well as in communication with others. Congruence means extracting the poison inherent in "the blame pain" and replacing it with honest expression of one's internal experience. It means conveying anger or pain alongside respect rather than with denigration.

Virginia wanted to link the entire planet with human beings aware of the intrinsic value of each specific person—that "inner core of each being" she could see so clearly in people with whom she interacted. The congruent connections would empower the "shining light of the spirit" so often "trapped in a thick black cylinder of limitation and self-rejection" (Satir, 1988a, pp. 340–41).

She was quite serious and deliberate in the purpose of making this a better world. Those who tell of their lives in this book are evidence of how deeply, as well as how widely, ran her circle of influence.

Passage to a New Life

On Saturday, September 10, 1988 at 5:10 p.m. in her home in Menlo Park, California, Virginia Satir's body and spirit gently parted from each other in just the way she had planned. Having decided she did not want to continue to put out the tremendous energy required to fight the pancreatic cancer with which she had been diagnosed in late July, she had written her friends a farewell note announcing her decision.

September 5, 1988

To all my friends, colleagues and family:

I send you love.
Please support me in my passage to a new life.
I have no other way to thank you than this.
You have all played a significant part
    in my development of loving.
As a result, my life has been rich and
    full, so I leave feeling very grateful.

—Virginia

Laura Dodson, MSW, PH.D., is a Jungian analyst and author. Ten years ago, after traveling with Virginia in the former Soviet Union, Laura formed the Institute for International Connections, through which she continues to lead Satir-model cross-cultural family camps in Russia. With her leadership, many persons influenced by Virginia have continued to develop international community and respond to needs and requests of Russians, Latvians, Lithuanians, and persons in Poland and the Czech Republic. This organization continues in the model of Satir.

—*Robert S. Spitzer*
Publisher

2

Dreams Unfold a Life

by Laura S. Dodson

I first discovered Virginia Satir when I was a frustrated graduate student of social work. I had taught school for a year, only to find that the "boxes" of educational theory and practice were too small for me. While social work held promise of being a better profession for me, a lot of my questions weren't very popular in clinical social work in that day and time. Why did graduate schools look askance at therapy for one's self? Why didn't they even require it? How could we learn to help others without examining our own lives? Why didn't they teach us to work with families? How could the profession know so much (or seem to know so much) about human beings that it didn't ask more questions of itself? Why weren't words such as *love, creativity, sense of meaning,* or *human spirit* found in the literature of this "helping profession"? Didn't meaningful things happen before the Oedipal time?

While exploring professional journals, I encountered Virginia's work with entire families. I combed the library for other writings in family therapy—maybe this was where the creative energy was in my new field. The year after I finished my graduate studies, I wrote to Virginia, Murray Bowen, and Nathan Ackerman, inquiring about their work and whether they conducted professional seminars. Virginia replied with an invitation to a family therapy training workshop that she promised would offer "something for the participant's mind, body, and soul." Never having heard such words in the context of training, I enrolled immediately.

The following March (1963), I was in my first seminar with Virginia. She held it on the central California coast at what was in the process of becoming the Esalen Institute. In keeping with the ambiance there, I discarded my formal conference attire and, in more casual dress, entered training with a dual focus: me as a whole person, and my skills and knowledge as a clinician. Virginia taught by lecture, demonstration, and experience, and I resonated with her approach. She considered *me* to be my best tool in my work, and knowledge of myself to be primary in my work with others. Every person possessed within all he or she needed to heal. Virginia viewed every person with respect, even awe, for the miracle of human life and the uniqueness that each person is. Rather than seeing us as patients or therapists, she saw us as individuals on a "common human journey of unfolding the self." Life itself was a process of growth, and psychotherapy focused on freeing "blocked energy" that inhibited this natural process. The process—not the "problem"—was the focus.

Images, seen as the language of the unconscious and experienced on many levels, were valued as necessary for insight or growth. While understanding events in one's life was important, the sense one made of such events was a critical key. The work clearly showed that past pains were often locked in the body as well as in the psyche. Action therapies and body awareness were important tools for psychotherapy. Virginia often went beyond Freud's Oedipal work to work with preverbal and even *in utero* experiences.

Here was a belief system and a way of working that I could embrace. I watched with amazement as this woman—tall like I am, dynamic and loving—seemed as if by magic to inspire and awaken the participants and families. I watched them gain more personal freedom and interact differently. How did she do that? I wanted more experience with her.

I returned to Esalen at least once a year for the next six years to study with Virginia. Every year for five years, I was instrumental in bringing her to Fort Logan Mental Health Center, where I worked in Denver, Colorado. Her work had significant effect on this experimental hospital's philosophy and approach. Each time she came, she joined me in my group of adult schizophrenics and their families, where she served as a consultant. She supervised me in my ongoing work with this group and with other cases.

Virginia had the art of helping people reexperience their family dramas so as to resurrect roots of their complexes in the context of past events. Reexperienced family dramas became understandable plays of life, viewed beyond blame. I had the good fortune to have her lead me through several experiences of this sort, including my own Family Reconstruction.

From our first encounter, Virginia contributed to awakening creativity in me. She was the first teacher I had who put values and common sense into the profession of psychotherapy, and who was interested in weaving professional life together with the whole of life. One of her greatest gifts was her ability to see and inspire the highest and best selves in people.

Our 27-year relationship had several phases. I met Virginia when I was 25, searching for meaning in my profession and for a richer personal life. For seven years, she was the central teacher in my life. Then, during my marriage and throughout my Jungian studies, she was on the fringe of my life. Later our lives intertwined again, this time more as colleagues, friends, and at times coworkers.

In those years, we shared our personal journeys and our puzzles and meanings about life.

One of the greatest gifts she gave me was letting me see her own life process, the edges of her growth, and her strengths and her limitations. I experienced her ever-curious spirit as she met life with reverence, respect, and courage. I saw her build her theories and her work, and elaborate on and change them as she learned more. I saw her stand up and fall down, committed to seeing her truth and living it. And I saw her blind spots. The pattern of her life, far bigger than the incidents, was noble.

For the first seven years, our relationship was based on her great knowledge, her ability to impart it, and her consistent valuing of me. Relating this way accentuated my strengths and opened my life to increased confidence and risk of creative expression. Then, as I began to see Virginia's humanness and imperfections, I stopped idealizing her—a process that often included pain as well as significant growth. I first felt this jolt when her own issues affected how she related to my dilemmas about relationships with men. I awoke to this with the realization that I was listening to her more than to myself! Only much later, after I had worked through more of my issues and after each of us had had many other experiences, did Virginia and I reflect together on these times.

When Virginia she was in Colorado, she was usually a guest in my home, shared in my political and community involvements, explored my philosophical interests, and met my friends. We had some funny experiences together, such as the time I gave her a foot-saddle boost through a high window to get into my locked house, and the time we danced down the middle of the street in Aspen. We exchanged addresses for where to order shoes and clothes for our long feet and tall bodies, and we shopped together. During this time of my life, I experienced a growing congruency among all aspects of my life and thought, as well as bursts of creativity. Virginia supported even the smallest of my ideas and intuitions, and her excitement and provocative questions helped me actualize them.

After these seven intense years of learning from her, our contacts were sparse from 1971 to 1977. In that period, I began and completed doctoral studies in clinical psychology, began my studies toward becoming a Jungian analyst, and absorbed myself in my marriage and efforts to have a family. Negative interactions occurred between Virginia, my husband George, and I; and I became fearful that whatever struggles Virginia had with men in general and with George in particular would effect my life negatively. This feeling increased my distance, though I visited her in Columbia, Maryland as I was on my way to Zurich in 1972. At that time, Virginia felt passionate about the experimental community she was working to launch. At the same time, she felt restless for California. She told me that somehow she must settle her life enough to get her "hands into the soil," to work with the earth.

In a telephone conversation in 1977, Virginia invited me to be a member of a collegial organization she was forming with persons who had trained extensively with her (an organization she then called Humana; later, the Avanta Network). These people would work with her and substitute for her when her own schedule was full. I indicated that my life and interests had shifted to include a spiritual, transpersonal psychology; maybe our paths were too different. As I shared more, she did too. Finding remarkable commonality in the shifts our lives had taken, we met again in a new phase of our relationship, more as peers and colleagues.

In 1977, I became a charter member of the Avanta Network. That same year, Virginia wrote a glowing foreword to my book *Family Counseling: A Systems Approach.* I began working with her periodically in public presentations, and taking consultations for her. When we worked together in a public presentation, she demonstrated therapy with a couple or a family, and I followed this by presenting conceptualizations about her demonstration in terms of process, theory, and technique.

Virginia expressed skepticism about the regimentation in my training to become a Jungian analyst, which I had begun in 1973. Then, in 1981, during a month-long training which I conducted jointly with my close colleagues M'Lou Burnett-Dixon and Bill Nerin of Avanta, Virginia came to lead the group for a few days. While there, she read my postdoctoral thesis. It was my first written effort to combine my own thinking about depth psychology and larger-systems change with Virginia's influence and the work of Carl Jung. After she read it, Virginia and I began an increasingly rich dialogue about the application of systems thinking to massive culture change.

This dialogue found some expression in a public presentation and workshop in 1987, "What Heals the Family Heals the World." Virginia, M'Lou, and I did this as a fundraiser for our anticipated work in the (then) USSR in May 1988. The dialogue continued as the three of us went to Russia, Georgia, and Lithuania. Virginia told me during this trip that her next intent was to study history more so she could apply her work to cultural change with more confidence and clarity.

In the USSR, Virginia's sessions started with a dynamic but simple demonstration of how she began her work. Calling up a volunteer from the audience, she had the person stand beside her and she held his or her hand. Virginia then spoke of centering herself by leaving previous thoughts and concerns on a "shelf," bringing her full attention to this moment. and aligning herself with energy from the heavens, the earth, and life on this plane. Next, she spoke of her attitude toward the person she was about to meet. She spoke of him or her as unique in all the world; no one before or after would be exactly like this individual. She spoke of a sense of awe about their being, commenting with humor, "I am speaking of the person's essence, not necessarily about their be-havior!" Then she turned toward the person and looked into his or her eyes. With eminence and warmth in her voice, Virginia offered a simple greeting: "Hello, Natasha [or whomever]."

At every presentation in the Soviet Union, this simple demonstration brought an intense round of applause. Sometimes the audience even stood while applauding. The universality of Virginia's concepts and her simple, direct way of communicating crossed cultural barriers. Such honoring of energies and of persons was, it became evident, key in the hearts of a people too long suppressed in their individuality and spirituality. Virginia then continued her work, weaving in comments about the equality of women, the birth of the self, how meeting of selves is core to marriage, and so on. As she spoke about and gave permission by her very being for people to think, to feel, to see, to hear, and to comment about it, those in her audiences made longed-for connections with self and other. As was usual in Virginia's audiences, a sense of well being, openness, and creativity grew to fill the room.

On occasion, I assumed my old role of process and theory commentator about Virginia's lecture or discussion. After Virginia's morning exercise or her work with individuals or families, M'Lou and I sometimes led separate breakout groups. On this trip, Virginia exercised control of all presentations even more tightly than usual. She even moved a KGB-infested audience from resistance to receptivity, although some of those secret police missed the moments of that transition. As I was returning to the presentation after visiting the bathroom, the KGB were attending to an Afghani man who had cornered me in the hall earlier with his concerns. I thought it rather humorous that they had been outside the meeting room during the real action.

After that presentation, Virginia said: "Who could ever do my work but me? None of my students could have done that!" Later, I understood this remark, her unusually tight control of the stage, as well as her remarkable work in the USSR as, perhaps unconscious to us all, a foretelling of her death. Her fatal illness surfaced within ten days of our return to the States. Our pregnant dialogue on cultural change and everything else in Virginia's intense life was suspended as she became consumed, first with a fight for her life and then with a process of surrender to death. Pancreatic cancer took her life three months later, in September 1988.

Being present with Virginia during her dying process was one of the most profound experiences of my life. Among many things she gave me then were a sense of death related to birth and more attuned ways to move beyond fear through intense focus and attunement to life's process, moment by moment. Only the most important things, however small, earned space in our attention, conversation, and action. A year later (1990), I wrote an article about this moving experience: "The Dying Process of a Conscious Woman."

Most of the years I knew Virginia, I sensed the profundity beneath her work's dynamic simplicity. Only more recently have I been able to articulate how I see her impact on holistic thought and the development of psychological theory and practice. Core elements in her work since the 1940s are only today becoming acceptable in mainstream psychotherapeutic thought.

In a Chicago children's home in the 1940s, for instance, she never hesitated to follow her orphan clients to the place of their pain. She and they went beyond the Oedipal period—where classical Freudian thought stopped—to the roots of early abandonment issues. Through breath and body work, she discovered that people store these preverbal experiences mainly in the body and in images. Working outside any then-recognized framework of psychotherapy, she practiced what many theoreticians have since described in attachment theory, self psychology, and object relations theory. In psychotherapy, these and other schools of thought have legitimized attributes that were always primary in Virginia's work, such as compassion, empathy, and the therapist's use of self. In her relationship psychotherapy, she drew back the curtains to awaken people's compassion, support, understanding, and healthy interdependence. These qualities had faded out of more classical Freudian work. (In some neo-Freudian work, particularly that at Stone Center at Wesley College, and in self psychology, these ingredients of healing are now receiving more recognition.)

Virginia spoke in a language of symbols and images. In an extroverted manner, she used the symbolic language of the unconscious—pictures, images, and metaphors—to help people integrate unconscious material into ego functioning. This was work that Carl Jung had done in an introverted way. While he worked with symbols from dreams, imagination, and cultural myths, she created external images in the form of family sculptures and psychodramas. As with Jung, her belief in the innate wisdom of all persons awakened the inner healer in those with whom she worked.

At the same time that she worked profoundly with the unconscious, she was infinitely more practical than Carl Jung in her awareness of everyday issues. She taught in a systematic, simple, earthy way, drawing examples from things that everyone had experienced. She made her teachings palatable with her humor, her normalization of the common human journey, and her loving, charismatic personality. She rarely missed an opportunity to alert her clients, often in humorous ways, to daily opportunities to practice what they were learning.

She practiced a rare combination of education, depth psychology, self psychology, object relations work, systems psychology, reality therapy, and hypnotic suggestion. In the last 15 years of her career, she entered more deeply into transpersonal psychology as she began to work with "energies within and without." Her family systems work then took leaps toward viewing the universe as an interrelated system and toward transforming whole cultures. Had she lived longer, I am certain she would have moved farther into applying her understandings to cultural transformation and cultural recovery from oppression. While the world recognizes her as a major contributor in the field of family therapy, I find this much too small a box for the work of Virginia Satir.

I miss her for many, many reasons. She influenced me greatly. Her work is the core of my own work, my philosophy of life itself. Yet what I miss most is what might have been—collegiality with her and leadership from her in today's rich time of major paradigm shift. I would like to puzzle with her about the archetypal shift as east and west realign, as wars torture the former Yugoslavia, and as the former Eastern bloc attempts to moves toward healing from oppression and incorporation of democratic principles.

It's the more personal things for which I am the most grateful to Virginia—the qualities of honesty, dynamic simplicity, straightforwardness, humor, and ability to be real with me about some of her own process. I feel privileged and grateful for our relationship.

Autobiography

In a life being lived rapidly and intensely, how does one pause to capture the journey's history and tapestry? Using the writing of this autobiography as a reflective process for myself, I hope to give you an impression of some ways I see myself: a picture of personal, family, genealogical, and archetypal influences on my life; a flavor of what I consider the most significant events in my life; and an overview of my professional work. I experience my life as an incredible journey, unrelated to any measurement of happiness, pain, or struggles (and I have had my share of them all—but they are simply incidents in a bigger picture). I hope you will see more the tapestry than be distracted by any particular story. At the end of this writing, I would like to have presented on personal and professional levels what I see as interplay of all systems. And I would like to have inspired some readers to think from new perspectives about the systems in which we live and the tapestry in all our lives.

Impressions and Overviews

I have something of the soul of an artist. I might have been one, had the economics of my life allowed it. I might still, and maybe I am, in a sense. I think in images. When I am most in harmony with myself, I move lightly through the world, allowing material from the unconscious to emerge and decisions or action to grow out of this state. I like sketching or working with water color, doing little things that make a house a home, creating art with my children, making pots or hand-building clay, and working with house plants or in the garden. It is sheer joy to have a companion with whom I can feel as good as I feel alone, while adding other richness to that base.

Monet, Chagall, and Gertrude Stein touch inner cords; Bach is in my dreams. My social consciousness and sense of justice resonate with those of Carl Sandburg, Pete Seeger, and Woody Guthrie. Thomas Jefferson, Eleanor Roosevelt, Anaïs Nin, Thomas Merton, Pierre Teilhard de Chardin, and Jesus are some of my heroes. I like the poignant, poetic description of truths, without judgment, with awe and love for life expressed by mystic/realist poets such as Rainer Maria Rilke, T. S. Eliot, the Sufi poet Kabir, Pushkin of Russia, and Borgess of Argentina. In addition to following the growing edges of knowledge in my profession and relating that to social and cultural change, I prefer reading biographies, history, fiction, or poetry that is a comment on society, is based in history, or in some way delves into life's journey.

Sports that let me feel my body and that allow quiet time with nature are my choices: biking, skiing, swimming, canoeing, hiking. My children and I are a part of a group of clown families, and we can be found on quadricycle or foot in Colorado parades.

In this, my 37th year of clinical practice and 30th year of teaching and consulting, I still thrill when my clients and I—or the group with whom I am working and I—come to the point when the experience of working with their material becomes as if we are artists together, placing their images on canvas for mutual examination. An image appears of the self or the system, or both. Then the energy blocks that inhibit growth or flow evidence themselves. As we look into the past and at the present, and work with dreams or our relationship, we at times look at the canvas from the perspective of a higher self, beyond time and space limitations. A peak moment is when we feel a movement similar to that when a picture in process takes over and begins, as artists say, "to paint itself." What appears is dynamic, descriptive, and fluid. It tells a truth not conscious before in this way.

I find myself working and living on the cutting edge of some issues. In my professional and personal life, these have emerged up to 15 years before they are in motion in the larger population, changing societal thinking. Examples of this permeate my history. Being influenced by Virginia Satir is one significant instance. I left elementary school teaching in 1959 because I couldn't move what I experienced as an antiquated system toward better ways to teach. I wanted to find new approaches to specific learning problems, work with emotional issues in learning strategies, and implement academics with a more humanistic view of children. These innovations came in subsequent years but were taboo in the time and place in which I taught.

In 1960, I was "block busting" for civil rights and then lived in that newly integrated neighborhood. I worked for the recognition of Red China—an activity that put me on the "pink list" for a few years until our government recognized that country. From 1977 to 1979, in the process of adopting my infant son, I pioneered legal regulations for single-adult adoption of infants. Innovations in psychotherapy (psychodrama, Gestalt therapy, psychosynthesis, and family therapy) were key in my career years before they became generally acceptable modalities of psychological treatment. In 1967, a colleague and I formed an institute to teach these methods to psychotherapists. To escape my leadership role on the cutting edge,

I went to Zurich to study Jungian psychology in 1972—only to discover when I returned that Jung was becoming a new popular psychology in the United States.

Pioneering innovations and changes was for many years an involuntary role. At first, this continual occurrence bewildered, burdened, or inflated me. More recentLy, I have come to see this fate as important in the meaning of my life—even as destiny—and now I feel surrendered to it as a core reality of my life. Most of the time now, this journey intrigues me, and I attempt to walk this path consciously with grace and balance in my inner and outer life.

Family Genealogy

My family heritage on both sides is that of the rugged pioneer. My father's forebears came from England on the *Mayflower* and settled in the east. When the territory that is now Texas was fighting for independence from Mexico, a several-times-great-grandfather went there by covered wagon as a Baptist circuit preacher and became well known and respected. After his death at a young age, his wife, Kate Morrill, crocheted bedspreads and sold them to assist more Baptist ministers to attend the newly established Baylor College. She was one of its first woman graduates. Kate is described as having been six feet tall, strong, and determined. I identify with her. Politicians and public servants peopled this side of the family, as did a number of school teachers and school principals.

My mother's ancestors include a woman six or seven generations back whom I've recently learned was a part of the early establishment of the Religious Society of Friends in Pennsylvania. It is a group I have been a part of for the last 22 years, although I had been unaware that the Friends were in my heritage. Another woman on this side of the family, a few generations later, was the daughter of a Georgia plantation owner. After marrying a hired hand, she was disowned and ran away to Texas. Her daughter married a Cherokee Indian; later in that bloodline, my grandmother Susie Dunbar was one-quarter Cherokee.

The matriarchy on my mother's side traces back to the late 1600s in the southern Scotland town of Dunbar, where Mary, Queen of Scots hid to escape being beheaded by her sister Elizabeth. While visiting Dunbar, I tried to imagine life there in 1100, with its matriarchal society that the Romans never conquered. I picture the women of my heritage as hearty Scots farmers.

Values of my family that go back for several generations and are important to me include a rugged, determined way of approaching life and a spiritual quality that lends a belief in the self and in the importance of family, human service, and community. I like the simplicity and earthy quality of the farming background on both sides of my family, the history of focused ability to accomplish what one sets out to do, and the courage to risk.

Archetypal Imprints

As much or more than our lifetime's events, archetypal threads may affect our life journey. With their positive and negative edges, the archetypes of my own U.S. culture have an impact on my psyche. I like wide open spaces, adventure, and the spirit of pioneering. As an eternal optimist, I find it difficult to accept limitations. Hard work, idealism, rugged individualism, and often naïvetè have been parts of my character.

I am curious about archetypal imprints from ancestors far beyond our known heritage. From how many generations back do such things reach into our psyches, our lives? This question can take us into the realm of the mystics and certainly into the thought of C. G. Jung. Some people think of them as past lives. I am not sure how to understand the meaning of impressions that could relate to this dimension, but about 15 years ago I had a profound experience of this sort. Whether my trance state produced a memory of a past life or the material came from ancestral memory or somewhere else in my unconscious seems less relevant than the strong numinous feeling I had. This is the imagery.

> I am a slave woman, walking all my adult life with a group of slaves on a long journey. I actually have two roles. As a member of the group, I am a slave; in secret, I am a mentor to the enslavers, who consult me about their decisions and about philosophical issues. (At times in the experience I am living it, and at times I look down on it from high above as if looking down on a relief map. At those latter times, I can see that we are walking from Scandinavia, across Russia to the Black Sea.) I have a sense of purpose about the journey and my role. Though the trip is difficult in all seasons, I feel contentment.
>
> At the end of the experience, we arrive at the Black Sea. I am an old woman. I lie down on the sandy beach, fall into a sleep, and quietly and peacefully die. In time my bones disintegrate into sand.

The experience was visceral and intense; yet without my really knowing what to do with it, it soon moved out of my conscious thought. Its memory returned in a rather shocking way 12 years later when, on the way to Russia for a third summer's work, I stopped with my children to tour England. While sightseeing in several areas, we chanced to visit a museum of Viking history in York. Walking through a room full of maps of various Viking invasions and trade routes, I found myself standing before a map of the same route I had seen in my dream. Below it was this caption: "As they moved from Norway, across Russia to the Black Sea, the Vikings took slaves along the way. The journey took a lifetime."

Chills raced down my spine. This map documented the journey I had been on in that whatever-you-call-it experience. So far as I know, I had never heard of this before. The knowledge made me wonder whether some connections to my own past lives or those of my ancestors sit in my very bones and are part of what has moved

me to work in Russia today. Did I have Viking and Russian ancestors, some of whom later went to Scotland and northern England?
Are they the forebears of ancestors I know about from that part of
the world? For now, I am content to say that the drama of any one
life likely extends far beyond the confines of the body that contains it.

Childhood and
Family of Origin

On this lifetime's plane, the tapestry of my life reflects my particular woundings and healings of childhood experiences as well as
the threads and knots I have made since. My mother grew up wanting to be married, but as she approached the age of 24, she began
fearing that connubial life might pass her by. When she saw my
father in a Southern Baptist church in Dallas, she felt "divine guidance" in their meeting and exclaimed that he was the man she
would marry. He was tall and handsome, embodying the perfect
masculine image held by a Southern lady. In addition, he was kind
and loving. Although her friends and his father helped make their
connection happen, my father was not a passive figure in this romance. In the church balcony one evening, he clipped a lock of
her naturally curly hair to keep in his wallet. (It stayed there all his
life.) As they walked together in the streets while courting, he carved
a slingshot for their hoped-for-one-day boy child.

A few months after my parents were married, my father's father—who had been a dashing extrovert and a politician, a true
patriarch of the family—suffered a stroke. It left him permanently
partially paralyzed and a bed patient. His long illness began drain-
ing the family money, aborting my father's college plans and some
of his zest for life. My grandfather died two years later, seven months
after my brother Tom was born. With the Great Depression deplet-

ing their money further, and with the responsibility of one child and hopes for a second, my parents and brother lived with my mother's sister, her husband, and their son. My mother took care of the children and did office work in the home while my father struggled with two jobs and looked for better work.

In this period of mourning and financial burden, when my father began suffering a mild depression that turned chronic, I was conceived. His depression as well as his tenderness and loving spirit were ever present in our household. I was born in Dallas, Texas in 1936, two years after my brother. Tom and I were like a second set of parents to my sister Gay, born ten years later.

Ultimately, my father worked his way past fellow employees who were college graduates to enter into management in a manufacturing company, where he worked from 1941 until his death in 1972. His confidence level, perhaps his depression, and the pressures to make money kept him from ever returning to college, though a part of him hungered for formal learning. We lived modestly, not having a home of our own until I was nine years old. Our first car came some years later. My mother supplemented the family income by home-office work, selling Avon products, and later being the "Welcome Newcomer" visitor for the city of Garland, Texas. Absolutely everyone in the community knew and loved her.

In the core of me, things have always been basically fine, despite life's pains and difficulties. On the familial level, I believe this has to do in large part with my birth process and my relationship with my mother in the first 15 months of my life. I was a full-term baby; no anesthetic was used; the birth was easy and quick.

"What is it, what is it?" she kept asking as I was being born.

"I can't tell yet." Then the doctor proclaimed, "Mrs. Dodson, you have a little girl!"

"Let me see her!" Although the doctor protested that I wasn't cleaned up yet, my mother demanded, "Just let me see her!"

I was wrapped in a blanket and presented to my mother. Her tender greeting was, "Hello, Laura Sue!"

My mother tells this story even today, at age 90, with twinkles in her eyes and endearment in her tone as she says my name—the names of my two grandmothers, chosen for me two years before my birth. Each time she tells the story, she conveys her sense of "something special" about my life. She tells me she always felt this about me, even before my birth. "Not that I don't feel that about all my children, but especially you!" she says. I am grateful for this wonderful beginning.

As life has it, my beginnings were too soon interrupted. When I was 15 months old, my mother developed pneumonia, which took her to the hospital for a month, brought her near death, and abruptly ended my nursing and tender care. My earliest conscious memory is of this time in my life:

> My father is holding me in a parked car as we wait for my grand-mother, who is visiting my mother inside the hospital. I want to nurse but, having no idea of this, he holds me in the air at arm's length and looks at me, admiring the beauty of his baby daughter. I scream, but he doesn't understand. In time, I give up on my need and, seeming to sense his, I run my fingers through his hair to comfort him in his worry, frustration, and guilt about my mother's illness. I remember, too, ragefully throwing my bottle out of my crib as Dad's mother, who cared for me, insistently offered it to me.

Complicating this first abandonment in my life were complexes in each of my parents that locked into our family system. Shortly before her illness, my mother had insisted on having a home separate from that of her sister. It was nearly impossible on my parents' meager budget. My father, likely, was not as committed to this goal as she. They moved to what she called a "cheap but filthy" duplex. Enraged at these circumstances and in her anger and disappointment, yet with determination, my mother cleaned the house long hours as a Northerner blew in. In the process, she contracted pneumonia. This event seemed to have locked her in an old complex, present long before she met my father—one containing the feeling that no one had ever loved her well enough. Now she felt my father would not, as well; she would never have her needs met.

My father's self-concept included a fear that he was inadequate to the task of providing for a family. Mother's rage moved right into this space in his psyche, affirming his fear. His response to his fear and subsequent guilt was withdrawal, a response that was probably an old behavior, too, arising long before he met my mother. As he withdrew more and more, my mother became more angry and blaming, believing her childhood fear was confirmed. Well before my father's death, my parents found their way out of this bind. Meanwhile, however, for my remaining years of childhood, neither our family nor I gained freedom from it. Aspects of the bind's residue remained in me and affected my adolescence and young adulthood.

The result was the formation of our family crucible. Every family forms such a crucible, creating the raw material from which we build our lives. For me, this "fertilizer" gave rise to my profession and my complexes. It also set the foundation upon which I could build a life and hone my soul. Every other incident of pain in my childhood seemed to be woven into this core web of distress.

Gradually, over many years, I came to understand each of my parents and their relationship better. Uncovering stories of my early childhood allowed me greater freedom from the bonds of their complexes, the family's complexes, and my early wounds. A first layer of this understanding came in relation to my body image, which I discovered in work with Virginia when I was 24. It was then that I began examining my feeling that I would never be quite okay as a person, especially as a woman, because of my height.

Fritz Perls, who was attending that workshop, played my father. As I sat on his lap as a "little girl," Virginia artfully took me from idealizing my father into the sadness of a change in my relationship with him when I was six years old. He had moved away from me emotionally, and I was heartbroken. I thought I must have grown too tall or must not be good enough for him to continue loving me.

In this drama I realized that this was the painful "sense" I had made through a child's eyes, and that this belief had imprinted my self-concept. I left the workshop feeling relief—and certain that there was more to this story. What had really happened with my father? I had more questions than I had ever known to ask. Intent on learning some missing pieces that could help me understand my life, I visited my parents and kept my mother up most of a night, demanding information.

After much insistence on my part, she told me that my father had begun an affair when I was five or six years old and continued it four or five years, until about the time she became pregnant with my sister. This was quite different from my childhood sense of the situation. I wept with relief, crying in a little-girl voice, "It wasn't my fault, it really wasn't my fault!" His unavailability had not been a statement about me.

In addition to thinking I was too tall to be loved, I realized I had thought I had caused pain, and that my inability to fix the pain— and my love for my father—had made me bad. My self-image went from bad to worse in those years. At six, I developed asthma, which continued until I left home for college (at 17). Attacks were sometimes acute and frightening, necessitating shots of adrenaline. Then, the spring after my sister was born, I was bedfast for several weeks with what was diagnosed as a kidney infection. (Later my parents discovered the diagnosis was probably incorrect. What it was, no one could or would say, but it was decided that my staying inside the house would be counterproductive; returning to school and playing in the sun were the revised treatment plans.) Meanwhile, during the time I was confined to bed, I would hear my parents playing gleefully with the new baby. The sense my young mind made of this time was that my sister had rescued them from pain simply by her birth—a job I could not do, no matter how hard I had tried.

As I neared 11, my parents became active in forming a new Baptist church. The church gave me a sense of community, an extended, positive family that cared for me. Desperate to be redeemed from feelings I couldn't put into words at that time—my sense of badness, of being too tall to be lovable, and of failing to help my parents become happier—I was baptized two or three times in this church (where my parents were becoming happier). Any effort to describe what was wrong or what my sins were never quite satisfied me. Nor did the attempt to be cleansed or forgiven.

I was old when I was young. To the outside world, I was a strong leader and a conscientious youth. I became a caretaker of my sister, super responsible in everything I did, and a leader in most things I undertook. I excelled academically. These were my most creative, sublimated outlets. The summer of my 13th year, I worked a 12-hour day, taking care of three young children, cooking, and cleaning house. Experiences of play, laughter, and testing skills with the opposite sex were not mine to be had. I taught Sunday school from the age of 14, won awards at school, and was a supportive, caring friend in whom many people confided.

I got no feeling of support in return. Although I yearned for someone to notice and speak with me about the unspeakable, no one seemed to detect my pain. I lived my adolescence feeling awkward in my body, often embarrassed, and being teased about it. At 14, I was six feet tall and only 105 pounds and wore braces on my teeth. I suffered somatic problems, some depression, and no socially acceptable defenses against my pain.

The Dam Unplugs

In college, my interests became more defined. They reached from drama and child development to anthropology and psychology, Russian, and international travel. After continuing to be elected to leadership roles, I gradually found them less gratifying. Neither friendships nor dating relationships were as rewarding as I wanted. My friendships lacked certain dimensions. I seemed locked at the level of either "the helper" or "the one being helped." Yet I felt bewildered about unlocking the next steps in my personal life.

After graduating from college, I borrowed money for a tour across Europe with fellow graduates. On returning, I lived at home and taught fourth grade for one year to pay back my loan. Restless emotionally and discontent professionally, I applied to a graduate school of social work and received a scholarship.

The more important arena for change lay in my personal domains. Getting away—first to Florida and then to Colorado for the second year of graduate work—let me experiment with release from previous confines. Student social work placements interested me, and the work went well, but I felt bound up inside. I wanted for myself the richer life I was learning to assist others in attaining. The religion of my childhood became too narrow for me; I left it and all religions. My dating choices were efforts to expand my life and embrace difference.

In graduate school in Denver, I found new and deeper friendships. I also considered therapy for the first time, when I learned that a new local school of Freudian analysis was beginning. I applied to be a control case for a psychiatrist in training. Although it took two and a half years for this process to begin, I felt hopeful just knowing it would.

In 1961, after receiving my master's degree in social work, I spent the summer teaching English to law students in Xalapa, Mexico under a program called Experiment in International Living. That fall, I took a position at Denver's new and innovative hospital: Fort Logan Mental Health Center. Two years later, after serving as member of the local Experiment board, I represented it at an international meeting in Germany. I then traveled with a friend on the Orient Express from Austria through Yugoslavia to Turkey. For several months, we had many adventures living with families and exploring on our own. My friendships, my work, and my inner and outer worlds were becoming alive and dynamic.

On my return in 1963, analysis began. Training with many pioneering leaders in psychotherapy, I also increased my training with Virginia. In the process, the waters of my unconscious began to flow. As when a sizable dam opens, unbounded creative energy surged within me as I made sense of and released some of my earlier pain. The family crucible became an alchemical vessel in which pain transformed into the very stuff from which the depth of my soul and life would emerge.

My mid 20s to early 30s saw dramatic transformations. Learning of my father's affair and debunking my supposed rule about height are but two examples of the many volcano-like movements in my psyche that occurred in workshops with Virginia or Fritz Perls, or in psychodrama. The Freudian couch where I worked for six years was my main place of integration for the unconscious eruptions during these more dramatic therapies.

I came to understand my childhood asthma as a reaction to the family stress and the "loss" of my father, and my illness at age ten as a reaction to my inability to save my parents from their pain, which I thought I had caused and must repair. Both physical symptoms were a somatization of my longing to feel more love. In my childhood mind, I perceived my sister as evidence that I was an inadequate being: I could not help my mother and father, but she could. She obviously had all the right ingredients as a person, as she could provide what was needed. (In truth, the affair stopped as soldiers came home from World War II. At age 41, my mother seemingly miraculously conceived my sister, and my parents recommited to each other.)

Virginia often said, "It is not what happens that causes our pain, it is the sense we make of it." As I became more conscious of what my young mind had construed, the confines of my family's crucible began crumbling around me. I made new sense of my parents' relationship, my father's distancing from me, my sister's role, and so on. I also gained some understanding that my mother's reactions to me as a teenager and an adult were frequently rooted in her fears. I stimulated those fears simply by becoming a woman different from her, by attempting to live a separate identity, and by moving my focus in life away from home—behaviors that she saw as threats to the family system and her sense of well-being. My father did not help me with these issues, for he sought peace by conforming to my mother's wishes. Neither knew how to speak about the "elephants in the living room."

The more I understood, the more I moved beyond conformity to console my mother, secrecy to protect her, or rebellion to escape her. An added, unexpected gain was that I saw another level of her being: the wise woman in her, her higher self, who supports my life and my dreams, and encourages me even when her everyday self doesn't understand me, or when my choices frighten her. I began having the pleasure of more of these kind of interactions with her, fewer of the old ones that stimulated complexes. I felt myself becoming more human, less defended, and less reductive in my perceptions. Wounds healed as the story of my family acquired more subtle dimensions and the soul of the family, which lives beyond the complexes, took life in my psyche.

In time, I came to see the family drama as being beyond the blame of anyone. My empathy grew for the human story and, most important, I freed myself more and more from the binds that had developed in me as a child. My body, my mind, my relationships, everything about me felt freer. My life was full and exciting. Creativity graced every aspect—my relationships, work, art, community involvement, the world of ideas, philosophy and religion, and even play. My artistic interest grew during this period as well, and I became a potter, worked in leather, and sketched.

In 1963 I met George Cronin, whose intensity and zest for life equaled mine. He was as involved in outer life—political systems and current events—as I was in inner life. An Irish ex-Catholic, he was a Democratic district chairman in Denver, ran for public office (losing by a small margin), completed a degree in economics in the early part of our relationship, and became coordinator of Vista Volunteers for the Denver juvenile court. Together, we worked actively on public issues important to both of us and were an active part of community life.

I could describe life with George as wonderfully positive or absolutely terrible, but it was always intense, dynamic, and passionate. Our values of compassionate living and service, our sensuality and love of life matched. One of our relationship's most dynamic aspects was the weaving between us of the two worlds of inner and outer life, which, not surprisingly, seemed to be a next step we both needed in inner growth and creativity.

With all these dimensions, our first five years together were really quite marvelous. Then, as we approached the question of marriage, I felt paralyzed. At times, I thought he was frightened by my successes and wanted to hold me back. (By this time, I was actively teaching and leading workshops over this country and Canada, including at Esalen.) I feared that my increased self-actualization and individuation could cost me this relationship, yet I couldn't seem to slow down my sometimes inflated circuit run. This was part of the issue.

I could neither leave George nor choose him as a marriage partner. Nor could I rid myself of my intense ambivalence. The gap grew more painful between my professional success and my personal growth: my ability to actualize my learnings in my relationship. My patients were getting better, my public acclaim was increasing, and my agony was growing. Desperate, I tried to resolve this through my Freudian analysis, times away in contemplation, consultations with Virginia, breakups with George, and—finally—marriage.

We had a beautiful wedding that reflected the best of us, but it didn't resolve my distress. Rather, distress grew between us. Two months after the wedding, I had this dream:

> George and I are building a house on an island where all my mother's sisters and brother and their spouses live. While I feel elated on the one hand as I am reminded of playful memories with extended family when I was a young child, I am also astounded to see the pain in the relationships of my aunts and uncles. I am standing on a slight incline just above their homes at the spot where the frame of the home we are building stands. A hurricane comes in from the sea and washes all their houses into the ocean. Ours escapes only because it is just a frame. Had the walls been built, it would have had no spots for the water to wash through and it would have tumbled into the ocean as well.

Indeed, our house was in danger—and the danger had something to do with elements of my family of origin in my psyche. I couldn't see it clearly.

In 1971, we gave ourselves a break from the unresolved distress and pursued further studies. George went for advanced degrees in social work and public administration at the University of Southern California in Los Angeles. I decided to seek a doctorate in clinical psychology and defined my field as the interface between depth psychology and larger systems. Finding no graduate program able to span these two areas, I designed a program of study that won approval as an external program by Union Graduate School of (then) Yellow Springs, Ohio. My program bridged sociology, political science, cultural anthropology, history and psychology so as to delve into the psyche as a system *and* explore the systems in which we live, particularly from a psychological perspective.

For the first three months of my program, I studied at the Center for the Study of Democratic Institutions in Santa Barbara, California with Robert Hutchens. In free time, I joined George in L.A. or he joined me in Santa Barbara. My program's second phase took me to the Jung Institute in Zurich for eight months of study and Jungian analysis, and to Florence for three weeks of study with Roberto Assagioli. The third phase, from the fall of 1973 to the spring of 1974, was an internship in Dallas, Texas with James Hall, M.D., a Jungian analyst who was also interested in systems and groups. From there, I often commuted to California to be with George. The last phase was my dissertation, written from 1974 to 1975 while George and I were in Washington, D.C. Having completed his two degrees, he had taken a job with the Senate Committee on Aging. I received my doctorate in May 1975.

We had wonderful times in Washington. Some of the unrest between us was quieting as his success and confidence grew. His world took me into a variety of political arenas and exposed me more closely to the pulse of national and international events; mine brought him to look more at inner life and relationships. We were appreciating each other more.

We both wanted to move our lives forward, and children seemed a next step. We had previously lost two pregnancies; that winter and spring, we lost two more. George grew restless about his work in Washington. Many years before, when he had envisioned being in D.C., he thought it would be gratifying to have a part in public policy in areas about which he felt strongly. While some of this was so, he was continuously stressed. Work demanded long hours and offered great pressures with small monetary rewards.

In the midst of all this distress, George and I began to have dreams about his dying. He would awaken in sweats. One dream of mine was:

> I am in Zion Canyon, on the pinnacle of a mountain, waiting for George. He is to come there from a fast-moving jet called "Senate Committee on Aging" that will fly over and drop a rope ladder for him to come down. He must time his descent so he is at the bottom of the ladder just when it reaches the pinnacle of the peak. He is successful! We are elated and begin to dance around each other. He loses his balance and falls to his death in the bottom of the canyon.

These dreams were enough to drive him to a medical exam and a second opinion. Nothing of significance was reported; he had no symptoms. We decided the dreams must be about an inner or outer life transformation needed, not a literal death. He began thinking that leaving Washington and possibly returning to Denver would be important to his well-being.

A week before George died, I had an imagery experience with music, guided by Helen Bonny (who wrote *Music and Your Mind* in 1973). I had this dreamlike image:

> I am dancing to a Bach symphony in a log cabin with large picture windows, in the woods. I have a young baby in my arms. Sitting around me on benches against the wall are a number of women in my life who are celebrating the child with me. I see George out the window, sitting on the steps of the capitol building. I want to go to him, so I walk out of the cabin. Now I walk alone past the Washington Monument and the reflecting pool to George. Suddenly, a spider web appears from the heavens to the earth between him and me, and I become tangled in it. My guide asks, "Would you like to go on?"
>
> "Yes!"
>
> "Who can help you?"
>
> I stand still and ask the help of God. The spider web falls off, and in that moment I see George climbing on the web, still stretched from the sky to the earth. He is agile and radiant, delighted in the task. For the first time I see his pleasure, comfort, artful skill, ease, and in-

trigue as he explores and masters the complex web, which I understand to be the political and social systems of Washington and of the world.

Recognizing more fully than ever before the differences between George and me, I experienced an overwhelming appreciation for the uniqueness of each of us and the complementary character of our differences. This was enlightening and freeing. My consciousness was shifting more from my ambivalence and uncertainty to a deeper appreciation of who we each were.

I never told George about this experience. I was waiting for the right moment, and I was afraid of how vulnerable telling him would make me. Three days after seeing Helen, I flew to Denver. A few days later, George came for discussions with our friend Dick Lamm (Colorado's then governor) about work possibilities in Colorado. George and I were elated to see each other when he arrived at the airport. Two nights later, he suffered a cranial aneurysm, became unconscious, and remained so for 30 hours until he died on September 9, 1975.

The day he died, I seemed to see the tapestry of George's life as clear as a bell. I could see our relationship better. What a dynamic weaving it had been of the outer and inner life! I realized that whether George was alive or not, even whether I had ever known him or not, this weaving of inner life and outer systems was my own journey. I realized, too, that at the time of his death, I was on the brink of experiencing intimacy and separateness at a new level.

I was startled, sad, and profoundly heavy with pain. How tragic that he lost his life at the young age of 41. I was mournful at losing him and at the incompleteness of our journey; the things unsaid, the things not yet understood or actualized. Daily for almost a year, I would have a severe headache if I stifled my tears, or feel sick to my stomach. Only weeks after his death did I realize that my earlier dream about his death included symbolism of the literal events.

I was also angry about being 38 with no child or husband. Being a wife and a mother were important parts of my journey, and now these roles were gone. I contemplated trying again to have or to adopt a child. "Yes!" I told myself. "But maybe I can't make such big decisions now."

I waited. I could take only one step at a time, and that in a fog of surrender. What to do? I made decisions from working with my dreams. This included the major decision to proceed with my return to Denver. To earn my livelihood, I taught psychotherapy and carried only a small caseload, as I was finding "talk" therapy taxing. In addition, I was giving massage and teaching yoga—skills I had acquired some years before.

I lived simply. Work in pottery and writing helped sustain me. Whenever I felt confused or overwhelmed, I sat on a cushion on the floor and looked at a particular dent in the plaster on the wall, which became a focal point for meditation. Thus I waited for guidance for the next moment. That next year was the most deeply reflective and solitude year of my life. Some missing pieces came to me for understanding myself and my relationship with George.

The eternal paradox of separate yet connected, interdependent yet independent had limited resolution in considering my parents' marriage and my relationship with them during my young, impressionable years. It was also an unresolved theme in the marriages of many of my aunts and uncles (as represented in the dream described earlier). These dynamics had affected my ability to individuate as a woman, to enter fully into relationship, and to have the courage to love. It was my story, twice gripping me in significant ways. I recalled the following dream about my analyst, which I had in the latter part of my work with her:

> I am looking for a way to get to the seventh floor of a building [the United Nations] where my parents are with my sister, who is a baby. I need to meet them there. I go to an information booth staffed by a

woman who in real life is my Freudian analyst. She gives me complicated and unclear instructions: "Go up those stairs over there, make a U turn, go down an escalator, walk to the north, look for another set of stairs."

I stop her and ask, "Would you just go with me and show me the way? I am concerned I cannot find my way unless you do."

"No," she says, "For you see, I have this yoke over my neck with heavy buckets on each end. I cannot walk there with this load."

I am terribly disappointed. I feel hopeless, unable to find my way.

When I told my analyst this dream, she recalled that a Chinese figurine with yoke and buckets like my dream image was sitting on her parents' mantel to that day. When she was three years old, she and her father had given it as a present to her mother. To my analyst, this figurine represented efforts to join her father in buying a gift that might appease her mother and thus lessen conflicts between her parents.

Experiencing and working through childhood conflicts reconstellated in transference/countertransference in the vessel of therapy can be perhaps the most poignant of psychotherapy's healing experiences. Or it can create more damage. Eventually, I came to understand that my analyst was weighted down with her own bind to her parents and so could not help me go farther than she herself had gone.

Judging from how Virginia related to me around George and other men I dated, and from watching her in her life with men, I wonder if Virginia hadn't been bound in a similar way, with her parents inhibiting her ability to love in an ongoing, long-term relationship. At least externally, our symptoms were similar: high energy for others yet limited openness to receive deeply and to commit. Neither my relationship with my analyst nor with Virginia—which had both instructional and therapeutic aspects—could adequately assist me in this area of my individuation and connectedness in intimacy.

While I gained understanding in that year of reflection, I had needed it earlier. Many years passed before I embraced and forgave that young woman trying to love that was me. Human tragedies exist, I believe, and this is one. At the same time, I believe tragedies need not be only tragedies. The use we make of them is the key to continuing our growth. They too can be the stuff from which one refines one's soul.

I was decidedly stronger from the "waking up" that death can bring. The experience deepened my spiritual life profoundly. In awe of the wisdom of dream life, I was humbled. New awareness of time's limitations gave me focus and courage to act. Life seemed beyond decision-making as I had previously experienced it. Now, I came to know what to do and, as I knew, I acted—crisply, clearly, and without ambivalence.

I yearned to have the opportunity to love again, this time better. That happened to some extent, but he didn't want children in his life. It became clearer that I could not pass up being a mother, so I chose to reverse the order of things. I'd become a mother first and marry again later. My feeling of intense focus without distraction continued, one step at a time. "I must find my children."

Children

In 1977, it was not easy for a single woman to bring an adopted infant into her life. Simultaneously, I explored three routes: agencies, artificial insemination, and private adoption. For various reasons, I eliminated the first two options. The law didn't provide for the latter, so I looked for a way around this problem. Studying the regulations of foster homes and adoption, I discovered that a child could be eligible for adoption if the birth mother placed the child in a licensed foster home, did not visit for one year, and then relinquished parental rights. If the foster parent applied to adopt the child, the adoption was sure to happen on three conditions: the foster parent had demonstrated care of the child and compliance with foster care law, and the birth mother had received counseling about forfeiting her rights. I could go that route for my child.

I wrote friends and colleagues across the country to inform them I was looking for a pregnant girl who might want to release her child for adoption. I stated that such a young woman faced certain decisions: Would she have an abortion? If not, would she keep the child? If not, she had two alternatives: placing the child via an agency that offered her no involvement in the decision about who would adopt, or soliciting adoptive parents directly. She could seek out various people who might adopt the child, ask for letters, meet them or not, and select the child's adoptive parents.

I suggested that for some young women, such letters might contribute to healing from their difficult experience. My letter made my plea to be the parent and asked my friends to spread the word to women they knew of who were pregnant and deciding their children's future. Over the next year, three pregnant women offered me possible situations for adoption, but each fell through.

At the same time, I interviewed lawyers in Denver until I found one interested in this process and in changing the law to facilitate single-parent adoptions. Knowing it would take time to craft new law, I was glad to have my back-door plan. Ultimately, after I shared all the data I had gathered with the attorney, he began working on the legality of the issue. Four years later, a legal process for single parents to adopt was in place in Colorado.

Meanwhile, after a year of searching, I lay in bed late one morning and had a frank talk with the Powers That Be: "Listen, if this is something really right for my life, You're going to have to help me. I've done everything I know how." Within seconds (honestly), the telephone rang, and a friend of mine asked me to go to a pottery show with her. Months before, she had dreamt of helping me in finding a child. When we met before the show, she told me that she had just learned her 13-year-old stepdaughter was pregnant.

We both understood that it was probably best for the young girl to have an abortion and, at the same time, best for me to have a child. Both of us were in tears. We left the pottery show and went for tea, bemoaning these painful realities.

Two days later, my friend called again, this time to say that her stepdaughter had seen a physician and learned that the pregnancy was too far along for an abortion. The girl's father was in an absolute dilemma. I became very clear that I would like to raise the child. I invited the girl's father to my house to speak about the matter.

He went on and on: How could he consider the girl keeping the child when she still slept with her teddy bears? He could not release her child to an agency and never know what happened with it. And if the child came to me, he feared he would be unable to stay uninvolved, though he felt that would be essential for his daughter's well-being.

I had only one line to say, which came like a mantra: "If everything can be all right, I'd like to raise this child."

He left after two hours, saying he would call me with his decision within ten days. When the call came, he announced that he had decided it was best for me to raise the child, and he had consulted his daughter's mother, who felt the same. Now the young girl would grapple with every angle in regard to her feelings, possible regrets, and so on.

After two weeks, the family invited me to their home. The young girl and I took a walk in the early November snowy night while she told me of her decision. "I've decided that my job is to raise the healthiest child I can in my womb, and find the best mother I can for my baby. I've decided you should be its mother."

"Wait!" I had to be sure everything was truly okay about her decision, as I explained to her.

Then she told me of her memory of the summer when she was six years old. Her mother had gone to be with another man, leaving her, her sister, and her younger brother with their father. Many evenings, George and I had ridden our bikes to their home, played with the children in the yard, read them stories, and tucked them into bed. She remembered the comfort and warmth she felt from me, and from that experience, she was sure now that I would be the best mother for the child.

Her statements jogged my recall. I was astounded that she had memories of those times and how they had led her to her decision. I wept with delight and relief. Yes, everything was okay— more than okay.

On February 2, 1978, Jonathan Anthony Dodson was born. He came straight from the hospital to me in the new home I had created by remodeling a stately old house. I nursed him using the LaLeche method of supplementing my colostrum (and eventually milk) with a bag of milk from which a small tube was taped to my breast. While it was hard to parent alone, it was wonderful all the same. A marvelous support system helped me.

I never thought I would adopt a second child alone, but a dream and continued images of a brown child with big black eyes and dark hair—a little girl—set me on a second search about three years after Jonathan's arrival. After attempting in vain to find this child in India, I shared my search with a friend in Denver who had opened a new agency. Within a few weeks, she called to say an orphanage in Peru was closing, and two children were available there. Would I like to inquire?

That evening, Jonathan and I went to the home of a Denver couple who had just returned from that orphanage with their new son. I had wondered if I would ever again have a deep knowing about a child being born to be mine, as I had with Jonathan. But that night, when I saw a photograph of Corina—the two-and-a-half-year-old little girl in the Peruvian orphanage, I felt that she was my daughter. On the spot, I showed the photo to Jonathan and told him that this was his sister. "We have to go and get her."

Then I wondered what I was doing, for I didn't know whether it would be possible. The couple told us Corina's story. About two weeks before, while they were in Peru getting their child, Corina's father had brought her to the orphanage. When he left her, she had wailed with grief. Three days later, when staff took her to a hospital to treat her parasites, she had stopped talking and refused food except for bread.

Although her agony distressed me, I was comforted by the fact that she was in mourning. To me, this meant she had been attached to her parents; so I thought she could attach again.

In a letter to Casa de Niños, Urabaumba, Peru, I asked to adopt Corina and said I would call at a certain date and time for their response. Exactly at that time, I attempted to call; but the one telephone line into the village was down. The Denver adoption agency went into action. Calling a family in Denver who were good friends of the couple who ran the Peruvian orphanage, they learned that "Papa" Klepper, the director, was at this family's home in Denver at that moment!

The family invited me to meet him that evening; he was leaving the next day to return to Urabaumba. When we spoke about Corina, he told me I would not have to endure any waiting list. The day before Corina arrived at the orphanage, he had written to inform about 50 families that the orphanage was closing; he would have no children for them. So it was fine with him for me to take Corina. He would clear it with his wife upon his return.

Three days later a telegram came, "Yes! Come as soon as possible." I began to work to secure all the proper papers, and arrange for a trip to Peru. I was anxious and afraid—overwhelmed at the task. The horror stories of the living situation, the quality of food, the lack of cleanliness and the parasites were all frightening prospects. Could I take Jonathan and keep him healthy? At a Thanksgiving party, I enumerated my needs to a friend: "I need someone to go with me who speaks Katchuan and Spanish, who could help with the care of Jonathan and Corina, who knows how to cope with legal procedures there, and who could help me find a place to stay in all the cities where I must go to complete legal papers; someone who could help us all stay healthy and help my daughter gain her health completely." I laughed at the seemingly impossible wish.

My friend sent me across the room to inquire of another guest at the party. Believe it or not, he helped me find a Peruvian woman in Denver the next day, who promptly called her brother Evan in Lima. Their family had grown up in the jungle not far from Urabaumba, so he knew Katchuan. They had a lawyer uncle in nearby Cusco and knew medical doctors there. Yes, he would be willing to take off from his work to help me. He had a son the same age as Jonathan, and he loved children.

Only eight days after meeting Papa Klepper, I left for Lima. I took a backpack of food, as if I were going on trail for a month. If I found it safe enough, Jonathan would join me in two weeks by traveling with an American couple who were going to Peru to adopt the last child at the orphanage. Meanwhile, I would have time to bond with Corina, help her get well, and check out how to keep Jonathan healthy.

After a royal reception in Lima from Evan's extended family, he and I flew over the beautiful Andes to Cusco. Papa Klepper met us and drove us to Urabaumba. We found Corina standing alone in the courtyard, withdrawn, eating dirt, her tummy swollen. She did not speak. In our first precious moments, I took her in my arms, prepared a warm bath for her, washed her body and her lice-filled hair, and then wrapped her in a blanket. She fell asleep in my arms.

I spent most of the next two weeks with her in Cusco, where she was cured of the parasites that were causing blood in her bowel movements. I spoke Spanish to her, but she didn't respond. Evan spoke Katchuan, but still no response. Then one day, as I was bouncing her in the backpack carrier that I had brought for her, she cried out: *"Me no bebé, me niña!"*

About two months before she came to the orphanage, when her baby brother was born, Corina had probably graduated out of her mother's *rebozo*—a cloth slung over the neck and back in which Peruvian mothers carry their children. Perhaps her mother told Corina that she was a little girl (*niña*) and not a baby anymore. Now my response was, *"Tu bebé, también tu niña!"* ("You're a baby, and you're also a little girl.")

She giggled. Our bond was growing.

Jonathan soon arrived, and the three of us began forming a sweet connection during our remaining time in Peru. It took ten weeks to procure all the proper papers for adoption and emigration, and to deal with the threats and bribes.

Five weeks after our return to Denver, Corina had her third birthday on March 12, 1983. I gave a party for her and invited and honored the 22 local people who had been instrumental in her adoption. It was and is incredible to me how just the right people materialized at every step of the way.

Events nothing short of miraculous led me to the two children whom I feel were born to be mine, though they grew in the wombs of other women. Finding Jonathan and Corina was an amazing journey in my life, so much so that I cannot imagine writing an autobiography, however brief, without these stories. My decisions to adopt them were among the best I ever made. Our connection has set the three of us on a rich, creative journey—a core of my life. The journey has not been without pain and suffering, but neither pain nor the freedom from it is the relevant issue in my life. The process of life itself is where meaning lies. As one of my Russian friends puts it, "Life is about finding that golden thread and riding it for as long as you can, then looking wide-eyed to find it and connect to it again."

In Jon's early years, I had worked less than half time with clients, wrote, and had a lot of time with him. Those were precious, gentle years. I was involved in a cooperative preschool program in our neighborhood; after Corina joined our family, my involvement in the children's schools increased. In 1983, I also taught at the Iliff School of Theology. Life became quite complex. I developed rheumatoid arthritis, which sapped a great deal of my strength. Finding no effective treatment, I felt ceaseless exhaustion. I took naps and went to bed early. These were trying times for all of us, as Jonathan was adjusting to the arrival of his sister and also experiencing his mother being less available because of health. After two years, my doctor finally hit on the proper combination of medications to control the disease, which restored some of my energy.

Seizing the moment of new energy and an increased demand for housing in a new area of Denver, I designed and built two Spanish style houses. My thinking was that having a strong financial base would give me more time with the children. Though I carefully sought the best advice, this project backfired. A radical decline in the Colorado economy, errors of the architect, arson fires, and theft by the contractor combined into a huge financial disaster followed by drawn-out lawsuits. Although I won, only the architectural firm paid a small amount of my loss. The most responsible party, the contractor, fled the country.

Our life changed dramatically. I doubled, then tripled my time at work. Despite this, finances forced me to sell our home. The experience compelled simplicity and realignment of priorities.

Though money was meager, our lives were interesting. Where I could, I combined work and family. For instance, I led the Satir Family Camp in California each year for eight years. There, the children had a rich experience in a redwood forest scarcely touched by humans. They experienced me working in community-building and psychodramas, and they experienced the Satir Camp community of families. Their experiences became the theme of many school papers. Later, in 1989, I founded the nonprofit Institute for International Connections, through which we have experienced cross-cultural family camps in Russia, Lithuania, and Czechoslovakia.

Jon is now an extroverted young man, witty and humorous, bright, full of life. He has been fully engaged in experimentation and in differentiating himself. This forced me to at least attempt developing shadow sides of myself: to be more suspicious and less naïve, and to set explicit structures and expectations. Corina, two years younger, enjoys exploring the worlds of reading, imagination, arts, and writing. Her life has a gentle, focused rhythm.

I am experiencing that precious process of helping young adults name, develop, and enjoy what they are discovering about themselves and being a part of their finding ways to relate with the world. Fourteen years after the financial disaster, we are recovering financially. And my life goes on with a sense now of anticipation for next beginnings. Managing my health gives my life a more even rhythm. I feel myself to be in the school of learning to love. As T. S. Eliot says in *East Coker:*

> Here and there does not matter,
> We must be still and still moving
> Into another intensity
> For a further union, a deeper communion
> . . . in my end is my beginning.

Professional Work

I was fortunate to have my first post-master's job at Fort Logan Mental Health Center. It was among the ten hospitals nationwide funded by the National Institutes of Health to explore innovations in psychiatric treatment. My nine years of work there in Denver included training in psychodrama, Gestalt therapy, therapeutic community, and family therapy. We studied with leaders in these fields: J. L. Moreno, Fritz Perls, Maxwell Jones, and Virginia Satir.

In 1966, with Virginia's encouragement, Carl Hollander (a sociologist at Fort Logan) and I formed the nonprofit Evergreen Institute for Personal and Family Growth. Incorporating what we learned from our training into our own styles, Carl and I worked together in Denver and across the country for seven years. Aside from working with individuals, families, groups, and organizational systems, we trained many psychotherapists in these innovative therapies. Through Evergreen, I sponsored Virginia in leading many public programs in Denver. In Glenwood Springs in the summer of 1971, I organized one of her first month-long trainings for therapists. With a three-year National Institute of Education grant, Carl and I also retrained school counselors nationwide to work with families using innovative psychotherapies. Out of this grew the 1978 publication of my first book, *Family Counseling: A Systems Approach*. Virginia wrote a glowing foreword:

> This book is really about music, human music as played by human beings as they struggle to live together in their family—inharmonious and unpleasant when things are going badly, and harmonious and pleasant when things are going well. I am likening the family to a mini-orchestra, for I see many parallels.
>
> Laura Dodson, as the orchestra leader (family counselor), tells us how she orchestrates new music, with the intent that the family will reach the point where they no longer have to hire an outside conductor because they have developed their own.

Laura's baton has many sides: patience; love; hard knowledge, especially about system operation and management; a profound grasp of human reality and an appreciation of human uniqueness; and a keen sense of timeliness, coupled with an ability to construct useful strategies. Because this emanates from a clear sense of her own selfhood and a clear sense of others, there is a flow and naturalness in her writing and in her description of how she works. . . .

Laura's method is to make the inharmonious, harmonious, thus creating balance and helping each member create his/her own unique music, while at the same time being in tune with the rest of the orchestra. She clearly knows what nurturing and harmonious music sounds like, feels like, and looks like, as well as being familiar with its opposite.

To continue my analogy, Laura understands that when family members are not making harmonious music, it is likely to be because some instruments have stopped playing, and therefore have no voice; some blare out only discords, which irritate; some just play loud and drown out the rest; some play out of tune, which frustrates; some will play only solo and some only duets. Laura obviously does not consider the problem one of bad instruments, but more of an education in understanding and using those instruments.

She shows the reader how she introduces each person to his/her own instrument *without threat.* She goes on to show how, as trust is built between herself and the family members, she creates a context in which each member is strongly invited to *want* to know how to play his/her own instrument. At the same time, he/she is being guided to an awareness of the depths of tone and the variety of expression that is his/her instrument's potential. She thus lays the groundwork for learning how to build and play with the other family members. . . .

Laura has shown in practice what I have urged all my students to do. She has taken in widely from the many rich resources that abound in our modern-day world relative to human growth and change. It is impressive that she has avoided the trap of being locked into any one theory or technique. She is not a GESTALTIST, a PSYCHO-DRAMATIST, a JUNGIAN, a SATIRIAN, or any other popular label today. Yet it is obvious that she has learned from and been influenced by these channels. Consequently, she can be free to use these learnings as resources when they fit, and build on her own experiences. The result is a rich, flexible, process-oriented, deeply humanistic, and realistic life-giving approach to helping troubled families, which I see as an approach that is every becoming, not having become.

Laura's personal qualities of gentleness, strength, caring, and congruence, combined with her lucid style of writing and her practical content, make this book a powerful (in the sense of a seed) and important contribution to the practice of family therapy, for both the practitioner and the family.

—*Virginia Satir*

As mentioned, the eleven years from 1972 to 1983 were a time of study, although I continued my practice and my teaching most of that time. In the summer of 1972 while I was a fellow with the Center for Democratic Institutions in Santa Barbara, our discussions focused on the problem of movement from dictatorships to democracy. Renowned French communists, theologians, and fellows at the Center participated in dynamic and informed dialogues, also producing papers on the topic. Along with observing these, I availed myself of the Center's library of tapes regarding various political and social concerns and trends. This greatly expanded my thinking about systems change, from social systems to the depth of the psyche's inner system. I spent a year in Zurich and took numerous classes at the Jung Institute. This part of my study culminated in 1975 with a doctorate in clinical psychology. Then, in late 1975, I entered the Interregional Society of Jungian Analysts as a trainee. In 1983, I became a certified Jungian analyst.

After my year in Zurich, I began working in 1973 on the relationship of Virginia's work and the work of Carl Jung—work I continue today. Lecturing widely on this topic, I conducted many supervisory sessions and therapist trainings that combined the work of these two masters and my own thoughts and style, as well as material from psychodrama and Gestalt.

In the 1983–84 academic year, I taught three courses in Denver at the Iliff School of Theology. These were "Jung and Family Therapy," "The Feminine in Personal and World Transformation," and "Dream Interpretation." In addition, I co-taught "Personal and Social Transformation." Students from the University of Denver School of Professional Psychology also attended these classes.

Throughout the 1980s, another main focus in my work was early childhood wounding and its impact on relationship. My own analytic and marriage experiences had sensitized me to particular issues: that one partner's analysis could affect the marriage adversely, and that intimate relationships comprised an interplay with early wounds and family dynamics. I saw these early childhood wounds as core issues in many marriages, and I incorporated working with them into my therapy with couples. As well as using classical analytic and Satir approaches, I expanded and deepened my work with preverbal wounding and pre-Oedipal conflicts through activating body memory, recreating scenes from childhood, and amplifying images. I also delved further into studying transference, countertransference, object relations, and self psychology.

I developed and wrote about integrating action therapies with systems and analytic therapy, and I wrote an article on dream work with families. All this work and thought generated dialogue with supervisees and colleagues, and was incorporated in lectures, consultations, and teaching. My second book, *Psyche and Family: Jungian Applications to Family Therapy,* which I edited with Terry Gibson (1996), is the first to connect Jungian psychology and systems work.

My foundations were set in Satir training, many innovative therapies, Jungian studies, the experience of both a Freudian and a Jungian analysis, nine years' work in an innovative mental hospital, and ongoing interest in relationship between patterns in the depth of the psyche and the systems in which we live. So it is not surprising—though I couldn't see the patterns at the time—that my career has moved deeper into the mysteries of the psyche and soul, and deeper into attempts to apply psychological understandings to the systems in which we live.

Zambia and Zimbabwe

My work with cultural systems began in1980 when I went into a six-month retreat at Pendle Hill, a Quaker center in Pennsylvania. My goal was to write up my six "control cases" for my training as a Jungian analyst and to begin my thesis on "Jung and Satir." I planned to compare and contrast their personalities and work, and I anticipated eventually writing a book by that title. (That book remains on my "to do" list.)

My focus shifted shortly after I arrived at Pendle Hill with my young son and our child-care person. First, I learned that several people from the newly independent Zimbabwe would arrive in a few weeks for a month's stay. Then a dream also helped me expand toward a broader arena.

> I am given a map of the world and on it, across Zambia, Africa, is a seven-digit telephone number having several threes and sevens in it. This number needs to be known by persons in power in the United States and Russia, as it will somehow contribute to world peace.

In number interpretation, threes and sevens are numbers of motion and change, as contrasted to multiples of four, which connote wholeness or being at rest. Knowing this, I inquired into major themes in motion in Zambia. I learned the Zambian people had won independence nonviolently from the British 16 years before. As many efforts in the other half of the former Rhodesia had not accomplished the same, Zambia later supported its neighbor's three-year war for independence. That culminated in Zimbabwe's formation in 1980.

This support came despite Zambia's conflicts about war. About the time of my dream, that country's president Kaunda (1980) published *The Riddle of War*, a book of his contemplations. It questioned war as a means for transforming political and social systems, as well as speaking of war's effects on individuals, groups, and nations. This book contributed to my understanding about how nations move from dictatorship to democracy—a theme that had also been important during my 1972 stay at the Center for Democratic Institutions.

A second theme I noted about Zambia was its resistance to control from super-powers as it explored various combinations of communism, socialism, and capitalism, within the context of its own history and culture. To serve the needs of its people, the country sought innovative forms of government and ways to help individuals develop with more focus on cooperation and teamwork, less on "rising to the top." They modeled exploring systems beyond polarities at a time when Russia and America were locked in bitter dualistic stances over communism and capitalism.

Looking back now, it is easy to see that both themes reflected pioneering efforts in dimensions now considered vital to world peace. Seeing them in the context of the former Rhodesia spurred my thinking about using psychological analysis to study change in societies and cultures. It gave me a context in which to explore how Satir- and Jung-based psychology might contribute to understanding and perhaps affecting cultural transitions. I saw my dream as pointing me in the direction of this inquiry. A few weeks before I left for Pendle Hill, I had this second dream:

> I am to go on a space ship to gain a perspective on the world and its problems that I cannot gain on earth. I am to choose persons to accompany me on this journey. I choose Margaret Mead, Houston Smith, Jean Houston, Kenneth Boulding, and an unidentified Taoist priest. We prepare to take off for outer space. Then I realize I can also select persons from the dead for the journey; I select Thomas Jefferson and C. G. Jung. We take off. I see our earth from space and am overcome with awe, compassion, and wonder. I can see more clearly than ever before, from this perspective. I have a sense of expectation that more will be seen and understood.

Rather than comparing Jung and Satir in my writing, I turned toward world issues. My postdoctoral thesis became "Toward a Jungian View of Cultural Analysis With Zimbabwe, Africa as an Example." (1975). It presented an analysis of myth and song (taken as indicators of the collective unconscious) that were popular in Zimbabwe during its war for independence. I began writing my thesis during my Pendle Hill retreat, and later drafts were enriched by a Zimbabwean *mbira* player and folk singer who visited us in Denver for some months.

Jung predicted that archetypal shifts would occur in many countries as we approach the year 2000. He thought the archetype of the self—symbolized in a rise of the feminine, or *yin*—would emerge, and that masculine and feminine energies would press us toward integrating them personally and collectively. Combining my own thinking about depth psychology and larger systems change with Virginia's influence and Jung's work, I developed the accompanying diagram of the process of change. I also attempted to apply that model to personal and cultural change.

Subsequently, I published two articles based on this model. This work has its limitations, as psychological analyses of culture often do; it does not reflect economic or political issues. It would be my pleasure someday to expand and refine my own thinking by dialoguing with persons well informed in these schools of thought.

Eastern Europe

Starting in 1984, my financial disaster somewhat diffused my focus on culture and psychology. Then, in 1987, M'Lou Burnett-Dixon organized a trip to the former USSR for herself, Virginia, and me. There I saw some of the same patterns of rapid cultural change as in Zimbabwe. Compounding my interest in exploring cultural systems and recovery from oppression were new friendships, requests

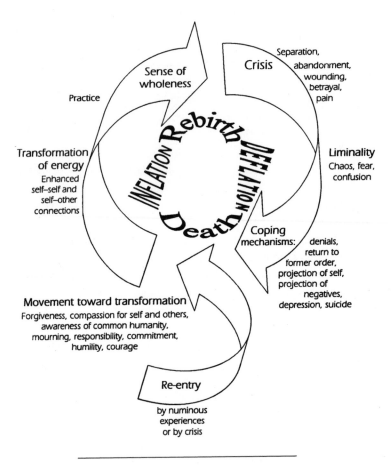

Process of Change

for maintaining connection, and new possibilities burgeoning in that part of the world. Later came a vacuum of response by Avanta in the wake of Virginia's untimely death and the network's ensuing immobility and chaos. All these things moved me toward further involvement in eastern Europe and Russia.

In 1989, I added a second full-time job to my life: the Institute for International Connections (IIC). I started this nonprofit organization with the encouragement of my Russian colleague Julia Gippenreiter, a professor at Moscow University, who founded a sister institute in Moscow. Oppressed for so long, these people of heart now flowed with energy and creativity, like water from manholes suddenly unplugged. We in the States needed to know them and connect with what had too long been forbidden to us, and they longed for the same. Catching whatever "balls" I could, I responded to some of the requests from various eastern European countries and carefully passed many to other professional colleagues across the country.

IIC is not simply a program for sharing Satir's and Jung's work. Nor is it designed for "doing good work" in formerly oppressed countries. We recognize that the world is undergoing fundamental transformation, and that the combined thought and work of persons of all cultures aids this transformation's potential health. Sharing the work of Satir and Jung in experiential ways deepens our contact and offers a common language for speaking, thinking, and working together. From this base, which crosses cultural lines in essential ways, we generate ideas, insights, and work that transcends what any of us can do separately.

From 1990 to 1993, we laid the foundation for further joint endeavors in eastern Europe through cross-cultural workshop formats and more Family Camps in Russia and Czechoslovakia. In Lithuania, I did Satir/Jung work. More than 200 U.S. professionals came along to eastern Europe for these cross-cultural workshops.

These intense, dynamic retreats built a base for our future work. Eastern European and U.S. families retreated to work and play together in the model of the earlier Satir Family Camp in California (which I led from 1986 to 1993). This included lectures on Satir communication skills; experiencing those skills in triads, dyads, and family groups; examining one's own ways of coping with stress; and working in front of the group in family units, as individuals, and in larger systems. For our group, action ways of working in psychotherapy seemed most fitting and natural. The Satir group process built community and involved everyone, from 45 Russians at the first camp to 85 at the last, and about 45 Americans at each camp in Russia.

Gathered on the floor each morning with their parents nearby, the children participated in Satir "Temperature Readings." They expressed appreciations for things that had happened the day before, spoke of hopes and wishes for the coming day, shared information, and expressed their complaints and suggestions for solutions. Some taught songs in Russian; some, in English. Often, as they spoke from the heart about thanks for little things, words that too often go unsaid, these children moved all of us—especially their parents— to tears.

After the children left the group for organized play, the adults had a similar Temperature Reading. Bringing out our hopes and wishes, appreciations, information, complaints, and possible solutions set the stage for our group's sense of well-being and empowerment to enact what *we* wanted to have happen. This is the Satir model. Our experience was rooted in this democratic, feeling-toned process, which encouraged individual creativity and initiative. Together, we were living what we were trying to teach.

Then came activities planned and usually co-led by Americans and Russians. These included family play activities and groups on various themes, such as specific social issues, women's issues, or exchanging information on our respective countries and family life. Russian children discovered bubble gum, and we had a bubble-blowing contest. U.S. children discovered new games with the jump rope. We painted T-shirts, played guitars and sang, laughed, and told stories into the night. For most Americans as well as Russians, this was a first time of meeting and getting to know persons from Russia or the United States. Thousands of misconceptions fell by the wayside as we opened to experiencing each other.

Meanwhile, I gave Satir-type lectures and led activities to experience their content, worked with families in front of the group—intensely and into the night—and worked with problems among members of the Russian nonprofit institute. A sense of community built among the people in these retreats. Our aim was to create a sense of safety to experience what Virginia called the Five Freedoms: the freedom to think, feel, see, hear, and comment on our experiences. Long hungered for, these basic liberties seemed possible now, given *perestroika, glasnost*, and the environment created by Satir group process. We listened raptly as people voiced what they had long been forbidden even to visit in their own minds, much less communicate in a group.

Every day held dramatic moments of intense emotion, connection with each other, and stretches to comprehend the profundity of the Cold War's impact on the world and each of us. We staggered sometimes under the realization that "Russians could not cry, for there would be a flood of tears." Living in oppression and fear, many of them had coped by simply repressing deep experiences, containing themselves enough to brace against the next trauma.

U.S. participants cried for the pain of their friends and—in this environment more intensely than at home—felt flooded with the emotions and memories of their own wounds. People felt safe enough to work through important memories they had never before allowed themselves to recall or speak about. Collective patterns surfaced of coping with trauma and oppression. Our bonds deepened.

In a country hardly influenced by Freud, we did not need to walk gingerly while incorporating human values, spirituality, and community into psychological thinking. A psychospiritual psychology focused on individuals as well as groups, community, and the world seemed a natural for the former USSR. Spirituality had grown strong underground, and people there held strongly to the ideals of community related to their history and communist ideation. They also hungered for validation of the individual. As some later expressed it, they were learning to reflect psychologically and develop a "psychological culture." To my delight, everything I had to offer was called upon. Comprehending what I was experiencing also posed a constant challenge. We were all having life-changing experiences. (Mine included learning from my eastern European colleagues about acceptance, humility, and dignity in suffering. This later sustained me through a long illness.)

Following each two-week retreat, American families stayed for several days with eastern European families, experiencing their family life and seeing sights.

The next year's retreat was organized similarly to this 1990 one. In addition, several participants from Czechoslovakia joined us. Hot topics included old wounds from the Russian occupation of Czechoslovakia and newer wounds from the Czechs reclaiming control and firing the Russians. Many Russian camp attendees had friends and family in Czechoslovakia who were now without jobs. Fishbowling to tell their stories, Russians and Czechs heard of each other's suffering, Russians mourned what their country had done—and wanted no comfort to minimize the wrong.

Without realizing it, we were creating a foundation for joint U.S.–Russian work that soon became possible. After the second Satir Family Camp, while we were staying with Russian families, many of us involved ourselves in the drama of the 1991 coup attempt. We helped put up signs in the subways that encouraged Russians to break curfew and come to the Russian "White House" that night. Going there with our friends, some of us watched the first young men who abandoned the army in favor of the end of communism drive their tanks into Moscow with their dogs and flowers. Realizing the confrontation between soldiers in tanks and ex-soldiers in tanks signified taking a stand against oppression—rather than being about Yeltsin or the army—people came out of the woodwork to support freedom and democracy.

Among camp participants, our trust with each other, our mutual respect and knowledge, and our now-common language of Satir growth model and humanistic work, shared values, and communication moved us into new possibilities after the fall of communism. Satir work did indeed cross cultural boundaries. That plus many shared experiences, including those with each other's families, had bonded our hearts.

Before we left for Lithuania and Czechoslovakia that year, our Russian friends approached many of us in the U.S. group to help work on various projects. They had begun some of these, and their creativity was bursting to begin others. Together, we designed the 1992 Russian–American Camp to have four foci: schools, human services, management consulting, and cross-cultural dialogue.

Within these areas, we began work on a number of goals. These included creating programs and textbooks focused on self-development and democracy in the classroom; developing psychotherapy skills and curricula, clinics, mental hospital day programs; adapting U.S. skills in management consulting to Russia's culture and new private businesses; helping establish creativity, initiative, and democracy in the workplace and in the public arena; and studying the process of rapid transformation in cultures.

After staying in touch by electronic mail and telephone, many of us met again a year later. Our friends in eastern Europe had incorporated an amazing amount of our experiences together into their lives and their work. They had been training teachers and writing new textbooks for them, doing management consultation, beginning private practices, and teaching what the camp had taught at Moscow State University's psychology department. Previously, that department had been only research oriented.

This third camp plumbed new depths. In each division, an American and a Russian led. We had recruited Americans who could be effective counterparts to our dynamic Russian friends. After the first camp, we had brought 11 of these Russians to the United States for three-month internships in the various areas of their interest. Now, and even more so after the third camp, it was evident that they and others were taking further steps to effect their changing culture in humanistic ways. In time, many became world-recognized leaders.

Out of this camp grew many joint projects between Americans and Russians. The IIC held three additional conferences in Russia on management consultation. Three years into our joint work, Russians and Americans were landing contracts as management consultants. Consulting firms formed by Russians used Americans as their consultants. Some Moscow University graduates based their theses and dissertations on our collaborative work. And the Russian psychologist Julia Gippenreiter published the first popularized Russian psychology book, a how-to volume on relationships among parents, grandparents, and children.

After receiving a UNESCO grant to train social workers, one of our Russian colleagues invited IIC to join her in this project. In the Ukraine, Belarus, and Russia, the trainees worked at nine UNESCO-built centers for helping children and families harmed by the Chernobyl incident. Interestingly, our colleague was skeptical when she began her study on "Application of Satir in Russia." This training experience convinced our colleague of its relevance. She later won the Satir award from the American Association for Marriage and Family Therapy. Another participant in this training project—a retired social work professor from Michigan—developed and directed another IIC project with the Chernobyl centers.

These are examples of how IIC continues to evolve. The passions of eastern Europeans and Americans continue igniting, and IIC's specific projects change according to emerging needs and interests.

Like many nonprofit organizations, IIC operates through the work of volunteers, grants, and a few immensely helpful donations. Since 1992, Avanta grants have been instrumental to offering Satir trainings in Latvia, Lithuania, and Poland. While we struggle financially, the energy and enthusiasm for this work continues in the persons who have gone on our trips. Their fees for the conferences, home stays, and travel are quite small compared to tour groups, but this funded our institute and sister institutes in the former USSR for the first three years. After the failed coup and ensuing chaos, however, the initial fascination with family camps in Russia waned for large numbers of Americans.

Although following a half-step behind is the only leadership that makes sense to me, my IIC work still almost swallowed me at times. In 1993, I withdrew from it because of illness. Two years later, I returned—this time with a solid force of board members and volunteers involved in leadership. The IIC is now a manageable and constantly stretching and creative part of my life. Many Avanta members and IHLRN members are involved. Taking Virginia's work to eastern Europe is exactly what is needed in building world community and humanistic leadership.

My greatest interest is in certain philosophical and psychological questions about the world's transformations. What can we

say about the psychological process of cultural change? What can
we learn about healing from oppression? What about restoring the
oppressed culture as a part of healing? How do the oppressed and
the oppressor recover from shame? What happens with the psychological defenses (such as dissociation and repression) that once
helped a country's people cope? The unconscious continuation of
such learned behaviors can hinder recovery. What parallels exist
between cultural oppression and an individual's trauma and recovery? Can knowledge of these things help nations in transition?

What key correctives is eastern Europe demonstrating for the
United States in general and for our psychology? How is eastern
spirituality and psychology influencing western spirituality and
psychology? Can we recognize and use the cutting edge of those
emerging developments? Can resurrecting an oppressed culture's
myths, symbols, and images contribute to healing from oppression?
Can exploring their dominant archetypes or motifs also help us
understand psychological elements that proceede oppression?

With the Iron Curtain open, we can meet as one world and
develop our thinking and practice, and our persons. Together, we
can go farther than any have gone separately. Combining our thinking, history, and experiences, we can develop new applications of
psychology for facilitating change in massive systems.

With the newly formed Jung Society in Lithuania, I have explored shame and dissociation and Lithuanian myths. I have known
and worked with many of the society's members over the past seven
years and five visits there. Some of my Russian friends and I have
also studied how eastern psychological schools of thought relate to
western ones. Through my work with individuals and families in
eastern Europe, I have collected many stories of oppression and
recovery. These arenas represent the current edge of my thinking,
writing, and work as I continue my practice, consultations, and

teaching. I yearn for more time to work and dialogue on these questions.

The more I live, the less I know that I know. Yet life grows fuller of nuances and subtleties. I keep looking for the paths with heart. As the Yaqui sorcerer Don Juan says in Carlos Castañeda's writings: "For me, there is only the traveling on paths that have heart, on any path that may have heart . . . and the only worthwhile challenge is to traverse its full length. And there I travel looking, looking, breathlessly."

Virginia's family, circa 1945
(Left to right, standing:)
Ray, Edith, Russell, Virginia, Roger
(Seated:) Minnie and Reinhold

Dr. Lori Gordon is the founder of PAIRS Inter-national, Inc., an educational program about relationships for couples and adolescents. Lori's work pulls together the teachings of Virginia Satir on relationships with Lori's dynamic ideas and lifetime study. This program has improved thousands of marriages throughout the world. In her autobiography, Lori describes developing PAIRS and Virginia's involvement from the beginning.

—*Laura Dodson*
Co-editor

3

Passage to Intimacy
THE ADVENT OF SUPER EDUCATION

by Lori Gordon

Virginia Satir was the greatest single influence in my life. For me, she became a surrogate parent, a friend, a mentor, and an inspiring pathfinder. She provided crucial support through years when I found precious little support elsewhere. She helped me discover my own value and encouraged me to develop the kind of unique contribution I might make to society.

My intellect was alive and excited in her presence. She freed me to be my whole self—all of me—to know me and accept me, to risk, to venture, to dare, and finally to stand up, to speak, and to guide others. Finally, she freed me to lead. She will forever be a part of me.

I was a young, untried therapist at a community mental health center in Northern Virginia when *Conjoint Family Therapy* first crossed my desk. I had never heard of Virginia Satir, but as I read her book, I felt welling up within me a heartfelt combination of gratitude, humility, and relief. For me, these come from discovering a remarkable teacher. Her clear logic and understanding lit up the sky and inspired me from the start. They continue to.

I first experienced Virginia in person at a workshop in Florida. Amazingly, she was even grander than her book. I observed with awe her warmly humorous, spontaneous, common-sensical, insightful therapy with two troubled families of adolescents. I was hooked. I knew I had to study with her. When I did, I found her to be as generous with her time as with her wisdom. For the rest of her life, Virginia remained the finest teacher I have had the privilege to know.

I organized a series of workshops for therapists in the Washington, D.C. area so Virginia could share her gift with all of us. The first week we spent with her was at Cacapon State Park in West Virginia. We presented her with four of the most troubled families of our clinic, and she created change before our eyes. These difficult clients became open, warm, responsive human beings. In touch with their own worth and power, they were able to use it positively. No one could hold on to his or her pathology around Virginia.

The most important moment for me came during a weekend marathon for our training group at my home in Falls Church, Virginia. Suddenly, without warning, a role-playing incident catapulted me into the loss of my own parents 25 years earlier. My father had died overnight when I was 15, and my mother died a year later of cancer. I had been very close to both of them.

The pain that hit me during that marathon was overwhelming. I felt if I let it out, I would never get up off the floor. But in her incredibly accepting, loving, supportive way, Virginia allowed me to let it go. A sign of her creative wisdom was that she didn't stop there. She enabled me to reframe my grief with understanding, insight, and even joy. She had the group reconstruct my parents' meeting and courtship. This portrayed for me a time when they were young and carefree, before I was born, before the Depression years, before responsibility and worry burdened them.

Something profoundly healing happened. For the first time in all those years, I felt that it was acceptable for me to be happy and carefree. Virginia's artistry did that for people. That episode marked a new beginning for me. She freed me to be myself, to risk, and to follow the true calling of my heart.

She encouraged me to found the Family Relations Institute (FRI). Once I did, she would offer her trainings here in the Washington area. Eventually, FRI grew into a treatment facility and postgraduate training center, where many of the cutting edge thinkers and doers in our field shared their knowledge.

Virginia was always warmly and personally responsive to my curiosity and supportive of my budding interests. She welcomed presentations of my ongoing work at her annual IHLRN meetings. (A form of open university, IHLRN met for a week at different sites around the world.) I was particularly intrigued with her remarkable and innovative Parts Party, her sensitive meditations, and her development of particular structures such as the Temperature Reading.

She became part of my thinking, my style, and my technique. She spent a number of nights at my home, the memory of which I richly treasure. I came to know her as a person—one who enjoyed bubble baths and loved having her back rubbed in the bath. She enjoyed electric blankets and shopping for shoes, and she took a warm interest in my children. They never forgot her. She was for real.

Everything she did was innovative, creative, and called forth deepened understanding in those around her. She encouraged my emerging curiosity about the transpersonal realm, guided imagery with music, past-life regression, altered states of consciousness, and the use of guided meditations. She was a courageous and fearless explorer of the known and unknown, venturing into new territory and willingly sharing her own journey.

At one training, I asked her for specific help with my "accommodating, placating self," the one who couldn't say no. After some moments working with me through group pressure to say no to everything, she looked at her watch and said, "I'm going to lunch. You may never eat!" and left. I learned.

In 1977, I offered one of the first presentations of my "Laundry List of Marital Mishaps, Knots and Double Binds" at an IHLRN meeting in Coolfont, West Virginia. Afterward, Virginia wrote encouraging notes and suggestions on the manuscript. She continued making cogent suggestions as it evolved. The most significant was to insist that I add the "Positives"—clues for unraveling the knots. These enriched the work enough to make it a book, *Love Knots*, which owes ever so much to Virginia's influence.

In September 1984, four years before her death, she conducted a four-day training that launched my new PAIRS Foundation in Falls Church, Virginia. (The acronym stands for Practical Application of Intimate Relationship Skills.) These are excepts from my introduction of her.

> In the Far East, in Japan, there are rare individuals who are known for their wisdom and their unique talents, and who are honored with the designation "National Living Treasure." Our guest tonight is such a treasure in this country . . ..
>
> She is a remarkable leader who has dared to question the unquestioned; to seek new, more human solutions to age-old problems; to dissolve barriers of culture, race, religion, and sex; to perceive the light in each human being, and to find ways for that light to glow. She has used her boundless energy and creativity to traverse the world, opening doors to understanding between family members, between groups, and between cultures. She has inspired countless fortunate individuals to take charge of their lives in more loving, sharing ways; to perceive the value of their own work; and to honor the work of others.
>
> She has a unique talent for making the obscure clear, for unraveling complexity into easily understood parts, for inventing

experiences that expand the horizon of human sensitivity and the capacity for solving human problems.

The late Adlai Stevenson said about Eleanor Roosevelt that she believed "it is better to light a candle than to curse the darkness," and her glow has warmed the world. I would propose that Virginia Satir . . . follows in these footsteps. She carries with her the torch of new possibilities, of mutual understanding, of love, and of growth wherever she goes, and she finds creative ways of bringing them to be.

It is my pleasure to bring to you tonight my teacher, mentor, and cherished friend, Virginia Satir . . .

My major creation, the Practical Application of Intimate Relationship Skills (PAIRS) program, is a monument to her legacy. Her work is integral to this training program and is woven throughout, conceptually and experientially. Synthesizing what I consider to be the strongest, most effective concepts and tools from Virginia's work and that of several other modern pathfinders, PAIRS is a comprehensive program for couples. Its goal is to enable partners to live joyfully and honestly within a framework of equality that meets our highest visions for the coming age.

Relationships are like puzzles, in many ways, and each method I incorporated from my teachers fit one more piece (or several) into place. This, I believe, is the way we pass on to succeeding generations the accumulated knowledge of our culture. We glean the most time-tested and relevant ideas and techniques from our teachers, organize them to the best of our ability, and add a thing or two from personal experience. Then we spread the word to all who will listen. Now, when I am receiving unexpected publicity and acclaim, it seems absolutely fitting for me to pay homage to those who guided me along the way.

Thank you, Virginia. I will always love and honor you.

My Life

I was born at the beginning of the Great Depression, in 1929, the younger of two daughters. My father, a dentist, had come to the United States in his teens from Lithuania. He was descended from a long line of rabbinical scholars, religious leaders, and philosophers—among them Martin Buber, who wrote eloquently of the I–Thou philosophy.

I learned none of this until many years after my father's death. When I was in my twenties, I read a newly published book, *The Unbroken Chain*, which chronicled my father's mother's family. She was the only daughter in a noted rabbinical family named Katzenellenbogen, which traces back to the fourteenth century. She died immediately before I was born, and I was named after her.

From what I hear, my personality is remarkably similar to hers. She was musical, loved theater, and loved people. She had four brothers who all became leading rabbis of their cities. One of the few mementos I have from my father is a written version of his family tree, which he created for his 13th birthday, when he was still living in Lithuania. He wrote it entirely in Hebrew and dedicated it to his mother, his "teacher."

This is the way our family passed along its history. At the time of his Bar Mitzvah, each son wrote down the direct lineage of his ancestors (which went back literally to the time of King David). The same history inscribed by my father later appeared in a greatly expanded form, translated into English, as *The Unbroken Chain* by Dr. Neil Rosenstein (1990).

Surprisingly, another branch of this family tree includes Karl Marx. I find this particularly intriguing because his notions about sharing—giving what you have to give and taking what you need— are also an essential part of what I teach about intimate relationships. In his way, Karl Marx brought to the political scene what Martin Buber brought to the religious/philosophical domain. It is also what I have sought to implement in practical fashion in the realm of couples and families.

This heritage was never passed on to me directly in words. I didn't hear about it from my parents. What I do know is that my home atmosphere was nurturing and affectionate, with a great deal of respect for the children.

My father, the oldest of three brothers, graduated from Columbia University as a dental surgeon. My mother was a loving, nurturing homemaker. With her, I experienced a great deal of non-verbal affection. Bonding, snuggling, and warmth were all taken for granted. I don't remember arguments, and I don't remember anger. I didn't learn anything from my parents about how to fight. I learned with my older sister, who had a temper, that I could never win a fight with her. This led me not to attempt it.

My father was a chess player—an excellent one—and a member of the Staten Island Chess Club. There, world champions were invited to play. He taught me to play chess when I was six years old, sitting on his knee. I'd watch him play with his friends. When I was 11, he began taking me to his chess club on Friday nights. Being the only child there, I became sort of a mascot. I happily attended with him for about a year.

I know he encouraged and validated my intelligence, my ability to think clearly and logically, my ability to seek alternative possibilities in any given situation. In chess, it's not over until you're checkmated. Until then, there are always other possibilities. This provided an early education in thinking logically and strategically. It taught me important lessons about patience and persistence.

From the time I could speak, I sang naturally. I have early memories of many times when my parents invited guests for dinner. They would ask me to sing a song, to perform for the guests. At a certain point, I became very shy about this. Decades later, I remembered why. It involved an incident when I was two or younger. I was being potty trained, and I was very proud of learning this special new activity. I can still visualize being in the bedroom, on a little seat, stark naked. My mother's brother, who was my favorite uncle, came to the house to visit. He was sitting in the next room. I had real feelings of love for him, perhaps because he used to babysit for me when I was an infant. I have a memory, as clear as the day it happened, of rolling myself on the potty chair into the living room, ever so happy. My uncle saw me and burst out laughing.

I suddenly knew how it felt to be betrayed and humiliated. I knew how it felt to be laughed at, to feel inhibited, to realize that I was unclothed and shouldn't be, and to feel abandoned by someone I had trusted and loved. I had ambivalent feelings toward that uncle for the rest of his life, although I didn't remember this episode until years later.

From that day forward, whenever he visited, I stayed in the background. I never moved close to him, nor was I ever affectionate to him again. Following that early experience, I would go down the hall to the farthest room and sing from behind a club chair whenever anyone asked me to perform. No one ever asked why I did that, and I wouldn't have known myself. I just knew that was the only way no one could see me. I had to hide.

At about age nine or ten, when we sang in elementary school, my voice apparently rang out above the rest. One day my teacher, whom I loved, told me that she would like to take me somewhere the next day. I was flattered to be singled out.

The next day after school, she drove me to a different school. We entered a classroom where 30 or 40 teachers were seated at desks. Standing me up in front of the group, she told me to sing a song she had taught my class. Taken by surprise yet wanting to please her, I opened my mouth. Absolutely nothing came out! I was voiceless, speechless, scared out of my wits. She matter-offactly had me sit down, and nobody said anything about it. From that day on, however, I wrote a decision in invisible concrete that I would never permit anyone to place me in the position of performing solo in front of a group. I sang in choirs, in choruses, and at home by myself.

When I was growing up, my father worked long hours. His dental office was in Manhattan, and we lived across the bay on Staten Island. He never arrived home before 9 o'clock at night. I have vivid memories of my mother, my sister, and myself listening to soap operas on the radio as we waited for him. Mother would curl up on a sofa, my sister would rub her back, and I would rub Mother's feet. Sometimes I massaged her back or her head, and then we'd change off. It was a bonding that I never questioned, a lovely pastime for the two of us. My dad would then arrive and, while my mother fixed dinner for him, he read the paper. I would curl up under his arm. So I snuggled and bonded with both parents easily and regularly.

The one other family time together was on Sunday, when my father took off from work. Time and again, we had music sessions around the piano. What we played and I sang were the love songs— those beautiful, melodious love songs—"My Hero" and "Because" and "Someday My Prince Will Come." My father played piano by ear. He sometimes played the violin. My older sister would play the piano and I would sing. When I was 11, I began piano lessons, primarily so I could accompany myself.

The tunes I sang and felt most deeply were the romantic love songs on which I was raised. I sang those lyrics and collected sheet music to the operettas of the day, the musicals, and the musical comedies. My notions of love and life grew out of learning the lyrics to these songs, which became imprinted in my memory. I believed without question that people indeed loved each other, were faithful to each other, enjoyed each other's company, and were committed to their relationships.

Music became a very strong element in my life. If not for my shyness and inhibitions, I might have pursued it as a career. Logistics were another obstacle. When I was 14, there was talk of my attending Julliard School of Music in Manhattan. That would have required my taking a ferry, a bus, and a train each way. My parents vetoed the idea.

I continued to love singing and playing, but I maintained my aversion to performing solo. Many years later, when Daniel Casriel became terminally ill, he could not continue leading his workshops on bonding. These had become a very important part of my clients' healing process, and I did not want to see them end. Colleagues told me, "You can lead these workshops."

I had sponsored Daniel for years, many times a year, and I had attended each event. Naturally, colleagues expected that I could step up to the lectern. But just as quickly, I would reply, *"I can't."* It wasn't even a question for me, it was a certainty. I had a very clear belief that I under no circumstances would I lead a group or perform in front of one.

After six months, the Casriel workshops came to a complete standstill in the Washington area. The offices we had acquired for them sat empty, and I had even placed them for sale. At that point, so many people were so persistent about their need to continue his healing process that I gave in. With the support of three colleagues who had attended Daniel's workshops and said they would help, I finally agreed to present it.

I wish I could say this was easy, but it wasn't. I was terrified. It was as if I had to reexperience all the terrors I had ever known about performing in front of people, being evaluated, failing, and feeling humiliated. It all went back to having been a timid, shy child. My early decisions had been: "Don't stand out. Be careful.

Don't ever put yourself in a position where you might be laughed at, humiliated, or made fun of. Be cautious."

My self-confidence was also deeply affected by my older sister, who made no bones about disliking me and never wanting to be with me. Whenever her friends were present, she didn't want me around. She dismissed me and rejected me. Many years later, when we were both grown and married, I asked her why she didn't like me. I was hoping that perhaps she'd say, "Oh, you're making a mistake. I really did."

Her answer was, "Because you were born." It was that simple. Until she was four, she had been the oldest grandchild, the only child, doted on and very special. I don't think it was only that I was born, but also that the Great Depression began. I'm sure things changed for my parents. My father lost his financial security in the Wall Street stock market crash, and he was burdened with worry. This in turn affected my mother. It's possible she was depressed, too, when I was born.

I grew up as a quiet, introspective, musical, placating, accommodating child. I never doubted the love of my parents, and I always had a best friend. But I didn't trust the world outside my home, in my ability or power to go out and carve a path for myself.

It's very possible that if certain events in my teens had never occurred, I would have remained quiet and passive for the rest of my life. World War II erupted. My father's extended family in Russia was wiped out completely. In the village of Kovna, where his older half-brother was the mayor, the entire Jewish population was shot and thrown into mass graves.

Through newspapers and radio reports, I learned about the Holocaust, of the incredible slaughter of the Jewish people. There but for the grace of God went I. People were murdered for having a relative somewhere who was Jewish or even partly Jewish. I felt incredible terror at this dangerous world.

Prior to the war ending, my father's youngest brother died suddenly of a coronary. He had been seen as the light of the family, a leader. When his car became stuck in the snow and he tried to dig his way out, he suffered a fatal heart attack. He was only 40. He left a wife and three very young children.

Soon after, my father suffered a coronary and died overnight. My mother's parents died next, as did two other uncles in their forties. A year and a half later, my mother died of cancer. With such a series of stunning losses from ages 14 to 16, I went on automatic pilot psychologically. I had no way to integrate, to absorb, to express these losses. When my father died, I spent hours at the piano playing the music he had loved. Once my mother commented that she didn't think I fully felt what had happened. She didn't know this was my personal way of grieving.

Immediately after my dad died, we moved to a new area. Over the next year, my mother developed symptoms that were diagnosed as arthritis. She experienced increasing pain and difficulty walking. One day, when my sister filled a prescription for her, the pharmacist told her that what was written on the prescription was "cancer." My mother didn't know. They told her she had arthritis, and that it would get worse before it got better. She believed that. So we never talked about the end, about dying. It was acknowledged but remained a painful secret.

My world view at that point included a decision not to trust fate at all. It's not that I didn't trust people. I certainly had trusted my parents. But I most emphatically did not trust fate. I had learned that you never know what's going to happen. I also didn't trust religion, and I didn't trust God. When my father was dying, I repeatedly screamed into my pillow, "Don't die! Don't die!" But he did. God didn't keep him alive. He died before the war ended, and I had a horrible feeling that he never even knew our side had won. And now my mother had cancer.

When my mother became bedridden, a practical nurse cared for her at home. She became a surrogate mom for me. Mother was eventually in such severe pain that I wanted to give her an overdose of morphine to end her agony. I told the nurse this. She told me that if I were to do such a thing, I would go to jail. I didn't do it, but I felt like a coward. I numbed myself and waited it out until my mother finally died. The end came almost after the fact.

My sister then decided promptly to marry the man she was dating and to move to Manhattan. As she was now my legal guardian, I would have to move with her. She had turned 21 three weeks before my mother died. I told my school counselor that I couldn't complete the school year as we would leave Staten Island in January. The counselor allowed me to double my school schedule, fortunately, so I completed all my required courses in mid-year and graduated second in my class.

Moving to Manhattan with my sister cut me off from everyone I had known. My boyfriend of two years had also just left to serve in the Marine Corps. He and I used to spend hours and hours on the telephone, talking every day. His parents were divorced, and he lived with his father. This was my first experience in confiding in a male, a boy. He loved to talk, to reflect (and later became a psychologist). A deeply romantic person, he wrote me beautiful poetry. He was highly intelligent. The day he was accepted at medical school—which was what his father wanted for him—he enlisted. He left right when my mother died, just before my sister married and we moved.

So I left my parents' home, my friends, my school, and my only boyfriend. It was more painful than words can express. I had profound feelings of emptiness and loneliness that never left. I played the piano and subsisted on voluminous letters from my boyfriend, who sometimes wrote as many as seven letters a day.

I applied to only one college: Cornell University. My sister had hoped to go there, along with her best friend. But when my father died, she had to drop out of school and go to work. It is one of the great ironies of my life that, if not for the loss of my parents, I wouldn't have had the life insurance funds to leave Staten Island or to go to university. Cornell accepted me. I began as a freshman in Ithaca in September 1946. I didn't know anyone when I got to the university, yet those first two years were a wonderful period of blossoming. It was my first experience out in the world. Until my parents died, I had never spent so much as one night away from home. I never went to camp or stayed at friends' houses. I was comfortable at home. Now here I was, cast out into a world that was totally strange, alien, unknown. I did well academically and went out for many activities: choirs and choruses, plays and theater. I dated a lot and enjoyed my major in child development and family relationships. I double-majored in psychology, which at that time emphasized animal research and proved less intriguing.

Meanwhile, in the background, my Marine boyfriend kept writing letters. After his hitch in the service, he returned to Staten Island. I wanted him to join me at Cornell, but without a lot of social confidence in himself, he seriously doubted his ability to compete with the sophistication he pictured at Cornell. When he decided not to come, in the spring of my sophomore year, I stopped answering his letters.

That June, I attended a fraternity party and met a guy who was handsome, had a beautiful smile, and was very friendly to me. We started dating. About two weeks later, he gave me his fraternity pin, which I didn't take all that seriously. He had the reputation of being quite a lady's man, so I found it somewhat amusing that he was pursuing me.

He was graduating and was double-registered in law school. He asked me to stay for the graduation ceremony and to meet his parents, who would be attending. I said I would. His parents had already offered to drive me home, and the day after that trip, his mother called my sister in great excitement. She said this was just the most wonderful thing, that she was so happy. I was somewhat flattered.

It was as if we had become engaged. My sister and her mother-in-law (an elderly German woman) both looked at me and said something to the effect of "Well, is he a nice person?"

"Yes."

"Does he have a nice family?"

"Oh, I think so."

"Does he have a good future?"

"Well, I guess so. He's in law school."

"Well, what's wrong with this?"

Inside of three weeks, he presented me with a diamond engagement ring (that his parents gave him to give me) and a diamond watch. We each had two years to go to finish college, so we talked about becoming engaged. If marriage still made sense at the end of the two years, we would marry.

Quite soon after, a discussion took place about how two years was a long time. If we really cared about each other, perhaps we would get married during Christmas break. His mother would talk to my sister, and then he would talk to me. Then another proposal came forth. "There really isn't much time available at Christmas," they said, "so you had best get married this summer."

In retrospect, several things were occurring rapidly. He was an only child of Jewish parents and apparently had not dated Jewish girls, though he had dated a lot. His parents were ecstatic that he had found a nice Jewish girl. On the part of my family, people must have considered that, since my parents were gone, it would be very nice if I had someone who would be there for me. And this young man seemed to have a promising future. For them, the marriage also seemed great. My father's remaining living brother, who was married and had three kids of his own, made the wedding. It was very beautiful, lavish. The reception was on the roof of the elegant St. Moritz Hotel in New York.

We had met in June, and barely three months later, on August 28, I found myself married. I was a virgin at marriage—it was an era when penalties for sex before marriage were terrifying. They included the "scarlet letter," pregnancy, and having to marry the person with whom you had sex (since no one else would ever want you). That we had never slept together may also have contributed to his desire to get married as soon as possible.

The day after the wedding, we drove to Maine for our honeymoon. On the way, I suddenly saw a very different side of this man. I experienced someone who was rude, angry, moody, insulting, and sarcastic. It was a shock. I had never seen him like this, nor had I seen this kind of behavior in my family. Nor had I seen it in my previous boyfriend. I wanted to jump out of the car.

When he saw that I was terribly upset, he changed his behavior. "We'll go on this trip," he said, "and if you still feel that way when we get to school, we can get an annulment."

We went on. What I discovered with him was that all the assumptions I had had about romantic love, friendship, trust, confiding, sharing, being best friends—none of these were true. None of that was possible with him. He didn't know anything about these qualities. Furthermore, he didn't want to know. So for me, that marriage meant loneliness. Looking back, I have no doubt that if I had had a home to go back to, I would have left. Instead, his parents were very devoted and loving to me, making it clear that they wanted me as their daughter. In a way, it was as if his parents became my home and family.

When I went back to Cornell University, it was with the abrupt realization that my entire life had changed. I had hitched my wagon to one particular star, and I had to go where he went and do what he did. I was no longer my own person.

Our daughter Beth was born two years later, shortly after we graduated from Cornell. Six weeks later, we moved to Washington, where he progressed rapidly in his career. From day one, he performed extremely well as an attorney. Many of his personal qualities were excellent in terms of career advancement in Washington. Unfortunately for me, they had no value in terms of intimacy. In private, he remained distant, aloof, dictatorial, and angry, although he demonstrated an amazing ability to assume a front for people, to be smiling and pleasant when others were around.

I didn't know what to do. I knew there was far more to life and relationships than this. I yearned for someone I could confide in, and for physical and emotional closeness. My husband perceived closeness as being controlled. Much more was possible, I knew, but it wasn't possible with him. Periods of seeming pleasantness were as close as it ever got. Long periods of distance and silence were common.

Through it all, I developed close friendships with other couples and women neighbors. By the time I was 25, I had a daughter and two sons, all under the age of five. I loved my children, and my friends gave meaning to my life.

My husband was distant and aloof not only with me; he wanted little to do with our children. He never helped with them or got up at night, never changed a diaper, and never fed them. If anything, he probably felt competitive with them. When I was tired from caring for them, he resented it. He wanted me to be the perfect wife, mother, and homemaker and then be fresh as a daisy. He was probably meant to live as a wealthy man with servants. However, we couldn't afford servants, and I had a hard time having the energy to do it all. It was an impossible situation.

He and I were an attractive couple and, as his career progressed, people probably saw us as a wonderful couple with adorable children. We went through years of appearing to be the ideal American family. He disliked going anywhere with the children, however, because they might be noisy or fussy or messy. Nor would he permit anything in the living room to indicate that children lived in the house. And he resented ever having to eat in the kitchen with them, preferring that I serve him alone in the dining room.

I dealt with this by placating and accommodating him. I felt depressed, was tired much of the time, needed lots of sleep, and developed various illnesses. During my frequent appointments, my physician never asked, "How's your marriage?" That was the question that most likely would have led to a correct diagnosis.

In time, I decided to return to school. My first interest had been medicine. At Cornell, I had done well in pre-med courses. I loved reading the medical and scientific journals. Learning how the body, the mind, and the emotions work still fascinates me. Being part of the healing arts held great appeal but, as a busy mother, I decided against medicine. I had to choose a less demanding entry to the field.

I chose to attend Catholic University in Washington for a master's degree in social work. Unlike medical school, social work school accepted part-time students. As a full-time wife and mother, it was my best available option. Eventually, I attended full time and was awarded a National Public Health stipend that covered tuition and household help.

Meanwhile, I became pregnant. My children were then seven, nine, and eleven. I loved homemaking and mothering my children. It was a very active life, needless to say. To fit it all together, I spread out my graduate studies over four years. Even so, it was exhausting.

Following graduation, I began working in a mental health center. There I learned that "Someone who goes along with a bad situation is as responsible for perpetuating it as the one who starts it." In other words, you are responsible even if you are not the one who "caused" it. If you accept it, you are perpetuating it. This lesson was profound for me.

This seems obvious now, but it had never occurred to me then. I had seen my marriage as my cross to bear. Now I realized I had never learned to argue or fight back. I just learned to be quiet, to acquiesce, to accommodate. I might be unhappy but I would not fight. Now it hit me that I had to stand up for myself. I had to argue, and I had to fight. On my ninth anniversary, I swore there would never be a tenth if I remained so unhappy in this marriage.

I remember many very unhappy times. I was tired much of the time. When I started attending graduate school, I remember wondering where I would get the energy to walk from the car to the building. If I had stayed much longer like that, I think I would have died. When I learned that by going along with the situation, I too was responsible for it, I decided that either my marriage had to get better or I had to get out.

Much as I had hoped for things to improve in my marriage, they never did. After some additional upsetting revelations, things finally came to a head. My husband never agreed to speak to a therapist until the very end, when I said, "This either has to get better or it is over." When he did agree to go, it turned out that there were no therapists helping couples. It just was not an option in the 1960s. I was referred to my analyst, and he was referred to his analyst.

My therapist was a very wise, grandmotherly woman, a dean of psychoanalysts. She was the one who explained to me how guilt worked and that my husband probably felt guilty. He saw an analyst who, two months after they started, took off the entire month of

August. By the time September came, the window of opportunity had closed. He wouldn't return to therapy.

After I decided to let him know how everything was affecting me, we had some major arguments. Once, I raised my voice and threw a lamp at him—something I had never done in my life. On the spot, I developed asthma. I began wheezing, couldn't breathe, and felt incredibly scared. At 1 o'clock in the morning, I left home. I intended to drive 200 miles to my sister's house in New York. But at DuPont Circle in Washington, I stopped and sat silently in the parked car. My children already knew they had a father they couldn't count on. Now, if they also had a mother they couldn't count on, what would happen to them? I turned around and went home.

My husband and I separated. He came back, saying he'd change things. It went round and round, until finally he came home at 5 o'clock one morning. I said I was going to take his clothes and have them delivered to his office. Ultimately, he moved out.

That began the next phase of my life. I was 35. I had four children, a master's degree, and no idea what would happen next. I didn't know how I would survive, but I knew the marriage had to end. Anything I did would be better than staying married to him. I would never again be with someone I couldn't be close to.

The divorce was not amicable. As an attorney, my soon-to-be ex-husband drafted the agreement. The settlement did not automatically include such things as education for the children or specifics about visitation. I certainly intended for the children to continue spending time with him, but I would have signed anything to get him out of my life. It had never occurred to me that paying for their college education would be an issue. His parents had always been very loving to me, and they had always assured me not to worry about the children's education. When the time came, they said, the money would be there. His father was a successful building contractor.

My daughter was in her junior year of high school and applying to colleges when we separated. When I spoke to her father about her education, he said, "Don't look to me. There's nothing in the agreement." I went to New York and asked his parents, who said, "Don't look to us, we're only the grandparents." I was clearly going to be without help in educating four children—three of whom would be in college at the same time. Working full time at the mental health center was not going to supply enough to meet our needs. I began a part-time private practice in the offices of a local group of pediatricians.

I then went searching for all that had been missing in my marriage. I wanted to find out how to heal and how to change my life. As in the alchemical story in which an irritant in the oyster initiates the formation of a beautiful pearl, my pain had its payoffs. Ultimately, my search for personal healing and changes gave me the substance of the program I developed later. PAIRS has now proven to be both healing and preventive for thousands of people. With tongue partially in cheek, I can credit my former marriage for this program.

Fifteen years later, my divorce also led to my being the first one in Virginia to sponsor divorce mediation. After going through a very ugly divorce of his own, an attorney named Jim Coogler had decided that divorce did not have to be that painful and bitter. In 1978, he wrote the ground-breaking book *Structured Mediation in Separation and Divorce*. Through the Family Relations Institute, I sponsored him in 100 hours of professional training in Virginia. He came for five weekends over the course of a year to train 12 other therapists and me in helping couples collaborate in writing their agreements. This avoided having two attorneys in an adversarial position, each fighting to get the most for his or her client.

I then founded the Center for Separation and Divorce Mediation in northern Virginia and personally conducted 15 mediations. I found that, in general, one member of the couple wanted a divorce and the other did not. On the spot, I invented a "marriage assessment" that offered clients the opportunity to explore with me—in an individual and an ensuing couple's session—what had gone wrong in the marriage and what might help. More than half the couples chose the assessment. Of that group, more than half chose to work on their marriage. I then threw my energy into developing the Practical Application of Relationship Skills program (PAIRS) to help couples heal their relationships.

The state of Virginia's Ethics Bar accepted the divorce mediation program so that divorcing couples could meet with one mediator to arrive at a settlement. Either the husband or wife can then file for divorce. Mediators are trained to include in separation agreements every single item that needs consideration. This includes the education of any children, visitation, and "shared parenting"—a term that did not even exist when I divorced in 1966. Once again, my own painful experiences had given me the impetus to contribute something to the welfare of others. In this case, it benefits spouses and children who all too often had been the victims of unfair divorce settlements.

I was searching for what couples needed so that I could help others prevent the kind of marriage I had endured. I went to marathons, lectures, and conferences. And I attended every workshop I could that had to do with helping couples. At our mental health center, I had started the first couples therapy group. I read as much as I could and had volunteered at the center's library so that I could get first crack at any new books.

The first book that came across my desk was *Conjoint Family Therapy* by someone I had never heard of named Virginia Satir (1967). I read it and, for the first time in my life, found answers.

With logic, sensitivity, and a humane attitude, the book spoke to me. Shortly after, a flyer arrived, announcing that Virginia was presenting a two-day workshop in Miami. After making all the necessary arrangements for somebody to be at home with my children, I flew there to meet her and learn from her.

In front of a large audience, she worked with four very troubled families. This woman was truly inspiring. She was even better in person, remarkably, than in her book. I arranged to get a tape of that session and brought it back to my mental health center. It helped convince the director and the chief social worker that we had to sponsor a training by her in the Washington area.

The director told me I had to guarantee that we wouldn't lose money. This was risky for me. Given my income, minimal child support, and a limited amount of alimony, I had no money to risk. But I went ahead and guaranteed it, knowing Virginia was brilliant. She came, and so did 200 therapists.

As terrific as she had been in Miami—and even more so— she worked with the most troubled, most difficult, most impossible families that we had at our clinic. She was so insightful, so connected, so warm and human and healing that I had no doubt this was someone from whom I wanted to continue learning.

Not long after that, a new residential treatment center invited me to become its first family therapist. The courts sent adolescents there for all kinds of outrageous delinquent behavior, and their families had to cooperate. (This center later became a prototype for the residential treatment of adolescents.) Around the same time, Virginia gave a talk at Catholic University, which I attended. I spoke with her there and, to my surprise, she remembered me. I had heard she was now the director of training at the Esalen Institute in California (this country's first human-growth think tank). She was giving a month-long family training there, but my many commitments prevented me from going to California for that long.

"If I organize it in Washington and make all the arrangements," I asked, "would you come and teach the Esalen training here?"

She said yes, she could do it over the course of a year. It might be in bits and pieces, but she could do it.

That was the start of the Family Relations Institute, which I created so that she could offer her training in the Washington area. I chose the name and then went through telephone books to put together a mailing list of therapists in the area. For my board of directors, I recruited Peter Ziebel, director of the new facility where I worked, and Charlotte Kaufman, the chief social worker of the center where I'd worked previously.

Virginia spent a week with us in West Virginia, and then she conducted a marathon at my home, followed by two weeks of training in Aruba. She became my source of nourishment, enlightenment, and understanding. Family therapy was a new field, and psychology's focus moved away from analysis. Working with the individual, with the family as a unit and as a system, and with the marital couple as a unit and a system—these were all exciting new concepts.

The Family Relations Institute came together in short order and became a postgraduate training center for professionals who wanted to develop skills in marriage and family therapy. I learned to administer all the arrangements, which provided me the opportunity to find other speakers as well. At conferences and workshops, I'd approach those presenters who I felt had something important to offer. I chose the most brilliant people in the field at the time, inviting them to present and train at the institute.

The psychologist George Bach was one of the first trainers I invited. He was incredibly colorful about dealing with anger, and he was very effective in teaching how to fight and negotiate. Since anger was in many ways my nemesis, his work fascinated me. I was fearful of anger, and here was somebody who was making a ritual of it and bringing enormous humor to it. The Fair Fight for Change and techniques for differentiating between fair fighting and "dirty fighting" became an important part of PAIRS.

Murray Bowen was then in Georgetown, developing something he called family systems theory. He came and spoke to us. Lyman Wynne, the chief of family psychiatry at the National Institute of Mental Health, also accepted our invitation to present a workshop.

At the Adolescent Residential Treatment Center, meanwhile, we were finding less success. Despite the good will and all the techniques of our very caring staff of therapists, these kids were still escaping through windows at night, taking drugs, and stealing cars. Since none of the traditional modes of therapy were creating change, I set out once again to find who had developed something successful in the field of addictions and adolescence. I believed in learning from those who had found answers and adding such answers to my own knowledge.

Along the way, I heard about Daniel Casriel, a psychiatrist in New York City who was doing innovative work. I arranged to visit his Areba Institute. People there seemed friendly when I arrived, warmly embracing and chatting with each other. And when I met Dan, he appeared to be a pleasant, quiet, low-key person.

Having arranged to sit in on one of his groups, I went upstairs for the session that was about to begin. About 30 people were chatting in a circle. Dan came in, sat down, and said something like: "I'm Dan, and I'm fine."

The next person said, "I'm Harry, and I'm fine."

Then the third one said, "I'm Charles, and I'm ANGRY!" Throwing back his head, this man let out a blood-curdling shriek. And then another and another—a whole series, the likes of which I had never heard. I was certain he had gone crazy right then and there.

I sat in shock and horror. I had heard impressive things about Dan's work, but I had never heard any specifics. This was a mind-blowing experience for me. Around the room, nobody else seemed the least upset as "Charles" raged and screamed. When he could talk, he described what he was angry about and how he was going to make some positive changes in his life.

In turn, other people used this same incredibly intense expression of feelings, screaming out whatever pain and rage and fear they felt. No one seemed put off by this, and no one went crazy. Some people stood up, walked over to whomever they wanted to support, and hugged that person. This intense emotional expression and bonding were things I had never experienced. Staying to interview people afterward, I heard incredible statements about the healing that had happened for them.

I decided to learn more about this work and to bring it back to the treatment center. We had very angry kids there, and the only thing we were doing with them was talk therapy and behavior modification.

At the next session of the Virginia treatment center therapy group that the director and I led, one 18-year-old was expressing outrage. He'd been thrown out of school for using drugs, and he hated everyone. I intuited that Dan's process would help him, so I tried to offer it in the group. The director laughed at my efforts to bring in this newfangled technique. The group members, including the angry young man, followed suit in dismissing my efforts. A week later, the young man committed suicide.

This had a profound impact on me. I had experienced an approach that I knew made a difference—however startling the method might have been—but I could not implement it without the support of my colleagues. I also knew that I had never been a leader in the sense of pioneering and proselytizing for something on my own. I had merely set out to learn what I needed to be an effective therapist. Eventually, I left that treatment center, knowing I could no longer work anywhere unless I could use *all* the processes that I had found effective. It was a matter of integrity.

Meanwhile, I had met "Richard" when he came to work on the piano in my home. My son's piano teacher had given us his name. At that time, I was struggling to teach myself Beethoven's "Pathetique" sonata. Not knowing that Richard was also a professional concert pianist, I said, "I'm working on this sonata, and I'm wondering if you can play it?"

He gave me a somewhat contemptuous look, took the sheet music, closed it, and placed it on the piano. Then he closed his eyes and played the "Pathetique" from memory, from beginning to end. When he finished, he invited me to go bike riding with him someday soon.

This was during that terrible time of on-and-off separation from my husband of 17 years, and I said no. But Richard continued to call every few weeks, inviting me again to go bike riding. When my husband and I finally separated for the last time, I said yes. I took along a friend, and after the ride we went to her home. Richard played the piano (a gorgeous Steinway grand). As he did, something happened. It was as if a door opened to a bottomless pit in my heart. All my longing for love, unfulfilled for so many years, awakened deep within me.

Driving away, I tried to close that door. It wouldn't close. I felt an unending longing that perhaps only music can touch. The next time Richard called, I agreed to go biking again. Within a short time, our relationship became romantic. He was in my life for the next seven years. We never lived together, but at times I considered marrying him. My two youngest boys loved him. On the other hand, my daughter hated him, and my oldest son merely tolerated him ("He would make a nice brother, but I can't see him as a father"). For me, this split among my children posed an impossible dilemma.

About that time, Virginia conducted a group marathon at my home. It happened to provide something very important in my own understanding. She used a lot of psychodrama, in this case with a psychiatrist who had some regrets as to whether he had been a good enough son for his recently deceased mother. She asked him to choose someone in the group to play the role of his mother, so that he could voice whatever he needed to. He chose me, and I sat as he said all the things he wished he had told his mom. Suddenly, I was overwhelmed with pain and grief. Like tidal waves, they poured over me. I had never known such pain, hadn't expected it, wasn't prepared, and couldn't resist its expression.

In her healing and nurturing way, Virginia had me lie down. She encouraged me to get out these feelings. It was absolute, un-adulterated grief—the pain from losing my mother and father 25 years earlier. Without even knowing it, I had carried it all that time. I had no idea that anyone could carry that intensity of emotional memory for so long.

Later, I realized the repressed grief had affected me significantly. I had always been easily tearful and sentimental, but I had taken it to mean that I was simply sensitive. By the time the pain came out at that marathon, it felt as though it had taken a lifetime. (My outpouring actually lasted no more than 20 minutes, I'm sure.) Then Virginia had people in the group play the roles of my parents as they met, during their courtship and early marriage, and up until the time I was born.

At the time, this was an unusual therapy. I had never even thought about doing anything like this. Nor had I ever thought about my parents' courtship and early marriage. I had known them in their middle years, in wartime, when they had many worries. I never saw them when they were happy for any length of time. Realizing that they had once been young and carefree, happy and loving, was healing. My memories, role-play, and emotional release combined into an important learning for me about how to offer healing.

Virginia illuminated behavior by understanding it herself and then creating settings for clients to understand their own styles of communication. It seems like such a simple thing now: the universal styles of the blamer, the placater, the super-reasonable one, the irrelevant one. These patterns exist in every language, in every country. And these coping styles compound whatever problems people have.

According to Virginia, it is not the problem that is the problem—it's the way we cope with it. She demonstrated the coping styles so that we could identify our own style, identify someone else's style, and deliberately set a course to avoid those styles. Doing so allows us to arrive at what she called the *leveling* or *congruent* style. Being congruent means that what we say fits with what's inside—without blaming, placating, ignoring feelings, or being irrelevant.

In my own journey toward self-understanding, Virginia's style of using the genogram was also invaluable. Murray Bowen had developed a method of mapping family influences by looking at the bare bones of the family structure: births, deaths, hometowns, and whether relatives were alcoholics or had criminal records. He focused on facts, but Virginia used the genogram in a much more personal way. It allowed for broader perception and therefore more complete comprehension. She'd take the same facts and ask us for descriptive adjectives for a relative. What had we heard about this relative or that one? She'd send us out to interview our family members and to find out what adjectives other people used to describe them. In this way, she brought to life the human drama of parents and other relatives. From the genogram, she often developed psychodramatic role-plays.

As she had done with me during my grief, she frequently had her groups experience what she called a Family Reconstruction.

Asking someone in the group to describe scenes from his or her family history, she'd have them select other members to enact the scenes. This allowed us to look at the drama and experience it, arriving at entirely new understandings. Personally and psychodramatically, Virginia brought a deep human dimension to understanding the many springs that have fed into us and make us who we are. She revealed our invisible loyalties and "emotional ledgers," catalyzing a fuller grasp of ourselves and the people who were significant to us. In this, she moved far beyond what anyone else in family therapy had done. I continued to learn profoundly from her.

Richard and I eventually parted. I fell deeply in love with another man. He was superbly gifted in the counseling field, and for a while we were able to combine work and romance in a way that seemed the fulfillment of my dreams. I started writing poetry—something I hadn't done before. My children liked him. When he proposed marriage, I felt like Alice in Wonderland, swept off my feet.

I could never have guessed that this was the beginning of the most agonizing four years of my life. This man taught me lessons more painful than even my previous pain had prepared me for. I'll summarize it by saying that what started with such romance and promise, such chemistry and compatibility, turned out to be a can of worms such as I have never known before or since. Suffice it to say that tied up in this relationship were lessons about friendship, working together, love, and betrayal. These lessons have been essential to my growth and understanding—and I would not wish them on any enemy.

Our relationship ended after he had an affair with a woman who had been my best friend and long-time confidante. Becoming the object of betrayal, jealousy, envy, and guilt brought me in touch with pieces of the human puzzle I had never thought about (or identified with at all). As a result of this ordeal, I experienced an acceleration and intensity of learning and of emotion. This came through in my journaling at that time, and I even began to write music. I was in a long process of trying to express and heal my inner anguish.

For about four years, I was alone. I felt as though I had gone through another holocaust. What an education in human relationships—love and loss, passion, jealousy and envy. I learned that sometimes we don't even know who to blame. Maybe we can't blame anyone. Things happen.

At one point near the end of the relationship, this man and I entered a certain pattern. He would leave and return, and then leave and return again. For me, this was an excruciating spiral of pain, hope, and uncertainty. In the midst of it, he remarked, "Don't you know that whenever I return, I'm already leaving, and whenever I leave, I'm already returning?"

That statement began a series of endless contemplations for me. In the coming years, the same thought process kept me up late many a night as I tried to understand this confused, unpredictable, and charismatic man. I began formulating the idea of the *love knot:* a circular mass of hidden assumptions and misunderstandings. Love knots develop when we assume things our partner doesn't know we are assuming, and when we expect something our partner doesn't know we are expecting. Here again, my need to understand and resolve thorny issues in my personal life spurred my professional growth.

I have since discovered that this is not unusual. The archetype of the Wounded Healer has roots older than written history. In many cultures, healers or shamans recognized their calling after recovering from severe, often life-threatening illness. The ability to empathize with a patient or client is greatly enhanced, I believe, when the healer or therapist has experienced the same kind of illness or problem. Perhaps the best contemporary example is the valuable contribution that ex-addicts and ex-alcoholics make to the treatment of chemical and alcohol dependency. At the very least, healers need analog experiences that provide valid reference points for relating to what their clients are describing or experiencing.

I attended Ira Progoff's Intensive Journal Workshop three times. Going through a guided series of journaling reflections on my life helped me sift out what I had learned in each period, clarifying my life's invisible script.

An exercise I developed for PAIRS draws its inspiration from his work. It's a compact meditative journaling exercise, in which you begin by thinking of a metaphor or picture to describe where you are in your life at the moment. (My picture of myself then was of being adrift in the middle of an ocean in a rowboat, alone, without oars.) Next, you identify when this period began, using a marker such as a marriage, a move, or a loss.

Then add the following four descriptions. First, add the PEOPLE who were important to you in this period. Then add EVENTS that were significant to you, positive and negative. Third, indicate the EMOTIONAL IMPACT that these people and these events had on you at the time. Finally, note any DECISIONS you made based on the people, the events, and their impact.

This last bit is essential. What conclusions did you reach about life, about yourself, about what you want, and about what you don't want? About trust, distrust, and changes? Identifying these decisions illuminates much of your invisible life script.

Years earlier, at Catholic University, we had said prayers before and after every class. At the end of one class—knowing that I was graduating soon and also knowing how much I still didn't understand—I asked for the gift of understanding. I wanted this so that I could be an instrument of help for others. For the next several years, it was as if a hurricane had picked me up, hurtled me through space, and then smashed me down. This happened over and over, and I was reeling from what happened. Now, in a flash of insight, I realized that my prayer had been answered. I had been given the gift of understanding. It came not from a book but from my life.

In 1975, American University began its first graduate program to teach marriage and family counseling. While that may seem rather commonplace now, it was a first in those days. As I had sponsored many excellent programs at the Family Relations Institute, and because I knew the field so well, John Robertson, Ph.D. (chairman of the university's program) invited me to develop its first course.

I decided to weave into this course everything I knew that might enable future counselors to help the couples and families who sought their assistance. As I saw it, certain factors conspire to sabotage intimate relationships. My task was to help student counselors identify the pitfalls, learn how to work around them, and help clients resolve them.

Fortunately, I had the time and space to reflect on what I had learned from my teachers and from my life. Spending great effort, I developed and refined what I called my *Laundry List of Marital Mishaps, Knots, and Double Binds*. These described some of the key hidden expectations we have of our intimate others. Because our partners don't understand, they don't react the way we want them to. We get upset, angry, or disappointed, and then we act on that. Our partners respond to our reaction, and pretty soon a knot is there—a tangled mass of hidden expectations, misunderstandings, and misperceptions on both sides. Here is a sample love knot and typical belief:

If you loved me, you would want to know what I feel.
If I tell you how I feel, you criticize, judge, give advice, or
    dismiss my feelings.
So I stop telling you my feelings. I distance from you.

I started writing as many variations of the love knots as I could. This served my own healing from the very intense relationship that had ended. Virginia strongly encouraged me, particularly urging that I compose answers to the many "knots." (Thirteen years later, Bantam/Dell released my book *Love Knots*, which fine-tuned and expanded the original laundry list. It was translated into Chinese, German, French, Russian, and Hebrew. In 1996, Science and Behavior Books released an even more expanded edition called *If You Really Loved Me . . .: Identifying and Untangling Love Knots in Intimate Relationships.*)

Teaching at American University, I was pleased when graduate students started telling me how the course was transforming their own lives. Student after student said that what they were learning was useful in their personal relationships as well as their work. Eventually, I realized that if constructs such as the laundry list were so useful for them, I should bring it to my own clients.

The course included all those things I hadn't known early in my own marriage, most of which my clients didn't know, either. Against very real obstacles, people today work hard to build good relationships. We don't have widely accepted and readily accessible models for relationships in new contexts, such as a two-career marriage with children. Couples who were coming to see me were saying, "It's too late. I wish I had known all that before."

No one else was teaching this material, so I continued developing it. In 1977 I started offering the PAIRS program as part of a range of services in my practice. Its unique role is to offer the opportunity to learn those understandings and skills that sustain love in a relationship. The program offers this in a psycho-educational model, over four months.

Using a classroom rather than a counseling format has been an essential factor in PAIRS' ability to neutralize resistance. Many people who resist therapy have made dramatic transformations in the quality of their lives and relationships. Men especially respond to the program's logical structure and time-limited sequence on how to sustain pleasure in their relationships.

The program often breaks through years of conditioning that is often unconscious but that keeps us from forming and sustaining an intimate relationship. The conceptual base, which sounds so simple, is in many ways profound. I tell people that we have three hopes and three fears when we enter an intimate relationship. Our hopes are that:

- All of the positive, pleasurable things I had in my life, I will keep.
- All the things I hoped for in intimacy, I will find with you.
- All the painful, upsetting things that have happened to me before will not happen with you.

Like shadowy mirror images of our hopes, the fears follow right on their heels. Our history and our vulnerabilities trigger these fears:

- The good things I had—such as power, autonomy, money, and freedom—I will lose.
- The good things I had hoped I would find, I am not going to find with you.
- The bad things that happened to me in the past are about to happen again, because I've seen a similarity between you and someone in my history who caused me a lot of pain.

This sounds simple, and in many ways it is. But these issues move the human heart. They lead us either to develop trust and confide, or to remain guarded and closed. People understand that, and we can show them that it is possible to learn what we need and to hold on to what we want. We don't have to lose it.

In my private practice, I could now see a person on an individual basis, a couple as a couple, a family as a whole, and any and all of these as part of a group. Being able to offer this course as an additional option has given me a sense of completeness. I have a full range of services to offer the help that people need. This has been liberating and has given me a kind of empowerment as a professional beyond anything I had previously known.

The same year that I started PAIRS, in 1977, I also decided to present my laundry list when I accepted an invitation to speak at an international conference in Jerusalem. I lost a fair amount of sleep while preparing my speech: waking up in the middle of the night, I'd think up yet another knot. Then I would check it out with my clients the next week. After much brainstorming, I presented the material in Israel.

A few months later, I spoke at an open-mike meeting of 150 therapists who had trained with Virginia. Blithely running through the list, I met dead silence at the end. "Well, they're bored," I thought, assuming that therapists would find nothing new in this list. They had heard it all before. "Anything I know," I tended to assume, "everyone knows."

Then people began speaking, and it turned out they were stunned rather than bored. The knots in my list had been like darts in their guts. By the time they had heard four or five, they said, they understood what had destroyed important relationships in their lives.

This was the first time I had any sense of the power of this list. For me, each knot had come separately as a kind of "Aha!" I had never considered what it might be like to hear them all in one fell swoop.

Aside from the love knots, another major conceptual innovation I developed is the Dialogue Guide, which helps break through communication logjams. In my practice, when I asked a nonverbal spouse, "What's the problem?," I often got the classic response: "I don't know." (This probably sounds all too familiar to every therapist reading this.)

I might then ask, "What's really wrong?"

"Nothing."

So, starting with the premise that people can't guess what we're thinking, I developed a carefully sequenced structure of sentence stems or starter phrases. The Dialogue Guide now has 16 categories that help people sort out perceptions, thoughts, and feelings that are necessary to confide fully in another person. At first, it may seem like an artificial structure. The goal is to enhance communication, however, rather than limiting it.

More information is available about love knots, double binds, and the Dialogue Guide in my book *"If You Really Loved Me . . ."* (1996). In short, these can be invaluable aids in avoiding misunderstanding and in arriving at workable solutions based on clear communication, with respect for the priorities and uniqueness of each partner.

By 1980 the last of my children had left home to attend college. They had become very important to me as friends. They were my closest friends. We had been through a lot together. Now I faced a time of "yeasting," a time of beginning to blossom. It was a time of beginning to exercise leadership and of venturing into the world.

The year 1981 brought my next important transformation, which began with meeting Rabbi Morris Gordon. Fate had finally brought me a person who was kind, generous, loving, playful, and fun; who loved people; and who shared many of my values. I had known or dated other people in those years, but no one remotely like Morris. He was stable and open and talked easily.

I could sing and dance and play chess with him, and I didn't have to guess about what was afoot. I had gone through so many extremes—finding some of these qualities and not others—that to find someone who offered all of them and who loved me was remarkable. I had come to a place in my life where I really could appreciate such a man. In 1982 we married.

Life held the next surprise. Our marriage has been more than I had ever hoped for. I have dedicated my writings to Morris and to Virginia. Of Morris, I wrote (1996, p. vii): "[To] my husband, whose remarkable, unlimited vision makes possible the impossible, and probable the improbable. His encouragement, patience, and love nurture and sustain me."

By 1983, the PAIRS program involved a four-month commitment of one night a week and one weekend a month. Morris decided to attend a class to see what I was doing. He already felt an important connection between his own spiritual journey and his desire to help people learn to treat each other in loving ways. Through his religious commitment in the rabbinate, he wanted to help people maintain their ability to love each other and to love their children.

During that class, he saw these things happening in PAIRS. He saw powerful transformations in the participants. He also sensed that PAIRS could help people arrive at a spiritual breakthrough of the sort he had rarely achieved as a rabbi. When he saw this being achieved in the work I was doing, he felt deeply moved. (I didn't know this at the time. All I knew was that he was coming to class and becoming very attached to the people he met there. They welcomed his attention and made it clear that they liked him.)

Without fanfare, he took this work upon himself as a new life calling. In 1984, he established PAIRS as a nonprofit educational corporation, designed to develop programs to prevent marital breakdown. He then prevailed on Virginia to return to the Washington area to offer a four-and-a-half–day training program to launch PAIRS. We videotaped these Master sessions and produced a 20-hour series. In reviewing them for PAIRS, Dr. Clifford Sager, clinical professor of psychiatry at New York Hospital–Cornell Medical Center, wrote:

> Virginia Satir . . . inspired three generations of therapists to become more effective, to love their work, their clients and themselves.
>
> This collection of fifteen tapes . . . reveals the indescribable spectrum of Virginia's versatility and understanding. Utilizing a family or couple in the audience, she creatively improvises living theater, which evokes the healing potential within that family or couple.
>
> To read Virginia's books is a great treat, but to *see* and *hear* her in action is to watch and learn from a great healer at work. She shared herself most generously. Virginia . . . releases the therapeutic creativity in each of us.

Morris also arranged for Virginia to become the first chair of the new corporation's advisory board.

His third key contribution that year was to propel me into writing a proposal to present my work at the national convention of the American Association for Marriage and Family Therapy. I had attended many previous conferences of AAMFT but never as a presenter. Now, with the indispensable help of Morris's energy and vision, I launched PAIRS into the world. (Afterward, many therapists told me that my material had spoken to a deep part of themselves. They had always thought they would find such a program; several had even thought of developing one, but no one ever had.)

For me, PAIRS is the culmination of my life's work. Using all my chess-playing ability and puzzle-solving skills, I have conceived and created a model of relationships that helps people. It's been like putting together a 1000-piece puzzle of everything that goes into sustaining a loving partnership while also being aware of what can destroy it.

It is important to me to evaluate the program not only on a personal and anecdotal level but also with standardized research methods. We began collecting data as early as 1984, and various professional journals have published findings related to PAIRS (e.g., Durana, 1994 et seq.). Several doctoral candidates wrote their dissertations on PAIRS research (e.g., Bielenberg et al., 1992; DeMaria, 1998; Durana, 1995; Goss, 1994; Turner, 1998).

These studies have found positive changes in participants' levels of anger and anxiety, self-esteem, empathy, self-confidence, and assertiveness; relationship satisfaction, compatibility, cohesion, and consensus; sexual satisfaction; and appreciation of and affection for partners. Positive changes also showed up in people's ability to communicate effectively, resolve conflicts, function on the job, and relate with children, friends, and family of origin. Participants also reported making better use of therapy as a result of PAIRS.

Remarkably, the course's participants range from those who have not yet married to couples married over 40 years. Others are single, separated, divorced, or cohabiting. Many are contemplating a new relationship or a possible remarriage and want to avoid the pitfalls that sabotaged their earlier relationships. A vital component of this program is not only correcting what has gone wrong in the past, but preventing the destructive patterns from emerging in the first place.

Thousands of Florida youngsters are now participating in PAIRS for Schools: The Peers Experience. Designed for students from elementary through high school, this 10- to 26-session curriculum for emotional literacy is spreading quickly to school districts across the United States. Audio and video teaching tapes are supporting the efforts of PAIRS-trained providers who are teaching various curricula (half-day, one-day, weekly, and monthly seminars; and the hallmark semester course) to thousands of participants in communities throughout the world each year. In a cooperative effort with the Catholic archdiocese, we are also piloting Pre-PAIRS Catholic Couples, an integration of PAIRS' technology with biblical and spiritual content developed to support premarital training. In addition, PAIRS is reaching out to bring knowledge and relationship skills to corporations, organizations, and military personnel in North America and Europe. Our award-winning internet website (www.pairs.com) offers visitors the PAIRS mission and vision, together with practical skills for enhancing relationships.

We have recently developed a new range of PAIRS programs: a one-day "If You Really Loved Me . . ." workshop; a weekend "Passage to Intimacy" workshop; an eight-week premarital and newlywed seminar, "PAIRS First"; and "PAIRS for Life Partners" for the gay and lesbian community. Under the leadership of attorney Lynne Gold-Bikin, the American Bar Association Family Law Division has developed "Partners," a ten-session videotape that incorporates PAIRS concepts and skills. Hundreds of high-school classes across the United States have used the "Partners" program videotape.

The pioneering work of my teachers, especially Virginia, provided the foundation for developing PAIRS. The Satir model appears throughout the course, most particularly in the sections on communication, family systems, family rules, self-worth, and psychosynthesis. The program integrates the work of other therapists and theoreticians, including:

George Bach	on conflict resolution, differentiating dirty fighting from fair fighting, and the "Fair Fight For Change"
Daniel Casriel	on bonding, the logic of emotion, emotional expressiveness and intensity, and levels of emotional maturity
Ira Progoff	on journaling and life periods
Bernard Guerney	on empathic listening and expressive modes
Jean Houston	on guided imagery
Eric Berne and Claude Steiner	on ego states and life scripts
Nathaniel Branden	on sentence completion and journaling
Ivan Boszormenyi-Nagy and Geraldine Sparks	on invisible loyalties and what I call the Revolving Ledger
Murray Bowen	on differentiation and family of origin
John Gray	on letting go of grudges
Barry McCarthy, Bernie Zilbergeld, and Pat Love	on sensuality and sexuality
Paul McClean	on the triune brain
Clifford Sager	on contracting for change
Richard Stuart	on social learning and behavior modification

The insights and techniques of these people, together with my own, form the basic content of the PAIRS course. More information is available in *Passage to Intimacy,* my epitome on the PAIRS program. Published by Fireside/Simon Schuster in 1993, the book is currently being revised and updated.

As a result of the recognition and appreciation that PAIRS received, a number of therapists asked to study with me. This presented a major challenge as PAIRS did not initially have a training program. It had been more than enough for me to conduct my full-time therapy practice, teach the course once or twice a year, and have time for my personal relationships. Yet, as of 1999, we trained over 700 therapists from around the world to teach our programs.

Each challenge contains the seeds of its own completion. Morris prevailed upon philanthropic friends for initial funds to create PAIRS as a corporate entity. To film my work in progress and outline its content, we engaged an educator who had taken the course. He presented me with an 85-page outline, which I refined and expanded into a two-volume curriculum guide and training manual. I also wrote an accompanying participant handbook. More recently, PAIRS added with a one-day workshop, "If You *Really* Loved Me . . ."; a weekend workshop, "Passage to Intimacy"; and "PAIRS First," an eight-session program for newlyweds and early marriages.

Today's cauldron of accelerated changes has demanded new models. It has been uplifting for me to teach PAIRS to therapists from around the world. To a surprising extent, PAIRS is not culture specific. People now teach it in Moscow, Paris, London, Israel, Canada, and throughout the United States. The list continues to grow.

Dr. Laura Dodson actively initiated PAIRS being offered in the Soviet Union and in Lithuania. Following a PAIRS training, Dr. Julia Gippenreiter, a senior professor of psychology at Moscow University, wrote: "I want to bring back everything I discovered here . . . the wonderful role models I found are a real empowerment for me and for our relationship." While it is too early to judge the full implications, the potential for offering the world new models for personal, social, and political structures energizes me with hope.

The breakdown of old ways holds frightening potential for anarchy and new forms of oppression, both politically and in our most intimate relationships. It also offers unparalleled opportunity for new models of human understanding and peer relationships in democracy. All of us—wherever we live, whatever our personal history—seek meaning and empowerment.

In 1986, we began professional training with ten therapists. They brought great enthusiasm to their training sessions. In 1988, we started two training programs, including an international group. As of 1998, we had trained over 700 mental health professionals who have incorporated the learnings into their practices.

Some tormenting and challenging experiences transformed my life. It is as if out of my personal anguish, fine wine has emerged— a wine that has been quenching for many. More than words can fully express, I find it deeply gratifying that this knowledge is a source of positive life change even for complete strangers. It is a privilege to pass my synthesized life learnings into very able, welcoming hands.

I confess to the grand hope that somehow, through this work, we will create a more loving world that is a safer, saner, and more loving, a place of healing for people, communities, and nations. Morris and I are devoting every ounce of our energy, our knowledge, and our time to move this dream closer to reality.

*Virginia's parents,
Minnie Augusta Marie Wilke and Alfred Reinhold Oscar
Pagenkopf*

Bob Spitzer is a renaissance man and a *mensch*; publisher, psychiatrist, peace activist, lawyer, film-maker, philosopher, and more. His creativity over the 25 years I have known him——since Virginia first introduced us—has led to a wide range of projects that he initiated and then allowed others to develop further.

His name often remained unknown in this process, so many people are unaware of his germinal role. These projects have included a major role in publishing Satir and Satir-related material, as well as those of other therapists and thinkers such as Bandler and Grinder's early work in Neurolinguistic Programming.

During these past three decades, I have had the pleasure also of being close to Bob and his wife Becky's family. We have even traveled to Europe together and still remained friends.

—*Maria Gomori*
Co-editor

4

A Fortunate Life

by Robert S. Spitzer

As my mother told me this story, she is standing in a hotel elevator when the door opens. My father is in the lobby. Mother modeled gloves and was probably dressed like a flapper. They flirt. Dad asks for a date. Mother is delighted but gives him a false name.

She is pleased when he tracks her down and asks her out properly. She knew who he was all along, as the Jewish community in St. Louis was relatively small. He is supposed to be an up-and-coming businessman, religious but not overly so. She thinks he is handsome and loves his dimples when he smiles.

This is how my parents first laid eyes on each other. Virginia Satir liked to ask couples how they first laid eyes on each other. This folksy question worked well for her. Often, the partners would reminisce about their past meeting and reexperience trusting feelings toward each other. Meanwhile, Virginia would be assessing their expectations of each other and later disappointments. What were the family myths, and how did the parents talk about them in front of the children?

I never heard Dad's version of the first encounter. He had a reputation for being a great salesman, but at home he hardly talked. He didn't need to. We all loved his smile. Mother was the story-teller. When I look back at their first meeting, I realize how privileged I was. My parents each came from intact families, all the way back as far as I know. All my life, I have felt committed to my family and my friends. I was never disappointed while growing up. It was a good time.

My favorite story takes place when the Rabbi died. Mother was in line to pay her condolences to the Rabbi's wife, the *rebetzin*. Dad had been dead for six months. The Rabbi had respected my father for his success in business, and the Rabbi's wife loved my mother. The two couples had been friends for 35 years. The Rabbi and even the *rebbnitza* were college graduates, whereas neither of my parents had finished grade school.

Mother wanted to say something special to her respected friend. Finally, the line progressed and it was her turn. She said, "I'll always remember what you said when Harry died and how much it helped."

The Rabbi's wife looked up with a puzzled expression. My mother moved on with the line. Her ploy had just the desired ef-fect. It distracted the *rebetzin* from her grief when she was in a public role, and it reinforced a positive image. Thereafter, she kept asking my mother what she had said that had been so helpful.

Mother would answer, "Oh, you know," and change the sub-ject. She never told her she had made up the whole thing.

She did tell me, and I often wondered about the morality of lying to the Rabbi's wife on such an occasion. In my book *The View from Space,* I wrote about my now seeing the scene simply as two women caring for each other. From this perspective, whether Mother was lying seems irrelevant. Our internal and external dialogue can be very misleading.

The next episode takes place at the Golfmore Hotel, a Jewish summer resort in Michigan. I am five years old, looking through the window in my aunt's hotel room, watching my parents, brother, and sister returning from the lake. They had left me behind for some reason that day.

I leave my aunt and go to our hotel room, getting there a few minutes before my family. I don't remember distinctly what happened next. They must have been in sandy bathing suits. There is talk about smoke in the room and burnt matches in the ashtray. Very rapidly, I become the center of attention. They are telling me how important it is that I tell the truth, and I should tell them about the matches.

I doubt I had ever lied before or was aware of anyone else lying. Looking back on it, we were a pretty unsophisticated bunch. They tell me that playing with matches is no big deal, but lying is different. One by one, each of them takes me aside and tries to reason with me. My mother and sister are worried that my father will end up having to spank me. This had never happened to me before. They worry that Dad will have an asthma attack and, with his diabetes and heart condition, he needs to be protected at all times. I agree not to lie, and we get nowhere.

My brother eventually tells me to lie so we can get out of this mess. He is eight years older than I and my hero in lots of ways. But I am stubborn and know I have to tell the truth.

Finally, my father ends up spanking me. I'm sure he hated it. As I am very modest, the worst part for me is having to pull down my pants. They send me to bed without my dinner, but I think someone snuck in some food for me.

By the next day, I have forgotten everything. I think my attention span was too short in those days to bear a grudge. And I probably concluded that in some way it had been my fault. At breakfast, there is an announcement apologizing for the ventilation system the day before. Smoke had been blown into some of the hotel rooms. My aunt shows up and confirms that I had been with her and would not have had time to play with matches.

It is as if the family collapsed. No one has the strength to apologize. They are drained.

Thereafter, I am treated as if I were special. Someone who spoke the truth and is later vindicated. I believe my parents decided that they did not know what they had on their hands and that maybe I am supposed to teach them something. Now that I've had my own children and grandchildren, I understand better how this could happen. Children do teach us, and at times they are very wise. It is as if they can see the obvious and sometimes can comment on it, giving us a new perspective.

Later, in my teens, I begin to experience *grand mal* seizures. My first one occurs while the whole family is listening to "Lost Horizon" on Lux Radio Theater. The radio program followed the film closely. Ronald Coleman was a war correspondent whose plane had crashed during a blizzard in the Himalayan mountains. He and most of the passengers survived and started to trek out. They were freezing and exhausted and about to give up when they went through a mountain pass. Suddenly, the wind stopped. (Radio sound effects were very good in those days.) Before them lay a peaceful valley known as Shangri-La. Everyone seemed happy and calm. (In the movie, the valley's people were dressed in Buddhist robes.)

As I listened to the radio program, I must have been reexperiencing the film. There is an image of a distant view of Shangri-La. The image begins moving to the right, and then many other similar images are floating like soap bubbles, also moving to the right. I become aware of my mouth twisting to the right, as well.

I wake up in a different room, but I am so groggy that I do not realize I had lost consciousness.No one ever told me what I looked like during a seizure. When I asked, they adroitly changed the subject, as my mother did years later with the *rebetzin*. After a few more seizures, I had a neurological work-up. The doctors ruled out a tumor, told me to take Dilantin, and diagnosed idiopathic epilepsy, *grand mal* type. (Later, in medical school, I was disappointed to learn that *idiopathic* means simply that we don't know what causes a condition.)

In high school, I read very little until the English assignment *Crime and Punishment*. Its author, Fëodor Dostoevski, was an epileptic; and in several of his novels, characters have seizures with visual auras similar to mine. This pleased me. I don't recommend epilepsy for everyone, but for me, the aura made it a special experience. Its ecstatic aspect seemed full of meaning.

My wife Becky and I first laid eyes on each other on a blind date. A buddy from high school thought we would enjoy each other and have a great affair. He was right. To our surprise, it has continued for more than 40 years. As I look back, it seems as though we just lucked into having children. Neither Becky nor I had any idea how wonderful it would be.

I didn't realize it until now, but I feel doubly fortunate about becoming part of Becky's wonderful family. It was Josie, Becky's mother, who first pointed out to me how extraordinary it is that all children acquire language so young. This was before computers and maybe before basic research on imprinting. We did not have those metaphors to build on. With marrying Becky also came Jane and Gene. Our families grew up together. Not to be maudlin, but I was and am fortunate.

I first laid eyes on Virginia when visiting the Mental Research Institute (MRI) in Palo Alto. It was the spring of 1960. Finishing up a year at the Harvard Student Health Service, I was looking for a job in the Bay Area. Having been stationed there in World War II, I liked the climate and the feeling of openness. Becky had worked on the *San Francisco Chronicle* and loved that city.

I could not stop arguing with Virginia. Everything she did with families went against my Bostonian psychoanalytic education. She was out front, leading the whole process—just the opposite of the nondirective approach I had been taught. Nevertheless, I hung around. I wouldn't admit it, but I was taken by her.

To my surprise, Don Jackson, Jules Riskin, and Virginia offered me the position of being Virginia's boss. This was the world's first training program in family therapy. To obtain government grants in those days, one had to be a psychiatrist, preferably male. The people at MRI may have been impressed by my earlier degree from Harvard Law School. Moreover, no other available psychiatrists had training in family therapy, either, although most of us were trained in group therapy. I accepted happily and soon had the enthusiasm of a recent convert.

Although I had never treated a family, it somehow seemed natural to all of us that I should learn by teaching. Virginia and I were a good team. At times, I thought she was brilliant. Other times, she could get defensive and seem grandiose. She was undergoing a divorce and has said she felt suicidal during that period. I saw my role as offering support and some continuity.

MRI had a reputation for its work in schizophrenia, so we had a number of fairly disturbed patients. In those early days, before modern psychopharmacology, we used conjoint family therapy for everything. This was also before Virginia had really worked out some of her basic ideas, such as Parts Parties and Family Reconstructions. Not until ten years later, when I attended a month-long training by Virginia, did I really appreciate her. I loved the feeling of common purpose that developed among all of us there, almost as if we were family.

I have felt this at other times—a sense of purpose, a common mission. I felt it in the incest project with Hank Giarretto [now the Giarretto Institute], the Veterans' Fast protest in Washington, the veterans' Peace Action Teams in Nicaragua and El Salvador, and in the early days of home birthing with Raven Lang. It was also strong during Vietnam protests, particularly when many of us went to jail.

In the month-long, Virginia encouraged people to draw a Circle of Influence, in which they put themselves in the middle and arranged significant people around them, showing how close or important they are. I would have been surrounded by my parents and siblings. My brother and sister were like another set of parents, helping me and enjoying me. In addition, I had my grandmother and my "Uncle Doc," who lived with us.

Beyond our household, I was especially close to my girl cousins Ellie and Bitzie. Best friends were Jerry Rubenstein, Jim Dreyer, Joe Glik, Bill Edison, Bob Wald, John Richman, and Gil Murray. My dog Sandy was very important. I found that out when I couldn't stop crying after he died. No one talked about commitment back then, but we had it.

Virginia facilitated my Family Reconstruction. I have all five hours on videotape, and I've gone back to it from time to time. The experience was profoundly amazing. She began by clarifying the context. Becky, my wife, and Lucille, my sister, were present; so Virginia asked whether they could agree not to interfere, to allow me to have my particular interpretation of what happened? They agreed.

Did I, Bob Spitzer, allow her, Virginia, to be in charge of the Family Reconstruction? She told everyone there that we had a complicated relationship: we had been teachers together, we were friends, and I was her publisher. I felt relieved that she had made our relationship clear and explicit, and I agreed to let her take charge.

I chose workshop participants to play various relatives. I could see the family communication system into which each of my parents had been born. In separate tableaux, the players portrayed important developmental stages of each of my parents.

My mother's family had immigrated from a *shtetl* in the Ukraine. My first sculpture of them showed a dominant group of three women: my grandmother, my mother's older sister, and my mother. My mother's younger sister was trying to join them. My grandfather, a cheerful cabinet maker, was placating my grandmother and reaching out playfully to his daughters. Everyone was pushing forward the youngest child, a son.

That was my Uncle Doc, the only child my grandparents sent to college. He became a track star and then a dentist. He married a socialite, developed a drinking problem, gave up dentistry, and continued to be the family focus, only now in a negative light. When I looked at this family tableau, I realized how much I loved this uncle and my grandfather, and how I shared my family's worry that I might have fatal flaws like my Uncle Doc.

My sculpture of my father's family was strikingly different. My father was the second of five sons and two incidental daughters. They were Hungarians who had remarkable status for Jews of that period. They raised horses for the emperor (of the Hapsburg Austro-Hungarian empire). The family myth—and probably reality—is that my grandfather killed a serf. Beat him to death for mistreating my grandfather's favorite horse. Because of family connections, my grandfather was given one month to leave the country.

Like my mother's family, he came to St. Louis, where I grew up. My father's family was strongly hierarchical and sexist. My grandfather sat down to the dinner first, then my father's older brother, my father, and the younger sons, in order of age. Then, of the women, some sat and some served. This ordering by age and gender did not rest well in the New World. Whether or not I approve of it, I too have significant parts that are sexist and hierarchical.

I watched the role-players act out key events in first my father's life and then my mother's. I saw the birth of each parent and watched the changes in each family. In a way, I was making a movie in my mind about each parent's birth, hopes, disappointments, and even death. Doing so changed my perspective. I started to experience my parents as fellow inhabitants of the planet. It helped get them out of the role of mother and father.

Virginia called this process *granting personhood*. She would end a Family Reconstruction by having the "star" (in this case, me) and all the players describe what they experienced during the Family Reconstruction. Then she would ask all those who had played a role to close their eyes, reach up, and take an imaginary hat off their heads that represented the respective roles they had played. Then they were each to put on the hat that bears their respective real names. in that way, we were all deroled.

Earlier, I talked about feeling fortunate when I look back and realize that I came from an intact family all the way aback as far as I know. I feel equally blessed when I look forward and see my children and grandchildren. Each one seems perfect. I wouldn't want to change any of them in any way, even if I could.

My parents handled death creatively. They said that the important thing was that the three of us—Jerry, Lucille, and Bob—continue to love each other. We should write their wills. They had helped each of us in different ways, and we were to settle all accounts among ourselves. At the time, I credited Dad with coming up with a good idea. I didn't see how simple and wise it was. Mother said she liked it this way because she did not like to think of death. You see how fortunate I was.

My first picture of Maria is of a beautiful red-haired 19-year-old Hungarian studying at the Sorbonne. Maria must have painted that scene for me, as I did not know her then. Only occasionally does she describe her impressive former life, which included being a member of the pre-revolutionary Planning Secretariat for health, education, and welfare in Hungary when she was a young economist.

As did a few other women with enormous experience and common sense, Maria provided a long-lasting emotional connection for Virginia. I think she was Virginia's closest friend. Together, they could be amazingly creative and amazingly silly.

Maria was devoted to understanding the depth of Satir's work and attended most of her seminars for almost 20 years. Adding her own unique perspective, Maria went on to teach Satir-based workshops internationally and to found several Satir centers worldwide. Maria, John Banmen and Jane Gerber have been Avanta's most famous teaching triad. Together with Virginia, they wrote the much-praised book *The Satir Model*.

—*Robert S. Spitzer*
Publisher

5

Finding Freedom

by Maria Gomori and Eleanor Adaskin

Born in Hungary, Maria Gomori earned her bachelor's degree at the Sorbonne in Paris, and her economics degree in Budapest. She then worked in Hungary as an economist in the Planning Secretariat. After the Hungarian revolution in 1956, she left her country with her husband and son and started over in Canada, where she earned her Master's of Social Work at the University of Manitoba (1966). For 19 years, she studied extensively with Virginia Satir. Since 1981, she has been a faculty member and advanced trainer in Avanta, the Virginia Satir network. She has been an Approved Supervisor and clinical member of the American Association for Marriage and Family therapy since 1979 and is a certified practitioner and master programmer in neurolinguistic programming.

Maria has an international reputation as a workshop leader teaching and demonstrating the Satir model. She has facilitated numerous workshops throughout Canada, the United States, Europe, South America, and Australia. In 1990, she founded the Satir Institute in Winnipeg. Since the mid 1980s, she has focused her work in Hong Kong, Taiwan, and Thailand. She was involved in developing Satir Centers in Hong Kong (1989), Taiwan(1991), and Melbourne, Australia (1991).

With Virginia and others, she coauthored *The Satir Approach to Communication* (Schwab et al., 1989) and *The Satir Model: Family Therapy and Beyond* (1991). Maria brings to her work a diverse background and a wide range of practice, teaching, and study with leaders in the field. These include Fred and Bunny Duhl, Yetta Bernhard, Milton Erickson, Carl Whitaker, Richard Bandler and John Grinder, and others.

The following chapter derives from an interview with Maria by her long-time colleague and friend, Eleanor Adaskin. It explores the values Maria held, how they were formed in her early life experiences, and how they drew her to Virginia (who was teaching and practicing many of the same values). This makes understandable the strong professional and personal connection that developed between them.

Extended Family

As an only child, I grew up with a mother and father who both came from very large families. My mother was the second youngest of six children. Both she and my father were born in the northern part of Hungary. After World War I, this became part of Czechoslovakia. So the rest of my mother's family—her sisters and brothers—lived in the northern part of the country, which was no longer Hungary.

My mother comes from a rich, very enmeshed family. She was financially independent from my father but was emotionally dependent on him. And she was even more dependent on her sisters and brothers. In her family, everybody's business was everybody's business. My mother spent her inherited money to support her brothers when they were in trouble. Her sisters raised her after age six, when their mother died. I think my mother was like the Cinderella in her family of origin. She always did what her sisters wanted her to do. One of the outcomes was that from age one to eighteen, I had to spend all my summers in my aunt's big farm in Czechoslovakia with my cousins, with people I was afraid of.

My father's family was poor. He was the oldest child, and he became a lawyer. All his sisters and brothers and their children were financially and emotionally dependent on him. He gave them money secretly. If my parents ever had arguments, it was almost always about money and extended family.

For both my mother and father, their families of origin were more important than our family. Sometimes I felt that I wasn't as important to my mother as her siblings. When I wanted to have a normal holiday at the lake, like other families did, she would say, "Well, you have to go to your aunt's in the country." So I learned early that the extended family was more important for my mother than I was. I felt extremely important to my father, for which I am very grateful. However, the power of the extended family seemed enormous in my growing up.

Freedom and Independence

When I went to school in the 1920s, we learned to refer to the ceded part of our country as the "Amputated Hungary." There was anger over this. We learned that we would have to fight the whole world in order to make Hungary one big country again.

That was on the political level. To fight for my freedom in my own family was very important for me because I was swallowed up by my mother's extended family. When I was four, and my three boy cousins were a few years older, ages five to eight, they would frighten me by playing war games, making me a prisoner. I was really afraid of being killed, and I did not feel free at all. Under their threats, I didn't dare ask protection from the grown-ups.

Elizabeth Kübler-Ross said that there are a few events in life that at a moment in time set your goals, objectives, and values into a certain direction. I think that's true. My first memories are of my cousins playing in Czechoslovakia in Indian outfits in the garden. In the middle of some bushes, I am in prison in this little space. Around the bushes, they have ropes. I cannot get out, because my cousins are walking up and down as guards. I really believed that I was the prisoner, and I also believed that my fate depended on their mercy.

Freedom in the political sense became a very important issue for me. The government was very rightist and dictatorial. There was trouble in the world, and Hungary was going to be on the German side, which certainly wasn't reflecting freedom.

Then, as my life went on, I was always looking for freedom. In 1938 I went to Paris to the Sorbonne, to enroll in physics at the Marie Curie Institute. I understood that people with physics degrees from that institute after three years were guaranteed of getting jobs in America. From early in my life, America represented a place where I could be free.

World War II interrupted this plan for seeking freedom. I found a new cause to fight for freedom—that is, to stay in France and fight against Germany. This goal of freedom was interrupted, however, by my father's insisting I come home because of the dangerous situation in France.

I never felt free in Hungary under the rule of the Germans, and later the Communists. Actually, I never felt free until I left Hungary after the revolution in 1956. I remember walking the streets in Vienna. I had no money. I had nothing, and I was very, very happy. I experienced what freedom was for the first time.

☆

Two important pieces influenced my search for intellectual growth. One was curiosity, the other was survival. They became connected through my experience with my three cousins, who were very intellectually oriented. When I was a little girl, they always read a whole list of books by the end of every summer. I'd go back home and read them, too, but I was always one step behind. So I read to catch up and to be accepted.

I was never validated for knowing enough. These three boys did everything kids can do to a little helpless girl to invalidate me and to lower my self-esteem. The family never knew about it because I couldn't talk about it. And I didn't realize how abused I was. I really believed that I wasn't good enough, and that I was stupid. The only validation I got was from my father—knowing that he loved me.

At another level, reading all these books was very helpful for my intellectual growth. Although I started reading out of survival motivations, I wanted my cousins to respect me. I never succeeded at that before the age of 18. By then, I had read all the classics that were available to me. Then I became very curious, really loved reading, and wanted to learn more. Later, intellectual growth became again a survival tool for me, because studying enabled me to leave Hungary and the constrictions of my family. So my intellectual growth is not so much related to something that I was born with, but what my life necessitated so as to get what I wanted. Both as a child and as a young adult, I wanted to get away and live in freedom.

My mother's hope was for me to learn all kinds of social manners, go to big parties, have nice clothes, find a husband, have children, and be a housewife like she was. So I decided when I was about 14 that I would never go to a party, and I never wanted nice clothes.

I said I would never get married for two reasons. First, when I was in my mid teens, I thought nobody would ever want to marry me. My cousins never took me to a party when they were grown and started going out with women. I had very low self-esteem as a woman. Second, I wanted to be independent, never to be dependent on a man or anyone, probably for fear of ending up like my mother, controlled by the family. Therefore, I chose to have a career for myself so that I could stay autonomous.

In the end, of course, I did get married to a wonderful man, Paul Gomori. At the end of 1940, before the Germans occupied France, I went home to Hungary for a visit. My student visa said I must return to France in 13 days, but I couldn't leave my father. He was afraid for my safety and said he would die if I went back.

So I started to study economics in Hungary, which was the only thing a woman could at university at that time. I hated to be there, and I was very angry that I didn't return to France. I hated the whole political situation. I was very much alone. But the German occupation obliterated personal worries and life became focused on survival.

In 1942 I met Paul, who really valued me as a person and as a woman. I didn't want to get married, but he sort of overwhelmed me with the idea that our marriage was written in heaven. He loved me on first sight. The evening we met, he decided that we were going to get married. This was all very mystical, very spiritual for me. Paul and I were very different people. He didn't focus on problems like I did. He knew how to live life. He saw the beauty in the world, in music, in animals, and in people. I think that he was the missing part of my soul.

After two weeks, we were engaged. After six weeks, we were married. I really learned from living with him that he had unconditional love for all living things, especially for me. I felt safe that I could have my freedom and independence in our relationship.

Fighting for Freedom

When I was very young, I was afraid of my cousins but determined to survive. Later, I had to fight my father—whom I loved very much—to get what I wanted. In 1938 for an 18-year-old woman from Hungary to go alone to Paris to the Sorbonne was absolutely a no-no for him, and he was realistically very worried about my security. So I was fighting him on all levels. He set up all kinds of obstacles. I had to have grade A's, I had to do this, I had to do that. To meet his expectations, I did everything that he told me. And because he was fair—he was a wonderful person—he had to let me go, even though he wanted me at home.

My determination to fight for freedom didn't change even in the darkest times of World War II and later under Communism. It was based on a belief, an idealism, that things can change. If I'd survived so far, I could survive anything. This was later the basis for having the courage to leave everything in Hungary in 1956 to start a new life in the west.

Two months after Paul and I were married, he was drafted. It was the middle of the war, and I was pregnant. Andrew was born on January 10, 1943. Thinking about what I went through—surviving the German occupation in Hungary and all the terrible things that happened—I am convinced that there was a purpose in my life, and that I was protected on a spiritual level. I had a little baby and did not know whether Paul was alive for two and a half years, but I believed that he would return.

The war ended in Europe in April 1945. Even though we wanted the Americans to free us, it was the Russians who did. Once I thought I was safe, my fighting spirit turned into working for change. In 1945, my hope and belief in a better world led me to believe the propaganda that people would be equal and everybody would be free under the Communists. To build my country in the areas of welfare, education, and health, I was determined to work hard as an economist. I did that from 1948 to 1956.

Paul finally came back in June, and again I wanted to leave the country as soon as we could. I had a small baby. Why didn't we? Paul, who was finally home after almost three years, didn't want to leave. The Russian occupation promised us freedom, equality, rights, equal rights for women—that everything would be just wonderful. They promised everything that we didn't have under the Nazis. So there was hope, and we believed things would be better.

We decided to stay and start a new life. In 1947, when very few women there had degrees, I got my degree in economics. The economy was a very important piece in Hungary's process of change from feudalism to communism. There was no capitalism in between. In 1948, I got a job in the Planning Secretariat, which was the country's highest government office. This was based on the Soviet system.

How I became part of the whole planning system is a story in itself. Just before that, I had a job that I didn't like. Communism had already started, and I was the secretary for the director of a big factory. I accidentally met Zoltan, the person in charge of the economic transition in the country. He later headed the Planning Secretariat and was one of the founders of the Communist Party in Hungary. At the time, his organization employed only men. But he also wanted to show the world that women are equal, that women can be used in high positions.

He gave me an appointment, and I went to his office in fear. This was a place we imagined to be an evil place full of Communists. Paul was waiting nearby to see that I came out alive.

When I entered his office, Zoltan said, "Well what do you want?"

I told him I wanted to work in the Foreign Ministry. I knew languages, and I wanted to travel.

He said he would see what he could do, and I should come back the next day.

For that second appointment, I purposefully put on my darkest suit—dark gray—and took off my nail polish and lipstick. I felt that talking with this big Communist, I should not really look very bourgeois. When I walked in, he said, "Don't you have a better coat? I can buy you one. This is an awful coat. And don't you wear lipstick and nail polish?" That was the first time I realized that he was a different person than our image of a Communist leader. His criteria for hiring were competence and professional expertise rather than Party membership.

In exactly these words, he went on: "Little girl,"—I was 28—"I will offer you a job here in this place for six weeks, on a trial basis. And *if* you achieve, after six weeks you have a job. If not, you can go back to the factory."

As the first and only woman in the organization, I was scared. To prove myself, I worked very hard. Six weeks later, I was employed. My first job was to give reports to Zoltan as to whether the country's ministers were implementing all the new rules and laws from the previous three years. It was now 1949 and the whole country was going through change. Change became the name of the game.

Later I got the most exciting job of my life. Zoltan authorized me to go around to the country's ten counties to find out what they needed in terms of health education and community resources. I was to choose two or three people to develop a small planning secretariat for each county. The process would rest on the principle of planning from the lowest local unit on up—just the opposite of the old top–down feudalistic system. To coordinate all these people and programs around the country, I became a department head.

The people I chose would be responsible to Zoltan, who had absolute signing power for any money that was needed. He had the greatest financial power in the country. So if I wanted a person to work for us, it was regarded as the greatest honor. The people I chose were really the cream of the country. (Later, they went on to become ministers.) With great excitement, we started to plan and implement a better life by building resources in areas of housing, bridges, health, and education.

As the Planning Secretariat mushroomed in terms of people and planning, my department became responsible for the whole country's health, welfare, and education. Plans came from the little villages, up through the counties, to the ministries, and to the Planning Secretariat to get money. At the beginning, this was a wonderful way to turn the whole system around. Especially under the leadership of Zoltan, who believed in freedom, I really had faith that our recommended plans would be implemented.

Certain events in 1951 changed my beliefs and idealism about the system. I was so idealistic and so involved at the top that maybe it took me longer than some other people to find out that this whole Communist system led by Russian advisors was full of lies. The ideas they advertised were not practiced. People were not free, and my plans would never come true during that very, very leftist Stalinist era.

Since 1948, I had worked very hard on the five-year plans in the areas I was responsible for. One of these was housing. Because we didn't have enough housing after the war, this was the country's most important project. After three years, we had only accomplished 0.2 percent of our goal, which I reported to Zoltan. We reported exact figures to the press regarding progress of the five-year plans, and my statistics had to be published.

The next day in the Party paper, the housing project was reported as having accomplished 102 percent. Going to Zoltan, I said, "There's a mistake in the paper" and told him what it was.

He said, "Do you want to live?"

"Yes."

"Do you want your family to live?"

"Yes."

"Then shut up."

That was the moment I realized that this was all a lie. Everything I was working for was really not true. How crazy and stupid I was to believe all that propaganda. Everything for which I was responsible was for propaganda purposes, and the people did not know the truth. I talked with other people, who said, "Well, didn't you know?"

One day, without warning, the Party dismissed Zoltan, who couldn't live with the lies, either. They sent him to work in a mine in the southern part of Hungary. The secret police soon imprisoned other people who were close to him. In the Planning Secretariat, my telephone was tapped and I was waiting every moment to be jailed.

Zoltan lived with a woman named Edith in a great, loving relationship. Edith's mother called me and urgently asked me to meet her. She didn't dare come to my office, obviously. In a local park, she told me that two days earlier, the secret police had taken Edith away. Since then, somehow, Edith had sent word that, under their torture, she might be forced to sign a statement against Zoltan.

I had to find a way to mobilize help. Zoltan was already in the mine and didn't know about Edith's arrest, let alone torture, and I knew it was crucial to get the information to him. He might have the influence to free her. So, in a country where I knew that everything and everybody was watched, I took the risk to drive my government car 200 miles south to find him.

He did not want to believe my news. It turned out that, when Zoltan was dismissed, the Party's leader had promised that nothing would happen to Edith. Despite his doubts, Zoltan managed to talk to this man again to confirm my information. He convinced the leader to release Edith, although she had to move outside Budapest as a *persona non grata.*

I was afraid to drive home, thinking my car might be followed. So I flew back. After that, I was paranoid whenever someone was walking behind me. I thought it was the secret police.

Zoltan became one of the chief leaders and promoters of the Hungarian revolution. When things changed under Kruschev, he came back as part of the prerevolutionary government. That was when Edith came back to Budapest. They were kidnapped when the Russians reoccupied Hungary after the revolution. The whole government was jailed for two years, somewhere in Romania. Some went on trial in Hungary and were hanged, including our prime minister. Zoltan survived because he was popular, but the Russians took away all his rights and his writings.

I need to add here that Zoltan was an important person in my life. I learned how change can happen for a whole country. He was an idealistic Communist, and he had courage. From him, I learned administration and an organic view of the world. An organic view is based on the principles of freedom, equality, respect, choices, self-responsibility, and humanness. Administration is not limited by red tape but is based on needs and on providing resources for fulfilling them.

Zoltan represented the value of believing that change can happen and things can be better. His downfall was that he believed in the basic idealistic principles of communism but tried to work for a Party system that eventually betrayed these principles in practice. He had the courage and determination to stand up against a whole party. They dismissed him because he didn't agree with the methods of Stalinism. He also had the courage to be one of the leaders of the revolution. To the end of his life, he was an absolute idealist. Later in his life, he expressed what happened when someone asked him, "Did you leave the Party?"

He answered, "No. The Party left me a long time ago."

Today his books are published in Hungary. He wrote a three-volume history of the Hungarian Communist Party and the Hungarian revolution. In 1991, that history was finally published.

I think I connected with Zoltan and Edith on the level of having the spirit to survive and to fight for change. I also learned from Zoltan that for purposes of good, rules can or should be broken. If money was needed for a purpose, he broke all the rules of the old parliament and legislation. He approved money based on need rather than rules. He hated dictatorship just as I hated it, and that was his downfall. He wasn't dictatorial enough for the Communist system. What I admired was his humanism. What I learned from him was a wonderful free-lance way of administration, not a bureaucratic way. It always gets me into trouble now. Bureaucracy is everywhere, and I am impatient when rules stand in the way of helping people.

Things in government changed after Stalin's death. There was more self-criticism within the Party, and Kruschev opened the door to criticize the Stalinist era. During that time, Zoltan came back to the government as one of the ministers. I was still working in one of the government ministries.

The revolution started in 1956. From October 23 to November 4, we thought it was successful. The Communist Party leaders left Hungary. It was wonderful. Our new government wanted to have freedom and to have connections to the east and to the west equally. However, on November 4, the Russians betrayed us again. We woke up at 4:30 in the morning with 4,000 tanks looking at us in a city where we had absolutely no ammunition or food stored.

For almost ten days there was fighting in the streets. We did not know what happened to the people in the parliament. We found out later that the parliament building was surrounded by Russian troops. All the government officials, including their families, were kidnapped and taken to prison for two years in Romania. The new

Hungarian puppet government later recalled some of our ministers, including our Prime Minister, and tried and hanged them.

Needing To Get Out of Hungary

The Russians had invaded us again. The old Communist Party survived again. This was a terrible, terrible disappointment for me.
Since 1951, I had hoped that somehow I could get my son Andrew
out of the country. I did not want to raise him in that system, and I
did not want to live in that system, either. At that time, Andrew was
13 and ready to go to high school. Even though I was responsible
for the whole country's education, I could not get him into the high
school because Paul and I were intellectuals. The quota system
was such that only the children of working-class and peasant-class
families could get into any high school or university.

Before the revolution, it was hopeless that we ever could get
out of the country. During the revolution, Hungarian freedom fighters
had removed the land mines around the border, so it was becoming
possible for the first time. We made the decision to leave. There
was no question of staying. People often think that this was courage. It was absolute desperation. I'd rather die than stay there.

After the invasion, the Russians had checkpoints every ten
kilometers between Budapest and the Austrian border. To move
from village to village toward the west, we would need false identification papers and a cover story. We couldn't come out as a family
together because that would arouse suspicion. I had to leave my
mother there—and everything else I had. We took our worst clothes.
We didn't take any jewelry or anything, not even a phone number.
And if we got caught, we could never return to Budapest, to our
home. The Russians either shot people or deported them to Sibe-

ria. Paul and Andrew left on November 20, and I left ten days later with another group of people.

Everybody who left sneaked out. We did not know what was waiting for us outside. We didn't know what was waiting for us on the road. We knew that, as a family, we could not go together. Paul was working for the government as a vet, so he had false papers pretending that he was to buy some horses and dogs on the border. Andy had false papers that he was a kennel boy.

When they left, I told Andy that I was going to try to get out and go after them, but I didn't know whether I could make it. I wanted him to know I would really try. I really didn't know whether I would ever see him again. And for the next ten days, I was crying nonstop. My tears just didn't stop, because I was very aware that I might never see them again.

We had decided that we were going to meet in London if we made it. Paul had a sister there, and we had to memorize her phone number, because we didn't dare carry it.

I told Andrew not to say "Daddy" to his father on the road. At one point along the way, Andy forgot and said "Daddy," so they were taken to a prison camp. There they saw thousands of Hungarians who had already been detained because they were suspected of leaving the country. Paul got himself out because he had such self-determination. He told the Russian officer, "How dare you stop me from going to buy something for my government?" They believed him.

I was trying to find a group to travel with, to leave the country. Most people wanted to leave, and people were talking about how to get groups together, how to get a truck, and how to get other things. The most important things were false papers, which were made from potatoes. In a Communist country, you're not a person without identification papers. Officials check these everywhere you go.

One day, I connected with a group of ten people. We left Budapest together. The women all were dressed like peasant women, wearing *babushkas*. For a while, we went on a truck. Every 10 or 15 miles, authorities stopped us and asked for our papers. Thank God they were always Russians who didn't know what real Hungarian identification papers should look like. Our story was that we were buying food in the next villages. So I had about 10 different pieces of identification, each one saying that I lived in a different place between Budapest and the border. At each checkpoint, we died a hundred deaths until they said, "Okay, you can go on."

When we got near the border, we left the truck . By that time, it was night. We had survived so far, but the biggest problem lay with the border ahead. The Austrian–Hungarian border is not straight. It is very irregular in shape. Some of the mines were still there. Many people stepped on them and died. It was night, and there were flashlights of the border police, who were also shooting. Because the road was not marked, we never knew which way to go. Many people lost their children on the road or went back to Hungary by error.

There was a man in the group who used to be a soldier, so he suggested we follow a railway track, which went out to Austria. We did. When the lights came on from the border police, we rolled down in the snow to the lower level. They didn't see us.

At one time, I really wanted to give up because I was afraid I would be shot in the leg, and that would be the most awful thing, if I were unable to move. They would probably take me to Siberia. I wasn't afraid to die, but I would lose my past and lose my future.

Eventually, we found out that we were in Austria when we saw our first Austrian soldier. I think that man got more hugs than he had ever had in his life. Then we also found out there was a wonderful organization, the International Red Cross, which took care of refugees. They offered us food and shelter and flew us wherever we wanted to go.

I wanted to get to Vienna alone. I wasn't going to go with the other Hungarians to a camp. I felt I might be restricted in the freedom which I had just gained. Instead, I wanted to find out whether Paul was alive. And since I spoke fluent German, I somehow got myself on a train and got to Vienna. It was the greatest day of my life. I had nothing but I had everything, because I was free. I also found out that my son and husband were on their way to London. The Red Cross flew me to London, and after an overnight stay in a camp in Scotland, my cousin helped me to get back to London, where I met Paul and Andrew. Oddly enough, it was one of the cousins who had kept me prisoner as a child who helped me become free.

So there we were in London for the first time. We had nothing else, but we had freedom. That was when my total value system changed. Money wasn't important. A job wasn't important. What was important was that I was with my family and in the free world, where I had wanted to be ever since I was young. The world was open to me, and we had choices about where we wanted to go as refugees. Ever since I went to the Madame Curie Institute, I had always wanted to live in California, so I thought, "Now is my big chance to live on the ocean in a warm place."

I had only one bias, and that was absolute. If I could help it, Andy was never going to be in uniform. I went to the American embassy and my first question was, "Do you have military service or the draft?" They said yes. So my dream about California went down the drain. As I found out later, if we had gone to the United States, Andy would have been drafted for Vietnam. I decided that I was not going to a country where they have compulsory military service. This was 1956, and Andy was nearly 14 years old. I asked,

"Which country does not have compulsory service?" and they said
Canada. So the choice was Canada.

We went to the Canadian embassy, and they put us on the list.
I still wanted to live on the ocean, so we chose Vancouver. They
said it would be similar to where I wanted to live, which was San
Francisco, so we signed up for Canadian immigration and were
told to wait a few months to get to Canada. This was no problem,
since we had many relatives in England. My husband had two sisters there, and I had four cousins. We were in England from
November 1956 to April 1957, when the Flying Tiger airplane
brought us to Vancouver.

Meanwhile, surviving in London was another interesting story.
I think my spirit of independence was certainly guiding me. As
adults, my cousins did not remember their abuse, which had terrified
me as a child. They had left Hungary for England in 1938. They
were all established, and by this time we were good friends. They
invited me to stay on the farm or in their house at the seashore. But
in spite of their offer, I wanted to be on my own with my family.

However, jobs were almost impossible to get in London. Paul
and Andy didn't know English, and I knew only some. We stayed
awhile, maybe a week or two, with my sister-in-law, who had lived
in London for a long time. Meanwhile, we put an ad in the London
Times that a Hungarian family would like to have a job while waiting for immigration to Canada.

Up came an old gentleman, a typical Englishman, who responded to the ad. He lived 30 miles outside London and went
with his umbrella and bowler hat every day to London to his office.
He was about seventy, so he was just doing this because that was
his daily routine. He phoned and said that he needed a housekeeper family and he would like to have a Hungarian refugee family
as temporary housekeepers until he found a permanent one.

So we said, "Fine."

I knew lots of things, but I did not know anything about house-keeping, and especially English housekeeping. I had never even seen a piece of toast in my life. I grew up in a culture where we had maids. My mother had two maids, as people do in South America now or Hong Kong, where women come in from the country and housekeeping gives them an opportunity. Maids did the cooking, babysitting, cleaning, and everything. So I always had maids; and in Hungary, with my job, I even had a chauffeur. I didn't have to learn how to drive or how to cook. And here is this man phoning to say that he needs a housekeeping family.

So this gentleman, Alex, came up and turned out to be decent looking. I was keen to be on our own instead of with the family and glad of the opportunity to earn a little money.

When Alex directed that we bring our luggage, we said, "We have none. We have nothing." I had taken only my worst coat and my beach bag when I escaped from Hungary. If I had come out of Budapest in a fur coat, they certainly wouldn't have believed that I was a peasant buying potatoes in the next village.

So we went out 30 miles from London, where rich people lived in little communities with very elegant houses. They took the train every day to go to London. This house was 500 years old and full of antiques, and Alex was very proud of it. It had central heating, which was very unusual in England, and hot water. Alex showed us the kitchen, which was the size of a whole apartment and had a huge, terrifying stove. Then he took us to the visitors' quarters, where we had two rooms and a bathroom, and a toilet in a separate place, which I really liked.

My role was to shop and cook. Paul's job was to make the boilers go, which we didn't know anything about. Alex showed us how to take care of three boilers, the hot water system, the heating system, and the stove in the kitchen. He was telling us in English how much coal we would have to feed those boilers, and Paul said for me to listen carefully to what Alex was saying, because Paul spoke no English. I tried to understand but I really didn't know what to do.

Alex said he wanted an English breakfast—toast, tea, and eggs—in the morning. Well, I had a sleepless night because I did not know how I could make those three things at the same time. So I got up at 6 a.m. and made the tea, and then I made the toast, and then I made the eggs. You won't be surprised to hear that Alex did not eat the breakfast. It was absolutely awful. So he left without breakfast.

I was terrified about what to cook for dinner. I decided to buy veal, because wiener schnitzel was the only thing I knew how to cook. Then, at noon, a woman came to do the shopping. We went to the butcher, but she refused to buy veal because it as the most expensive meat in England. She insisted on steak. I found out later that the whole village heard that Alex's new housekeeper was so extravagant that she wanted to buy veal. What I hadn't admitted was that I didn't know how to cook steak. Now I had to find out. So I said, "How do you make the beef?"

She told me, "Three minutes on one side and three minutes on the other side." (In Hungary, we cooked beef in a sauce for hours and hours. We had no steak there.)

Back at the house, I said to Paul, "Just feed those boilers. Put as much wood and coal into them as you can." The boiler got choked on too much fuel, so of course everything stopped. By 5 p.m., there was no hot water and no heating, because we had overfed the boilers. By the time Alex came home, I had been cooking the beef for about three hours. It was like a shoe. The house was cold, and there was no hot water. We had also overstoked the kitchen stove, so it wouldn't work either, even to make the tea. I was desperate. I knew I had failed.

Alex said, "Don't worry about it, let's have a drink." Paul loved that. Soon we were sitting in a nice living room with a fireplace, and there was no food for dinner. We had our drinks, and Alex said, "Don't worry, tomorrow I'll send somebody out to fix all the things." He suggested that we go out for dinner the next evening.

Three days passed this way. Then Alex came home and said, "Well, I found a housekeeper family, the Joneses, and I don't know when I will find another one, so I've hired them."

I said, "Oh, that's fine. I can go to my cousins'."

"Oh, no, you are now going to be a guest and live like an English lady." He was really thrilled, having a Hungarian family there. Alex was sort of on Andy's level. He liked watching Robin Hood with Andy in the afternoon. He also liked to have a glass of whiskey with Paul. We found out later that he had a drinking problem. Meanwhile, he said, "You are my guests, and I have only one condition: that you cannot go near the kitchen. Mrs. Jones is going to serve you breakfast in bed."

Here we were, refugees with no money but having a life like I had never had before. He wanted me to know what an English lady's life was like. In the morning, the breakfast comes on a silver tray, the toast and everything. Mrs. Jones had to cook extra for Andrew to gain weight. And after we went out to London in the evening or to visit our friends, we came home and dinner was there, perfect.

After two weeks, Alex stopped going to London to the office. He took us to Cambridge; he took us to Oxford; he had a ball with us. What we did not know was that at night he was drinking in his bedroom. His son, Sandy, came one day and said that Alex had to go to an alcohol rehabilitation program. Alex said, "Well, you will be the lady of the house now. You are staying here. You are my guests."

During that time, while he was away, we were in charge of the whole household, including all the servants. We began to connect with the neighbors and eventually invited everyone to a party at Alex's house. Around 11:30 people said, "We have to go because the ghost is coming. The ghost is coming!"

We said, "What ghost?"

Well, it turned out that there was a ghost in Alex's house who came at midnight. The story was that somebody had killed herself there earlier.

Alex's life had been very sad. We learned that when Sandy was three months old, Alex's wife left him. He raised his son alone. He never made any connection with anybody in the village, and they knew that he was an alcoholic, so they didn't want to socialize with him. We were the first people in his world who were living in his house and enjoying it.

When Alex came back, we said, "We want you to have a party. We want you to meet the people in the village." He said fine. So we connected him with the people, and they saw that he was a nice person.

☆   ☆

☆

We left England with four big boxes of warm clothes, socks, and a fur coat. Everything came from the villagers. We were the refugees of the area. They brought us warm socks, as if we were going to the North Pole.

Alex used to take us to Cambridge. We learned later that gave him the opportunity to meet with the widow of an old friend who had died 20 years before. After we left England, he married her and sold his house. I visited them once, and our hope was always to invite him over once we had a house in Canada; but he died before that. We got a letter from Sandy. Alex had cancer of the throat. We were sad to hear this because he had provided a wonderful piece in our lives, fostering security, recovery, and a loving environment at the most difficult transitional time in our lives.

Moving to Canada

From England, we finally headed for Canada. With over a hundred other Hungarian refugees, we flew on an American military flight called the Flying Tigers. Most people signed up for Montreal and Toronto because they had jobs and relatives waiting there. In Goose Bay, the pilot announced that he was not going to stop in Montreal or Toronto because the camps were all full, and they wouldn't take more Hungarians. We all had to go on to Vancouver. We didn't mind, because we were signed up for Vancouver, but there was almost a revolution on the flight.

The Canadian government paid for us to get to Canada, and from then on we were on our own. Those diverted from Montreal and Toronto to Vancouver didn't have the money to get back to the East. When we arrived in Vancouver, they put us in a van to go to Abbotsford, where there were already 6,000 terribly upset, angry Hungarians because there were no jobs in Vancouver for them. These people were stuck there. They had heard about jobs in the East but they didn't have the means to get there. The camps were full of a mixture of people, including Nazis, Communists, criminals, and others who all claimed to have been freedom fighters.

The one person I knew in Canada was Susan, my oldest Hungarian friend, who lived in Vancouver. I had not been able to correspond with her for nine years; we couldn't, under the Communist system. I opened the phone book and found Susan, who had a Hungarian name. I phoned her, and she came and took us out of the camp.

I found Vancouver a beautiful place, so I said, "We will stay here." The problem was to find a job and to investigate veterinary licensing for Paul. The veterinary association in Vancouver said to go east. (They needed 26 veterinarians but wanted only British.) So we ended up in Toronto, where Paul found a job in a veterinary hospital as a kennel boy. At that time, Paul was 50 years old and an excellent veterinary practitioner. I think it broke his heart that he could only clean the kennels and couldn't really treat a dog for about three years. But he got 50 dollars per week, and that we needed.

I got a job with the Canada Life Insurance Company in one of those rooms where seventy-five "girls" were sitting, and where we knew about nothing except what was on our own desks. I got checks on my desk, and I had to put them in alphabetical order for eight hours a day, with half an hour for lunch and ten minutes for coffee breaks. I think that was the hardest task in my whole immigration. I did not have to use my head to do this job, but I needed the money. That was the job I got, and I could not really get another at the time, because I didn't know enough English to write an appropriate letter.

My knowledge about economics had to do with planning, and I very much wanted more challenge. I went from employment office to employment office and begged them to find me a job where I could use my head a little. Six months after we were in Toronto, I got a phone call from one of the employment agencies. She said I had an appointment next door. She told me it was a new life insurance company, established with German money, and they needed an actuarial assistant.

I didn't know what an actuary was, because there was no life insurance in Hungary in my lifetime. I had never heard about this company, so I didn't want to go. I was afraid that if I didn't go at least for this interview, however, the employment agency wouldn't recommend me for any other. So I went.

It was a new life insurance company, and the actuary of the company was a young, talented man who was in charge of establishing the whole life insurance premium book. He had this fantastic calculating machine in front of him. He said he was making formulas, and I would have to apply the formula for each age group. I was really afraid. I said, "I cannot do that." In addition, this office was plush, with blue carpets and a few very elegant looking people. I came from a country where one became suspicious, one didn't trust anybody. I was sure that they were selling women there, and that this was not a life insurance company, this was a cover story. Plus, there was German money in it, so it could not be good.

So there was no way I was going to give up my little job for this kind of setup. The man asked me, "How much money do you make now?"

"Thirty-seven fifty a week."

"How would it be if I could pay you a hundred a fifty?" This was double what Paul and I made together. I went home to think about it. Paul suggested I take it.

But I was more suspicious, and I went back to my superintendent at my existing job and told him about this new job possibility. He was flabbergasted. I said, "Did you ever hear of this life insurance company?"

He said no. I told him what I had been offered, and he said he had been there 15 years and he still didn't make that kind of money.

So I became even more suspicious. About an hour later, the personnel manager called me up to the eighth floor. For the first time, I knew there was a personnel office on the eighth floor in that building. The personnel manager was an absolutely delightful old lady who didn't know about this new company either. She said,

"Well, if 35 years ago, when I started working here, I had had that offer, I surely would have taken it." She asked what I was afraid of.

"Well, my present job is my bread and butter. I'm afraid that if I don't like the new one or they don't like me, I won't have a job."

"Would it help you if I promise you that you can always get your job back here?" She was the first person who really helped me in Toronto.

So I took the new job. It turned out to be wonderful. I always wanted to know what was happening in the life insurance building. In my previous job, when I tried to find out where the checks I sorted came from or went to, I was always told it was none of my business. In the new company, I not only found out these basic things, but I grew with the company: from being an actuarial assistant to being an underwriter to being the office manager. They were wonderful people. I had a very good income, so that Paul didn't have to stay in that veterinary hospital. I did intellectual work as best as I could, considering that I still could not read and write English very well. But I could work with figures. I worked there until we came to Winnipeg in 1960.

Settling in Winnipeg

We came to Winnipeg because Paul wrote his veterinary exams in Manitoba. Therefore, he was only allowed to practice here. By that time, we had gotten my mother out of Hungary. It wasn't easy to get a visa for her, because we had very little income.

In the process, I experienced for the first time that a federally elected member of parliament (M.P.) could be trusted and was there to support his constituents. I had to go to Ottawa to ask for help. I used to be afraid of the parliament building and M.P.s, because in my past experience, they were the enemies of the people. This time, I met my M.P. in the parliament building and he listened to me. He said there were always exceptions to the rule, and he put my mother on the list of the 100 people who would be allowed to immigrate to Canada within three weeks. It took me years to get used to realizing that I was in a free country I knew in my head that I was free, but I had to experience it.

In Toronto, we had been concerned that our son Andrew would have the best possible opportunities, since that had been our biggest motivation in coming to Canada. Education was a principal value for us. We were concerned that, with us both working during the day, speaking Hungarian at home, and not knowing Canadian people, Andrew would not learn proper English or the Canadian ways of life. My plan was to get him into a boarding school. I found out that one of the best schools in Canada was the Upper Canada College in Toronto, which was five minutes from us. That meant we could see him often.

In an elegant borrowed hat, I walked into the principal's office and said I would like to enroll my son. Andy was going into grade 10, and I wanted him to be a resident. We really could not pay, so it didn't matter to me how much it cost. I wanted to enroll Andrew now and pay later. The principal asked me, "How do I know that you can pay later?"

I said I just knew it. We were both professional people, and I wanted my child in the best school. That's where I would have had him in Hungary if Hungary were a normal country.

He said they had never had a request like that. I said there never was a Hungarian revolution, either. The main reason we came away was to get my son a good education and a future. So he said he would have to take it to the board. I did not know what a board was. We didn't have boards in Hungary. So I said, "Take it to the board." I came out of there very discouraged to hear that they had never done this type of thing before.

Three weeks later, I got a message to go and see the principal. He told me that the board decided to have a Hungarian refugee boy, and Andrew was admitted. Paul was very worried later, when we found out that this school might be snobbish. However, it proved to be a wonderful school. Andrew finished two grades in one year. He learned English and found some Canadian friends. He gained a secure identity in feeling he belonged in Canada. He finished grade 13 at this school and when we moved to Winnipeg, he was able to enter university. Over the years following, we made good on our promise to repay the school.

Moving to Winnipeg was a big step. Paul was finally able to work at his profession, and I could finally choose what I wanted to do. I had wonderful letters of reference from the insurance company, but I knew I did not want to pursue that field. I had always wanted to work with people. That's why I had had all of welfare under my hand in Hungary. I never could work with people directly there, because that was not something that you did under Communism. Families and individuals are not important in a Communist system. So I wanted to do something for and with people. I was considering social work.

The University of Manitoba accepted my degree in economics as a bachelor's degree, and they said I could go to the School of Social Work. It had a two-year master's program at that time. I got a mental health grant and enrolled in the master's program from 1964 through 1966. I got my social work degree because I had vowed to have nothing to do with life insurance ever again, not even to buy a policy!

Before I went to the university in Winnipeg, I needed a job. Although I only had the equivalent of a bachelor's degree, St. Boniface Hospital accepted me in its social work department. At that time, there were three social workers there. I assessed financial assistance, which wasn't the type of work I wanted. I really thought that social work could do more for people.

After I got my degree in 1966, I wanted to go back to the hospital. Because I had a mental health grant, the chief psychiatrist accepted me back to St. Boniface to work on the psychiatric ward. A few months after that, the hospital's medical director asked me whether I would be the director of the department of social work.

It wasn't a very big department. At that time, we had three social workers, while I had had 40 people under me in Hungary. I took the job because I didn't want anybody else over me. I soon decided to do something different with it. There was more to social work than assessing people for financial assistance. I wanted social work to become more integrated into the whole hospital system and treatment planning. The concept of systems wasn't new for me, because I had worked with systems with Zoltan.

By the time I resigned from that department 14 years later, we had 27 people and were integrated into the whole hospital. I think I did a good job in developing the department, which had been my main interest. It was a challenge to teach people and to encourage social workers not to be afraid of doctors but to feel equal as people.

Social workers felt just like the nurses at the time, very much inferior to the doctors. Whatever the doctors said, that was absolute. I couldn't accept that, because I valued equality. I wanted my staff to feel equal to the doctors. You cannot inject feelings of equality, and you cannot blame the doctors either. I had to find people who wanted to value themselves and to validate their worth.

My experience in influencing the system in Hungary helped me contribute in Canada. I was also on the Health Services Commission from 1971 to 1975 because the Minister of Health heard about my planning experience in Hungary. He asked me to be a commissioner on the Health Services Commission for about four years.

It was a very interesting situation. I was wearing two hats (which I liked, because I'm a Gemini). One was as a member of the Health Services Commission, which funded the hospital. The other was as an employee of the hospital. The hospital's president supported me to use my integrity to serve in both ways without a conflict of interest. I really learned a lot and found I could use my Hungarian government experience even in a very different environment.

Meeting Virginia

Working with psychiatric patients on the wards, I had a feeling that these people's hospitalization had a lot to do with their family life. I also knew from my parents' families about how powerful the family can be. One day, the head of the department of psychiatry came to me and brought Virginia Satir's book *Conjoint Family Therapy*. He said, "This is a fantastic person. I saw her on the weekend in Minneapolis. She is a social worker, but she is really unusual. You'd better read this book."

When I read it, I didn't understand it, but I had a feeling this was something I had never learned in the School of Social Work—something good.

A friend of mine phoned me one day and said Virginia was giving a workshop in Minneapolis soon. That was 1969. I wanted to go, but Paul didn't want me to go away on the Easter holidays. I didn't.

When my friend Anna came back from Virginia's workshop, she was a different person. She was sharing her experience and talking about her feelings—which she hadn't done before. There was so much change in her that I said to myself, "If I ever again get a chance to go to a workshop like that, I will go."

Soon after that, Virginia did a workshop in Brandon, a five-day workshop, and that's where I met her the first time. That was in

June 1969, and in those five days, I experienced all kinds of magic I'd never seen before. I watched a deep process of change going on in people that I hadn't known could happen before.

Like most social workers of that time, I had been taught to focus on changing behavior through advising people. Virginia helped people to change themselves based on self-acceptance and responsibility, rather than telling them what was good for them. Magical things happened to people, and I was just speechless. I had never learned anything like that.

I remember I went to Virginia at the end of the five days and said, "Well, only you can do this. Nobody else can learn it!"

She said, "I hope it's learnable!"

"How?"

"Well, why don't you come to my month-long training workshop? I do those once or twice a year." She gave me the name of the contact person for the next workshop, to be held three months later in Minneapolis.

I was obsessed to go and find out more about it. And so I found my way to the next workshop and to many, many more from 1969 to 1980. I followed her workshops all over the United States, and from Israel to Tahiti to West Germany. I also invited her for three months to Manitoba, which was the greatest opportunity to experience her work on many levels with different systems.

Virginia started her Avanta Network in 1976, and I became a trainer from 1981 on. From 1969 to her death, I was very closely connected with her. First as a student, and then as a colleague, and through this time we also became very close friends. We spent many, many times of learning, working, and being together.

I managed to invite Virginia through the Manitoba government for a three-month period to Winnipeg to work on all levels of systems with government, with university faculties, with professionals, and with parents and children. The program was developed together with a committee representing all the university faculties.

What really connected me the most with Virginia was her belief system, which was similar in so many ways to mine, from the time I grew up in Hungary. The recurring theme in my life was the search for freedom and for people being treated and seen as equal and having dignity. Virginia not only was believing and teaching these values, but she was also practicing them. That was the first time in my life that I met someone who was practicing what she was teaching and also believing in it totally.

So much of what she taught touched on my valuing of freedom. Her written statement of "The Five Freedoms" encouraged us to say what we want to say, hear what we hear, see what we see, take risks, rock the boat when necessary for change, and ask for what we want.

As I look back at my life, I always wanted to have freedom and the right to rock the boat, both for myself and for others. I already believed in this, and Virginia provided the tools to achieve it. This was the gift I got from her. The Communist system does not believe in individuals and families, but only in the overall goals for society as a whole.

Through my work with Virginia, I found that our families of origin can keep us prisoners, just as political systems can. So the way toward freedom and peace is first of all to find our own self-worth and freedom. This was a wonderful discovery for me, because that kind of thinking and connection was not in my awareness before. Virginia believed that the "freedom within, freedom between, and freedom among" is the process toward peace in the family and in the world. She said, "The family is the microcosm of the world. Healthy families create a healthy world."

Her magic was how she connected with people, how she made contact. This was based on her belief system. She could connect with somebody for five minutes, and for that person the world had changed in terms of how they would value themselves for a lifetime. And that was based on her valuing every human being as she connected with them in a way that conveyed her belief that they were basic miracles as manifestations of life. As people felt her deep validation and respect for them, they responded with a genuine valuing of themselves.

Virginia "found the gold" in people. She didn't look at pathology or what was wrong with people. She looked at strengths and positives and what we can learn from any experience. She really believed that people have all the resources they need. She believed that all behavior is learned and purposeful, originally adopted to help us survive. Therefore, no matter how negative a behavior seemed on the surface, she could always discover its positive intent.

For example, I discovered I had a skill at persuading people to do what I wanted them to do. I did not like this behavior and labeled it manipulation. I learned from Virginia that "manipulation" had been a way to survive for me and therefore to appreciate this ability as a resource. I no longer needed to use it in the same way but could use this resource as one among many strategies.

It was at first very difficult for me to accept that there is gold in everyone, because of my experiences during and after the war. I felt very angry about the cruelty and inhumanity I had seen and experienced. With Virginia in a workshop in Germany, I learned about trying not to be judgmental, and discovering the humanness in all people. I learned that even people who perform destructive acts are part of the human race. We all have the potential for a range of good and evil. The question is how we use the resources, and we have to make positive choices.

Teaching the Satir
Model Abroad

From opportunities to observe and participate with Virginia in international teaching, I gained a greater sense of the essentials that join all humans. Human processes are universal, feelings are universal, ways of coping are universal. Anywhere I go in the world, feelings like fear mean the same thing, whether in China or Hungary or Canada. Feelings are universal no matter what the color, the age group, or the race of peoples. Therefore, we can teach and practice the Satir model all over the world. It deals with universal human process, and not with content.

This is now the 12th year that I've been working in Taiwan and in Hong Kong. At the beginning of our workshop, sometimes people say, "Well, this is an American system. It's not going to fit in Chinese culture." I have learned not to argue or explain as my response. Instead, I wait for an opportunity to utilize people's own experiences for making the point. So, every time a feeling came up, like feeling depressed or rejected, or happy, or sexy, I asked this person, "Is this an American feeling, or is it a Chinese feeling?" After a few hours, he said he understood my point. Working with process is also very connecting because we understand each other on a human level.

Virginia ultimately moved from focusing on peace in the family to peace in the world. Processes in organizations, countries, or nations are not very different from the processes in families. We can use the Satir model to help people in any system to communicate and to connect on a human level, rather than on the level of power struggle and who is right or wrong.

When Virginia went to Israel, she brought Israeli and Arab families together in one room. Doing their Family Reconstructions and playing each other's family roles connected them on the human level like nothing else could have. Her idea was to do the same in Ireland.

I know that this is possible because on the family-of-origin level, we all have common human experiences such as yearnings, expectations, feelings, and relationships. In Virginia's work for peace, she felt convinced of the importance of connecting people and nations on the human level, knowing that we are all born little, and all have samenesses and differences. We all have parents, we all want to fulfill our human dreams. She felt if these connections are developed throughout the world, that peace is a real possibility. This vision was what drove her tireless teaching all over the world in her later years, and why she regarded it as so important to carry this international work forward.

Virginia influenced my life deeply in many wonderful ways. I feel very grateful and very privileged that I met her and was able to teach with her and experience her as a friend and as a human being. It was a cherished connection in that I respected her very highly, and she validated my ideals and hopes for people.

I know I have the resources to continue the work she started. I use her concepts now in my own way, and that was the growing up in me: that I no longer want to do it her way, but to do it in my way and to trust my way. The greatest thing I learned through this whole process of working with Virginia's concepts is that the magic is in everybody. Everybody can find his or her own magic, and I certainly found mine. No matter how much knowledge I have and how many things I learned, the most important thing is to trust and use myself in sharing myself with other people.

My greatest interest right now is to share what I know and believe, including doing this in countries where people are hungry for these concepts. The focus of my work has expanded from seeing families at the hospital to doing family-related workshops all over the world. That, too, was a process that grew out of a super time working with Virginia. I was director of the social work department in a teaching hospital in 1969, when I met Virginia. I was very lucky that I had the opportunity to continue to go to workshops while keeping my position. When she came for three months to Manitoba, she had an impact on the university level and also the hospital level, where I work. And so I had a lot of support to start teaching her concepts in my local community. She had been in Manitoba many times, teaching diverse groups, from Native Indians to professionals, to parents and children.

Ten years later, in 1979, I felt that continuing my administrative work no longer fitted me. I really wanted to get back to working directly with families. Also, I wanted to start a teaching program in my community, based on the guidelines developed by Virginia. I joined the Department of Psychiatry in the same hospital and found a small group of people who were interested in training with me to work with families.

I got freedom in that department to go on and work with families, sharing what I knew. This developed into a training program for residents in psychiatry. Today we have a family therapy training program in the Faculty of Medicine. I'm very proud of it.

While I was doing all this in the last few years, I also had the opportunity to start moving out and developing training programs in Hong Kong, Taiwan, Thailand, Australia, and earlier in Venezuela. At the same time, for the last eleven summers, I was a trainer working in Colorado in Virginia's month-long training program. With my own colleagues in the Avanta Network and with Virginia, we developed and ran the advanced training program from 1983 to 1989.

Three of us—Jane Gerber, John Banmen, and myself—also worked together in Hong Kong and together wrote and published the book *The Satir Model: Family Therapy and Beyond.* In 1998, it was translated into Chinese and published in Taiwan, where I had trained a group of professionals. It's very beautiful to see how profoundly people all over the world are growing as they apply Virginia's concepts in their work and lives.

For example, many Asian women have not used their full potential due to rigid social rules that demand total servitude to their families. They have devalued themselves as well as being devalued by society. One of my students there took care of her parents 24 hours a day and denied herself the possibility of a career or even a holiday. She came to the workshops regularly for four years and is now the administrator of a large foundation for professional education. She still lives with and helps her parents, but she lives her own life as well.

Close to a hundred people enroll in each of our workshops in Asia. Since Virginia's death, Satir institutes have begun developing all over the world. I am very much involved with the center in Hong Kong, Taiwan, Australia, and Winnipeg. In Winnipeg, we started a Satir Professional Development Institute in October 1991.

Virginia and My Family

My intense commitment to learning and teaching Satir approaches affected my family life. When I went to the first workshop in 1970 in Minneapolis, Paul was upset. It was the first time I went away without him and did something that he wasn't part of. When I came back after one month, I wanted him to learn in a half hour to be congruent and to practice all the things that I had learned.

He was really scared, and after I gave him my lecture, he asked me if I still loved him. Then he was running around telling everyone, "I'm not afraid of Virginia Wolff." So it didn't help my family life at first.

Six months later, I wanted to go to another one-month workshop. I wondered if my marriage was going to survive. Luckily, a two-week workshop with Virginia in Tahiti was advertised. I knew Paul had always wanted to go to Tahiti. So he agreed to come, and my hope was that when he met Virginia, he was going to fall in love with her.

Before we left, he told me he would go to Tahiti but he wouldn't participate in the workshop. Amazingly to him, but no surprise to me, he didn't miss a minute once he met Virginia. They became very, very good friends. So from then on, it was no problem for me to follow Virginia and to have her visit us often, because the two of them connected so well. What she really loved in Paul was that he did not love her for being a therapist or because she was famous. He just loved her for herself, and that was really her dream to find in friends. Paul wasn't really into Satir for therapy; he just loved Virginia as a human being.

Our life was so very Hungarian—loving and hating each other at the same time. We learned how to find freedom for ourselves and at the same time be connected within our relationship. Paul and I had very different interests. We learned how we both could have our individual preferences and yet be really connected on a deep human level.

We learned to have freedom within the relationship, and growing with each other. Partly through her influence, our relationship deepened and became much more beautiful. At the end of our living together for 32 years, we had achieved an intimacy that was not enmeshed anymore but loving and free.

As to Virginia's own life, she talked very often about her family and was very open and honest about it. The reason she wanted to be a "children's detective" when she was five years old was because she couldn't make sense of her family. How could her parents hate each other and argue at times and then love and dance together?

A friend of mine commented so appropriately that if Virginia had had an ideal family life in her growing up, she wouldn't have become the family therapist that she was. So, she talked often about the relationship between her parents being confusing for her as a child. She spoke of leaving home at age 16 and going to college and going on with her own life and not having much connection with her family until later in life. My feeling was that she had two families: one was her family of origin and her children; the other was the family she chose—her friends.

For myself, I know that much of my interest in families came from experiences in my own family. If I hadn't been sent away those summers as a child and felt so powerless to change that, maybe I wouldn't have rebelled so much. I really believe that the negative things that happen to us can become assets. As I look back in my life, I don't regret anything. I wouldn't want to do some of it again the same way. Since I survived (and survival is a big thing in my life), I think I'm very lucky because I lived so many lives in so many worlds. In all that I experienced, my connection with Virginia was life-changing and profound. I will always be grateful that somehow our paths joined.

I first heard of John Vasconcellos from a psychiatric patient who volunteered at his campaign office. He was an inspiration for her and for a remarkable number of gifted, energetic people.

Virginia and John enjoyed each other. A robust, loving humor played between them, as in the incident this chapter describes with the IIIFFI Club.

—*Robert S. Spitzer*
Publisher

6

Toward a Politics
of Self-Esteem:
JOHN VASCONCELLOS

by Diane Dreher

For California state legislator John Vasconcellos, Virginia Satir was "a modern day Christopher Columbus and Charles Lindbergh put together, voyaging the world round and round, seeking to help everybody discover their own new worlds of self-esteem" (Vasconcellos, 1988).

John met Virginia in the early 1970s when her agent Bob Shapiro invited him to come and watch her work at the old Jack Tarr Hotel in San Francisco. John found himself fascinated by her message of self-esteem and her powerful family workshop style. They kept meeting over the years at conferences of the Association of Humanistic Psychology. In the early 1980s, as John says, they "started to hang out together."

Virginia lived in Menlo Park, just a 20-minute drive from John's home in Santa Clara. They had a common interest in humanistic psychology and politics. Despite their respective heavy travel schedules, they made time often to share meals and conversation, deepening their friendship. They went out for Chinese food or walked over for a light meal at Late for the Train (a restaurant near her home). They shared books, ideas, a deep belief in the transforming power of self-esteem, and a sense that they had some significant work to do together.

After John's heart attack and seven-way coronary bypass in 1984, he spent a month recuperating at the Menlo Park home of his college friends Bill and Jeanne Weseloh. His first visitor was Virginia, whose doctor had just told her she was losing her eyesight. During the next month, John says (1988), "Virginia and I coached each other through very difficult and tenuous times and, in the course of that, developed an uncommon and precious bonding and relationship."

They each recovered their health and seized a second chance to live their lives with heart and spirit. As John says, they became "buddies, teammates, real dear to each other." With her, he "learned about being authentic and genuine."

He discovered a great deal about himself from his close friendships with Virginia, Carl Rogers, and Sidney Jourard—three pioneers and leaders in humanistic psychology. They offered John valuable lessons. "Carl," he says, "was more cerebral, Sidney was earthy, Virginia was most immediate. She played more ... of all the wonderful leaders I had the good fortune to know and witness in action, Virginia demonstrated the most capacity to come right at you, insisting that you open up and come on out, all in a way that served to assure you that you were literally safe in doing so."

He admits that Virginia and he were both workaholics. They embraced their respective work as a vocation, a personal mission to spread the message of wellness and self-esteem, both personally and politically, as far out into the world at large as they could manage.

They also realized that they had to learn how to play. So John took her to a George Winston concert, and she took him to purchase his very first finger paints. They went for walks, talking and laughing together. "We became playmates in a lighthearted way," he says—thanks, in great part, to her outrageous sense of humor.

In the fall of 1984, as he was recovering from his bypass surgery, he was to introduce Virginia before her speech on the Sunday morning of a conference in Sacramento. She was scheduled to speak to over 200 counselors from teenage pregnancy programs throughout northern California. When he arrived, the desk clerk told him that Virginia had asked John to come upstairs to her room.

They greeted each other warmly, and she told John with great delight that she had just founded a new group called the IIIFFI Club. When she invited him to become a charter member, he asked what the name stood for. She explained: "If It Isn't Fun, Fuck It."

John laughed and agreed: "Of course, I'll join your club, Virginia. And why don't you invite all the persons at the brunch downstairs to join our club as well?"

Laughing, she said, "Oh, no, I couldn't do that!" They went downstairs and enjoyed a champagne brunch with the counselors.

Afterward, John gave her a rousing introduction: "Well, it's presidential election campaign time, and we surely need a president who is warm and cares about people and who is inspiring and who is a great speaker. So I want to present to you my candidate for President of the United States, Virginia Satir."

During a round of applause, she went to the podium and over to the person running the videotape. "Turn off the machine," she asked. "They [future viewers] won't understand what I'm going to do now." Smiling out at her audience, she said, "John and I want to invite you to join a new club I have just recently invented. It's called the IIIFFI Club. We're having T-shirts made with that inscription on the front and back. Each of you can have your own chapter right where you live."

The audience leaned forward curiously, wondering what the acronym meant. Virginia announced ceremoniously what IIIFFI stood for. Two-thirds of the audience doubled up and howled with laughter. The others looked around sheepishly wondering if it was okay to be seen laughing publicly at such a phrase (Vasconcellos, 1988).

No doubt, the powerful political leader had met his match in Virginia. She could be just as serious, just as dedicated, just as powerful as John. And she had a way of breaking down barriers within and between people. Tall and strong, she would look him right in the eye and tell him what she thought. "She was utterly disarming," he recalls fondly.

They became members of each other's close family of friends. John brought her to his best friend Mitch Saunders' graduation, to family birthdays, to Thanksgiving dinner, even to his annual fundraisers, where she'd sit at the head table next to his mother.

Both were leaders, innovators, pioneers in a new humanistic approach to life that combined psychology and politics. In his notes after a dinner with Virginia and other friends at Menlo Park's Flea Street Cafe in December 1985, John recorded a question they had discussed:

> How can we develop
> a core of persons in politics
> who are focused on this positive human alternative—
> who can offer a clear attractive program—
> an alternative to the traditional cynical politics
> of both left and right, liberal and conservative,
> Republican and Democrat—which is going on today?

As chair of the Assembly Ways and Means Committee, John sought to ask and to answer this question in his life and throughout his work.

He and Virginia worked tirelessly to help each other and all others realize their full potential as human beings and so transform our society. They gave each other the understanding and support that pathfinders need, what John called "company, comfort, and confirmation." In February 1986, he arranged for her to lead a successful workshop on communication for 18 Democratic Assembly members. Later that year, he also arranged to have her appointed to the California Task Force to Promote Self-Esteem and Personal and Social Responsibility, along with his friends Emmett Miller and Jack Canfield. Of the 25 diverse and dedicated Task Force members, John says, "Virginia was the most spirited of all of them, the most exotic. She set the pace."

And what a pace it was! The visionary, against-all-odds endeavor (which John created and Virginia helped inspire) first faced the scorn of cynical editorial writers, the fright of the fundamentalists, and three weeks of satire by Garry Trudeau in *Doonesbury.* Undaunted, the Task Force proceeded to convert notoriety into opportunity. Conducting almost 30 public meetings and hearings, and resolving their own enormous internal differences, Task Force members ultimately produced their historic and hopeful final report, *Toward a State of Self-Esteem.* It identified self-esteem as a social vaccine (with the analogy okayed by Jonas Salk) whose presence enables a person to be less susceptible to social diseases. Confirming the family as "the crucible of self-esteem," it served to legitimate self-esteem throughout California and across the country. More than 50,000 copies of this report have been distributed throughout the world. Public dialogue has since turned from whether self-esteem is vital to how we get, lose, and regain our self-esteem.

As the Task Force's work was being completed, Virginia's life drew to an end. The remaining members unanimously decided to dedicate their January 1990 report to her memory. And so it was that when she died of pancreatic cancer in September 1988, John

(1988) gave a *Peninsula Times-Tribune* reporter this statement for her obituary:

> Virginia was the Number One Princess Charming in the entire world. More than any other living person, she touched more of us frogs and awakened us to our own beauty and worth and self-esteem.

John's Early Years

John Vasconcellos was born on May 11, 1932 at O'Connor Hospital in San Jose, California. He was the first child of John and Teresa Jacobs Vasconcellos. His mother was the daughter of German immigrants. His father, whose family was Portuguese, had come to California at 19 from his birthplace in Kahului, Maui (Hawaii).

John's mother smothered her first son with attention, even more so after his next brother died at birth. Five years later, his brother Jim was born (who later became an engineer). Their sister Margaret (now a school administrator) was born when John was ten.

As John was growing up, his family moved from one small town to another in the San Francisco Bay Area. They lived in Irvington (now part of Fremont), Hayward, Mount Eden (now part of Hayward), and then Crockett in Contra Costa County (when John was eight). Later, when he was 12, they lived in Rodeo.

John's father, whom he calls a "very dutiful, self-abnegating Catholic man," was a math teacher, school principal, and superintendent. John, always bright and inquisitive, became a model student. His traditional Catholic background gave him a strong ethic of helping others, of serving the community. His father was active in the church and many fraternal and service clubs, and he emphasized this lesson in talks with his children as well as through his own commitment.

John began his political career in the eighth grade when he ran for class president and lost by one vote—his own. "I was a good Catholic self-abnegating boy," he says. That meant putting others' desires before his own and never preferring himself. As echoed by Virginia in *Your Many Faces* (1978, p. 45), young John was developing a classic case of high academic achievement and low self-esteem:

> Most of us live in an emotional jail because we want to be good. We surround ourselves with a whole network of "shoulds" that are often in conflict with our wishes and our abilities. This almost always results in a sense of failure, needless frustration and disappointment.

John's strong-willed mother was so protective that even with the best of intentions, her actions often contributed to his sense of inadequacy. John was never allowed a bike or skates—his parents were afraid he'd hurt himself. When other kids his age were out playing, he was left to himself, by his own recollection: "a good Catholic boy: no body, no feelings." Awkward and self-conscious, he didn't bond with boys his own age through the usual games and sports. Having internalized his mother's protectiveness, he never learned to swim well and could not bring himself to jump off the diving board. He was even more self-conscious because he was left-handed. So he concentrated on his studies and on pleasing Teresa, "becoming her proof that she was good mother."

Today, after years of therapy and body work, he enjoys playing racquetball almost daily and often defeats persons 20 or 30 years younger than himself. But as a youngster, he buried himself in his books. His math skills were phenomenal, and he invented ways to practice them. Listening to the radio, he would tally up numbers in his head and in logbooks, keeping records of everything from baseball box scores to movie stars to songs on the hit parade. For years, in his job as chair of the Assembly Ways and

Means Committee, he kept track of the complex California state budget. He still does math in his head, at times amazing colleagues with his speed and accuracy.

John's father was very formal and lectured his children on self-control. "We never get angry," he told them, developing a family myth that kept John's emotions repressed for the first third of his life. His mother emphasized humility, telling the children not to use the pronoun *I*: "it's so egotistical." So he grew up "utterly contained," out of touch with his body and unable to express his individuality or his feelings until his emotional awakening in the explosive 1960s.

When John was 14, his father shipped him off to Bellarmine Preparatory, a Catholic boarding school in San Jose. He did this to help John outgrow his too-strong attachment to his mother, but John felt banished and betrayed: "It felt like being expelled from home." He resented his father for years.

At Bellarmine, he excelled in his studies, always being first or second on the honor roll. But he says he "had no self-esteem at all" and still looked to others to tell him how to be. He also often sabotaged himself in his attempt to seek acceptance. For example, he tried out for sports but then spent most of his time on the bench. When he ran for class office, he was so shy that he choked up in front of the other students and could only stutter, "V-v-v-ote f-f-f-f-for m-m-m-e." They didn't. He lost two more elections.

After graduating, he went on to Santa Clara University. It was, he says, "a safe place," another private and (at that time) all-male Jesuit school. It felt a lot like Bellarmine to him, and many of his friends and family had gone there. During his four years of college, he earned top grades but changed his major every six months or so

("I had no idea what I wanted to do"). He finally graduated with a degree in history.

Always questioning, searching, he had many long talks in the dormitory with his closest friends about the nature of social commitment, the routes for Catholic action, and the ethics of that action. His strong sense of duty only increased his anxiety about what to do with his life. He wondered how to use the talents he had been given, how to serve the greater human community and, as the Jesuits expressed it, how to contribute to the *magis*, or the greater glory of God.

His accomplishments hid the fact that he was still painfully shy. He became freshman class vice-president, sophomore class president, and then student body president, valedictorian, and Nobili medalist for the outstanding graduate—the only Santa Clara student ever to attain all three recognitions. (Years later, in 1985, when John was proposed as the first alumni initiate of Santa Clara's *Pi* of the California chapter of Phi Beta Kappa, the membership committee was amazed by his academic accomplishments.)

Still lost in low self-esteem, however, this high-achieving student had buried his feelings under a mountain of "shoulds." He recalls his then-closest friend and former university roommate telling him in 1961: "You don't know what it is to feel." John says he was "dutiful rather than responsible, intellectual rather than whole."

Political Beginnings

When he graduated from Santa Clara University in 1954, his dorm counselor, Steve Earley, a New York Jesuit, called him into his room to discuss John's future. "You should go into politics," Steve said, recognizing John's potential, his political values, and the fact that he had been a good student body president. "Pat Brown [then Attorney General of California] should know about you," Steve said.

All of this came as a total surprise to John, who shrugged his shoulders in uncertainty, mostly relieved that Steve had not asked him to join the Jesuits.

Steve used his clerical collar to get an appointment with Brown (who had been raised a Catholic) and told him that John was a hot prospect with a great political future. Brown wrote and invited John to visit him in San Francisco. But John lacked Steve's conviction and confidence, and his half-hour interview with Brown was uneventful. They talked mostly about the fact that John had once dated Brown's daughter Cynthia. Brown said he'd some day give John a job.

After graduation, John spent two years in the army to fulfill his ROTC duty, then returned to Santa Clara for law school. He graduated in 1959 with his Juris doctor degree, with honors, and again as (law school) student body president. Twice again he met with Pat Brown (then governor), with just about the same conversation. The last time, Brown called him Jim, his brother's name, and John "didn't have the sense of self to correct him." Brown encouraged John to attend the 1960 Democratic convention in Los Angeles and got him an entry pass.

One day in the summer of 1960, while John sat dutifully watching the convention, Brown decided to go to Mass (he didn't go regularly). He went to a nearby Catholic Church where, by utter coincidence, Steve Earley was saying Mass. As he greeted people after the service, Steve followed Brown out and asked him point-blank, "When are you going to give John a job?"

By then, John was practicing law in San Jose with former mayor Al Ruffo, whom John calls "a grand man" and a "second father." One of John's close family of friends, Ruffo helped him develop his potential. The Monday after the convention, Ruffo walked into John's office bittersweet. After an hour of dodging, John asked, "What aren't you telling me?"

"The governor called and wants you to go to work for him . . . and I don't want to lose you."

Torn between going and staying, John took a tortured week to decide. Finally, he was swayed by his friend John McInerney's urging: "Pat needs good men. You should go help him."

He spent a year on Brown's staff as his travel secretary, helping the governor with his trips as well as with John F. Kennedy's presidential campaign. Gaining plenty of experience and exposure, he outgrew much of his shyness. Then he returned to San Jose to practice law for five more years. But by then, just about everyone—except John—knew that politics was his destined career.

Shortly after, he and his businessman friend and godson Rob Miller promised to run each other's political campaigns. With John as his campaign manager, Rob was elected to the San Jose City Council and thereafter became vice-mayor of San Jose. Soon, longtime Democratic Assembly member Al Alquist left his district seat to run for the State Senate. John thought about running but took no action. One Sunday morning he got a call from Rob Miller: "What are you doing today?"

"Going to the beach," answered John.

"Well, I've got 20 of your friends coming here to my house to plan your Assembly campaign. You'd better get your ass over here."

John went, as much from not knowing how to disappoint his friends as anything else. They coalesced around him, and he campaigned for an entire year. He won the election in 1966 and has been in state government ever since.

As with that first campaign, his political career and much of his success in life have been supported by a devoted family of friends. They have recognized his potential, often before or more clearly (or both) than he did, helping him see beyond his early conditioning and reach toward becoming more fully himself. John has always been deeply grateful to his friends, who have become a second family. They reinforce one another for continued growth and hold out a more dynamic, humanistic vision of life than John learned from his very traditional family of origin.

Through the years, his second family has expanded to include many persons in education and the helping professions throughout the state, as well as supporters in his own district. Each year, a group called Friends of John Vasconcellos organized his fundraisers. For other politicians, this "Friends of" might be just a name. In John's case, it is literally true.

The late Ken Blaker, the professor of education who started Santa Clara University's graduate program in counseling in 1965, remembered when John drove his Mustang through the university's main gate to enlist support for his first political campaign. John excited the faculty because he was "very growth oriented," said Blaker, who walked precincts for John in the early days. He told me that John was "very committed to what he was doing." John was often a topic of conversation in the faculty club because of his vision and values and the power he could wield in Sacramento, the state capital (Blaker, 1993).

Led by a vision of political change in the early 1960s, John and 15 other young Catholics formed a Santa Clara University professional men's sodality named the La Mancha Fund (after the musical *Man of La Mancha*). Its goal was to address the problems of hunger, poverty, farmworkers' rights, and social injustice. In 1966 John and eight other La Mancha members joined Cesar Chavez on his historic Good Friday march from Delano to the state capitol. La Mancha was an early example of John's personal commitment to helping those most in need. The times have changed, but commitment to social justice has remained a vital part of his political philosophy.

John's Personal Revolution

In 1966 John was favored to get the San Jose Junior Chamber of Commerce "Young Man of the Year" award. When he did not, he was devastated. Shortly after began his rebirth, his struggle to find himself, to become a person and simultaneously to become a legislator. In 1967, the Sacramento press corps voted him "the best freshman member of the Assembly." Yet beneath all of his accomplishments, he—like the nation and society around him— was coming apart at the seams. The old values and traditions no longer made sense to a generation of young Americans. They marched for civil rights, protested against the war in Vietnam, and listened to Bob Dylan sing "The Times They Are a-Changing." Rebelling against the status quo in everything from politics to religion to personal life, they began searching for new identities and alternatives.

Against a backdrop of college protests and the summer of love in San Francisco, John was caught up in a temblor of repressed emotion. It shook the foundations of his belief system and shattered the very basis of his identity. "As I approached the end of my 20s and early 30s, I grew more aware of my alienation from the church, from myself, from life," he recalls. In 1966, he had "hit rock bottom" and gone to Tenny Wright, a Jesuit priest he had known at Santa Clara. Wright referred him to Leo Rock, a Jesuit trained in Rogerian therapy; he had founded Santa Clara's Counseling Center the year before. John was desperate to discover who he was beneath this hard-working, "high-achieving, people-pleasing robot."

Seeing Leo Rock was a new experience for him. Whatever he said, whatever he did—scream, go silent, break into tears—Leo listened empathically, his eyes glowing with unconditional acceptance of John as a person. Leo told him he had a right to express himself authentically, encouraging him to break through a lifetime of repression and to release the layers of fear and guilt that were holding him inside. Rejecting his early conditioning as a "self-abnegating Catholic boy" from a family that did not express anger, John now dared to show his feelings, sometimes with volcanic intensity. To get more in touch with himself, he started going to psychological workshops and seminars. In 1969 he attended personal growth workshops with Richard Farson, Sidney Jourard, Abraham Maslow, Jim and Liz Bugenthal, Jim Fadiman, Rollo May, and John Heider. He followed this with a weekend with Carl Rogers in January 1970. "It was a stunning year," he recalls, "a year of reaching for my center, time and time again."

In an intense struggle to rediscover and recreate himself, he worked through his childhood conditioning, his family myths, the "shoulds" that had kept him from being congruent, from acting and speaking as he really felt. To accept himself as a valuable person, he had to confront and abandon what he calls "our old vision": the traditional Christian definition of human nature as sinful, guilty, imperfect, and untrustworthy. In his poem "The Dawning," he wrote:

> old ways of being
> which lock us inside
> leave us all crippled
> without inner guide.

Looking back at his childhood in a home where anger was not allowed, John came up with years of resentment and rage at his parents. For a time, he stopped seeing them in order to process all the rage. Then he started to reconstruct his life and relationships. Trying to get beyond strict filial duty and begin a new, more personal relationship with his father, he started calling him by his first name, John (rejecting the title of "Dad"). "He was very hurt by that," John recalls. Despite the reactions of others, however, he persisted in expressing what he felt. To do anything else would have been to go backward, to surrender to a life of repression and inauthenticity, to give up becoming a person.

Before his death, Leo Rock said that what changed John was learning to follow his heart. "John is one of the most intelligent men I've ever met." Therapy opened him up to a powerful new source of knowledge. He began "letting his heart into his life. He started to pay attention to his heart, to understand how much our feelings tell us about who we are" (Rock, 1993). Looking within helped this shy, brilliant, achievement-oriented young man turn his whole world upside down and all around.

John's personal revolution amazed the Legislature. He had come to Sacramento with dark, conservative suits, narrow ties, a crewcut, and a tightly wound, controlled personality. Suddenly, here was this person who refused to wear a coat and tie, wrote poetry about his feelings, stopped capitalizing letters, and raced off to weekly bioenergetic sessions. His speech was punctuated with psychological terms, his new energies exploded in outbursts of rage against what he perceived as political sellouts, and his hair was a mass of dark curls that he did not cut for four years.

With his open shirts, long hair, and colorful personality, John didn't fit people's stereotype of a politician. He looked more like a rock musician or a campus radical. He tells a story about a southern California judge who wrote him, wondering if his state car—a red-trimmed white Mustang convertible—had been stolen. The judge had seen it driven on the San Bernardino freeway by a "swarthy young man." John wrote back, thanking him for his concern, and explaining simply that "I am a swarthy young man."

He did all he could to learn, to grow as a person who could live more fully and represent California with greater depth and understanding. He spent a weekend in Watts with black Assemblyman Leon Ralph, volunteered as a teacher's aide in a high school remedial reading class, and filled his capitol office with books on humanistic psychology, politics, and philosophy until it resembled the home of a graduate student.

In an attempt to go deeper, he had begun doing body work in 1971 with Stanley Keleman, a bioenergeticist in Berkeley. After John was well along in treatment, Keleman called a time-out and informed John that he still had a great deal of rage inside. If he opened John up any further to release it, he wasn't sure but what John might lose control and ruin his political career.

Although politics had become his life, John responded, "I have no choice. Let's go on." Willing to confront himself and risk everything, he says it was more necessity than courage. "My pain was so great that I couldn't afford not to go after whatever it was." And so he exploded in rage one day on the Assembly floor. His peers assigned two colleague monitors to help him through it whenever he exploded.

In 1972 he invited five powerful colleagues (including Willie Brown, Bob Moretti, and Leona Egeland) to join him for a group weekend with psychologist Will Schutz at the Esalen Institute in Big Sur. He became known as the "touchy-feely legislator," and some of his innovations aroused people's interest. The word got around in Sacramento, and other Assembly colleagues asked to join him in various excursions.

In his quest to become a healthy human being, he sought out an alternative family to support him in his alternative vision of human nature. His political mentor Al Ruffo (and later, Carl Rogers) became like a father to him. Virginia Satir became like another mother, offering a view of family systems, interactions, and self-esteem that helped support his personal transformation. She also further shaped his progressive view of politics. Already committed to progressive politics, Virginia became even more involved, offering workshops to members of the State Assembly and later taking her message of self-esteem to Russia.

John cast aside his old emotional baggage about human depravity and original sin. In his new vision of life, he realized that "neither money nor human nature is the root of all evil." As he says in his book *A Liberating Vision* (1979, pp. 132–133), "The root of all evil is our belief that we're evil, and our resultant efforts which serve to make us so." In his personal and political development, he has progressively emphasized our "original grace" as human beings, overcoming the old vision of sin and guilt with all its concomitant cycles of shame, guilt, fear, insecurity, and fragmentation. His politics have been an ongoing effort to create an awareness and environment for healthier individuals and healthier family systems and to recreate society in the image of a healthy family. His view is that many of our personal and social ills result from an alienation from ourselves and one another. Western societies, especially the United States, have emphasized independence according to the model of the rugged individualist. They have done so to such a degree that we have become a society of strangers instead of an extended family, a supportive community. Through his politics, John seeks to inspire individuals to heal themselves and rebuild community—valuing each man, woman, and child, and celebrating both our individual uniqueness and our essential interdependence.

He also sought out leaders in the human potential movement—Jourard, Heider, Rogers, Maslow, May, Satir, Schutz—because he found in them kindred spirits who moved beyond the old, limited definitions of human nature into new realms of becoming more fully human. He read their books, attended their workshops, engaged them in conversation, and developed friendships with them. With this new extended family, he enjoyed what the Hindus call *satsang,* the communion of like minds. This sharing enriched them all and cycled back into a new vision of politics.

From Personal Growth
to Holistic Politics

John's quest for wholeness has made him a more effective political leader, not only by giving him a more holistic view of life but also by changing the way he relates to people on a day-to-day basis. Because he's always been open about his therapy, it has never become a political liability. U.S. Senator Thomas Eagleton's career was destroyed when news came out about his therapy for depression, but this resulted from his efforts to hide that fact. With John, there has never been anything to expose simply because there has never been anything to hide.

Through the years, he has transformed California politics with lessons derived from his explorations of personal growth. This transformation developed over two different yet related dimensions: his relations with other political figures, and the substance of his approach to social issues. All the while, he has retained—indeed, strengthened—his core commitments to those most in need in our society.

For John, years of therapy have expanded his sense of compassion and taught him to respect the person beneath the political label. Ken Blaker (1993) said that in a therapeutic relationship, "reciprocity is essential." The therapist listens empathically and, in so doing, reinforces the client for greater self-esteem. For Blaker, active listening was "an act of deep respect." John listens carefully to both liberals and conservatives. "I've lived both lives, lived in both our traditional (even approaching fundamental) culture and our nontraditional culture of liberation, and so I have more appreciation for those who still live that old culture," he says. He no longer dismisses the opposition as belonging to an alien group. His inner work has developed his intuition, insight, and skills of negotiation and mediation. This gives him "a deeper insight into the heart of myself and the heart of all of us."

In addition, humanistic psychology and therapy have given him a more positive paradigm of problem-solving. Rather than blaming others or wallowing in self-pity, he looks beyond the problem to the solution. With a belief in our ability to grow, to learn, and to heal ourselves and one another, he asks how he can help heal the situation. In what has been called holistic politics, his agenda has become to promote wellness. This is a preventive view regarding the state's role, appropriate programs, and intervention in society.

For him, political and personal responsibility "are one and the same, for the politics we do are truly an expression of who we are." To be an effective leader, he realizes he must attend especially to his own personal development. Beyond that, he sees "my every belief, act, and statement" as political. He explains that our personal beliefs and values are essentially political; they mold and reinforce the world in which we live and act. This holds true for everyone, according to him: "Our most important public policy is our personal policy, vision, belief, value system—regarding human beings and our own nature. It underlies *all* our other public policies. How we humans most healthily grow and develop is the central political issue of our times" (1979, p. 154).

His friend Mitch Saunders (1993) says, "There is no politician in this country who has endeavored to translate his values into public policy as much as John." Like his father, John is an educator. Politics for him involves teaching people to redefine themselves and create healthier ways to live and interact. In December 1974, he and two friends started a group called Self-Determination: A Personal/Political Network. At its peak, it consisted of 1,800 Californians dedicated to both personal growth and political action. Concerned with creating healthier family systems, in 1977 he helped set up the California Task Force on Positive Parenting and Celebrating Families.

In 1979, to investigate the causes of violent crime, John wrote legislation establishing the California Commission on Crime Control and Violence Prevention. The commission found that most violence was alcohol-related and most violent felons had been abused as children. Using the political arena to help us better understand ourselves and the roots of social problems, John's commission demonstrated the close relationship between the personal and the political. Again, the family system emerged as a crucial causal factor. Years of childhood neglect and abuse exact an inevitable price from citizens in massive suffering and anxiety, as well as the spiraling costs of the criminal justice system.

Years later, in August 1993, the American Psychological Association announced the results of its research into the causes of violent crime. Those results echoed the findings of John's commission. To him, the lesson is clear: how much healthier, saner, and safer society would be if we could only promote healthier family systems. What people learn in their families of origin carries into all their relationships—beginning, of course, with their relationship with themselves. All this affects how they view the world and the kind of world they create.

Transcending violence with active compassion, and cynicism with abiding faith, John works to build a politics of trust. Through his own example, he calls on people to trust themselves and one another. For instance, I recall my own surprise when I first received his district Assembly reports. I had just moved to northern California, and I wondered about this unusual person who not only represented me in Sacramento but embodied some of my most valued ideals in the political arena. Since then, I have been intrigued and inspired by his efforts to extend the lessons of humanistic psychology into the world of politics.

Shadowing John in Sacramento for a magazine article years ago, I witnessed an example of his openness. He shared his day with me, including a budget hearing, a Pritikin lunch in his office, brisk walks to various meetings, and a jog up four flights of capitol steps. After we returned to his office, he also shared his phone calls. One of them struck me as the kind that, for most people, would have meant a private conversation behind closed doors, so I got up to leave. John motioned for me to stay, all the while expressing in strong language his heartfelt displeasure at a colleague's decision. Whatever his feelings, he had nothing to hide.

As I later learned from Ken Blaker, John's behavior was that of congruence. The more open, honest, and authentic we can be with everyone—from a close family member to our boss, the governor, or the president—the more congruent we are. Rejecting the need for artifice, posturing, and phony politeness, daring to be genuine in any context—that, for Blaker, was the definition of mental health. It is certainly John's way of life, as well as his way of facilitating a healthier state of politics in California.

In the high-risk environment of state politics, his gamble is that complete honesty will create an opening to produce greater trust, cooperation, and actual results. During virtually any day in Sacramento, one or more of his colleagues comes to him with a thorny problem, a dilemma in which the contestants presume it's dangerous to show all their cards. His skills as a negotiator are legendary; his experience includes negotiating a settlement of the prolife/prochoice Medi-Cal abortion funding impasse. These skills are rooted in his willingness to put the stakes right out on the table (Murphy, 1993).

In 1980, the Democrats in the Assembly asked him to mediate between Leo McCarthy and Howard Berman, contenders to be Speaker. This position is arguably the second most powerful in state government. If anyone had the skills to resolve this conflict, they thought, it had to be John. He did his best, thinking for a while that he'd managed to get them together. But he could not effect a peaceful resolution. (Ironically, the result was that both sides gave up hope of a solution and called a truce until the following election.) John's efforts won him the respect and gratitude of those colleagues, however. After Leo McCarthy became the Speaker, he named John to chair the powerful Ways and Means Committee.

Many Assembly members wondered if John could handle the job. That chair oversees the massive budget of California, the sixth largest economy in the world. But his outstanding math skills and hard work convinced them in a fairly short time, and his reputation in the capitol changed. He became known for his political pragmatism as well as his progressive ideas.

In June 1984, John received a letter from Carl Rogers acknowledging his unique approach to politics. "You operate in an arena which is much rougher and dirtier," Carl wrote, than anything he had experienced. "It must be very difficult to bear at times, but you stick to it. You are a symbol of what can be accomplished in the world of politics as well as in education and other fields. You have the courage to fight for a human point of view." By his own example, John creates his own ongoing evolution within state government, affirming a more human politics in his process as well as his policies.

Leo Rock (1993) said that "we invite people to be trustworthy in trusting them, and that's what John does." It's a powerful lesson. According to Leo, intelligence and caring are hallmarks of John's politics as well as being "two essential elements in his personal growth." The caring goes along with his courage, in the sense that (in its most radical meaning) *courage* comes from the French word for "heart" *(coeur)*. He has the courage to explore new dimensions, personally and politically, the courage to take risks, and the courage (as Ken Blaker said of him) to be "who he believes he is and [to do] what he believes is right."

As Leo felt, this goes beyond courage: "John has nothing to lose." He has already done the courageous inner work to get to where he is; his ego is not invested in his politics. He seeks something beyond that: the right for us all to become more fully human, more fully ourselves. As San Jose businessman Robert Podesta, Jr.

explains (1993): "Other politicians practice politics as it is. John sees politics as it should be."

Despite his many commitments and heavy political responsibilities, John still practices politics with a personal touch. He stops to talk with people when they recognize him—on the street, in restaurants, in grocery stores—and records their requests and suggestions. His pockets are filled with notes scrawled on scraps of paper. He listens to people he meets at conferences and takes to heart their ideas, their lives, and their challenges. Later, he sends them handwritten notes from his office, often followed by articles and information he thinks will interest them. He has touched thousands of people by such gestures. Reaching out like this, he recruits people as partners in his ongoing campaign for a healthier society.

As Gandhi once said when asked about his philosophy, "My life is my message." In the fast-paced world of politics, too often filled with media hype and hollow appearances, John lives what he believes. "You can find out what he believes by simply observing him. It's written in the way he acts," said Leo Rock (1993), adding that it's "a travesty in our country, how rarely it is the case that a politician is actually a public servant, even though they claim that. John truly wants to serve the public. That's primary. It's not ego or personal power but service that drives John." Politics as usual, negative campaigning, insulting the opposition—these practices have no place in his vision of politics. John was, for Leo, "the one living person who prevents me from saying politicians are crooks, and [from] being swallowed up in that cynicism."

The Politics of Human Potential

John first set forth a comprehensive statement of his political philosophy in his 1979 book, *A Liberating Vision: Politics for Growing Humans.* After this lengthy analysis of our lives and times, problems and challenges, he described his action program, "A New Human Agenda." It is a vision of politics informed by the human potential movement. In the early 1980s, he began translating his New Human Agenda into legislation and programs. In March 1982, his newsletter to the 46,000 voters in his 23rd District described what he believed to be government's responsibility to the people as well as their responsibility to themselves and one another.

Part of government's responsibility, he explained, deals with tasks "we cannot effectively accomplish as individuals (e.g., funding for our schools, public hospitals, highways, sewage treatment plants, keeping our air and water clean and pure)." Yet government's responsibilities have escalated as citizens have progressively abandoned their personal responsibility. "Most of the rest of what government does," John wrote, "is a substitute for our individual inaction (e.g., crime, battered wives, child abuse, litter)." Greater personal responsibility would thus strengthen our society while reducing the cost of government. "That's why," he explained,

I consider it essential that we recognize as extremely critical the question, "How do we grow healthy human beings?" The question is better stated: How do we provide environments (including human relationships) which enable persons to grow themselves into healthy human beings—persons who are:

- self-aware and self-esteeming
- self-realizing and self-determining
- free *and* responsible, competent *and* caring
- faithful rather than cynical, open rather than closed
- gentle rather than violent, ecologically responsible, motivated rather than apathetic
- moral rather than immoral or amoral, and
- political rather than apolitical

A major task of government, according to John, is to encourage healthier human development. His vision claims as well for politics and government the moral and ethical responsibility formerly limited to the church and the family. Informed by systems theory, his approach addresses the root causes of unhealthy human behavior and encourages us to seek healthier alternatives. As we do so, his newsletter continues,

> we humans will become more self-sufficient, better able to take care of ourselves. We will also become better able to relate to our fellow human beings in ways that enable them to grow healthy in the first instance and/or, in the second instance, to recuperate from their unhealthiness. We'll hurt each other less, help each other more.

To help his constituents begin their own personal and political journey toward healthier development, his 1982 newsletter included a recommended list of books by Virginia Satir, Carl Rogers, Sidney Jourard, Marilyn Ferguson, and others. These were books on personal development, futurism, humanistic psychology, and existential philosophy. It is perhaps the only time a political mailer has included recommended readings, but then John is no ordinary political leader. He sees himself as an educator, a facilitator for others' personal and political growth as well as his own.

He also included a list of resources: names, addresses, and phone numbers of humanistic programs in birthing, parenting, marriage and family counseling, sexuality, hunger relief, education, energy, holistic health, mental health, violence prevention, community building, law enforcement, prison reform, management, aging, dying, and world peace. His is a vast political agenda incorporating all phases of human development from birth to death. At every stage of life, John's holistic, humanistic approach to politics supports our essential human dignity and fullest personal development.

This newsletter argument captures the essential political lesson he had gained through taking seriously the social implications of humanistic psychology. That is, the state's role in a decent society is to do more than protect us from one another, or provide resources for the after-the-fact expenses of the social or economic environment. The state can serve a powerful role in facilitating the development of responsible citizens and responsible citizenship through investing in those environments that enable us to grow whole and healthy.

The implications of this insight for the man whose professional responsibilities include drafting California's annual budget—over 57 billion dollars in 1993—have been enormous. For years, John asked his staff to include in their analyses the degree to which programs increase or retard a preventive strategy to social issues. Preventive health programs, children's health and welfare, decent and effective education for our children—these have been the regular touchstones for his politics.

His commitment to these and other programs stems from an articulate argument about providing the social base for individual responsibility and self-esteem. As chair of Ways and Means during the terms of two conservative governors, his capacity to defend and protect classically liberal programs on this unique basis is one of his enduring legacies. He points to the Task Force on Self-Esteem and Personal and Social Responsibility as the apex of his political work because it speaks so directly to his view of the relationship between the heart and the healthy self. Yet millions of Californians would point to other programs he saved, lives he made more healthy, and classes and clinics and counselors who have survived because he fought to save their budgets or their programs, or both.

From Personal to Global Responsibility

John's vision of humanistic politics is global in dimension, like those of Virginia Satir and George Brown at the University of California at Santa Barbara, whose confluent education program attracted the attention of the Solidarity Movement in Poland. John (1982) says that

> there's no reason—except our own lack of sufficient faith—that each one of us cannot . . . [envision] ourselves and our world in much more hopeful and loving ways, attending to our own continuing personal growth, and acting publicly so as to help it all happen. It isn't enough for you and me to sit back and wait for someone else to fix our world. If we choose to take no personal responsibility for what is going wrong—and no part in improving it—then we forfeit our right to complain. If you and I instead choose to recognize our personal potential and responsibility, and involve ourselves—we have a whole new world to gain.

Any potential for responsible action requires an underlying belief in ourselves. John's most important contribution as a leader, according to Leo Rock (1993), is calling "public attention to the critical role that self-esteem plays in democracy." Much of his vast legislative agenda over the years has been to promote self-esteem and personal and social responsibility. Sample projects include Californians Preventing Violence, the Senior Partners project, Parents as Teachers, California Leadership, the California Human Corps, the Latino Advancement project, the Select Committee on Ethics, the Joint Legislative Committee for the Review of California's Master Plan for Higher Education, the Assembly Democratic Economic Prosperity Team (ADEPT), his 60-point California–Japan Citizen Action Agenda, and his Task Force to Promote Self-Esteem and Personal and Social Responsibility.

The Self-Esteem Task Force effort is typical and illustrative of John's way of being and working in politics and government. First, he brought his own experience (and resulting insight and vision) into the search for a solution to major social problems: violence, drug addiction, teen pregnancy, child abuse, and educational failures. Then, he began recognizing clues and possibilities.

Originally, he proposed the Self-Esteem Bill in 1984. The Assemblypassed it, but the Senate voted it down. Later that year, after a heart attack, he underwent seven-way coronary bypass surgery. His extensive recoveryincluded treatment at the Pritikin Longevity Center in Santa Monica, autogenic hypnosis and visualization with Emmett Miller, Gestalt and bioenergetic work with Lou Pambianco, and a whole new regimen of diet and exercise.

In 1985, he doggedly renewed the Self-Esteem Bill, refusing to abandon its name. It passed in both houses, only to be vetoed by Governor George Deukmejian. Seeking to convert him to the cause, John met repeatedly with the governor over the following year to explain how preventive work on self-esteem might well save millions of dollars in the state's criminal justice, welfare, and health-care systems.

The governor recognized the value of that hope, and the bill finally passed and was signed on September 23, 1986. It set up a 25-member task force charged with compiling all available data on whether self-esteem is implicated causally in the aforementioned social problems. The task force received an unprecedented 350 applications for the 25 positions.

John was active in the membership selection. Then he addressed the task force at its first organizational meeting, charging them with their profound opportunity, responsibility, and mission. The task force named him an *ex-officio* member, and he participated in all but two or three of its approximately 18 meetings. At one point he served as facilitator, enabling the task force to heal an internal division.

Once the task force's report was ready in January 1990, he dug into his campaign fund to employ his long-time friend Bobbie Metzger, an expert in promoting public causes. John appeared on the national media circuit and promoted the task force report on self-esteem in more than a dozen states. He even flew to Little

Rock to deliver a copy of the report to a recent acquaintance, Bill Clinton. Then governor of Arkansas, Clinton immediately recognized it as a preventive strategy. Throughout California, John continues promoting laws furthering the self-esteem vision and seeking sponsors and support for national self-esteem legislation.

The Self-Esteem Bill was vital to his larger program, "Toward a Healthier State." He began it in 1985 in the wake of his recovery and lifestyle changes pursuant to his heart trouble. Reflecting his comprehensive vision of government responsibility, his program included proposals for reforms in public health, the economy, family counseling, child care, public education, environmental protection, political campaigns, public management, violence prevention, and world peace. It is a stunning list of programs, a "real agenda, not an election agenda," according to one lobbyist. The program dramatically illustrates his definition of leadership: working to "educate and lead people to a healthier vision of themselves."

All the while, John engaged himself and his friends and fellow pioneers in nonlegislative initiatives. In January 1984, he organized a weekend retreat in Cupertino (northern California) at Dorothy Lyddon's Seven Springs Ranch. It was to serve as a brainstorming team for Carl Rogers, who was ready and wanting to carry himself, his vision, and his practice into the world peace movement. Twenty persons met, including Carl and his friend Ora Brink; Gay Swenson and John Wood of the Center for Studies of the Person; Michael Murphy, the founder of Esalen; Jim Hickman and Dulce Murphy of the Esalen/USSR program; therapists George and Judith Brown from Santa Barbara; Willis Harmon, director of the Institute for Noetic Sciences; and Mitch Saunders, future director of California Leadership. They came together to discuss new patterns of politics and peace-making.

After much discussion, Judith Brown summed up their approach (Vasconcellos, 1987):

the very same rules apply in all human relationships—whether it's between spouses or lovers, or between the Americans and the Russians. The rules are universal: either we trust, accept, invite and include each other and become partners, or we distrust, reject, distance and exclude each other and become enemies.

In November 1985, John joined the directors Carl Rogers and Gay Swenson in Rust, Austria, for the Carl Rogers Peace Project's first international person-centered workshop on "The Central American Challenge." It was cosponsored with the United Nations University for Peace. Some 65 prominent political and lay leaders from 17 countries met for four days, attempting to transcend personal and political differences and touch what was human in them all (Swenson-Barfield, 1993). The Rust experience inspired John to write this poem:

RUST . . .

We arrived
amidst a heavy fog, which gradually
lifted to become
sunny by the conclusion of our workshop;
on Hallowe'en yielding to the day of all saints;
in a town whose steeples house the nests of storks,
we hopefully midwifed the birth of more faith and
hope for, and a process leading toward,
peace!

In December 1985, John invited Tom Peters, Virginia Satir, Emmett Miller, Dirk Fulton, and Mitch Saunders to join him for dinner at the Flea Street Cafe in Menlo Park. As they sat down, a woman at a nearby table recognized John and had a bottle of champagne delivered to their table. After smiles and toasts, he went over to thank her. She told him this was to show her appreciation for his support of the nurses' strike at O'Connor Hospital several years earlier.

The dinner party was a festive brainstorming session about new possibilities in politics. John recalls, "Our conversation was nonstop and high energy such that persons at adjacent tables were looking around at us, watching and leaning our way, almost as if drawn to the energy vortex we were creating."

As the evening wore on, a man at a nearby table finally asked, "Are you folks all Democrats or Republicans? Because you are very persuasive, and I am certainly intrigued by the politics you are discussing."

Virginia smiled and responded: "Let the jury stay out." John's notes from the evening reveal that they were creating a new idea in politics:

> How can we design a political vision and program and platform
> and do it all with integrity—
> that will serve to both
> separate the conservatives from the reactionaries, and
> separate the progressives from the left-wingers—
> such as to pull together an effective third (humanistic) force
> in California/American politics today?

> We human beings—people—are innately good—
> and the more our good gets denied and depressed and distorted,
> the more our love energy gets frustrated—
> the more we become monsters.

> How can we inspire people—
> and lead them to hope—
> while appealing to realism,
> without pandering to their fears,
> and not at somebody else's expense?
> We can only accomplish that by teaching people to
>   believe in themselves.

It was evident from their group dynamics that they were practicing the same inclusive politics they were describing. Virginia said to the group that night and repeated to John on the phone several days later that she "certainly found it wonderful to be amongst you five men—you were all so loving and noncompetitive" (Vasconcellos, 1985).

Combining local and global arenas, John continued promoting this blend of psychology and politics. In 1986, he proposed his six-point "Peace Package" to the California Assembly, advocating arms control and a massive student exchange with the Soviet Union. The next year, he became co-president of the Association of Humanistic Psychology, along with psychologist and sexuality therapist Lonnie Barbach. John was certainly the first politician ever to hold that office.

Major Losses

In the late 1980s, John lost two dear friends within a year and a half. In February 1987, while he was in Orange County for a legislative and political meeting, he learned that Carl Rogers (who had been hospitalized for hip surgery) had suffered a heart attack and lay dying at Scripps Hospital in La Jolla. John rushed to his bedside for a last farewell. When John entered the room, Carl stirred visibly, although he was in a deep coma. His daughter Natalie and his granddaughter Frances gave John some time alone with Carl.

With tears in his eyes, John sat down by Carl's bed, took his hand, and, although his friend was still unconscious, thanked him for the profound impact he had made on John's life. Carl died shortly thereafter. Later, John was one of the speakers at his memorial service.

In July 1988, Virginia's doctors discovered that she had cancer of the pancreas and liver. She died two months later, but not before saying her last farewells to her close friends—"dying," as John says, "with an elegance that mirrored how she lived."

He visited her four times during her final illness. The first time, he took her a gift package of a rainbow sun visor, magic color particles, and a copy of *The Weaving of a Dream,* inscribed: "for Virginia, co-weaver of so many wonderful dreams of so many of us—with so much love—Always—John & Cindy & Mitch [Saunders]. 7/31/88." John had put together this package to echo Virginia's 1986 speech to the Association of Humanistic Psychology in San Diego, during which she had taken her audience on an inward journey, each having his or her own "self-discovery kit." She immediately saw the connection with John's gift and told him she loved it for its symbolic value.

The next time he visited, he brought the David Roberts photograph of the two of them from his September 1987 fundraiser at the Winchester Mystery House in San Jose. She put it on top of the television set in her living room, where it remained until she died. (He has ever since kept it on his front room endtable.)

On Thursday, September 8, he went to Millbrae to attend a two-day meeting with the California Task Force to Promote Self-Esteem and Personal and Social Responsibility. When he called his office to check messages, John learned that Virginia's condition had suddenly taken a turn for the worse. She had only a few days left to live. He called her house and asked if he could come by. As the task force concluded its activities that evening, members told John to send Virginia their love and unanimously voted to dedicate their final report to her. Andy Mecca, the chair, told John to give the news to her.

John drove down to Menlo Park, arriving at Virginia's house about 9:15 p.m. A sign on the door said, "Please don't ring the bell. If you're expected, come on in. Otherwise knock, and I can hear you." John began to knock and then realized she was expecting him. Walking in, he was greeted by Virginia's doctor, Jonathan

Stolzenberg. Knowing of John's closeness to Virginia, he invited John to go in and visit her.

She was asleep, so John sat quietly by her bed. After a while, she opened her eyes. She was very weak and could barely speak. He told her that the task force would be dedicating its final report to her, and she smiled. He then left the room so that her nurse could attend to her. In the living room, he joined her doctor and several of her friends.

The nurse came out and said, "Mr. Vasconcellos, Virginia wants to see you." He jumped up and rushed to the room. As he walked to her bed, she said very assertively, "Give me a hug." He took off his jacket and leaned down. She reached up and gave him a long hug, then told him, "You are doing wonderful work."

"I learned that from you," he replied, leaning down and kissing her on the neck.

She looked into his eyes, raising her hands to his cheeks. "You are a beautiful man."

He thought to himself that if she was saying that, it must be true. "Thank you," he said. "You are beautiful, too."

"What day is this?" she asked, "Wednesday or Thursday?"

"It's Thursday," he answered, "Admission Day." He wondered whether it would be the day she was admitted to another experience.

"Tell the task force thank you for me. That's a great honor."

"It's fully deserved." He leaned down with tears in his eyes, to kiss her good-bye. Then he stood there for a long time, just holding her hand. As he finally moved to leave the room, she smiled and waved at him, then sank back on the bed and closed her eyes.

A couple of days later, he checked in on her and found her sleeping peacefully, slowly drifting away from them all. On Saturday, when he was in Los Angeles at a dinner for Assembly Speaker Willie Brown, he received the news: Virginia had died. He told his friends, including Willie Brown, who shook his head in sadness.

The next day, John flew back to northern California for her memorial service. He concluded his remarks with: "Virginia was a wonderful and remarkable presence in my life, and she always will be. I miss her and, I expect, I always will . . .. Can you imagine the workshop she is now leading wherever she has gone?"

Leadership as Cooperation

Like Virginia, John leads by engaging people on a personal level. However, he did not always transcend partisan politics. His book (1979, p. 28) describes how, when he first went to Sacramento, he avoided the conservatives in the Assembly. He was concerned that "they might contaminate me. As I grew personally, I came to recognize my avoidance as a symptom of my personal insecurity. As I grew secure enough within myself to risk exposing myself to them, I found them to be humans, just like me."

Since then, he has formed partnerships with Republicans and Democrats alike. For instance, he enlisted Republican Assembly leaders Pat Nolan and Gerry Felando as main coauthors of his Self-Esteem Task Force legislation. Also, he designed his ethics and higher education committee process to gain ownership by his Republican colleagues. Because John does not polarize issues, he usually does not blame others or make enemies. He may disagree passionately with people's ideas, but he almost never attacks them personally. He goes for principle.

Knowing that California was fast becoming the United States' first mainland state with no racial majority, John saw that the state needed a new model of leadership. In 1985, he worked to create the organization California Leadership with his best friend Mitch Saunders and with John O'Neil. It set up forums and ongoing programs incorporating multiple perspectives and using the latest patterns of cooperative leadership to solve current problems.

Participation was both inclusive (involving women and persons of color) and collaborative. Saunders served as the group's Director of Programs; O'Neil, as president. And in line with his inclusive beliefs, John Vasconcellos also invited Republican Senator Becky Morgan to serve on the board.

In September 1988, Cal Leadership sponsored an intensive 44-hour educational experience on water use in California. It involved 12 of the (all-white) top water leaders and 18 (multicultural) emerging leaders. Discussions and planning continued over three years. Cal Leadership also cosponsored a workshop at Asilomar with the California Economic Development Corporation. This workshop launched an 18-month process of discussion and decision making, leading to a commitment to the California Compact for realizing the promise of a multicultural democracy.

Democracy simply cannot work, in John's view, unless we believe in ourselves. He mentors people, directly and indirectly, by living and promoting his message of empowerment: by trusting himself, trusting others, and daring to trust in our human capacities to learn, grow, and take charge of our personal and political lives. For the survival and realization of democracy's promise, it is essential to redefine leadership in terms of empowerment.

Another example of the new leadership John inspires is the Assembly Democratic Economic Prosperity Team (ADEPT). He and ten other Assembly Democrats first met in 1991 to confront California's economic problems. Eventually they saw they could overcome these problems only by healing the historical rifts between business and government, and between Democrats and business leaders. The problems were too large and too complex for polarized politics as usual. The time had come to combine resources and perspectives so as to create new solutions.

Applying principles from humanistic psychology, the ADEPT team went out and met face to face with more than 80 business groups across California. These ranged from fishing and tourist industries to insurance, aerospace, electronics, oil, and grocery business; from construction to fashion, banking to biotech. Instead of talking politics or holding press conferences, ADEPT held focused, two-hour sessions for the legislators to listen (rather than preach) and to learn (rather than presume to instruct).

A year later, the resulting report stated "that traditional ways can no longer suffice in today's complex global economy. Neither the standard, stereotypical Republican *laissez-faire* model nor the standard, stereotypical Democratic command-and-control model works any more." Echoing John's earlier brainstorming with Virginia, the ADEPT report advocates a "third force" in California politics. "We learned that only a third way—the way of trust, partnership, and collaboration—offers us any hope for our future" (Assembly Democratic Economic Prosperity Team, 1992, p. 9).

The challenge is new, but the words ring with a familiar cadence. Believing in our human positive inclination, using active listening, and building trust, partnership, and cooperation, ADEPT applied the strategies of effective therapy directly to California's economic problems. Advocating a preventive, proactive approach to problem solving, the report states that we must respond "to our changes and challenges before they grow into crises." It also says that "leadership in California must be explicitly inclusive, visionary, and inspiring" (p. 31).

The context of humanistic psychology runs throughout John's innovative political ventures. Realizing that polarized politics-as-usual no longer works, he strives to create the equivalent of new family systems on the social level. This means facilitating new environments in which people can listen, learn, and work together to address and overcome the new challenges emerging in our complex world.

In spring 1993, the ADEPT report was translated into a legislative package. It proposed reforms in government structure and attitudes, taxes, worker's compensation, and environmental regulation. It also laid out a strategic plan for economic development and conversion, business incentives, improvement in the state's infrastructure, and preparation for a multicultural work force. Bipartisan support enacted two-thirds of its recommendations.

As is often the case with John as he grows personally, one effort led to another. The Japanese government's Ministry of International Trade and Industry picked up ADEPT's "signal to all the world that California was again open for business." Through its San Francisco Deputy Consul General Toshi Kato, the ministry invited John to come to Japan to become familiar with the country and its people, policies, business, and industry.

Seeing its significance for promoting his humanist vision of inclusion and collaboration, prevention, and problem solving, he accepted the invitation . He prepared himself thoroughly, reading several key books about Japan and arranging more than a dozen briefings in California with Japanese nationals and Japanese-Americans. Then, aided by two long-time friends living in Tokyo, U.S. Navy Commander Ken Patterson and Tanya Neil-Tanaka, he enjoyed 19 days there in a charmed adventure during the fall of 1993.

By the time he got home, he had written a 60-point California–Japan Action Agenda. As is characteristic of John's efforts, this proposed program built trust and practiced collaboration. His host, Toshi Kato, acknowledged it as "Amazing. This could well become the foundation for a new Japan–California relationship."

John's Political Legacy

In the spring of 1989, while flying back from a talk on self-esteem in Orlando, Florida, John was reading Tom Owen-Towle's book *New Men, Deeper Hungers*. He was struck by a passage about examining our lives, asking how we'd like to invest the time that remains to us, and what kind of legacy we'd like to leave behind. On May

11, his 57th birthday, he recorded his answers to those questions, looking back at what he'd done and ahead at what he still wanted to accomplish.

By then, he had chaired the Assembly Ways and Means Committee for ten years, seeking to create "a balanced human budget" while educating Californians about their state's fiscal situation. Amid progressively demanding economic conditions, his work had become increasingly sophisticated and sure. Indeed, hardly anyone in the state better understands California's sprawling budget. And one day of sitting in Ways and Means meetings would be enough to disabuse anybody who thinks that caring about self-esteem makes John soft and fuzzy.

He had followed through with his long-term commitment to education. He had twice chaired the Joint Legislative Committee for Review of the Master Plan for Higher Education (and earlier, in 1971–74, he had chaired a previous version of it). This body helped enact Assembly Bill 1725, which provided comprehensive community college reform in 1988. Now, with his good friend political philosopher Brian Murphy, John had just completed his second major blueprint report for higher learning, *California Faces . . . California's Future: Education for Citizenship in a Multicultural Democracy.* It argued that higher education would have to play a critical role in ensuring that the democratic prospect was a reality for the "new majority" who would create California's future.

Through the California Human Corps, John wanted to redefine the boundaries of higher education, encouraging every university student in California to engage in ongoing community service. This endeavor won the support of the Campus Compact (a network of college presidents from public and private universities), which extended it to the national level.

As chair of the Assembly Select Committee on Ethics, John worked to develop the nation's leading legislative code of ethics, an ethics education program, and an ethical behavior sanctions process for the California State Legislature. Again, he combined his commitment to education and personal development to improve the political process.

Another innovative project of his is the California Senior Partners program, which encourages active seniors to volunteer their services to assist less able retired persons. By creating a community assistance network, they earn credit which they can call up when they in turn need assistance. In this fragmented modern society, this program brings people together to help themselves, help one another, and build community. Changing demographics are set to produce an unprecedented age wave in the 21st century, and such programs may be vital not only to the health of senior citizens, in John's view, but to the future health of our society.

Since 1986, when he successfully introduced AIDS vaccine legislation in the State Assembly, he has worked to support research in this crucial area. In addition, he created the AIDS Budget Task Force to determine each year how much money California needs to appropriate for the growing AIDS epidemic. Here again, his compassion combined with pragmatism to meet a grave societal problem.

On the other hand, he also celebrates. In 1989, he worked to establish the first California Peace Day. Held annually on the third Sunday in May, it recognizes persons and practices that help people develop an atmosphere of peace in their lives and in the world.

Knowing the vital importance of family life in forming healthy citizens and a healthy society, he has long promoted programs for children, early childhood education, and the family. He set up the California Task Force on Positive Parenting and Celebrating Families in the 1970s. Later, he helped establish the Alternative Birthing Committee. Along with Republican Senator Becky Morgan and State Superintendent of Schools Bill Honig, he cofounded Cal Kids to move children to the top of California's agenda.

Through the Latino Advancement Project, John sought to help educate and support the future success of Latino children, especially in his own Santa Clara County. And in 1989, he set up Parents as Teachers to provide in-home education for new parents, together with health screening and follow-up advice.

In related directions, he initiated successful legislation requiring a course in human sexuality for all new California doctors, family therapists, psychologists, and psychiatric social workers. And he helped enact new, more humanistic licensing for family therapists in California.

Calling people to assume greater political responsibility, he set up "1990 Leading Californians: Demanding Leadership for a Change." This group challenged voters to voice their opinions and get involved in the 1990 gubernatorial and other elections. Both this project and John's personal vision of leadership draw from the maxim that "When the people lead, the leaders will follow."

Oddly enough, he gives the lie to his own maxim, for he often has been way out in front of "the people" as well as their representatives. He must be on to something: the people in his district keep electing him. He served 30 years in the State Assembly and has been in the State Senate since 1996. His career proves a political truth that Virginia Satir and Carl Rogers would have loved: trust your own instincts, and trust others to be in your face if you are wrong. And *then* be flexible and open enough to craft a solution others can accept.

Politics in a Healing Crisis

With his systemic approach to political problems, John looks beyond any current crisis to search out its root causes and cures. From his book's title, *A Liberating Vision,* to his latest programs and speeches, he is a visionary leader who looks for and calls our attention to the larger patterns.

In his 1993 inaugural speech for Raymond Orbach, the new chancellor of the University of California at Riverside, John eloquently described his vision. In many ways, he explained, our society is like a dysfunctional family. We are finally overcoming our denial and experiencing a breakdown that may also be a healing crisis. He pointed to the four major revolutions that have shaken up our old world order: the computer revolution, the revolutions in race and gender, and the humanistic revolution (in the way we see human nature and ourselves). He concluded:

> in these times of chaos and breakdown which evoke so much fear, it is our challenge as leaders to try to help have the vision, to help paint the pictures to enable other people and ourselves to see what is happening not in terms of negativity and fright, but instead to recognize these transitions as not so much breakdown and terrible but as breakout, break up, breakthrough towards some more hopefully whole, healthy, more diverse, and inclusive society.

Describing the massive changes in society's fabric, he portrays them in a way that offers hope to many persons who would otherwise retreat into defensiveness and anxiety. He offers a highly sophisticated, systemic view of our evolving society. He is able to see beyond apparent breakdown to posit the emergence of a new social order.

After saying that his father had taught him that "you can't give what you don't have," he concluded: "Only the person who is willing to be living authentically and creatively, with integrity, with vision, with boldness and wholeheartedness and passion and risk taking, can lead a life willing to meet the challenge of our times."

John's Family, Then and Now

John's greatest challenge, he says, has been "to reclaim myself, to accept myself." He recalls a dream he had at Esalen in which he saw a Ferris wheel turning, burning up more and more of himself. He has been living that dream for years now, bringing more and more of himself to the surface, accepting himself and, in so doing, engaging and helping others to accept more of themselves as well.

He has made peace with his parents and his past. For two or three years in the late 1960s, when he was in intensive therapy, he didn't see his parents at all. But he has long since worked to rebuild and redefine his relationship with them. In recent years, he joined his parents for the usual family visits and holiday meals. Since they lived halfway between Santa Clara and the state capital, John would stop by once a month or so. He'd join them for Sunday dinner, have a short visit, and stay overnight on his way back to Sacramento. He grew able to address them by the titles so crucial to their sense of themselves.

His father died in 1983. His mother, Teresa, is now in her mid-nineties. John says that she's "finally come to terms with my being myself" and they've "developed a real friendship over the years." His brother Jim is an engineer with General Electric and lives in Pacifica. His sister Margaret lives in Guerneville and is a teacher and director of programs for non-English–speaking students at Mission High School in San Francisco. John sees them, but rarely, at family functions.

John's path has taken him to new frontiers, leaving little time to spend with his family of origin. Like Don Quixote, he has been on a quest for most of his life. With offices and households divided between Santa Clara and Sacramento, and commitments spread all over the state—and now the nation and beyond—he has never married. His quest has given him a strong sense of duty, long hours, and a hectic schedule. During his flights around California, he occasionally looks down to contemplate the land and the millions of people he helps govern. He recognizes that "It's an awesome responsibility" to be a legislator. "There are only 120 of us and 32 million people in the state."

When asked how he has managed to maintain himself and his faith, strength, and balance through all these years in the rough-and-tumble world of politics, he smiles. "Good friends, good therapists, and good staff." His staff are like family, he says. They are mature and diverse, smart, well informed, and generous. They operate with openness and trust, share information, and represent him so well that he can "be a dozen places at once."

Since his 1984 heart attack and bypass, he has lived more deliberately, striving to find a balance between his own life and the demands of his work. He does daily bioenergetic body work, plays racquetball, reads a great deal, listens a lot, and learns more about his life each day. Most of all, he values his closest friends: Mitch and Cindy Saunders and their daughter Megan. What began as a mentorship has led to their becoming his primary family. John's greatest-ever service was locating Mitch's father (in Texas) after 27 years of utter separation and silence. The resultant healing opened Mitch to his own becoming a father.

The young Megan has an honest, loving nature and a wisdom all her own. When she was three, John read this note on her pre-school report card: "Megan has an unusually developed sense of self-esteem." This touched him to tears and to smiles. "Uncle John" spends holidays with them, and Megan has become a special friend.

To relax, he sometimes just "hibernates with friends." He particularly enjoys conversations and strategy sessions (as well as an occasional family vacation) with another close friend, the political philosopher Brian Murphy. And sometimes John takes off to Hawaii for a few days or weeks. Mostly he stays on Maui, his father's birthplace and likely to be John's retirement destination. Then he returns to the intense atmosphere of the state capitol.

For a man who spent much of his adult life rebelling against his early family conditioning, family has become very important to John. This includes a close family of friends and his extended family which, in one sense, includes all Californians. He says that he and Virginia had a lot in common in this regard, and that in his work he seeks "to make real the vision she had." In a way, as John sees it, they were both family therapists working to facilitate healthier family systems. They did lots of the same things, except that "she worked in smaller family groups. My family to do therapy with is California: 32 million Californians. That's my area, in which I seek to understand the dysfunction, and give them some vision of growth and possibilities." In their talks about politics, psychology, and life in the 1980s, he and Virginia had agreed that it was "time to go from family reconstruction to social reconstruction." She expanded her message of family and interpersonal dynamics and went on to do peace work in Russia. He has worked in the California Legislature to strengthen education, community, social justice, and the state of self-esteem in California. Both reached out with hands and hearts, combining the personal and the political into a vision and affirmation of healthy human development that embraces community and offers hope for a more just and peaceful world.

John's ambition and hope are that enough persons will recognize and be ignited by his liberating vision to mobilize into a cohesive, effective new mainstream movement. For the 21st century, this could create a humanistic, healing, and hopeful new force in politics.

About Diane Dreher

Since moving to northern California in 1974 to teach English at Santa Clara University, I have been intrigued and inspired by John Vasconcellos's efforts to extend the lessons of humanistic psychology into politics. I recall my surprise when I first received his district Assembly reports. Who was this unusual person? He not only represented me in Sacramento but embodied some of my most valued ideals in the political arena.

During the 1980s, I placed many English department interns in John's district office. With John as a role model, I have also struggled to discover and affirm a healthier sense of self in my own life. Since completing my doctorate at the University of California at Los Angeles, I have been continuously redefining what it means to be a teacher, writer, lifelong student, woman, and person in this world of challenge and change.

I have sought to apply the lessons of modern psychology in various ways. Beginning with my dissertation, my scholarly research has combined literature and developmental psychology. I have also published popular articles on peace, self-esteem, and personal growth. In 1977, I founded the Faculty Development Program at Santa Clara University, directing a series of interactive workshops on teaching and research. In 1988, I codirected a regional workshop on self-esteem for parents and educators in San Jose, with John as the keynote speaker. I have also benefited from my friendships with Mitch Saunders and Gay Swenson-Barfield, whom I met in the 1980s while doing research on conflict resolution.

As a means of breaking through the limits of the Western mindset, I look to Eastern philosophy in addition to humanistic psychology. Asian art, culture, and philosophy have influenced me subtly ever since early childhood, when I lived in the Far East. My book *The Tao of Personal Leadership* (1997) records the personal blend of Eastern philosophy and humanistic psychology that guides my life.

I now teach literature and creative writing at Santa Clara University, where I chaired the English department from 1992 to 1997 and served as president of the Faculty Senate in 1999–2000. In my writing and academic work, I seek to explore more humanistic forms of leadership. In my personal life, I enjoy cultivating my garden, training in *aikido,* and sharing life's adventures with my husband and best friend, psychologist Robert Numan.

For years, Virginia held an annual month-long residential training workshop in Crested Butte, Colorado. By 1988, it had grown to 90 people and 15 instructors, and none of us had given a thought to the possibility that Virginia might die. She said she'd live to 120.

When Virginia became ill that summer, she requested Jean McLendon stand in for her as Director of Training for the Process Community. I was surprised, and then it seemed only natural. Jean was no longer the young 26-year-old eager student I first met in 1971 at the second IHLRN conference in Mexico.

When I thought about it, Virginia's choice made sense. Jean had been good at the work for years. She gets very clear, simple, and intuitive, and she works with remarkable control and ease. It's like hearing a wonderful solo from time to time. Other Avantans hit other notes or keys that distinguish them among the choir, but Jean has a special, clear voice—the kind of voice that inspires trust.

After directing the Process Community for two years, Jean set out to create a Satir system training program modeled on the Crested Butte design. The program, after more than ten years, now attracts people from both clinical and organizational occupations and from all over the world. No one has used Virginia's approach across more varied settings and contexts than Jean. Virginia chose well.

—*Robert S. Spitzer*
Publisher

Mount Crested Butte, Colorado
site of Virginia's annual Process Community
and other trainings

7

Starting from Within, Here and Now

by Jean McLendon

Virginia taught me that the most important place of contact is where one's current life connects with the old familiar, perhaps almost forgotten childhood experiences. That is the home of "within" and the place I will travel to with you. My hope is that you will get something useful for your personal or professional life. Ideally, if I do a good job, you will also be pleasured. For me, I hope for a sense of relief and satisfaction for a job well done. Starting "here and now" requires, as Virginia knew so well, a description—a definition of the word context. For me, *context* is about place, purpose, season, sounds, colors, and culture. Context is not so much about time unless "time" means the angle of the sun or the swell of the moon. These are personal to me. Too much sun, and I wilt; too much moon, and I want to howl.

Purpose and Place

I have been dual tracked for a long time and have often wondered if being born a twin under the astrological sign of Gemini accounts for this. As long as I am able to manage the reality that I have (and always had) two parallel professional interests, then things go pretty well.

My clinical office, where I see psychotherapy clients, is about three miles from my home, in an office condominium. What I like most about it is that the windows are the old-fashioned kind that you can pull up and open. Next, I like that I have the wonderful assistance of Ann Austin, who has been supporting Chapel Hill psychotherapists for many years. Ann does her work with not too much to say, does it well, and is extremely dependable.

In my home office, I handle my nonclinical business, matters of training, and consulting. My primary support staff is miles away in Maryland, so we usually have multiple daily e-mails and a weekly phone conference that can last up to three hours. Elly Williamson handles all the administrative matters that have to do with my Satir System training programs. She is good with numbers, knows computers intimately, writes well, works hard, and is very generous to me with her many talents. Before she took me on as her favorite and "most in need" client, she was a veteran measurements expert with DuPont for 17 years. Having participated in two Congruent Leadership Change Shop trainings and two year-long Satir System Performance Development Programs, she is Satir literate, to say the least.

I work on training and consulting at my mahogany rolltop desk on a used, no-back, on-your-knees, new-fangled chair that is supposed to be good for your posture. I bought it in my hometown— Timmonsville, South Carolina—for five dollars. I like most that it is on wheels. If I had my way, all furniture would rock, be on wheels, and swivel. Flexibility, versatility, and convenience are very important to me and essential for doing the kind and amount of work I do.

I guess my desk and chair have a lot to do with my being a sentimentalist, spend thrift, bargain lover, and eternal optimist about there being an answer to my ever-present challenge to get organized. I get pleasure from sitting at the desk Daddy "bought" for me. With his farm business, my father had a fair amount of paperwork, which he dealt with at the kitchen table. When Mother needed him to remove it for a mealtime preparation, he would pack the stuff up in his very organized fashion and return it to a drawer in his bedroom. After Daddy died, I treated myself to this wonderful rolltop desk. I imagined he would have given an eyetooth to have one, had he been able to fathom such a piece of furniture or such an aid to his work.

It was 1980. I had left my husband, my father had died, and I was returning from a nearby county to make my home in Chapel Hill. I needed a desk. When I went to a local antique store, I was asked if I would like to see a recently acquired solid mahogany roll top. That sounded expensive to me.

"I'm looking for something not so expensive, maybe a couple of hundred dollars," I replied. The lady helping me understood. Once I had found something that would do, I said, "I'm curious about the mahogany desk you have in storage. Can I see it?" Since I had found what I needed, I assumed I could see it and not risk drooling or doing anything impulsive.

She willingly took me back into the warehouse where this majestic piece of furniture was stored for safe keeping. It was completely covered by a large dark maroon velvet ceremonial-like blanket. If I had had to guess, I would have assumed the special blanket was protecting a casket or maybe an organ. She slid the blanket off, unveiling a really handsome desk, though I would not have been surprised to see organ keys as she rolled back the top.

She invited me to sit, and I did. My first words were, "A woman owned this desk!" She was surprised and confirmed my suspicion. "It fits me," I noted. I opened one of the many little organizing drawers and found it filled with buttons, needles, and pins. We laughed. "My father sure could have used this," I told her.

It all happened fast, like a lot of things in my life. I asked about the price. She checked. "Two thousand dollars," she said.

"Eighteen hundred if you deliver it," I offered. It was a deal.

I'd just spent the only inheritance I would spend until the next summer, when I made a down payment on a house. I did, however, run into a slight problem. When the desk arrived at my apartment, it was too large to get through the doors. I have since taken it apart screw by screw four times, each time proclaiming it to be the last. I figure I may have to do it once more, but that is it!

It has 21 drawers of all sizes and shapes, with pull-out shelves and one that actually performs as a large work table. I use it for George, my friendly and impressive portable computer.

Color and Culture

I have a spectacular view from my desk. There are three door-size windows side by side in my office, and one is a sliding glass door. I sit at an angle to my desk so I can reach the printer and still face the outside. The outside is something to behold and something that feeds my soul.

When I look out, I see a lot of green from the oaks, maples, hickories, dogwoods, and pines that separate me from a lovely 54-acre lake. The lake draws my attention—and that of most other people, too. I have always loved water. I'm often awed to look from my office and be reminded of the sweet and rich body of water that calls to me daily. Our lake has its own personality and inner system, just like all other life. Sometimes it is like the finest silk, so even and smooth I cannot resist being wrapped and bathed in it. Sometimes it is so alive with movement that I feel a little trepidation.

Last summer was our first summer in this house. I was standing on the dock. The water that particular day was in its mostly silken state except for a swiggly movement coming directly toward the dock from up the shoreline to my right. Carol, my partner of 15 years, was sunning. She sat quietly and very still. I stood not even breathing. It was a snake.

I do not like snakes. I know God gave them their own rightful place in the ecosystem, but my swimming in this lake is the only reason we went through the massive energy drain—not to mention other kinds of costs—to renovate a little dark, flat-roofed, cement block cottage into a three-story, stuccoed, pitched-roof, fully modernized, upgraded "pleasure palace" (the term Virginia used for her modernized and luxurious bathroom).

I had been seconds away from diving off the dock into the lake, but now I wasn't breathing and I wasn't moving. The snake swam no more than two feet from the dock, still not noticing Carol or me. "So what now?" I asked in my look to Carol.

Her look said it all, as it has so many times: "This is your thing, so it's your call."

As I readied myself and put on my swimming goggles, I got yet another personal lesson in acceptance of life as it is: surprising, varied, and challenging. I stood watching the snake swim by. I felt absolutely gutless, a bit heartless, and, truth be told, a little sick to my stomach. I knew I could not waiver; I had to make my point. "Move over and make room, because I'm coming in. This is my lake, too!" I dove in and soon learned that there was a free lane for me down the center of the lake headed east to the wooden floats that lie several hundred yards off the homeowner's association park beach. Though the lake still contains potential traffic—fish, snakes, turtles, muskrats, ducks, geese, and whatever else I'd just as soon not know about—I've not had contact with anything but an occasional floating stick or leaf.

The Adirondack chairs on the dock are a ready invitation for "Y'all to come on down." And we do, a lot—with our books, friends, fishing rods, or weekend cocktails. The area around the dock is my favorite place to garden. There's no direct sun until the late afternoon. By then, the sun is even more delicious, and I can drink it up without fear of harm.

A rainbow flag waves happily from our dock. It's a special reminder that important people have made room for me in this world—from the beginning, when I shared my mother's womb with my fraternal twin, Jane. To me, the rainbow flag is not really a political statement, but rather a reminder to stay in touch with gratitude and pride for the freedom I have been given and have created.

Here in Chapel Hill, I feel the now familiar excitement of seeing possibilities. On my first day here, this feeling was about sensing I had found my Southern paradise. I arrived in Chapel Hill in 1971 with my husband, J. D. Pickering. Having repaid my debt to the South Carolina Department of Mental Health for its support of my two years of graduate social work training in Hawaii, I was in Chapel Hill to enter a post-graduate interdisciplinary program in the Community Psychiatry Division at the University School of Medicine.

Walking down the street in Chapel Hill that first day, I was fascinated to see the diversity in a Southern town so close to my home. Chapel Hill was more textured, colored, and cultured than the Southern towns and cities I had known. As J.D. and I walked hand in hand, showing our own diversity—he was dark-skinned and Mexican-American, I was red-haired, freckled, and Scottish-Irish—I remember my excitement and my energy. I believed I had found a Southern home that would work for me and for us. It was a place where lots of things could come together.

I expected to see different kinds of people in Chapel Hill. I was not, however, expecting my reaction. Though silent about my feelings, on the inside I was stirred, challenged, excited. The feelings were not too different from those I experienced while in college at Winthrop and during graduate school in the melting pot of Hawaii. These were the places where I first met peers who were Catholic, Jewish, Yankee, atheist, agnostic, etc. The explorer in me was having a feast, and my feelings that day in Chapel Hill were deeply personal. Chapel Hill—like my family, my friends, and my profession—would prove to be a wonderfully accepting container for my growth, my healing, my learning, and my changing.

Sounds and Season

My home office is enriched by two radios. One is a standard radio/tape-player, but my favorite is the earphone radio. I can tune in our local classical station, and tune out just about everything else. I give credit for my love of classical music to my father's eldest sister, Lucille, or Aunt "T," as we all called her. I took piano lessons from "T" from second grade until I went off to college. She had high hopes for me as a pianist. Given my "light touch and nimble fingers," as she used to say, she couldn't understand why I didn't devote myself seriously to my practice.

She was particularly disappointed one spring when for weeks my knuckles stayed a dirty brown. I had earned enough money to buy my first really good baseball glove. I oiled the pocket daily and worked it with my fist. It softened right up and was part of a good baseball season that year. It was a great glove for as long as I needed it. I don't remember when I last used it, but probably I had learned that "girls don't play baseball" at least by the time I entered high school. (Thankfully, we are making progress in opening up more possibilities for little girls and big girls to follow their bliss.

Perhaps it is true for boys, too. I hope so.) Meanwhile, listening to "T" telling me one hundred ways to get my hands looking better was no fun. Besides, I tried several of her ideas and they didn't work.

Even with my loud music, I can hear the alarms from our "babies." No other animal that I've heard can sound so much like a terrorized child as Ivan and Murphy, our cats. When I hear their "call to arms," I head outside and answer in my known-to-the-neighborhood yelling voice. In the most recent example, Ivan responded to my call and showed up quickly, looking puzzled but fine. I cajoled him into the house and continued calling for Murphy. Shortly, I saw him sauntering through the brush toward me. Every few steps, he would turn and look back as if to say, "Mom's here now." Or, maybe he was just checking to make sure he wasn't being followed. In either case, I suspect he was grateful to have the excuse of my summons to exit whatever altercation had commenced. The incident ended like most things with the boys: they got treats and took naps.

I did not grow up with pets. My father always had a special bird dog or two, but they were his dogs and not family pets. In my adult life, I've learned how a pet can be a true member of the family with equal rights for justice, self-esteem, and freedom of speech. Our pets have also taught me about the "soul pleasure" of sharing love and loyalty. I've learned to endure vet bills, accidental scratches, flea bites, and the poison ivy that Ivan sometimes brings to bed with him. Their need for attention is sometimes difficult for me when I am busy and into my own affairs, but they are patient and persistent teachers.

Between the lake and my office, the property slopes dramatically. The most direct path is lined with azaleas. In the spring they are gloriously fragrant and a lovely, spectacular sight. Today, they are readying themselves deep inside their cells for the next change of season. At 51, I am readying myself for life-season changes. Having as many interests as I do, I consider myself very fortunate to still find joy, challenge, and deep satisfaction in the career I began nearly 30 years ago. These days it is an anomaly, and more than I knew to wish for.

I have seen plenty of people floundering and starting over in their mid-life career changes. My wish is to stay the course and have it open up more and more to me over time. It has—and I knock on wood, pat myself on my back, and thank my lucky stars, God, and Otis Robbins for introducing me to Virginia Satir.

Family of Origin

I feel very fortunate in that my parents were good people. I didn't have to deal with abuse in my life. My family helped me be ready for what Virginia had to offer and gave me the ability to do something with it.

My father, Ralph McLendon, was nicknamed "Speck" for his freckles, and also "Red" for the color of his hair (both physical traits that I inherited). He was raised where I grew up—in Timmonsville, South Carolina, a small agricultural community of about 2500 citizens. It is located in the flat, hot, northeastern part of the state that was and is predominantly rural and economically poor. He was the youngest among his five sisters and became the only male in the family at age 14. His father, a banker, was killed when a train hit his automobile. My father finished high school and managed to get in one year of college before he was called back home to help with raising cotton and tobacco on the family farm.

My mother, Geneva Atkins McLendon, came from a little town called Campobello, near Greenville/Spartanburg, in the foothills

of the South Carolina mountains. So in terms of culture, my mother
was raised very differently from my lowlander father. When she
moved down to the lowlands to join this genteel family where she
was supposed to be a lady, her shyness served her well. We used to
kid her about being from "the hills."

She came from a large family with five sisters and two brothers. Her family had a lot to deal with. She had a sister and a brother
who were blind. Her family fits the stereotype in my mind of mountain people—hard-working and closed. I think her family members
were pretty easily angered and showed it.

Though it was unusual for their time and background, she
and her sisters all went to college. She received her degree in home
economics from Winthrop, a woman's college in South Carolina
(where I eventually did my undergraduate work). Ultimately, my
mother was the only one of her siblings who did not return to her
native foothills. She met my father when she was substitute teaching in the Timmonsville area. He drove by the boarding house where
she lived. They laid eyes on each other, and that was it.

As it turned out, my father would become the sole male in the
household of his marriage, too. They had three children: Joan (Jo),
Jane, and me. Jane and I were born on June 5, 1945; Jo was four
years older and very precocious. She was very verbal and learned
to read at a young age. People in town thought she was the brightest,
most wonderful child. I gather she got lots of attention from my
parents, the community, people from church, and my father's
relatives who lived in and around Timmonsville. On the day we
twins were brought home from the hospital, Jo ran away to a
neighboring black woman's house and stayed for a couple of nights.
I don't think she ever found a way to enjoy having younger twin
sisters.

Jane and I were a bit of a surprise. My parents were expecting
twins, but had assumed that at least one child would be male. They

would name that child "Ralph," and the other name they'd chosen was "Jane." When we both arrived as daughters, "Ralph" became "Jean."

We were both little skinny things, but immediately distinguishable: Jane was very blonde with blue-green eyes, like my mother's. I had very red hair and these brown eyes, like my father's. Our differences remained apparent during infancy. I was a very agitated, colicky cry baby while Jane was placid and content as an infant.

I remember as a young child hearing my mother respond to people in our little town who asked why she did not dress her twin daughters alike. "They are different," she'd explain with a clear kind of knowing wisdom. Years later, I overheard Jane telling friends that we were very different. "Like silver and gold," she said.

Growing Up in Timmonsville

Timmonsville consists of a Five and Dime, a grocery store, a hardware store, the town hall, and the post office. That's about it. Daddy would be disheartened by the condition of Timmonsville today. He served as mayor for over a decade while I was growing up and cared deeply about the town of his childhood. Mother said he loved Timmonsville more than anybody else. He never liked to leave it and hardly ever did.

My father was cautious, conservative, honest, and "henpecked"—the word he used. He took a lot of pride in standing against the crowd, but when it came to his wife, it was a different matter. My father did not quarrel with my mother. He never got a chance to put up a fight. My mother was real fast on the draw. I think he must have been angry at times, but he acted more like a hurt puppy. My mother primarily did the discipline in our house.

My sisters and I attended the First Baptist Church on Sunday mornings with my father while Mother got a little "peace and quiet" and prepared our best meal of the week. Aunt "T" was the organist and a real matriarch in the congregation, and Daddy was a deacon. "T" should have been a deacon, as she had lots to say about anything having to do with the church, from the finances to the decorations. (They still exclude women from those leadership positions. It seemed strange to me then, and now I find it offensive and stupid.)

I think my father suffered from depression—or maybe it was just grief. His sister, my Aunt Abby, committed suicide when I was really young. I have only the vaguest memories of her. Unlike "T," she played the organ by ear and could really "cut loose," as Daddy used to tell me. The youngest of my father's sisters, Aunt Virginia, whom I really loved, also tried several times to kill herself. Supposedly, she died of some kind of natural cause—a stroke or something—but I'm not sure I believe that. I have also wondered about my grandfather's "accident" with the train, which might well have occurred very near the time of the 1929 stock market crash and the onset of the Great Depression, when many people lost their fortunes and as a consequence took their own lives.

I don't remember feeling stigmatized by their suicidal acts, but I do remember wondering what could have been bothering them so badly, so deeply that they didn't want to live. I understand now how a person's life force can be so wounded, pained, and drained that death might feel like a blessing.

Daddy was a farmer and tobacco was the cash crop. Christmas was small or moderate, depending on how well the tobacco sold. What my father did on the farm was coach, supervise, check in, and hunt. He and I did things that were special—from riding horses to hunting to gardening. We would do the garden parts that Jane, Jo, and my mother didn't do: he did the planting and weeding, she harvested; he mowed the grass, she did the flowers.

Mother is a kind of Martha Stewart–type: she likes gardening, cooking, putting things up (canning), and tending flowers. She has taste, from expensive shoes to nice clothes. Shopping with her was always a treat for me. "I learned to get things that matched and would last—nothing cheap or cheap looking—though getting a bargain was especially satisfying and fun. She is not up for shopping these days, but she used to like to buy nice things.

When I was growing up, Mother was first and foremost a homemaker. She loved for things to look pretty, especially the flowers in her yard. Her therapy was to get her hands in the dirt. "Farm girl" didn't appeal to her as a description, but "gardener" did.

I think my father's life was more interesting to me than my mother's. Early on, I remember wishing I were a boy. It's still a family legend that I tried to kiss my elbow, hoping that, magically, my gender would change. Though I played with the toughest among the kids in the neighborhood, I don't remember any boy ever challenging me or dismissing me for being a girl (though perhaps I've forgotten).

The older brother of one my girlfriends regularly taunted her while she practiced piano. In the middle of a piece, he'd run into the room and slam the keyboard cover on his sister's fingers. She'd be crying yet still playing, and she would push that keyboard cover back up and say, "Stop that!" Then he'd do it again. All the while, I'd be standing there thinking, "How does she take it? I would have creamed him."

Summer, when most families traveled or did some kind of vacation, rarely worked for us. With the tobacco and all, it was the busiest time of the year. Daddy didn't much want to go anywhere, anyway. The only significant trips I remember making when I was growing up were to Columbia, South Carolina's capital, about a three-hour drive from Timmonsville. The family made the trip to Mother's eye doctor (she has glaucoma) and to find the special shoes Jane and I needed for our tiny, narrow feet.

My parents were of the Depression era and weren't much for fun and frolic. I have vivid memories of Mother taking us twins to Florence, a nearby town, to go to the swimming pool. We were about six years old. I think Mother thought it was her responsibility to see that we learned to swim, as Daddy never did know how. He was probably as scared of water as Virginia was. Neither of them ever took me up on my offer to teach them about the pleasures of being held up by water.

It was a very special treat to have Mother drive us to the Florence pool. We never went enough to suit me. Since we were only about two and a half hours from the coast, I learned about the ocean early. But, I don't think Mother felt the same responsibility to teach us about the ocean, so we seldom went.

I do remember one trip to the South Carolina coast when I was four or five. When it came time to leave the beach, I was furious. I loved the ocean, and I wanted to stay. When my mother forced me to head for the car, I said, "I don't know why little girls need mothers anyway!" Mother also remembers this incident, and though she can laugh about it now, I know it hurt her feelings. I didn't talk like that to her that I can ever remember, so the water must have been a really strong pull for me to express myself in such a way.

Today, I think my mother would say that little girls need a mama (and a daddy) to teach them the difference between right and wrong. One of the things Jane and I used to do was leave our bikes out somewhere in the neighborhood when we decided to go to the movies several blocks away. Once the movie was over and it was dark, some friends' parents would usually bring us home, and our bikes would still be wherever we'd left them.

One morning after such an occasion, my father collected his twins for a little trip to the town hall. He walked us right past the area in the building that held all the bicycles that had been found or recovered as stolen property. Jane and I both pretended not to see our bicycles sitting right there. He didn't say a word; he didn't have to. We got the message.

At age 14, I got my first summer job running the calculator in the tobacco warehouse. None of my girlfriends were able to have real jobs, and in those days, the tobacco warehouse was where the action was. I actually had spent a lot of years working in the tobacco industry by then. Though I never cropped nor strung "bacco," as the tenants on the farm called it, I used to follow the big trucks on my bicycle as they carried the harvest purchased by the tobacco companies to their large warehouses in preparation for shipment to cigarette factories. I peddled up behind the trucks in case a tobacco bundle fell off. When one did, I picked it up. Sometimes when I was really lucky, alert, and riding well, I could just lean over and scoop up a fallen bundle, tuck it under my arm, and keep peddling. That way I could scoop up another bundle or two as they fell like dominoes off the truck.

"Picking up tobacco" was pretty competitive, and there were lots of little and not-so-little boys in town who chased the trucks along with me. Sometimes the "colored" men who sat on the truck to make sure the bundles didn't fall enjoyed watching us kids chase the trucks. When several of us got into the competition, racing each other and calling out to the men to throw us a bundle, they joined in the fun and tossed us a bundle or two.

I stored my tobacco in the "junk house," the cement block storage and gardening shed in the back yard, until summer's end. Daddy then took it to the market and auctioned it off with his.

My career in the tobacco industry ended at age 16 when Timmonsville put in a swimming pool, and I got a summer job as a water safety instructor and lifeguard. I worked there several summers, and the job gave me the opportunity to learn what it really meant to be in authority and to earn, require, and accept respect.

Messages of Childhood

A psychic once told me I would never have to worry about having rice in my bowl. Her take on me and my life validated the faith I began wearing at a very young age and now feel increasingly inside myself. I will be okay, no matter what. I will do okay, no matter. And I will always have enough, no matter. I think my parents tried to teach me how to make all that work. I translated their efforts into this: If you work hard, be good, and save, then everything will be okay. I don't doubt the value of those teachings, and now I have a faith that supports my belief in myself.

It seems to me that as fast as doors close, others open. It doesn't seem to matter whether the doors are closed by me, by someone else, or mysteriously. Being born human, I assume that God has taken care of the basics; we all have enough. I just have to stay on my path, be the best me I can be, and help others to be their best. The rest will fall into place.

One childhood message was: "Hold onto your dreams." Dreams are a lot like butterflies. You can't hold them too tightly. But knowing your wishes is like being an entomologist with a net always handy. I know about the vulnerability of sharing hopes and wishes, and I know about the empowerment of saying, "I want . . ., my wish is . . ., my dream is . . .." The Salutatorian speech I presented to my high school graduating class, "Bridges to the Moon," was about the power of hopes and dreams for building strong futures.

I came into the world wanting a horse. You might think that would be a simple request for a farmer to "make good on" with his daughter. And Daddy did, but I was a sophomore in college when he finally heard my wish in a way that led him to act. I was home from college for Easter and relaxing with him and Mother at the kitchen table. He told me to look on the back porch. "There's something out there for you."

I opened the door and my eyes landed instantly on a brown leather riding crop hanging on a nail by the porch door. I grabbed it, and it felt in my hands like I had always imagined it would feel—great! Thirty minutes later, we were out at the farm and I was meeting "Who-dat." Before the end of the summer, Daddy traded Who-dat for a younger stallion named Juba, and Daddy got a nice Tennessee walking horse named Mac. Jane, Jo, and Mother pretty much left the horses to Daddy and me, and we had many fun times riding together.

One version of another childhood rule was: "Have your emotions, but don't show them publicly." Growing up in Timmonsville in the late 1940s and early '50s, I got a message common to the time and my family's status in that Old South community: "You don't call attention to yourself. You don't shame your family by acting out, showing off, or losing control in public."

Both my mother and father were people of few words—whether words about their pleasures, pains, problems, or plans. My parents did not show their feelings in obvious ways; rather, they demonstrated them to you. They were reserved. Daddy was more social and seemed to enjoy his men friends very much. They were not boastful or loud about anything. I think my father would have been mayor of Timmonsville until the day he died, but he eventually lost an election and did not run again. I never saw him show any emotion over that loss.

I remember my mother showing anger on occasion, but only twice do I recall seeing her cry while I was growing up. She cried when each of her parents died. It was like I wasn't supposed to see her do that, and I felt some discomfort.

I got mixed messages about my temper from my family. In some ways, my temper fired up the family system. I (along with Mother and Jo who also had tempers) would be teased in a loving way about my temper inside the house, but I knew it was not okay to show it outside the family.

I must have been in the first or second grade when this older boy—somebody I looked up to and wanted to think I was wonderful—referred to me as "Spitfire." I was shocked. I felt as though I had been exposed, as though some private part of me was hanging out in public. It was as if a deep secret had been revealed.

At home, I felt freer to show my temper. Once, my mother even gave me a china cup to take outside and shatter against a concrete wall as a way to vent my frustration about something that had happened at school that day.

The clearest message on showing my temper in public came in the ninth grade when I was playing basketball on the girls' high school varsity team. I was this teeny player—five feet four inches and almost 100 pounds when wet. I played pivot and was known well beyond the boundaries of my little town for my incredible hook shot. It enabled me to score against guards who were a lot bigger than I. One morning after a game, I was reporting at the breakfast table about how angry I had been when the referee let this other girl ride my back the whole night before. My father said to me, "If I ever hear that you showed your butt with your anger on the court, that will be the last time you play basketball."

Somehow I got the message that the way you looked good, the way you achieved emotional maturity was to hide your feelings. I don't think my family would have ever said that emotional maturity is the absence of emotion. I think I just learned that from watching them. "You manage your emotions so they don't call attention to yourself, hurt anybody, or interfere with your being productive." Today, my concept of becoming emotionally mature is very different than that limited take I had on it growing up, though I'm still learning that lesson. I'm still about that search.

A third childhood lesson involved accomplishments: "It's okay to star, but don't overshadow." I developed a capacity to lead in many different contexts. Among the 30 people in my graduating class, I didn't feel I lacked intellectual or cultural stimulation. We had plays, a band, a choral group, a school newspaper, and the yearbook. I was a star basketball player and an academic star.

I understood very early that boys could do more than girls. I believed as a child that my life would have been better, richer, more exciting, more fun if I had been a boy. I also learned, perhaps a bit grudgingly, that girls were not supposed to "overshadow" boys. (I came to remember the competition between boys and girls during the Supreme Court confirmation hearings for Clarence Thomas. I was very agitated when I watched that on TV. Feeling angry at men in a way that I have not felt in years, I thought, 'Gee, this must be like something I felt when I was nine years old.")

Jane and I had four girlfriends, all about the same age, who lived on our block. I quickly became the ringleader, with a bigger circle than just the girls. Three of the four little girls had older brothers, and with my native athletic abilities, I was quickly drawn into their baseball games. In fact, I became a star player. Jane, who was not athletically inclined, was part of the neighborhood group, but I don't think she ever felt very central.

During our high school years, Jane and I began to move into different social groups. I was the athletic/academic star and president of the junior class. Jane, the follower, was not as academically inclined, but more socially adept. She and I always wanted the best for each other. Jane was, in many ways, my biggest fan. For as long as I can remember, she has enjoyed my successes and bragging about me. I still both like and dislike this. By the time we reached high school, I felt uncomfortable with some of the things she did. For example, she wanted to hold my basketball warm-up suit during my games, like that was a big deal for her.

Over the years of my childhood and adolescence, I developed an automatic, programmed response to the compliments from Jane and others. I learned to respond with modesty and understatement, pass the credit, remember to smile, and say "thank-you." This system has its payoff. I always know that I have an acceptable if not gracious response. Over time, I have come to know that the system also has its cost. It is difficult to harvest the fruits of my very hard work, and I often overlook or dismiss celebrations. It can be a kind of "put-down" for the other person to meet with such denial of my obvious influence and competence, and in that way, it is distancing. Professionally, it is dangerous not to recognize the power associated with the level of trust I am so often afforded. It behooves me to be aware of and accept my status as a star.

If Jane ever resented my achievements, she never let on. She has indicated that there were ways in which I did not meet her expectations for demonstrating my affection. After all, if someone is going to put you on such a pedestal, you have a responsibility to acknowledge that honor. I know that she takes pride in my accomplishments, although she forever says she still doesn't know what I do. She'll ask, 'Tell me again, how do I tell people what you do?"

I think Jane and I still have very different aptitudes and, I would have thought, different attitudes. But now, as we grow older, I am seeing how much we have in common. After Jane returned to Timmonsville as an adult, she worked in a center for the psychological rehabilitation of learning-disabled children for about two years. It was an environment that I'm accustomed to—a social service agency—and I've heard her say things that sound like the philosophy and attitudes that I have.

People in the community and in our high school were always looking for a way to differentiate or stereotype the two of us. My stereotypes in high school and college were "senior superlative," "most likely to succeed," "best all round," and "most dependable."

The place that people carved out for Jane was that she was going to be a homemaker, mother, and wife.

Indeed, her dream was to be a wife and mother. She married and left Timmonsville. They lived in Las Vegas; her husband was into show and money and cars and things. He gave Jane a different kind of experience. Today, she is divorced and the mother of two grown children. Several years ago, she left Nevada and her husband of 16 years to move back to her hometown. My father died in 1980, and Jane and Mother are now taking care of each other. I think they do that without realizing how much care they are being given. Somehow, thankfully, it works, and I try to stay out of their dynamics.

Jane is very active in the church and in town beautification projects. She has begun to find an important and active place for herself in the community of her childhood. Jane's youngest daughter and her husband have moved to Florence (about 15 minutes away), and Jane is thrilled.

Jo also chose the lifestyle of wife and mother rather than a career path. She married her high school sweetheart, who became a dentist, and they have two children. Mypath was less traditional. When I was in college, my father told me a secret: from when I was very young, my mother always thought that I was going to be a missionary. I was not particularly surprised at hearing this. The notion seemed to fit my self-concept. I had seen very early on that I was telescoping to some place farther than my family knew.

My mother doesn't remember the missionary story. Recently, when I asked her about it, she told me: "I thought you could be anything you wanted to be—even a farmer! I hoped and was willing for my children to do whatever God's will was." As it turned out, all the same, the life of a missionary is not far off from what I do today. Someone recently asked me, "If money were not an issue, and there were no other barriers, what would your profession be?" I thought I would like to be funded by some foundation to be an anthropologist. I would travel around to obscure islands and far-off countries to study the people. I would stay a couple of years and then move on. Fascination with other cultures and lifestyles has been an interest of mine for as long as I can remember.

I always had an appreciation for the different. It has developed into an affinity for eclecticism, whether as a style of decorating or the approach I use to do my work. It took only a little encouragement toward the unfamiliar for me to be fascinated with how being different and having differences make life more real and meaningful.

Timmonsville was such a provincial, circumscribed world: 50 percent white, 50 percent black, one Jewish family, one Syrian family, and one Catholic couple. The Catholic couple would, on occasion, come to our church and sing. It was a very big deal. You wouldn't miss that—Catholics singing in a Baptist church!

My exposure to other geographies had been extremely limited even by the time I got to college, because my father simply had no inclination to travel. But I always knew I would travel. That was never in question.

As it turned out, I stayed in South Carolina to attend Winthrop, the women's college my mother had attended. Early on, because of my love of athletics and my competitive spirit, I thought I might become a physical education instructor. But a kidney problem (diagnosed in early high school and later found to be insignificant) caused me to look at other possibilities.

I was astonished by the diversity of women I found at Winthrop. It was where I met difference for the first time, or at least where I first noticed it. Drawn to the differences among people in a powerful way, I studied sociology as a natural consequence.

Two influential professors at Winthrop offered their opposing views about what I should do professionally. My sociology professor argued against social work and in favor of a more academic route. Dr. Dorothy Jones, my professor for social work, said, "Open up your horizons." She was my favorite college professor and my first woman mentor. She thought it would be wonderful for me to study about people and to have the experience of going to the University of California at Berkeley. There were many options, she advised. The social work field was very broad.

I imagined that I could work in administration, or in recreation, mental health, hospitals, or corporations. It seemed like a very big world out there. But I knew that the activism and experimentation going on at Berkeley in the late 1960s were beyond what my small-town, Southern, conservative background could handle.

I got a stack of booklets about accredited schools of social work and tossed them on the floor. One orange and black one jumped out at me: the University of Hawaii. I opened it up and said, "This is it!" I also considered Tulane and Columbia, but I felt that the University of Hawaii would be a culturally different experience for me—and I wouldn't have to freeze in the winter.

I told Dr. Jones, who understood and thought it was a great idea. No one else seemed to "get it," though. The college president told me that going to the University of Hawaii was fine if I just wanted to play. My parents thought Tulane would be better. With her lips kind of pinched and puckered, Mother told me it "was plenty far off enough." My wanting very much to go to Hawaii didn't make sense to my parents, and I didn't know how to tell them. Their disincentive was to declare that they would support me at Tulane or some other closer school, but not at the University of Hawaii. So I checked into the South Carolina Department of Mental Health stipends, which said *any* accredited school in the United States—and that included Hawaii.

Once I was in Hawaii, my parents did help me. They even made what was for them a heroic trip. The first and last time they ever boarded an airplane was to fly to Hawaii to visit me in graduate school in the late 1960s. My mother said to my father, "I'm going. You can come or not, but I'm going." He got on the plane. It was a miracle.

Graduate School and Marriage

*It was during this period of my life that I began
to acknowledge my fascination with cultural
diversity, as evidenced in my marriage and
choice of graduate schools. It was this preoccupation with the differences among people that
would create such resonance with the Satir
philosophy when I finally learned about it.*

I did choose social work and had a definite agenda in deciding to
do my graduate work in Hawaii. I wanted a very different cultural
experience—an early echo, perhaps, of my fantasy of escaping to
an island to do anthropological research.

The value of differences is a basic tenet in the Satir System.
For me, it was more than just a valuing. It was a delight, an infatu-
ation. For example, two books I recently read and really liked were
The Education of Little Tree and *The Joy Luck Club*—both about
other cultures. These books speak about universals, and they take
me home and to someplace else all at the same time.

It was in Hawaii that I came face to face with being a South-
erner. One of the Japanese women heard me say something about
having a date. She asked me, "Did you bring letters of introduction
to meet men? Isn't that the way Southern ladies meet men?" She
also wanted to know if I used a parasol at the beach. I learned later
that *Gone with the Wind* had been playing just before school started.

I went to see *In the Heat of the Night*. When it was over, I
didn't open my mouth for fear that everyone would say, "There's
one!" My Southern accent was very foreign to the islanders. I ran
into a lot of prejudice about "Southerners" and went through a
period of self-consciousness about it. It was my first real experience of being a minority—conscious about differences and how
much of it I wanted to expose or disclose.

Within two to three weeks of my arrival at the University of Hawaii in Honolulu, the faculty decided that I was as much a foreign student as the students from Japan. I was told to change "pods" (the groups to which we were assigned for companionship and to ease the "ice breaking" during orientation). They put me with the students from Japan, Korea, the Philippines, and Samoa.

Katie Tyson was my first field placement instructor. She was powerful. She wanted us to meet our client families and let them know about the upcoming eligibility review (a standard social work survey to determine eligibility for benefits). I went to a highrise apartment building, where I met my first client, a young mother. Inviting me in, she asked, "Aren't you going to ask me the usual questions?" I told her that I didn't know the questions yet. She did, so she led me through them, and I wrote down her answers. That amounted to the eligibility review.

Katie Tyson said it was the best report she'd ever read. She passed it on to the second-year students as a model of rapport building and how to work with clients. She knew that I didn't have a problem with power, condescension, or prejudice toward my clients. This was very compatible with what I learned later from Virginia. (Not that Katie was a fan. My husband and I used to go up to her house on Mount Tamales and drink brandy and play classical music. She told me, "I don't have much truck with Virginia Satir." Years later someone told me they had seen Katie, who had asked about me: "Is she still hanging around with that Ginny Satir?" The only time Virginia bombed was in Hawaii. I always wondered if Katie had put some kind of Hawaiian voodoo on it.)

It was in Hawaii that I met my husband-to-be, J. D. Pickering. Our first meeting was something out of either the movies or a comic book. One night I was at a party in this apartment filled with people, and out of nowhere, from across the room, comes this voice that says, "I want her!" I could see a finger going up and pointing toward me. Then, this handsome, dark man walks over, looks at me, picks me up, throws me across his shoulder, and heads out the door and down the stairs of the building. He carried me across the sidewalk and put me into his MGB convertible through the window. Then, getting in the car and rolling up the windows, he said, "My name's J.D. Pickering. What's yours?"

I was frightened and astonished. Our friends from the party were all standing at the door watching and calling for us to come back. I introduced myself. When J.D. asked me where I wanted to go, I told him "back to the party."

"Okay," he said. He drove the car around the block and back into his original parking space. We sat on the grass, leaning against a tree, and talked until the early morning. I fell in love with him, his potential, and my fantasies of him.

His Christian name had been Jerome Damian. His legal name was Jay Dee, but he preferred J.D., which he later surmised must be some kind of karmic evidence that he should become an attorney (*Juris Doctor*).

J.D. had an alcoholic father and had lived a very transient childhood in California, moving from town to town and school to school. He served during the Vietnam War, and when we met, J.D. was a photographer in Army Intelligence. He was also Mexican-American and Catholic—a religious background that especially worried my Baptist father, who feared that J.D. might give away all our money to the Pope.

There was something very freeing about J.D. for me: he opened up an appreciation for the aesthetic. He was a nonconformist, an artist type, very intelligent, and very creative.

After I finished my graduate work for my master's in social work, I moved back to South Carolina to work in a mental health clinic. That had been my agreement with the South Carolina Department of Mental Health, which had given me my full scholarship for graduate school. J.D. returned to California.

He and I soon discovered we missed each other too much, however. We married in December 1969, and after a month together, J.D. returned to California for the last semester of his undergraduate program. Then he rejoined me in South Carolina—yet another new territory for him to try to fit into. He taught school until his temper got the better of him. One day in class, he threw a book at a surly student and nearly lost his job. At that point, J.D. knew he didn't have the patience to be a teacher.

Meanwhile, after two years at the mental health center, I wanted to do postgraduate studies in a special program in community psychiatry at the University of North Carolina. So, we moved to Chapel Hill. Once in North Carolina, J.D. decided he wanted to go to law school, and he was accepted at the law school of prestigious Duke University. As I put him through law school, I got involved in the possibilities of new forms of therapies. My career began to involve more and more travel; he practiced law and raised goats at the old Girl Scout camp we bought outside Chapel Hill.

In time, we grew apart, and the relationship wasn't working anymore. Things that once seemed like small differences between us had escalated to major problems. J.D. was a slob. When we went down to South Carolina, he would look like somebody I dragged in off the streets. (Actually, at that time, nobody on the streets of Timmonsville even looked like J.D!) He was out of his culture. He didn't get his taxes done. He had no ambition; I thought of him as pretty lazy.

The last straw came when he had been in California, and I had been away. He and I returned home to the Girl Scout camp, and for the second time, the goats were in the house. The door was wide open, and it looked as though they had been in there for a couple of days.

J.D. never gave me a sense of security that he could take care of me—or himself, for that matter. I had been on him for the longest time to get the goats fenced in. People sometimes called the courtroom where J.D. was practicing law to have the judge tell him that traffic was stopped in front of our house because of the goats. We were in therapy at the time, but I just couldn't handle it any longer.

One day, I picked up a few of the papers lying in the middle of the floor and said "I am leaving. I don't know if or when I'll return." I went to stay at a mutual friend's house. J.D. went there, too. Two days later, I moved out and never went back to him. We divorced in December 1980, and J.D. moved to California. He has since remarried and has two children. I always thought he needed someone who would really come down on him to get his act together, but a "nagging wife" was the last thing I wanted to be.

The Years with Satir

Virginia Satir took me beyond
places I could go with my parents.

I heard about the work of Virginia Satir from a colleague at the mental health center in South Carolina. I was involved in patient education, clinical work, management, various outreach projects, and program planning. Otis Robbins, a staff psychologist, had known Virginia for a long time and was one of the hundred or so people chosen to join the International Human Resources Learning Network (IHLRN) at its first meeting in Mexico in 1969. One day, he said, "There's somebody you've got to meet." As it turned out, Virginia was coming to Charleston, South Carolina for a two-day workshop.

I drove to Charleston and got there early so I could be in the front row of the audience of 200 or so at the Medical College. In the middle of her presentation, Virginia called for volunteers to do a family simulation. My hand shot up and my butt flew off the seat before I knew what was happening.

I don't really remember how the stage was set for the role play, but I was the "mother," and probably one of our "kids" was having problems. What I do remember about the simulation is suddenly seeing myself on the path to becoming a martyr—a bitter, depressed, unfulfilled, and unsatisfied person. I had never had that experience before. It was as if Virginia saw me and I felt me. And the more I felt me, the more of me she saw, and the more of me I felt. To use Virginia's lingo, here I was, this super-reasonable person, pretty tightly wrapped about my feelings.

Something opened up for me in that moment of connection. During that role play, Virginia somehow touched me in a way that I felt seen, and there was this path out—both from the role I was playing on stage and from what could have become my life.

I spoke to her after the conference and mentioned our mutual friend, Otis Robbins. Later that year, when Otis attended the IHLRN meeting in Mexico, Virginia asked him if he had any suggestions for future meetings. He told Virginia that the meeting had been a success, but one thing was missing: "Jean Pickering needed to be here." Reportedly, Virginia remembered me from the Charleston meeting and said, "Let's make sure she's here next time."

Joining the Satir Family

My trip to Mexico for the second annual IHLRN meeting was my first trip out of the United States. I was one of the younger people at the conference and had the feeling that everyone else had known Virginia forever. Many of the people I met at that conference became my most significant friends and colleagues. One of those friends, Maria Gomori, invited me to a month-long workshop she and Virginia were planning for late 1974 in Canada.

I thought, "What am I getting into?" But when leaving Mexico, I was sure that I wanted to go to Canada. I knew it was right. I would need a month off from my duties at the mental health center, and I wanted leave with pay. If there was any flak, I would quit my job. It wasn't that I didn't like my job—I loved it. I was just that clear.

I got the leave with pay, no questions asked. From that point on, my connection with Virginia and its intrinsic value to me, both professionally and personally, was never in question. She quickly became my mentor and remained so until her death in 1988.

In many ways, Virginia's genius (and certainly my attraction to her and her work) was her ability to explicate universals that went beyond culture and time. She said, "Each of us is unique and though we come together from our common ground, we grow from our differences." She believed people's yearnings offered more light for illuminating human behavior than assessments of who was right or wrong, good or bad. My personal experience and longings were immediately validated. She said things I had never heard but knew to be true. It was as though my inner thoughts and feelings had found a spokesperson, an advocate. I knew immediately she was to be my teacher.

The month-long workshop in Canada was an intense experience for me. It included what Virginia named Family Reconstructions. In this group experience, participants role-play different members of an individual's family of origin—including grandparents, aunts, uncles, siblings, and parents. They enact family events according to the information the client provides and what unfolds from the role-players. The technique gives permission for the client to see his or her relatives in situations before and after his or her entrance into the family system, to witness what may have happened, or to act out what could have happened but did not. The healing effect and outpouring of grief from old wounds and losses can be dramatic. As might be obvious, this kind of theatrical and emotionally charged role play requires an excellent director, skilled in the pitfalls and power of evoking such a potential show of emotions.

When I arrived, my friend Maria Gomori said I should get Virginia to do my Family Reconstruction. Maria said, "She will not do everybody. You must see her immediately and tell her that you want yours done." She hounded me to talk to Virginia. I was scared and excited at the same time.

I finally marshaled the nerve to ask Virginia. She received me in her room early one morning and agreed to lead my Family Reconstruction. Then about a week passed and she still hadn't gotten to me, so I went back to her room and told her I didn't want her to do it. I would do it myself. I asked her if she ever knew of anyone who had directed his or her own Family Reconstruction.

Ever open to new possibilities, Virginia admitted she had not seen it done, but she supposed it was possible. She told me she believed in me, that I could figure out how to do my Family Reconstruction myself. Maria thought I had lost my mind, and I panicked. I realized I couldn't do it and went back to Virginia on my knees.

Once again, Virginia agreed with good humor to lead the role play. One powerful episode came when she had me give my "mother" (played by Maria) a foot massage. It opened up the world of touch, of demonstrative affection that had not happened for me in my family. Watching the other reconstructions was also potent for me. The only family I had known intimately was the one in which I grew up. Now I saw my experience validated in the different stories.

By the last week of the month-long workshop, I believed I had finally gotten it together and understood what all this was about. I went to Virginia's room again, this time to declare that Satir work was all about the universality of emotionality.

Virginia said, "Yeah." And she looked at me as if to say, "Now what?"

I had come through the month feeling absolutely fine about who I was. I felt as though I was in my natural environs at last. We had had a powerful common experience that left us with a shared language and beliefs about being human, an understanding of our yearnings and motivations and how change happens. I was already going through separation anxiety. I told Virginia that the group needed another month.

Patient but honest, she replied, "Well, you know, after a month, I feel like I have pretty much shot my wad."

"Precisely," I said. "If we kept going, you'd be right in there with us, on the same level. What do you think would happen?"

Intrigued by the idea, she told me to propose a format for another month-long, sometime later, perhaps in Mexico. Plans fell through for that meeting, and I tried to organize a workshop to be held North Carolina. I wrote Virginia a long letter about the design I had in mind: some supervised training, an applied practicum, and having some clients in. I felt well connected in North Carolina and believed I could pull it off.

She wrote back that she wanted to build a new organization around my idea and that the first meeting of the group would be in California. A core group of about 40 people from all over the world who had significant training and experience with the Satir approach joined Virginia in giving birth to Avanta.* Part of the intent was for these individuals to become sufficiently competent to take referrals from Virginia's own practice, which had grown larger than she could manage herself.

---

*Some years later, the Avanta group began holding month-long trainings with Virginia "on the hill" in Crested Butte, Colorado. These "process communities" (later called the Satir International Training Institute) became a regular summer workshop open to the public. Virginia was Director of Training, and the staff included six to nine others from Avanta.

Early on, Virginia attempted to empower a governing body for Avanta, and we formed a membership committee. To that point, a person became a member by asking to be a member, or as the result of a spontaneous act on Virginia's part. I agreed to chair the committee under some pressure that "I was the one to do it," and on a handshake from Virginia and agreement at a board meeting that she would not invite new members without at least telling me.

At the first European IHLRN meeting in France, I met new Avanta members I knew nothing about. At the Avanta meeting, I confronted Virginia about "breaking her word." For two days, she did not speak or interact with me. All I got was "icy eyes."

During those two days, Nechama Levy—a very wise, elderly Israeli colleague and friend, and a grandmotherly type—gave me a big lecture on how I had been "out of place" to talk to Virginia that way. She said that Virginia could do what ever she wanted to do.

Joan Winter also took me aside to say, "You're more naive than I thought! Did you really think Virginia could abide by that agreement?"

I remember the discomfort of having Virginia so disapprove. I called her on the evening of the second day to ask if I could have some time with her. She told me that she was busy, but I assured her that it wouldn't take long. I was shaking in my boots.

When I arrived, she went into the bathroom, and I followed her. I said, "I came to apologize. I feel like I kicked you. I did not mean to hurt you, and what can I do for us to make up?"

She looked at me briefly, this time without the icy eyes, and said, "Sometimes that's what I need."

Then, she gave me her feedback on me. She said, "One thing I like about you is that you are sometimes as soft as cotton, and other times as hard as steel. And you can kick like a steer." We hugged and never discussed it again. I was thrilled to be back in her good graces. I never again challenged her in any kind of public or group setting.

The ingredients for what became my current professional practice were coming together. The Canada experience with Virginia gave me the yeast, the ingredient that had been missing in my work: personal emotional freedom. Once that got in with the rest, I could really rise.

At the mental health center, my work had already demonstrated my innate gifts in a variety of therapeutic contexts with a wide array of clients. I had dealt with school phobia, and black–white teacher–student relations; I'd worked with couples and families, autistic children and developmentally disabled ones—whoever walked in the door. Both my therapeutic successes and my co-workers' praise strongly validated my work.

I didn't realize it at the time, but the variety of those experiences would stand me in good stead as I learned more and more from Virginia and as I began to take her technology into new situations and contexts as a young pioneer for the Satir System.

Along with my growing involvement with Satir's work, I had begun working with the National Training Laboratories (NTL), a more orthodox, traditional, experiential education organization. NTL was more acceptable to my mind than what was happening on the West Coast through Esalen.) I traveled to Bethel, Maine to participate in NTL workshops on power, organizational change, human relations training, and small-group process. I had begun to believe that the world would not be changed just by psychotherapy, the one-on-one process. Group and systems work intrigued me more.

I was invited to join the faculty in the Advanced Training Program in Mental Health Administration at the National Institute of Mental Health Staff College in Washington, DC. There, I began conducting workshops on team building, management effectiveness, preventing staff burnout, and other systems issues for mental health directors from across the United States. Soon I was invited to conduct such workshops with clinicians and administrators in mental health centers across the country. I was applying the Satir method, in effect, to teams of mental health workers whose jobs were to provide the same kinds of therapies to their clients.

In 1975, I was elected President of the North Carolina Group Behavior Society and began my brief but enriching experience in academia. For five years, I taught at the School of Social Work at the University of North Carolina. In 1980, I launched my own business, Innersystem Services, which continues to serve as the umbrella for most of my work with individuals, groups, families, and organizations. Teaching and clinical work seemed familiar and very natural to me, but adding work with the corporate sector challenged my creativity in new ways.

In the late 1970s, Virginia also invited me to participate in longitudinal study of the effectiveness of three modalities of therapy with juveniles and their families. Through a grant awarded to the Family Institute of Virginia in Richmond, this study compared and contrasted the therapeutic techniques of Murray Bowen, Jay Haley, and Virginia Satir. She invited me to work as liaison between the team of Satir therapists, the Family Institute, and the community service providers. As community coordinator, I worked with the social workers, probation officers, family members, judges, and other court officials. This let me observe the Satir System at work as never before. By asking me to take this role, Virginia seemed to be guiding me and putting me next to her in an "airport control tower." I couldn't have been in a better position.

Recently, a faculty member of the Satir Institute of the Southeast asked what I thought Virginia saw in me that allowed her to trust me so much. I said I thought Virginia saw me as "good help." I knew how to step into a situation, not cause too much ripple or ruckus, see what was happening, and pitch in with something positive and constructive. She relied on me for all kinds of things, from helping her pack her personal belongings after a summer in Crested Butte to giving her impromptu exercise designs which she carried out in workshops and at Avanta meetings.

Virginia taught me to trust my "wisdom box," as she would say. She was convinced that we all have the capacity to know vastly more than our usual conscious minds indicate. I remember one time when she was in Chapel Hill and decided to have her hair done. It was kind of a last minute thing, so she didn't have an appointment and had to settle for finding a salon through the yellow pages that could take her on short notice. Arriving at the salon, we were greeted by a young and very nervous girl who was obviously a trainee as a beautician. Virginia was pretty particular about her hair, and the prospect of putting herself in the shaking hands of this youngster visibly disturbed her.

So, Virginia did what Virginia did best. While the young woman went to work on her hairdo, Virginia went to work on the young woman's self-esteem. She coached that girl to deliver beyond her best and somehow, together, they got through it.

Putting Down Roots

Sometimes Virginia helped me resolve things without even knowing I was pondering something. I think that is one of the powers (and traps!) of strongly felt mentorships. Transference and countertransference can be a quiet force, moving and shaping one's insides without much noise at all.

I remember one delightful morning with Virginia at her home in Menlo Park, California in the spring of 1981. On that damp gray morning, we both agreed that a fire would take some of the chill out of the air. With Virginia, there was always something for me to learn around the next conversational bend. This time it was teaching me how to make newspaper kindling rolls. She laid out a page of newspaper and folded a corner into a strip about two inches wide. Folding the rest of the page accordion style or just folding it over on itself, she then made a big knot with it and pulled tight. (Actually, Virginia was skilled enough to make two knots.) In what she called her "cuddle room," we stoked up the little stove with the kindling rolls. Virginia sat in her cane-back rocking chair while we talked about one thing and another. I took in the joy she seemed to be experiencing relaxing in her home.

In the midst of my own success and the increasing demand for my services, I began feeling that something was missing in my life. Traveling as a consultant, I had gotten spoiled. People took care of me. Then I went home to find stuff in the fridge that had turned green, and I had to take my own clothes to the dry cleaners.

It wasn't that I wanted to give up the travel, but I'd been doing a lot of it. That year I'd been out of the state more than 50 percent of the time. My life was actually beginning to look like Virginia's. She had a house, but she was rarely there. Her home was wherever she was. There was a loneliness about that kind of life that really scared me. When I left Virginia and her house and returned to my apartment, I suddenly realized that I had lost my root system. My friends were shrinking to a handful of people. I wanted roots. I wanted a home to cuddle in, a nest to rest in, and a partner with whom to share my life. ☆

By this time, I'd met Carol, who had finished her master's degree at the School of Social Work at the University of North Carolina (UNC) in Chapel Hill. Earlier, when she had looked over the faculty and course list, searching for an elective to complete her degree requirements, she had had a strong impulse to take my class on consultation. And once in the classroom, she knew her instinct had been correct; she found herself immediately drawn to the instructor. By the end of that course, she knew she wanted to get to know me better. She did so two years later.

Carol grew up in Gadsden, Alabama—a town much larger than Timmonsville (population: 50,000), but with similar community values. She had been to college at Jacksonville State University, earning a bachelor's in secondary education, and was married and divorced after seven years. She was an outspoken, feisty, and sometimes hot-tempered activist. By the time she met me, she had spent a great deal of energy organizing and lobbying for the passage of the Equal Rights Amendment in North Carolina. She had also served as Coordinator of Special Projects for the North Carolina Governor's Council on the Status of Women.

After Carol's graduation from the School of Social Work, she invited me and another friend to go hear Marilyn French, the incendiary author of *The Women's Room*, who was speaking in Chapel Hill. Carol introduced me to feminism. In fact, we spent a lot of time, early on, arguing about it—my ideas of humanism versus her stand on feminism. As it turned out, being with Carol was the beginning of my claiming more of myself as a woman.

It was also the beginning of a change in lifestyle that neither Carol nor I had seriously considered before, at least not in the context of a committed relationship. Carol picked me up from the airport after the visit to Virginia's. On the way back to my apartment, I proposed that we make a home together. After a couple of weeks of persistent persuasion, she agreed. A few weeks later, I found the perfect house: with a wrap-around porch and woods on two sides. I got Carol's approval, bought it, and moved in along with her in July 1981.

Being in a nontraditional relationship forces me to be clearer and stronger in myself. It also puts particular stresses on other relationships. For me, it was always the question: who needs to know about this? Privacy in a therapist's life is, by nature, a tricky question. For Carol, a certain vigilance about personal privacy was part of her public position (she soon became the director of the Campus Y at UNC, a job requiring that she counsel and guide undergraduates).

Carol had studied with Virginia in British Columbia and served with me as co-sponsor of a Satir workshop held in North Carolina. When I told Virginia about my relationship with Carol, her only comment was to express her hope that Carol would not come between us and our work. Later, while I was driving Virginia to the airport after her visit to my mother's home in South Carolina, I asked her advice on how to tell Mother about Carol and me. Virginia said, "You don't have to say anything. She knows. At some level, she knows."

The question stayed with me, though, and I kept asking people's advice. At a subsequent planning meeting of Crested Butte trainers, Virginia put me with Gerhard Lenz as the only dyad; she assigned everyone else to work in triads. I wondered at the time, "Why me?" I then had a great experience. And when I asked his advice, he said to me, "How can you not tell your mother?"

Of course, I did tell Mother. She put her hands on my shoulders and said, "I love you." I asked if she wanted something to read about lesbian relationships, but she said she had seen and read enough. She said, "Just don't be on the Phil Donahue show."

Carol and I had created a unique and sweet family, and I was really enjoying my new home life. I will never forget Virginia's intervention into one of our family crises with our wonderful dog Rebel. We got an angry telephone call one morning from a neighbor whom we didn't know but who obviously had come to know Rebel. She was pretty upset about Rebel getting into her trash can. Virginia, feeling a special affection for Rebel and probably seeing our "oh, my God—what do we do?" looks, suggested we all go to meet the neighbor. Together, we could assist Rebel in learning that his behavior was not acceptable.

Carol and Rebel sat in the car's back seat, and I drove as Virginia laid out her ideas of how we should approach this matter. When we arrived at the neighbor's, Rebel didn't want to get out of the car. Nor, it seemed, did the neighbor want to come out of her house. (We had decided not to ask permission for the visit. Since the woman had just called, Virginia thought it would be fine to head on over.) Finally, we got her to open the door and we introduced ourselves. She had, of course, already met Rebel, and she didn't seem too happy to see him.

Virginia began to explain that she was sure that Rebel didn't understand the impact of his behavior and that he was a very bright dog and could learn to be more thoughtful. The lady looked puzzled but did not shoo us off. Virginia went on to say that we could all walk over to the trash cans along with Rebel and discuss the matter with him. If we all told him in a firm and loving way that he was to never bother the trash again, she was certain he would get the message.

We all followed Virginia over to the trash cans. Rebel's head was down, and he was pretty sure something bad was about to happen. We all told him, each in our own tone and words, never to get into the lady's trash again. By the time we left, the neighbor was apologizing and telling us what a wonderful dog Rebel was. Virginia thanked her for assisting us in training Rebel, and we bid farewell. We never got another call from her or anybody else about turned-over trash cans.

The roots I put down with Carol were what I had been looking for. She's a good partner—a good fit. As our relationship grew over the years, we decided to affirm our commitment to each other publicly. Virginia, of course, was the person we wanted to lead us in a nontraditional ritual and celebration of our bond, and she agreed.

At the end of a summer institute in Crested Butte in 1985, surrounded by many of our "brothers and sisters" in the Satir family, Virginia led the group in an affirmation of the commitment and love between us.

I found out later that the day had been something of a stretch for Virginia. I know in her head she believed in our relationship and could validate it in her mind, but she needed some reassurance the night before the celebration. Virginia talked it over with my close friend Maria Gomori, who would carry the relationship rings in the ceremony. Maria assured her that she was doing the right thing.

Choosing to live in a nontraditional relationship has been another piece of the puzzle for me as I have come to terms with my own identity and my penchant for diversity. Acknowledging in myself what a large portion of society would condemn as too big a difference—a lifestyle that even Virginia Satir had to search in herself to accept—has required another leap that can only create a deeper empathy for those who are "other" in terms of ability, background, or cultural norms.

Virginia's Last Days

For the summer of 1988, Carol and I had planned a trip to Europe—a long overdue vacation. My work had continued at a brisk pace; I was ready for a rest. Carol had just finished law school,* and I had decided not to participate in what had become Avanta's annual month-long summer training institute in Crested Butte.

---

*I don't know what it is about me that compels my partners to go to law school. Neither J.D. nor Carol were lawyers when I met them. If something ever happens to Carol and I am on the hunt for a new partner, I plan to wear a button that says, "Beware: you may have to go to law school!"

Then, in June, came a phone call came from Avanta's president, Marilyn Peers. Virginia was ill. She had come back from a trip to the Soviet Union with stomach problems. I had seen her that spring in Toronto for an annual Avanta meeting at Geneva Park, where she dismissed her discomfort as the result of food and the stress of the long trip to Russia. But by June, Virginia knew she was too ill to serve as director of training at Crested Butte. She had asked the Avanta council to invite me in her stead. The diagnosis was not yet definite, but the doctors suspected cancer.

I talked it over with Carol. There was no question: I would go to Colorado. Meanwhile, I needed to call Virginia and hear her expectations first-hand. Her voice already reflected the battle that was to take her life. She told me, "I had to leave [Crested Butte]. I'm feeling too bad to be there. You're the closest thing I've got to an heir apparent. Can you cover for me?"

I stopped breathing, denied her claim, and told her I would be happy to help her. I offered to come to California, but she said, "Maybe later." Then, "I need you in Crested Butte."

I told her I would be there if she would give me phone consultation. She agreed, but her energy never allowed for those consultations. It was a good summer, but a tough one. Some days, we'd get information that Virginia was better and getting a new treatment; other days, the news would be bad. She did send me messages of encouragement after reviewing some of the videotapes we sent her. Her messages indicated approval and confidence, and that was what I needed from her.

Following the month-long workshop in Colorado, Carol and I flew to California to be with Virginia. It turned out to be a good week. Virginia had just given up her medications—some 70 to 90 pills per day. The doctors had given up on her, so she was left with only alternative therapies. We were with her on what might have been her best and worst days. Going off the medication had created a temporary improvement. On her best day, she asked Carol and me to go through her mail with her, and she wanted to see a funny movie, so we rented a Groucho Marx film. Virginia also wanted to see a recently received video made especially for her by Jean Houston, an international leader in the human potential movement. It was a video of Houston talking to and about Virginia. Virginia hadn't felt up to watching it, but that night she said she needed a lift. In the video, Jean talks about the impact Virginia made on the world. Houston once came across a tribe in Africa doing a family conference. When she asked how they knew these techniques, the tribal leaders said, "Satir."

I could see and feel the shift taking place in Virginia that night as she watched the video. She was so thrilled that Jean acknowledged her as her mentor and teacher. Part of the puzzle of Virginia is that she often did not recognize the impact she had on people. It kept her human.

About the fourth day we were there, some of the high was gone. That night, Virginia couldn't get to sleep. When she needed assistance, she'd ring a small brass bell that Becky Spitzer had loaned her; I'd help her to the bathroom or come in and read to her. On that very bad night, as I had done each night, I read from *The Course In Miracles*. Still agitated and anxious, she could not sleep. She was, I think, dealing with losing the battle, losing control. She kept saying, "I don't understand what's happening."

I helped her into the living room, read a few more pages to her, and then gave her a foot massage—the same expression of affection and connection that, so many years before, she had suggested that I perform for my "mother," Maria Gomori, in the role play at my Family Reconstruction.

I asked Virginia, "Do you feel scared?" She said yes. I asked her if she wanted me to stay with her, and she said yes. I slept beside Virginia on that difficult night, which turned out to be the beginning of her final physical decline. When we left, I told Virginia I would see her in a few weeks. Another Avanta meeting was scheduled for September in California. Just before then, when we heard that Virginia's condition had continued to worsen, I called her to say we would come early. Virginia said she didn't plan to be there by the weekend.

When Carol and I got to Virginia's that Thursday night, she was clearly on her way to another place. She asked all of us not to have our tears in her room, and she also didn't want to be touched.

At first, Virginia's unwillingness to be touched seemed very peculiar. She was the pioneering therapist who held her clients' faces tenderly in her hands to teach them about the value of such a connection when words failed. I began to realize, though, from the little bit she said—and she didn't say much at all—that she wanted to go on, and she didn't want us holding her back. Virginia was very kinesthetic. Touching her was like bringing her to where we were, and she didn't want that. She wanted us to help her go home.

Virginia died on Saturday, September 10, 1988, in the late afternoon. On Sunday, her circle of friends, family, and colleagues gathered for champagne and a ceremony to celebrate her passing. Years earlier, Virginia told Carol that when she died, she wanted her friends to have champagne and a party.

I think sometimes her life was taken away from her. She planned her personal appearances three and five years in advance, and she hired someone to manage her schedule. But with her death, Virginia took a lot of control. She didn't let anyone take her death away from her. I really felt like she taught me about dying. We just stayed present with her where she was.

☆   ☆

☆

☆

Becoming Myself

I said many times after Virginia's death that I was not prepared. As I look back, I can now say that I must have been. My life is too full and rich for me to assume that I didn't know what to do, how to do my life's work, without the living support of my teacher.

Committed mentorships can rival parental modeling. One of my most memorable experiences was when Virginia came to South Carolina for a workshop. She stayed at my mother's home, and I was very appreciative of Mother's being open to Virginia's visit. I walked into the kitchen while they were chatting. Rummaging around in her plastic bag of pills, Virginia was talking about the Wisconsin farm. I saw and felt the contact between the two of them. At some level, the connection was distant, competitive, both of them checking each other out. I stopped breathing, turned, and walked out of the room.

Often, it wasn't so much anything Virginia said but what I felt from her and with her as we rocked or talked or did whatever we happened to be doing. When she died, I came face to face with the fact that I had taken her in more deeply than I realized. I had known about learning that I don't have to be like my mother. Now I was learning that I would have to go through the same thing regarding Virginia— taking her "clothes" off me.

Soon after Virginia died, I stood in for her at the European Congress on Mental Health in European Families, held in Prague. A very wise older psychologist from London, Josephine Lomaz-Simpson, had known Virginia and was one of the people who attended my workshop. She later wrote in her newsletter:

> I sat next to Jean McLendon at the Opening Ceremony. She and I both watched the autobiographical film on the life of Virginia Satir to

> complete my own mourning. I attended her special workshop with a
> group of Czech professionals. But like Maureen Lipman's portrayal of
> Joyce Grenfell's *"Rejoice,"* I feel Jean has introjected Virginia Satir
> and it will take time for Jean to become herself.

Josephine was correct. With my mother, there is also the powerful
biological connection, but I will always have these two models for
being a woman embedded deeply in my soul.

Releasing the Mantle

When my father died, his last words to me were: "Take care of
Mama and Jane." When Virginia told me I was the closest thing
she had to an "heir apparent," I heard her ask me to "keep the
work going." In both cases, I accepted a request. In both cases, I
felt a responsibility. Over the years since those losses, I have come
to know that my work has to be about me, something I'm doing. I'm
no longer looking for a release from the responsibility nor checking to see if I'm doing it right. Their requests were concerns they
had rather than commitments that I have.

My stint as training director for Avanta's Process Community
at Crested Butte the summer before Virginia's death had been a
stretch for me and also for my brothers and sisters: one, because
Virginia was sick and we were frightened; and two, because to have
me acting in her capacity created in people both the desire to support me and normal feelings of jealousy and competition—all the
things one would see in any family in which roles are suddenly
shifting.

I served in the same role again the next summer. For me, it
was like carrying precious china on a slick silver tray over unpredictable and dangerous terrain. Avanta's organizational structure

had developed around Virginia because of who she was. It fit Virginia and her time, but it did not fit me. We all made an effort to hold things together, but some things had to fall apart.

It was not my china and not my tray. It had become too heavy, both in my body and in my spirit. I had faced angry, resentful, and jealous "siblings"; received undue praise and adoration; lost too much sleep; and grown too distant from my own inner self and life. I had to say, "Look, I can't carry it."

That fall, in my home in Chapel Hill, I conducted a board meeting for the newly formed Satir Institute of the Southeast (SIS). Virginia had known about this fledging group of therapists who were establishing a regional center for Satir training and consultation. She had given the new organization her blessing at Geneva Park in Toronto, when I saw her immediately following her return from Russia.

Earlier on the morning of the board meeting, September 10, 1989, I had been out for a walk with P.J., our Dalmatian. As I crossed the dam of the nearby lake, I was filled with more spirit than usual. I felt uplifted, ebullient, and tearful. As I let myself cry, I felt myself believing that I had done all I could do to carry Virginia's mantle. And I sensed Virginia telling me that I had done enough.

I couldn't get home fast enough. I told Carol I had done what I needed to do for Virginia, and I was going to take back my life. The experience was of something being released from me.

Before the formal meeting later that morning, the institute's board members gathered on the screened porch and passed around photos of Virginia's gravesite in Crested Butte. I was preoccupied and did not register the anniversary of her death. We began our meeting, and during our check-in time, I shared that I felt released from a burden. I told the board that I felt more committed than ever

to the institute's goals and objectives, and that I wanted to focus
my energy on things close to home.

I remember people seemed happy that I felt so good about my
awakening, but mostly I remember being particularly ruffled at not
being able to get oriented to time. I kept fumbling through my calendar and asking, "What is today's date?" I couldn't keep the
number in my mind.

After we adjourned, I left with one of the board members. We
were flying to Arkansas, where I was to do some team-building
work at her father's company. In the Atlanta airport, I asked the
date again. My colleague said, "What is wrong with you? We've
been telling you all day! It is September 10th!"

At last I made the connection and burst into tears. I realized
that my denial around the anniversary of Virginia's death was also
connected to my experience that morning on the dam. Now the
dam had burst, so to speak. Had I been able to recognize the day
and acknowledge it, I probably would have been thinking about
how I could help the group do more of its grief work. Instead, I was
working through my own grief.

The next morning, I realized that I did not want to continue as
training director for the summer program in Crested Butte. I made
a couple of key phone calls, and when the words came out of my
mouth, they felt true, right, and good.

I continued working as a member of the Satir Learning Committee
(a committee of seven named in Virginia's will to steer Avanta, the
primary benefactor of her estate). Along with John Banmen and
Jane Gerber as Avanta's Training Directorate, I continued providing
strategic and administrative leadership for the Governing Council's
training programs. Both the committee and the directorate were
transitional structures and were phased out when the Governing
Council recovered its footing and vision. My participation in Avanta
is now more from the sidelines.

Virginia passed off two opportunities to me that continue in the same form they were over ten years ago. One is membership on the Learning Resource Council of the International Institute for the Study of Systems Renewal. Founded by Don Swartz, the institute is a nonprofit educational corporation to honor the lives and works of Gordan and Ronald Lippitt. This institute and Antioch University collaborate to offer a master's degree in Whole System Design (in the north and southwestern United States). My contribution is working with the students around a final workshop weekend on Leadership and Transformation.

The second opportunity is a nearly ten-year association with Jerry and Dani Weinberg. Unlike Don Swartz, the Weinbergs were Avanta members. When we received word via Avanta's executive administrator, Rochelle Ford, that Virginia hoped Jerry, Dani, and I would proceed with the development of a week-long leadership training program that she had agreed to do with the Weinbergs, we were not "gung ho." Were it not for Rochelle's strong, positive, and persuasive talks with us individually and collectively, I don't think we would have agreed to take on the project together. Until then, we were like distant cousins who would see each other at family reunions but never bothered to deepen each other's acquaintance. There just had not been a compelling reason or a strong enough attraction.

We three met and wondered out loud to each other about our reservations. To test the compatibility of our styles and skills, we agreed to facilitate a conflict-resolution meeting between Rochelle and the onsite Crested Butte coordinator. I recall thinking we seemed to operate differently externally while coming from similar internal places. I think Dani and Jerry felt something akin to this.

We also agreed to meet in Nebraska for a few days in the early fall to get planning underway for the Change-Shop. The Change-Shop was a "coming out" for me. In my early days of applying the

Satir System to organizational consulting while I was teaching at UNC, I had felt a lot of intimidation. No one else was using Satir in this kind of way. To "sell" it, I inserted the Satir beliefs into something already acceptable, such as the Blake/Mouton managerial model or Tuckman's group development work. Now, at the initial planning meeting, the Weinbergs and I decided against hiding under some other model. Wanting what would be most exciting and congruent for us, we went straight-out Satir. In tribute to Virginia, we developed the highly successful seven-day "Congruent Leadership Change-Shop: Creating the More Fully Human Organization." We now offer this program twice a year in Santa Fe.

Building Support
for the Transition

The first couple of years after Virginia's death were wobbly times for me. I had never before faced such uncertainty about my professional abilities. I had credited most of my many successes to what I had learned from my famous teacher. Prior to her death, I had accepted referrals from her and had pinch hit for her during other illnesses. Now, I was standing too much on guard over Virginia's china and silver tray. It was really only when I put the tray down that I reclaimed my own personal and professional stride.

The next couple of years were very busy. My stride, my pace, my rhythm, my breathing were returning in a significantly empowered way. My professional thirst for broad, almost anthropological experiences in the lives of individuals, families, groups, and organizations was almost insatiable. Fortunately my energy equaled my drive, and the people who cared about me shared my vision. I had three primary professional support groups who knew me, appreciated me, and understood that I had a mission.

They didn't necessarily understand where I was headed. Neither did I. Yet they did understand that I believed that what I was doing was important.

One of my supports was the Cuddle group. In the early days of Avanta, in many different contexts with Virginia, most of us were involved in intimate sharing with each other. As Avanta got off the ground, we were always working when we were together. We were changing the world, and there was no end to it.

These people were precious to me, my "chosen family," but my time with them was never quality time. That was not all right with me. I was looking for a primary group where I could feel seen and could stay in deeper contact. I wanted to build a group out of unanimous consensus. To start such a group with me, I approached Joan Winter. We decided to invite Ken Block to join us, and then the three of us decided who to invite to be the fourth member, and so on. We stopped at nine.

We held our first meeting in conjunction with an IHLRN meeting on the California coast. The real tension was that half the people said they would join if Virginia participated, and half said they would not. We wouldn't hide—couldn't hide—from Virginia. We designated Becky Spitzer to let Virginia know about the meeting, to get her blessings for us, and to share the belief and regret that Virginia would not have time to join us.

Two of our original members dropped out, and the rest of us decided to meet twice a year. We have been doing so now for nine years. Three are no longer members of Avanta. The only person we attempted to add since that initial group formed was Carol, and she turned us down.

There was not much we didn't know about each other. Cuddle was one of my better ideas. It came out of a need I had, a need everybody had. There was no persuasion, no selling. It just happened. Now, if Avanta and SIS went down, Cuddle would remain.

My second supportive group has been the Satir Institute of Southeast, Inc. (SIS). It began when several participants in the Module II program told Virginia that they wanted to continue their training. Virginia told them to negotiate something with me. Members of this small group came from Florida, West Virginia, Alabama, Arkansas, South Carolina, and North Carolina. I first agreed to meet with them in Chapel Hill, at my home office, in the fall of 1987. They later became the founding board members of SIS and, eventually, for the most part, its core faculty.

After our first meeting, I met with them every six weeks or so for a long weekend of personal and professional development. In 1988, we decided to bring in an external Avanta trainer and present a public workshop. I invited my dear friend Maria Gomori to be our first presenter.

That workshop was a smashing success, and the next fall we opened the training group to colleagues who we believed would contribute and who were hungry for the kind of experience we were creating. In the fall of 1990, we opened the training group to the public and accepted applications for enrollment. We were coming of age.

The third part of my support system started out as Champion, Kiel and McLendon, Management Consultants. In 1985, I joined two colleagues—Doug Champion and David Kiel—to found an organizational consulting firm. We were a great triad (although it did not last). After Doug Champion decided to leave the world of free-lance and return to something more stable, David and I continued on as Kiel, McLendon and Associates.

In 1991, we invited two new partners to join us. This might seem insignificant in terms of change dynamics, but for me, the time and energy required to reconfigure our method of operation was more than I could afford. Everything from the most mundane to the most significant issues seemed to need addressing. I think the firm suffered from my divided attention, as I continued to work with SIS as well as my private psychotherapy practice.

After talking with David, I wrote the partners a letter. It was clear to me that my soul energy was with SIS, I explained, and I had decided to leave. David and I remain colleagues, and he is now a regular guest faculty with the Satir System Performance Development Program.

I think it is true that there are seasons to one's life; for me, 1992 was a season of planting far and wide. Leaving the consulting firm was part of securing more land to sow. It was a year of travel and expansiveness. I moved the vision of my Satir work to another level, and I became strongly cathected to developing a human-potential retreat center. To put it mildly, I was engrossed—some would say crazy—with my desire to take the plunge into what I believed would be an artistic manifestation of a long-term dream.

I found the perfect piece of property (I believed at the time that it had found me) for the 106-acre Virginia M. Satir Lodge and Conference Center. As I wrote then, it was

> a place where people come to renew their spirit and relationships, a place where congruence can be learned and practiced, a place for family reunions, family camps, family theater, family reconstructions, strategic planning retreats for businesses and corporations, team building sessions, management development training, writing, movement, art and meditation retreats. Congruence requires caring not only for the self and others, but also the context. People trained in congruence are natural and effective care givers to our wounded world. They are activists and leaders who know the importance of starting within and close to home. At one level my dream is big, at another it merely represents a drop in the bucket.

Within nine months, it was clear to me the project was too big. I did not have the resources, personal or otherwise, to make it happen. At least I couldn't make it happen with the people I cared about most. Those people had come to the same conclusion for themselves much earlier and had been put off by my insistence that we continue. It was a time when, as my father might have said, I had gotten "too big for my britches." For me it was a major loss. It was the second time I had tried to pull off a retreat and the second time I had failed.* I suffered with the embarrassment and resentment of failure and grieved the loss for a long time. I look back now and smile at my honest and naive exposure of myself.

At another time, I may get smitten again with the dream, but I think I won't take on the role of developer, fund raiser, and business planner. I want to be the in-residence therapist, trainer, consultant, author, and gardener. There are times when I'm feeling particularly grateful and fortunate for the life I have, and I am thankful that my retreat center did not happen. I remember one morning during my Satir System Training Program when the cook did not arrive at the retreat center. I realized this was not my problem to deal with. I could focus on what I wanted to teach, not where I could find the cook.

Deciding to leave the consulting firm had awakened me to my limitations, and the retreat center experience humbled me. Two weeks of work in Lithuania in the summer of 1992 surfaced my vulnerability. Laura Dodson, Bunny Duhl, and I did, I believe, a phenomenal job of presenting ourselves and Satir to an audience of about 30 therapists from the area. Our time with this group was deeply spiritual, almost beyond my capacity to contain. I was particularly pained, however, by the poverty that pervaded this white, highly educated group. The poverty I had known had always been about color or lack of education. It was eye opening to my white American naiveté, and at some strange level it shattered my grandiosity about my invincibility.

I experienced my most enchanted evening ever in a forest park in Druskininkai. This was a day of celebration—their Independence Day. About 20 or so locals dressed in traditional costumes hosted about 15 of us Americans to a late-afternoon picnic. They told the stories and shared the poetry and songs that had kept their souls alive while they had been imprisoned in Siberia. They teared and we wept.

Just as I thought I would fold into sobs, an elderly woman stood up in front of us and gave us the warmest and most gracious smile imaginable. She raised her arms, opening her palms in invitation to us. We all stood and the locals took us by the hands, one by one, leading us to a circle dance around the fire. The longer we danced, around and around, the more bonded we seemed to become, the more we cried, and the more we laughed. I thought I would drop in a heap from the sheer fatigue of emotional expression.

As it became dark and cold, we left—but only after the biggest and best hugs I've ever had. These people knew passion, and they shared it with me. I will not forget them or the challenge, the struggle, the rewards of congruence in that oppressed but richly textured culture.

By spring of 1993, I was back in full swing and planning three significant programs. (All the while, of course, I was also managing my consulting, supervising, and psychotherapy practice.) The first was perhaps the most innovative project I have been involved with as a clinician. It was engineered by my good friend and colleague Teresa Adams from New Orleans. She, her husband Jesse, Bunny Duhl from Massachusetts, Hugh Gratz from New York, Frances Mills-Yerger from Arizona, and I facilitated a one-week residential family camp program for about 100 people. Called Camp Beignet, it was a follow-up to a residential couples program that some of us had done in New Orleans a few years earlier.

We worked with the participants in about every combination possible: we mixed up the children in the families; we met with mothers and daughters, fathers and sons; we separated the children and adults; and we met in the large community. Still, we had time for fun.

Teresa and Jesse modeled realness in the most courageous way, inviting members of their own family to participate, along with colleagues, friends, and clients. It was truly a gift they gave to people they cared about. Staffing such an amorphous and sometimes unwieldy conglomeration of wonderful humans was no small accomplishment. Having worked with the New Orleans folks on three different occasions, I'm reminded each time that there really is something called Southern hospitality. It is real fine. These people taught me about the dynamic and flexible quality of healthy human boundaries—the kind that exude genuine caring and willingness to meet another human.

Later that summer, I helped with an equally gutsy program. I helped Pat Callair, an African-American SIS faculty member, engineer Camp Pegasus. This three-week Satir-based residential therapeutic camp was for children at risk. We did this program in partnership with the Department of Social Services and the local mental health center.

Most of the kids came from very abusive and neglectful homes; they were kids for whom basically nothing was available. At every corner, they tested us, our structures, our resources, and our good sense. We all survived and I think are better for the experience, but it was a program that could not be sustained with the limited resources of SIS. I learned that sometimes we go ahead even knowing we are not covered adequately. We go on faith and hope and, if we are lucky, the charity of others. Camp Pegasus survived one more year before it, like many other innovative therapeutic community projects, failed to have the kind of professional administrative support required.

The third project concerned our home on Dixie. While my most fabulous home office was working well for me professionally, the house served less well for Carol and me personally. When it became clear to me that Carol was not happy with the personal space, I started to face the prospect of moving—with dread.

One of my clients gave me a "golden nugget" as she left our therapy session. She mentioned how much she enjoyed the beauty and serenity of my office on the lake. I told her that it was not working for me as a home, and that I feared I would have to leave. As she stepped across the threshold and onto the rock path to her car, she turned and said, "Well, I suggest that you don't leave until you've found something better."

What a wild and refreshing idea! I followed her advice and began my search for a suitable home on another lake. The one I found was tiny and not very attractive, but it was on a high lot overlooking a wonderful and swimmable lake. Our significant renovations included adding a third floor, and Carol and I moved in on Christmas Eve, 1994.

Even with the renovations, there was no adequate space for a clinical office, so I reluctantly agreed to rent office space elsewhere. Some colleagues wrote me about office space they had available. My worst fear was that I would have no window and nothing green to look at, but when I met with the group and looked at the office, I decided to make the move. They were all people I either knew or knew of, and the office had a window with a green hedge that made a great place for birds to live.

By 1992, the SIS public workshop had evolved into the Satir System Training Year-Long Program. Gaining national recognition as a place to learn both the theory and the practice of the Satir model, it was now large enough for me to split the training community into two levels. I took the advanced group and gave the entry-level group to five trainers with whom I had worked closely for several years. I believed I had to find training opportunities for people I had trained to give staffing development programs. I became increasingly torn as to who needed and deserved what opportunity, all the while juggling the requirements for growing a quality program.

Program year 1993–94 reflected my increasing commitment to stay local, my renewed energy, and my ability to accomplish more now that I had the support of an administrator. Under my direction, SIS offered two year-long programs. The annual Satir System Year-Long Program began October 21. Three days later, the most significant collaboration to date between Avanta and SIS began with a year-long program for trainers. (I think the board members felt this training for trainers put too much on the plate and risked our own program, but they went along with it.) It made for an intense year for me, and I haven't offered to do it again. Lots of things are worth doing only once.

The tension was released when in 1994 the board of SIS agreed to contract out the training program to me. I had over the years helped grow an organization that had now become burdensome. In many ways, SIS was built on the model of Avanta; and I had already burned out trying to operate for and with that system, which had been created to support Virginia. Despite differences in situation, people, and times, my feelings about SIS were similar. In 1990, I had said to Avanta, "I can't be the driver of this system." In 1994, I told SIS: "Give me the reins and let me drive this thing." I recognized risk with both decisions but knew they were right. I've had no regrets.

☆

Teacher, Consultant, and Therapist

Today, the Satir System Training Performance Development Program is the best experiential process Satir training available. While it reflects the Satir International Crested Butte Process Community, its design is improved. The year-long format with three different "coming togethers" offers interim time for trainees to practice and integrate their training experience. The personal, clinical, and organization development applications groups offer trainees an opportunity to deepen their learning by focusing on the unique issues related to different applications of the Satir System.

I have the distinct pleasure and good fortune to have three former students assisting me with the program. Sheri Hanshaw is an exemplary therapist, vocalist, and song writer. Her music anchors our right brain to the community's experiences and to our inner selves. Bill Davis, a skilled therapist who specializes in the area of substance abuse, brings his analytical sensibilities to the particulars of applying and teaching Satir. He notices time, temperature, and gaps in reasoning, along with offering friendly support to me and the participants. To top that off, Elly Williamson handles all the numbers, contracts, money, and most of the paper with her impressive professionalism and generosity. I have love and deep respect for each of them.

The payoff for me is that my self-esteem is rarely in doubt, and I can be creative, present, contactful, grounded, and willing to risk. It would be wonderful if all the teachers of our children could feel as supported as I do. With this support, nearly 20 years of mentoring with Virginia, and almost 30 years of experience in the business of helping systems grow, change, learn, and heal, it is no surprise that this program now attracts people from all over (and outside) the country.

In my organizational consulting practice, I have worked with all kinds of businesses and companies: manufacturing, government, hospitals, universities, human service agencies, and insurance companies. Only the most anthropologically oriented change artist would care or dare to deal with such a mix of managerial, cultural, structural, and organizational issues, problems, situations, and goals. I have been involved in team building, project retrospectives, succession planning, change-management training, conflict resolution, strategic planning, and leadership development.

The truth is, the systems and the issues are much more alike than different. I enter with a great deal of confidence that any system with an acknowledged boundary can learn, grow, change, and heal. I learned that first from Virginia and now know it from my own experiences.

Many managers and consultants think that dealing with the future is sufficient. You must start where the client is. We cannot help anyone by disregarding or dismissing another person. Therefore, as we move vertically and horizontally through relationship and role structures in organizations, we must move with all due care. Feelings are the land mines of corporate America.

I know no better way to build trust than to model and operate from honesty. Honesty and harshness are not synonymous. It is not always easy to be honest when the sides are polarized. In the kinds of atmospheres I find in organizations, I know I am moving forward when I get agreement from shared understanding on anything.

In a universally inclusive fashion, I usually comment on the pain and price of dysfunction in individuals, teams, and organizations. This helps diminish blame for the current situation. Diminishing blame helps reopen the pores of closed systems so relationship and cognitive connections can begin. Reopening a system that has cut itself off or has cut off others in a reactively defensive way requires two important pieces. First, those who feel victimized need to acknowledge the pain of their wounding. The others must listen to and accept the expression of that pain. There is no shortcut to this stage of healing.

Positive change is not sustained if the heart is not invested. The heart cannot be invested if it has to hide out for fear of being ignored, criticized, dismissed, or rejected. It is a simple fact. Change is not easy. There is always a price. And paying that price is a requirement for learning, growing, and healing. The process is constant and beyond our human ability to stop.

Too often we assume that external changes—whether in role, incentive packages, or hierarchy—make the difference in organizational effectiveness. Not true. At the root, organizational effectiveness relates directly to the level of system esteem: the cumulative levels of esteem of all the individuals and groups comprising the whole.

We are hampered in our social, cognitive, physical, and spiritual lives when our sense of our unique value is low. When we do not have the experience of being a contributor to a team and when we do not have a place where we feel we belong, we put ourselves, our employees, our partners, and our children at risk for low self-esteem and low performance.

My most engaging work has been in working with family-owned businesses. No other work accesses so much of my training and experience. Having an owner and family present their struggles is a precious gift. These struggles are always wrapped intricately with old hurts, unmet expectations, disappointments, resentments, deep longings, basic yearnings, and hope that is often covered over with scars.

Family members in these businesses work in the context of intimate vulnerabilities associated with being family. It is not easy, but the successes are incredibly sweet. At its truest level, owners are dealing with the most powerful triad in their lives: their own mortality, the survivability of their life's work, and the need to love and be loved by their families. There is no more sacred territory than this.

As for my role as a therapist, I have to say that I do not think therapy is for everyone. I find it of minimal value when someone is madly in love, when someone has no awareness of things they want to be different in their life, and when someone is too depressed to put energy into exploration. Some people do their therapy with music, some with friends, some with God, and some with the support of a professional therapist.

People often call to ask me what approach I use and what kind of people I see. If they know of Satir's work, then we have a starting place. When they don't, I say I work with individuals, families, and couples. I want all organizations to know about the external stressors and satisfiers in their lives. I want time to explore the internal conflicts, feelings, and perceptions that have their roots in their family-of-origin experience.

I believe that we are all wounded by our family-of-origin experience; it is unavoidable even in the best families. It is in large part from this wounding that we learn to take care of ourselves so we can survive. When we become adults, the way we need to take care of ourselves in our new families is almost the opposite behavior. And that is terrifying to us: "Do it *how?*"

What we learn when we are young forms our attitudes and behaviors as adults. Without awareness of these forces, we deny ourselves full choice and permission to be whole and present in our current lives. On the other hand, if we dare veer from the old familiar program that helped us deal with challenges as a child, we have to learn to risk the worst happening to us. (It usually doesn't, but that paralyzing fear was also part of what we learned as a child.)

If I had to give up all my work but one kind, I think I'd keep on being a therapist. For me, nothing is as satisfying as listening with an open heart and a free mind to the story of another human. The stories always show me the person's courage, and they all ooze with the human longing for connection and meaning. To offer connection and provide compassionate light for their search for balance, intimacy, and joy is the greatest work I can imagine.

To do it in the familiar surrounds of my office without having to get on an airplane or sleep in a hotel is better than any training group or high-paying consultation. While I enjoy the challenging situations of teaching and consulting and traveling to interesting places, I think twice before I say yes to the invitations. And I am always glad to be back home at my office, sitting quietly, respectfully, and warmly in the energy field of someone whose soul wants more space to be.

Bud Baldwin took Virginia on a float trip down the Rogue River because she was afraid of water. Somehow, he got her into an inner tube along the way. She had a good time and continued teaching the rest of us even while drowning.

No one is better than Bud at dealing with high-pressure situations. He writes four to five scientific articles per year. Yet what he really loves are the long stretches of land in Nevada and teaching a collaborative approach to rural medicine.

—*Robert S. Spitzer*
Publisher

8

Memories, Myths, and Metaphors

by DeWitt ("Bud") Baldwin, Jr.

Several times in my life I've wondered if my true calling wasn't to be a storyteller. I love to tell stories—true stories, that is—and I have a rich store of them, thanks to an adventurous set of parents and an exciting life. In fact, whenever I was off skiing or camping with the guys, there was always a call for another "Baldwin saga" before the campfire burned out. Some of these revolved around my romantic exploits, but most described a childhood rich with exotic experiences. I think my storytelling was—still is—my way of creatively integrating a vivid visual memory, an unusually rich set of experiences, and a deep personal search for meaning.

In *Care of the Soul,* Thomas Moore maintains that our lives are made up of the stories or myths that guide and enrich our lives— that enable a sense of order and sustain us through adversity. Beyond facts and chronologies are the narrative stories, the sagas, the myths that bind things together, so that in some immutable way, every myth is a story and every story is a myth. In this sense, my story represents my myth—not a fabrication, but rather my perception, my truth, "my story." Like every autobiography, this is to some extent also a remembrance of yearnings, perceptions and feelings, filtered through the meanings I made of my experiences.

Beginnings

My childhood *was* pretty unusual. It began when I was born in 1922 in a small town in northern Maine. Apparently I cried a lot when they brought me home, so my autocratic paternal grandfather insisted that my mother send me back to the maternity home until "that baby stops crying." She told me that I cried for two straight days before I finally stopped, and she and my dad claimed that I didn't cry again for many months. I guess I was a fast learner.

My parents were very special people: attractive, intelligent, kind, idealistic, sensitive, creative, and visionary. They sang together beautifully . My mother had been a drama major and a junior Phi Beta Kappa in college—and the first woman ever to win the annual Northwestern University oratorical contest, which she won four years running.

My dad was a kind, gentle man—a true "gentleman." He probably was the most patient and totally accepting person I've ever known. Honest to a fault, he was hard-working and committed. He was universally beloved. A number of people have said that he came as close in his life as one could to emulating Christ—not an easy model for me to live up to.

I knew all four of my grandparents. My grandfathers were both strict, opinionated men, almost harsh in some ways. I remember both grandmothers as soft and gentle. I didn't know any of my great-grandparents, although the family history has always interested me. I now have almost all the family photographs and records on both sides.

Family Facts

The Baldwins apparently arrived in Connecticut before 1636. In that year, two Baldwin brothers sailed across Long Island Sound and up the Passaic River to settle in what today is Newark, New Jersey. My ancestors later fought in the Revolutionary War (Grandma was a member of the Daughters of the American Revolution). By the early 1800s, the Baldwins were farmers in northern New Jersey, and both my grandfather and father grew up on the family farm in Verona. That era ended just before World War I when my grandfather sold the farm.

They were a devoutly religious family, and my grandfather was a pillar of the church. Although he was a religious man, I never thought of him as a very spiritual or loving person. He was scrupulously honest and very justice-oriented, but in a punishing sort of way.

He and my grandmother had three children. My dad was the middle one, born in 1898. About 1904, the family moved to San Francisco. After the famous 1906 quake, my grandmother insisted that the family move back east.

On my mother's side, my Grandpa Aikin was born in 1865 and grew up on a farm in central Michigan. After trying farming, carpentry, and clerking in a store, he became an expert engraver at the Elgin Watch Factory, where my grandmother also worked. They courted, which for her meant going to church together. Eventually, he decided to become a minister and so completed high school, college, and seminary—all at Northwestern. I remember my maternal grandfather as witty, sarcastic, and quick-tempered—rather harsh and forbidding. All the same, I think it amazing that 40 years of my life overlapped with someone born during the Civil War.

Grandpa Aikin married two sisters—sequentially. The first, my maternal grandmother, died when I was about eight. I remember her as quiet, calm, warm, and supportive. I've heard that she took marvelous care of me during my first year, when my mother was in graduate school. Apparently, she gave me much of the gentle caring and trust I experienced as an infant and in all likelihood was the most important figure during my first year. A year or two after her death, my grandfather married her younger sister, who had lived with them for some 25 years.

My parents first met in 1919 in Columbus, Ohio at the Methodist church's Centennial Celebration of Missions. They later met again at Northwestern and worked together in a mission church on Chicago's West Side. On Valentine's Day in 1921, they became engaged in a manner that attracted attention from the International Associated Press. She kept him outside all night on a bitter cold Chicago night until he managed to propose. She then turned in a fire alarm to announce the good news. The story appeared in newspapers all over the world—even in Burma, where my father's sister read about it!

Later that year, they got married and moved to Maine, where my father was serving a rural parish. Meanwhile, the only advice on family planning that my grandmother gave my mother was, "Never stay in bed in the morning." Apparently, this was insufficient. Within two months, I was conceived on a morning when they lingered a little too long, and I was born the following July.

The advice my mother received, while it may not have helped her, has given substance and form to my life. Perhaps it came through to me *in utero*, because I am a morning person—I seldom feel like lingering in bed. Being energetic and active, I welcome challenge and look forward to new experiences. Nearly everything that goes on around me and nearly every person who enters my ken arouses my interest.

The truth was that my mother didn't really want to become pregnant—certainly that early in the marriage. To conceal my advent from her younger siblings (one didn't talk about such things in those days), my mother began to refer to me as "my buddy"—a term that was very popular during World War I, which had recently ended. The nicknames "Buddy" or "Bud" persisted after I was born.

Shortly after, my parents made their commitment to the missionary field. In July 1923, we sailed for Rangoon by way of England, the Suez Canal, and the Indian Ocean. I had my first birthday in Scotland.

Burma

My earliest memory, as confirmed by my parents, is of our first bedroom in Rangoon, Burma, where all three of us slept. I was between 18 and 24 months of age when we lived there, and I never saw it again, but I can describe the room extensively to this day. I have always been an extremely visual person, and I can recall scenes with amazing accuracy after many years. It seems as if my mind is like a camera lens, seeing all the objects in a scene and reproducing them on command. This helped a lot when I was in school.

I lived at home with my parents—in several homes, actually—only a few years. During the "hot season," when the temperature in Burma reached 120 degrees or higher, parents sent their children to a cooler clime if at all possible. So, when I was four, I went away to a boarding school in the hills, two days away by train and car. Except for a year in Chicago at age seven, when both my parents were in graduate school, I never again lived at home with them during a school year.

Meanwhile, when I was three or four, my mother decided I needed to be circumcised because I was "touching" myself. She arranged to have it done during my afternoon nap. She and the doctor began—and she claims I never woke up (!)—but they gave up when I started to bleed profusely. (It turned out that I was a "bleeder," so it's lucky they didn't try to finish the job. I have hemophilia—classic Factor VIII deficiency.) Just as well, I like my foreskin, scar and all.

I learned early that I had to take care of myself. As the youngest child and only Caucasian in the first two boarding schools I attended (at ages four and five), I had to learn to get along as a minority in the rough-and-tumble dormitory and schoolyard life. This served me well later, when I was six and my folks left me alone on the Trans-Siberian Express while they went into a station. The train pulled out without them, but I knew enough to pull the emergency cord. The train stopped, and my parents appeared. A month later, they left me on a ship from Japan to the United States and went ashore on an errand. The ship sailed away—again, without them. They did eventually manage to get on board when the pilot got off at the harbor mouth.

Some years later, a friend wondered why I didn't "get the message." I suppose someone today might even make a case for some sort of child neglect or even sexual abuse. (My *ayah* [nurse] in Burma used to put me to sleep by masturbating me—a not uncommon Oriental practice—at least until my mother discovered it and sent her away.) However, I never felt victimized in my relationship with my parents. Nor did I feel unloved—even during the early separations, although I must have experienced anxiety and resentment at being left alone. It was as though I was never a child to my parents—just a bright little adult who had joined the family. I recently came up with the metaphor for this. My parents were like a pair of fine horses drawing a carriage (looking straight ahead, of course). Tied on behind was a spare horse (for long journeys, in case one of the team threw a shoe). The extra horse had to keep up somehow, even though he had no control over where he was going—and got a lot of dust!

My parents had gone abroad in 1923 to be "change agents"—
the first of a new generation of educated, sophisticated, modern
missionaries recruited after World War I. Too much so, apparently,
for the older generation of resident Methodist missionaries. Largely
evangelists sent to convert "the heathen," that generation saw my
parents as upstarts and promptly punished them for their new views
and efforts at cultural understanding. My parents were assigned
the most menial and difficult work in the field—work previously
done by three missionaries. Dad was patient and long-suffering. Not
so my mother. She was never silent—or discreet—which didn't help.

My first boarding school was on a former tea plantation in
Thandaung, high on a ridge in wild country near the Thai border.
Looking out the windows at night, I remember seeing tigers and
leopards in the schoolyard where we played during the day. That
summer, my uncle and aunt vacationed near the school. One evening
as they dined, the cook stepped out of the house to go to the kitchen,
located several feet away to distance the smells and dirt. As he
left, there was a loud roar and a scream—and then nothing! The
men rushed from the room—but, unarmed, declined to explore farther into the night. Only in the morning did they discover the cook's
body several hundred yards away. This was merely one among many
scary stories about wild animals on which I was raised.

Later that year, I slipped and fell, cutting my head. I nearly
bled out before a retired local doctor, Dr. Coté, sewed up the wound
with ordinary thread. I still have a vivid memory of a bed covered
with bloodstains. It became clear to me only recently, however,
that I could not have seen the bed if I was lying down on it. Instead,
I was seeing it as if I were high above, looking down. Perhaps it
was an early "out of body"—near death—experience.

At the year's end, the school closed down and reopened the
following spring in the town of Kalaw. This was farther up country,

in a lovely vacation resort area with wooded hills and pine trees—
and not as many wild animals. The school was still under
construction, so we boys slept in a thatch-roofed, bamboo shelter
with an earthen floor. One night I awoke needing to go to the bathroom. Our outdoor privy was located some distance away, and it
was raining hard. Between that and my vivid memories of tigers in
the night, I was afraid to go outside. In desperation, I looked about
and noticed a puddle on the floor near my bed from the leaking
thatch. "Ah ha," I thought, "I can make my own puddle and it will
never be noticed in the morning." Elated, I edged over to the side
of the bed, lifted up the covers, and let fly.

Alas, I had forgotten to remove my pajamas. This left me with
a soaking set of pajamas and a wet mattress. I moved over to the
other side of the bed for the rest of the night and in the morning
went out to "face the music." Punishment at the school was swift,
severe, and public. Each morning, school officials lined up any
offenders, identified each one's particular "crime," and inflicted
the scheduled punishment. In that particular school (as in most
British schools), it consisted of so many switches applied to the
back of the legs or to the bottom. It was not the physical pain that
hurt as much as the humiliation in front of all our schoolmates.

That was not my only "crime." One day I was caught by a
sudden attack of diarrhea and didn't make it to the bathroom. Standing at the bottom of the stairs in the main building, I froze in horror
as excrement dripped down my leg and puddled at my feet in front
of everyone passing. I felt deeply humiliated. All I wanted was to
bury my face in my mother's lap and be loved and forgiven. Instead, the next morning I faced the line-up. The feelings associated
with this memory still bring tears.

Along with my age and prior events, I think these experiences
made me feel very much a loner, a marginal person. Although people
generally perceive me to be a congenial extrovert, I have always

felt apart, different. In some ways, this "different" piece of me has been both a cross to bear and a source of creativity.

Family Adventures

My parents were certainly adventurous. When it came time to return to the United States on furlough in 1929, they cashed in the tickets the church had provided for a safe second-class voyage home. Instead, they embarked on an itinerary so incredible that Thomas Cook and Sons, the premier travel agents of the day, said it was impossible. It was—but we did it anyway.

The plan was first to go east, across Southeast Asia to Saigon, traveling by boat, train, and car. On the way, we stopped at Angkor Wat, one of the great wonders of the world. At that time, very few people knew about, much less visited, this great lost city. Abandoned in the 15th century, its buildings lay covered by the jungle until the end of the 19th century, when a French explorer rediscovered the ruins. In 1929, when we visited, it was magnificent—and spooky, especially when I became separated from my parents. Such was the jungle's overgrowth that one could not hear a person in the next room. And snakes and tigers roamed the ruins.

In Saigon, I saw my first movie. Actually, I only remember the newsreel. It showed a football game between Notre Dame and Southern California. As an impressionable six-year old, I equated playing football with being an American. This apparently set the stage for my lifelong fascination with the game.

Just before arriving in Shanghai, I broke out with chickenpox. While I was isolated for three weeks in the home of two older missionaries, my parents went off on their scheduled visits elsewhere in China. When they returned, we started for Peking on the famous "Blue train." That was unusual in itself, as the train had not run for over two years due to ceaseless fighting in the interior, mainly between Chinese warlords. This was to be its first run. The minute we left, we realized we were in trouble. The order of the stations differed from the schedule. We were the only Caucasians on board and, for most of the trip, the only people speaking English, which felt less than comforting under the circumstances.

It turned out that fighting had recommenced, and the train was being routed far to the west. During the next two days, we passed many troop trains and even went by a recent battlefield full of cannons and carnage. At one point, my mother peered out to see where we were. As she turned away, bullets passed through the window where her head had just been!

Late on the third night, the train stopped for several hours on the banks of the Huang-He (Yellow) River. Eventually, we started slowly across a rickety and obviously repaired bridge. As we reached the other bank and started north for Peking, we heard a huge explosion. Soldiers had blown up the bridge. Needless to say, we were relieved the next day at our first sight of U.S. Marines guarding the embassy in Peking. From there, we went north to the Siberian border, then down to Seoul, Korea, and by boat across the East China Sea to the southern coast of Japan.

My mother yearned to see Mount Fujiyama. To reach it, we had to take a train inland, arrange for a car to meet us, and get to the Mianoshita Hotel. People had told us that hotel had the best view of the mountain. Arriving at the railhead in a driving rain, we discovered that a British couple had commandeered our car. We had no choice but to take the local bus through the mountains. Jammed with people and animals, the old bus eventually took off, crawling over wet and slippery dirt roads. Once in a while, someone called out, the bus stopped, and the person went off into the pitch-black night.

After a while, we were the only people left. The driver eventually said he didn't dare go farther in the rain, and he took us to a small Japanese *ryokan* (inn) off the road. We were exhausted and disappointed. Our ship was leaving the next afternoon from Yokohama, so in spite of coming all this way, we would miss seeing Mount Fuji.

We awoke (if we slept at all on our *tatami* reed mats with their wooden pillows) to a foggy, drippy dawn on the edge of a lake. As we waited disconsolately for the bus to depart, the mists suddenly parted. Towering above us in brilliant sunshine was Mount Fuji. We were on the shore of a lake at the base of the mountain. After five minutes, the mists closed in again. Later, the bus took us past the Mianoshita Hotel—which was shrouded in fog and mist—and on to Yokohama.

As mentioned, I sailed from Yokohama without my parents. I've often wondered how things would have turned out if they hadn't caught up with the boat. In those days, there were no planes. I guess I would have landed in the States unaccompanied—and without a passport. I think I would have coped, somehow. As it was, we came ashore in California and crossed the country to my paternal grandparents' place in Maine, camping out in an old Studebaker that cost $150.

To this day, camping is my favorite kind of vacation. I owe a lot of this to my parents, who liked to rough it. Those adventures are among my fondest childhood memories. After our trip through Asia, we could handle almost anything—including picking up a bank robber in Arizona and struggling with nine flat tires in one day in New Mexico. It occurs to me now that coping and survival were to become common threads for my many later travels and adventures.

While on furlough, my parents both pursued further graduate work at the University of Chicago, my mother in religious drama and my father in theology. I attended the local public school. Unlike Burma, school years in the United States began in September and ended in June, so I was able to complete a full school year while we were in the United States.

Back to Burma

After spending the summer of 1930 in Maine, we returned to Rangoon in the late fall. It was too late to enter boarding school for that year, so I attended classes at the Methodist Girls High School next door. One particular teacher excited my interest in literature. It was in her class that I learned the story of Arnold of Switzerland. In the 14th century, during the Swiss fight for independence, he supposedly broke through the phalanx of Austrian troops by sacrificing his own body to as many of their spears as he could encompass within his outstretched arms. His act opened a gap in the line, through which the Swiss farmers entered and defeated the Austrians. To this day, I cannot tell this story without tears. It has influenced my life tremendously and engendered a belief that it is my duty in life to take great personal, even self-destructive, risks for causes in which I believe.

The following February, I entered my fifth primary school: Taunggyi American School. For the first time, I would stay at one institution for more than a year. I was lucky to get in at all, as it was operated solely for Baptist missionary children. After considerable discussion of whether to admit a "foreigner" from another church, the director finally said yes because my father's sister was a Baptist missionary and her two daughters—my cousins—were already in attendance. Once again, however, I felt like the outsider.

High in the mountains near the border of China, Taunggyi was even farther north than Kalaw. It sat high on a shelf above a large valley on the edge of a Shan village of about 2,000 people. Built of gray stone, the school was a large two-story building. The fairly large grounds included a soccer field behind the building and a large playground. Below the school, facing the valley, the hill fell away to a series of gardens, a large banyan tree, and a hillock of stone. Covered with brush and trees, the knoll contained a number of small caves. Several of us had turned the caves into little "homes," until one day we were told not to play there. Shortly after, we heard a shot and saw some men carrying out a dead tiger from one of our caves. The animal measured ten feet long—half of it tail.

Life at Taunggyi was pretty spartan. Once a week, school officials doled out one or two pieces of candy per student from goodies supplied by parents and the church. Imagine what it means to make two small Chiclets last a whole week. Once I traded one of my Chiclets for a green olive from one of the other children and likewise made that last a week. I'm sure this whole experience led me to appreciate small things—especially olives.

Although we ate well and had adequate time for study, play, and worship—especially worship—we had to fend for ourselves when it came to diversion. The first year I did not have a bicycle and could not go riding with the bigger boys, so daily play depended almost entirely on what nature presented. Fun times consisted of such activities as carving wooden boats to float down the local drainage ditch after a rain, and making tractors out of discarded spools of thread and rubber bands. We collected multicolored butterflies and exotic, odd-shaped beetles and bugs. Aside from playing "zoo" with them, we often took them to bed with us so they could amuse us in the early morning.

We also loved climbing in the big banyan tree, playing "house" in the caves, tending the gardens, and hiking to "The Crag" and various temple sites nearby. Sometimes we visited the local markets or went to the Thamsang caves and the nearby swimming hole at "Mile 16."

We boys kiddingly talked about girlfriends. We each had a favorite girl, toward whom we could not possibly express such feelings, and about whom we would have been unmercifully teased if we had ever let on. About that age, my measure of a girl's attractiveness had mostly to do with her intelligence and her strength. My first exploration into the differences between boys and girls occurred about that time with my cousin Alice, who was my favorite playmate. One day, we both stripped naked in the bathroom and examined each other. Our startling conclusion was that we were exactly alike, except that I was "inside out" and she was "outside in."

I recall going home on vacations, filled with excitement and anticipation. For the first 48 hours, things were wonderful. Then parental preoccupation with work and attempts at discipline began asserting themselves. Suddenly it was no longer the joyful reunion I had anticipated, and I thought of nothing more than getting back to school with my friends. For missionary children, "family" often consisted of other children at boarding schools. Many of us preferred the stability of a school and the loyalty of friends to the comings and goings of distant and busy parents.

At a recent reunion of some of the missionary children with whom I had gone to school in Burma from 1931 to 1933, some even confirmed that they had little sense of belonging to their parents when they were reunited later in life. One woman, who had been separated from her family at two, mentioned that when her parents finally retired to the United States when she was 17, they assumed that they all would resume "family life." She had other ideas. "No way was I willing to go back and become their 'child,'" she said, "They were not my family."

I'm sure it was hard for parents to send their children off to live with strangers. Even the furloughs that occurred every six or seven years did not always result in joyous family reunions. Children often resented being uprooted from their regular lives and friends for a year and placed in a strange new environment with unfamiliar people—their parents—before being left again.

I think many missionaries regarded children and spouses as necessary sacrifices to "the cause." Most missionaries were deeply religious and committed to service. They worked under difficult circumstances with self-sacrificial dedication to an ideal or vision that denied personal gain or gratification. Perhaps preacher's kids know something of this, but they seldom experience the prolonged isolation and loneliness of foreign assignment.

End of an Era

Starting in the early 1930s, my parents began questioning not only the mission of the church but, as a result, their own faith. This began a long review and search for their own basic values, beliefs, and future. It was an interesting experience for me as a young child to see them go through this. I learned a lot about change—and I have always respected them for their open and shared struggle.

After reading and talking extensively for many months, they regained their faith but decided to leave the foreign field. They believed that their real mission was to inform people in the United States about the world's other vital cultures, religions, and beliefs. My mother hadn't really wanted to go back to Burma in 1931, but my dad had felt bound by his commitment to build a new church for his congregation. He worked terribly hard, and I saw his hair turn nearly white that year.

By 1933, the new church was built and my parents were eager to return to the States to activate some of their ideas about "one world" and a new approach to missions. The Great Depression was on, and the Board of Foreign Missions was recalling missionaries because of finances. My parents were supported locally in Burma and therefore not facing this threat. However, when the Board re-called an agricultural missionary who was doing something really worthwhile, my dad asked to go in his place. The Board was not pleased and refused Dad's request.

What board members saw as a purely monetary decision—recalling a home-supported missionary—did not make sense to my parents. They felt far more concern over the ideological issues of the future direction of missions and America. Dad kept insist-ing, and the Board finally said that he could go home, but they would have no job for him.

Despite this, he and my mother bravely set off into the un-known—and, as in my earlier metaphor, I followed. Once again, they turned in their tickets and used the money to design their own route. This time, they planned to go home by way of India, the Middle East, and Europe. In February 1933, we boarded a boat from Rangoon to Calcutta. One way to save money was to purchase deck passage, as the local people did. It cost next to nothing. Of course, such passengers received nothing except a space on the open deck, where every function of life went on in all kinds of weather. People brought their own food and cooked it right there on the deck, and slept there as well.

When my parents tried to book our passage, the British agents objected strenuously to the idea of any white person (even an Ameri-can) traveling in such a fashion. According to them, this would lower the stature of whites in the eyes of the "natives." My father and mother persisted, and the agents gave in. The only stipulation was that my mother sleep on the "white" side of the railing that separated deck passage from the rest of the boat.

My parents' purpose for crossing India by train was to explore the history of the Mogul empire and British colonialism. I remember getting off in the town of Cawnpore late one night, hiring a *tonga* (a little horse-drawn carriage), and riding out to see a famous well where a number of British civilians had been butchered during the Sepoy Rebellion of 1857. We heard gunshots that night and had an eerie feeling that the uprising was happening again. The next morning, a bright sunny day, we proceeded into Lucknow in time to hear the bagpipes of the returning Campbell Regiment— the very regiment that had lifted the siege of Lucknow three-quarters of a century before.

We continued across northern India to New Delhi and through Agra, with its scientific gardens and all the mathematical and astronomical wonders built by the Moguls. Another example of my parents' remarkable venturesomeness was their bribing the Taj Mahal gatekeeper to let us sleep on the gatehouse balcony overlooking the pool. Throughout the night, we watched the Taj in bright moonlight. Waking in the early dawn, we saw the white alabaster dome and the four minarets gradually come alive, a ghostly purple slowly turning into the rose of alpine glow. Then, suddenly, the sun's first rays struck the top of the dome like a bolt of lightning and cascaded across the white marble, nearly blinding us. The sight was magnificent.

In late February, we landed in Basra, Iraq and began the central theme of the trip. My parents planned to follow the story of the Bible, beginning in the city of Ur, where Abraham was born. (Mohammed apparently also was born there, making this one city the source of three of the world's great religions.) Looking at the famous ziggurat outlined against the immense sky and desert, we could appreciate why the original Chaldeans worshipped gods of the sun and the moon. Other than the desert, those were the environment's most prominent features.

From Ur, we traveled to Baghdad and then across the desert by bus to the Holy Land via Lebanon, the snows of Mount Herman, and the source waters of the River Jordan. At the Sea of Galilee, we stayed right on the shore in a charming little monastery run by European monks. I walked down the beach to a place I called "the glen." Completely surrounded by trees, sparkling water flowed out of a large spring into a pool with a sandy bottom. It was quiet and cool in the heat of the day, and I could imagine Jesus and his followers finding such a place of solitude and peace.

In an open touring car, we continued into Nazareth, a sleepy, dusty Arab town without much distinction. As we drove, my father would often quote from the Bible—in an historical rather than religious sense. He'd say, "A city that is set on a hill cannot be hid"—and there it would be. Or, as we observed beautiful blooms among the abundant rocks, "Consider the lilies of the field, how they grow: they toil not, neither do they spin." In this fashion, we arrived in Jerusalem, where we visited the Garden of Gethsemene and the Church of the Holy Sepulchre. I still have a piece of mosaic from the floor of Jesus' supposed tomb. From there, we followed the flight of Joseph, Mary, and the baby Jesus from Bethlehem through the Sinai to Egypt. After visiting the pyramids, we embarked on a small freighter to Greece to continue our pilgrimage to the scenes of early Christianity.

Greece fascinated me from the standpoint of both church and ancient history. After seeing the famous monuments in Athens and the lower peninsula, we went through the Corinth canal to the island of Corfu—surely one of the most enchanting sights in the world—and thence to Albania and Italy. We arrived on Easter weekend in Rome, which was jammed with visitors. I ended up sleeping in a bathtub, the hotel's only available space.

Our voyage through the history of the Christian church was nearly over as we proceeded north to Switzerland. There I learned about the rise of Protestantism and about John Calvin (an interesting role model for an impressionable child). Paris meant museums, not a little boy's forté. Little did I know that I would someday return and love Paris and its museums as much as I do. I also laugh at the fact that I was in Paris a full three years before my wife Michele was born there.

Welcome to America

Having alienated the Board of Foreign Missions, my parents arrived in New York with no welcome and no job. One net result of our coming back in April was that I was too late to begin the school year with other fifth graders. Since my parents were desperately looking for a job, they housed me with my grandparents in Maine while they traveled around testing their ideas. Just to occupy my time, they put me in the fifth grade anyway. When I passed the final exams in June, I was duly promoted into the sixth grade, making up a whole year.

A wonderful summer ensued at Green Lake—a crystal clear, deep lake surrounded by hills and mountains in Maine, with a lovely summer climate of warm days and cool nights. "The Camp," as we called my grandparents' place, was a sprawling building with a wide porch, on which were located six or seven beds. On those wonderful cold nights with no central heating, I snuggled beneath lots of blankets in the largest bed I'd ever seen, listening to the water splashing on the rocks below and feeling the breeze blowing across the porch.

Dawn came quickly, as my early-to-bed Grandfather Baldwin was also early to rise. Everyone was expected to go for a swim when he got up at six, so it was out of that warm, cuddly bed and into the cold, cold lake. Later, before lunch and in the late afternoon, we took more delectable swims under the warm sun. In between, we built rafts or played "store" with the fancy whiskey bottles from the pile behind Rule Higgins' place. That pile was impressive: probably eight feet across and two or three feet high, made up solely of bottles whose contents he had consumed during the preceding winter. The bottles were attractive and interesting, and after filling them with various colored substances we concocted by soaking crepe paper in water, we used them to play "drug store."

When my grandfather found out that these were liquor bottles, he confiscated them and chastised us all for consorting with the devil. Some 25 years later, when he was retired and traveling between Maine and Florida (where he wintered), he stopped by to meet my wife, Michele, for the first time. Remembering his and my grandmother's abhorrence of liquor, I told Michele to hide our one liquor bottle. She expressed utter disbelief that something like that could be so serious. I assured her that grandfather was a highly judgmental man and would think ill of both of us if he came across anything of that sort.

The next morning, as was his usual parsimonious habit, my grandfather asked Michele if she would make him a sandwich for lunch on the train and pour the leftover coffee into the bottle that he always carried with him. Glancing over, I recognized it as one of the liquor bottles that he had confiscated from us years before. When I attempted to kid him about this, he angrily rejected the idea that this had been a liquor bottle (and continued carrying it with him on subsequent trips). What poetic justice—that this self-righteous teetotaler frugally drank leftover coffee from it for all those years while onlookers who recognized it as a liquor bottle probably thought he was a secret tippler.

Farm Boy

As the summer of 1933 drew to an end, my parents were still job hunting. Visiting college campuses around the country, they promoted their view that young people in the States needed to know more about the rest of the world. I couldn't go with them, so my parents arranged for me to spend the following school year in Wisconsin with a farm family recommended by a friend. The farm was in the rural township of Rochester, which had no school, so that year I walked five miles (each way) to Burlington, my seventh elementary school.

In the mid 1980s, when Michele and I visited the school, she turned to me and said, "Now I want you to show me exactly how far it was to the farm." Knowing my propensity for telling a good story, she thought I probably had been embellishing things all these years. She insisted on monitoring the odometer as we rode down well-remembered back roads to find the farm. I was frankly concerned that I would be caught out and never able to live it down. It was with great relief that I saw the odometer turn 4.9 miles as we entered the farm's driveway.

One didn't think anything of walking to school in those days. Busing did not exist. During the bitter cold—sometimes minus 20 degrees BWC (before wind chill!)—I'd stuff school papers into my corduroy knickers to keep out the wind. At times I had to walk home in the dark after being kept at school. Occasionally, I would get a ride on a farm wagon or from someone who happened to be going on that particular road, but these were rare: only one other farm lay between us and town.

That year, I started out in sixth grade, but within a few weeks it seemed that I knew almost everything. The school promoted me into the seventh grade, where I again seemed to have mastered most of what the class was studying (because of our travels, I knew quite a bit about geography and history). At mid-year, I was promoted into the eighth grade and graduated in June 1934. So, in one calendar year, at age 11, I literally went from fourth grade (in Burma) to eighth grade (in Wisconsin).

My parents probably paid something for my room and board on the farm, but I was also expected to do chores each day, shovel manure, and care for horses, pigs, and cows. As I took a bath only once a week—in a metal tub in the kitchen—I undoubtedly smelled like a barn. Some kids had negative feelings about me because I was bright, much younger and, as always, an outsider. One day, when one of the big boys made fun of me in class, I hit him. He was just standing up, so it looked to the rest of the class as if my blow had lifted him out of his seat. I had very little trouble in school from then on.

My Pioneering Parents

My parents were broke and unemployed for two years as a result of declaring that the idea of missions was all wrong, and that we Westerners had as much to learn from other cultures as we had to teach. Calling this *world-mindedness* (in 1933!), they set out to persuade an insular, isolationist America to begin understanding its connection with the international community.

After touring college campuses, they took their unsettling report of student disinterest in world missions to the Board of Missions, who decided to hire my father as Secretary of Student Work. Believing that one could not just lecture about world-mindedness and expect significant change, my parents then came up with a unique experiential educational summer program for college students.

Lisle

The Lisle Fellowship was a six-week cooperative living and work-ing experience. It got its name from being located in Lisle, New York. Featuring a miniature world community, the program was international, interracial, interfaith, interdenominational, and in-tercultural. Four days each week, teams of students provided services to nearby communities. The other three days, the students returned to the center and talked about their experiences. (To founders of Virginia's Avanta Network, this may sound like Forest Knolls.) This approach followed Harvard philosopher William Ernest Hocking's educational principle of *alternation*: alternating living/learning experience with reflection.

To describe their process, my parents invented the phrase *laboratory in human relations* (in 1936) and attracted some of the great educators of the time: Ken Latourette and John Clark Archer from Yale, L. Thomas Hopkins and T. H. P. Sailor from Columbia, Mark Rich and Dick Edwards from Cornell, and S. R. Slavson from the Jewish Board of Guardians in New York City. They all served as mentors and facilitators of the group process.

My parents also drew around them a group of fellow world citizens, all attuned to the newly interconnected, interdependent globe. Night after night, visitors and guests at our house would talk until midnight around the dinner table about new cooperative, ex-periential ways of what is now called service–learning. Later, when I was home for the holidays from college, I would stick around with my date for dinner (to save money), only to find that we both be-came so fascinated with the conversation that we stayed there instead of going out. My parents were exciting people, leaders, and role models for many others, young and old—and I admired them.

One hazard of this exciting and stimulating environment was the feeling that since I had been exposed to so many opportunities and privileges, I was a failure for not achieving more. How could someone who had grown up knowing such remarkable people— evangelists such as Dwight Moody, Homer Rodeheaver, Stanley High, and John R. Mott; and people such as Jesse Owens, the Olympic champion; Langston Hughes, the poet; and Rufus Jones and Thomas Kelly, philosophers—have turned out to be such an ordinary person?

Yet, while I reveled in and grew by my parents' idealism and creativity, I often felt left out, just one of the many hundreds of people who wanted to be around and near them. I even acquired "siblings" during these years, young people who adopted my parents and became closer to them than I. They called my parents "Aunt Edna" and "Uncle Si." Starting in my teens, I too had to use those names, as they didn't respond to "Dad" or "Mom" anymore. In some ways, this was good, because it freed me to be myself and a regular member of the group.

Lisle was an important part of my life, even though I later took very little part in its activities. (It continues to this day with international, interfaith, intercultural experiences all over the world.) In its early years, this truly unique learning environment combined the service features of the Quaker Work Camps and the learning aspects of their International Seminars, providing life-changing experiences for many of the students. Several "graduates" returned to their native lands to become national leaders. After the 1936 program, in what may have been one of the first "freedom rides," black and white students from the South returned home in buses together, defying Jim Crow laws. Even in conservative upstate New York, it was quite a shock for townspeople to see blacks from Africa and Japanese from Asia walking around arm in arm and talking about the world's problems.

Blair

In the fall of 1934, my parents had to find another place for me, as they were still unemployed, traveling extensively, and not going to leave me alone in New York City. Seeking a boarding school that would give me a full scholarship (that was essential), they settled on Blair Academy, a fine college preparatory school in northern New Jersey. Its beautiful campus included wooded, rolling hills and athletic fields, large trees, and historic gray stone buildings. Its faculty comprised older, life-long secondary school teachers together with a few young doctoral graduates from some of the best Ivy League schools who could not get other jobs during the Depression.

I was just 12, and Blair was my eighth school. Besides being the youngest student, I was once again an outsider, the different one. I was even still wearing knickers instead of long pants (I wore church hand-me-downs until I was 14). Coming from Burma and then from a farm, I was totally unprepared for Blair's sophisticated, upper-class student body. Young, naive, and vulnerable, I soon became a victim of my desire to become one of the boys. Meeting classmates the first day, I attempted to ingratiate myself humorously by saying, "Just call me Nitwit" (instead of DeWitt). They seized on this and made my life miserable with it for the next five years, especially when I made better grades.

At the end of the first year, I was miserable. I hated the school, or rather, the superficiality of my schoolmates and their cruel taunts. This was partly because it contrasted so greatly with my summer experiences with college students at Lisle, partly because I was small and smart, and partly because I insisted on being my own person. Other rejections related to the fair amount of homosexual activity going on at Blair (as in all such schools at that time), which I found both unappealing and unacceptable. Years later, when interviewed by Dr. Kinsey of *Kinsey Report* fame, however, I had to count myself as having participated in such activity. Meanwhile, I wanted desperately to change schools; but I was on scholarship, so I stuck it out.

Blair's seniors made up the largest class. Most were high school graduates needing an additional year of work before college. To import athletic glory, Blair also recruited top high school athletes who wanted to raise their grades. The irony of this was a student body made up of small boys like myself, surrounded by six-foot giants who came in for one year to play football or basketball. Competing for a place on the athletic teams was really difficult.

My hemophilia limited me to sports such as swimming, wrestling, and tennis. I was pretty good at swimming but could hardly compete with the talented "ringers." In those years, Blair's outstanding swim team won both state and national championships and set a number of national and world records. Over time, however, I developed technical skills that enabled me to compete with and even coach some of these bigger, better athletes.

The guys at Blair talked constantly about girlfriends. I had none, except for my cousin Alice, whom I loved deeply and with whom I spent every moment in the summers when I wasn't at Lisle. Both of us felt we were soulmates, but our parents made it clear to us that first cousins did not marry or do other things. All the same, I think we were always secret "lovers of the heart."

To hold my own in the nightly bull sessions, I kept a picture of a girl from a missionary home in Ohio where I had stayed briefly. I'm not sure if I took it or found it. It was inscribed: "Lovingly, Vera," and I'm not sure if I had written that or she had written it to someone else. (Later, I met that same Vera at a reunion and showed her the picture. She was delighted.)

At the rare school dances in my junior and senior years, other fellows brought in dates for the weekend who occupied our rooms.

Sunday nights, I'd return with the delicious excitement of knowing that a real girl had slept in my bed the night before. At our senior prom, we had the Glenn Miller and Charlie Barnet bands (live!). As usual, I didn't have the money or the girl—and didn't know how to dance.

I got no allowance, so I earned spending money any way I could. For instance, during the 20-minute break between the end of our evening study period and "lights out," I gathered food orders from classmates, ran to the soda fountain in town (over half a mile away), and carried the orders back. I made a nickel on each transaction, which usually gave me enough money to pay for a weekend movie and a milkshake.

Blair was difficult and demanding scholastically. What I remember most were good teachers who challenged me. My transcript doesn't look much like college-level work by today's standards, but at that time, even an 80 (out of 100) was a top grade. I recall handing in my final exam in English History to the professor, who had never given anyone as much as an 80 in the course. Knowing that I knew my stuff, he asked me if I would take an 80. I said, "No, I'm better than that"—and got an 81.

It was a totally absorbing life, with many extracurricular activities. Most of my good memories are of sports and scholarly challenge, a chance to try everything and succeed at many. I participated in everything from drama to newspaper to yearbook to debate society. And my senior English class consisted of making the 90-minute trip to Manhattan on Wednesday afternoons to see a Broadway play. However, the wound from my time there was so deep that I turned down scholarship offers at all the colleges where my schoolmates might go. Instead, I chose Swarthmore, a small Quaker liberal arts college where no one from Blair had ever gone.

☆

Awakenings

When I went to college, I intended to major in psychology. My interest grew out of meeting some of the outstanding psychologists who were friends of my parents, such as J. L. Moreno of psychodrama fame and William H. Sheldon, the famous somatotype psychologist, who was a neighbor. Swarthmore's psychology department, though top notch, turned out to be totally alien to my interests. Its faculty included Edwin Newman and Robbie McLean, known for their work in operant conditioning; and Wolfgang Kohler, the great German Gestalt psychologist. However, their courses bore little resemblance to the psychology I knew. They focused on mice and measurement. So I turned to economics, mainly because we had a professor who taught social economics, which was the closest thing to sociology— a field that has held my interest ever since.

My college years were wonderful. My excellent preparation at Blair made it relatively easy to get by—which was about all I did. I'm afraid I didn't take full advantage of my world-class professors. I recently came across some things I wrote when I was in my late teens. It was humbling to see the fecklessness of my youth. Throughout, the common theme was of being interested in and intrigued by things but unwilling to put in the hard work or discipline necessary to master them. I seemed always "becoming"— rather than "being."

Nonetheless, I exploded socially. I arrived at college with little experience and lots of inhibitions. I had never learned social dancing, the dating scene, or other things that young men generally encounter during high school. Anxious to learn, I went along with my classmates to the social hall for a mixer the very first evening. I'd heard that there was going to be dancing, and I assumed it would be folk or square dancing, which we did at Lisle and at which I was quite good.

As we entered the door, someone handed me half of a playing card and told me to match it with the card of one of my female classmates. As I met the young woman who held the matching card, music from the Glenn Miller Band started. Other couples paired off and started to dance cheek to cheek. I panicked. Excusing myself hastily, I left my partner, hoping she could find someone more suitable.

Ashamed and embarrassed, I feared another poor start like the one at Blair. The very next day, I started a concerted effort to learn to dance. Swarthmore had at least one formal dance every weekend. Later I joined a fraternity that had two weekly dances, records on Friday nights, and a live band on Saturdays. I went to parties, square dances, and outings. Given the ample opportunities, I rapidly became one of the better dancers at college.

I was soon dating heavily, exploring a whole new side of myself. Swarthmore's major contribution was socializing me to a world of boys and girls, men and women, male and female, and enabling me to feel accepted and part of American society. In that wonderful, open, accepting, coeducational environment, I no longer felt like an outsider. I could date as many girls as I wanted (or had time and resources for), and I proceeded to do so.

Aside from dancing, dating, working, and—oh, yes—taking classes, I pursued my love of sports and struggled against my hemophilia. I was an excellent swimmer, so I felt I had to go out for the team, but my heart wasn't in it. I wanted to try football (separated my shoulder), soccer (hurt my leg), and lacrosse (broke my nose and my leg). The doctors were right about avoiding such pursuits, but I wasn't a bad athlete and I wouldn't trade those experiences.

Money was a problem. I was so poor that I came to college with only one sport coat and two pairs of (long) pants. About a month later, the cleaners lost my best pair, so I was really stuck. I noticed a football contest in the Philadelphia *Inquirer*, in which the prize was a tailored suit of clothes. I entered, won, and went to collect. They said I could get any suit I wanted.

"Even a formal set of tails?" I asked.

"Sure."

That did it. I wore those tails throughout college and graduate school. Of course, that didn't solve my clothing problem—but the *Inquirer* kept having similar contests, and I entered and won again. This time I asked for a regular suit.

For other expenses—spending money and the rare trip—I worked as much as 50 hours a week at various jobs, including cleaning the fraternity house and waiting tables in a local restaurant. One summer I worked as a stevedore, another on a factory assembly line. This generated enough money to date the girls with whom I was experiencing the joys of coeducation. I finally had found a home—at Swarthmore. I loved it so much, I never left the campus unless I had to. I stayed there even on most vacations and summers.

The one exception was during the summer of 1942, when I took off across the country and found myself flat broke in Colorado on Labor Day. It was round-up time, and I asked for a job from a rancher. The man asked if I knew how to ride. I said yes, although I'd never ridden a horse in my life. Telling me to mount up, he dashed off across the meadow to corral some stray cattle. Happily for me, my horse knew what to do and I managed to stay on. The rancher ended up offering me a job and left me alone in a mountain cabin to finish rounding up cattle that had been feeding in the high country all summer. I ate by hunting rabbits. A month later, I drove the herd out over the mountains in a snowstorm. He offered me a permanent job. I wonder what life would have been like as a cowboy.

Meanwhile, in the middle of my junior year, the Japanese had bombed Pearl Harbor. College life as we knew it began unraveling as draft notices arrived. Within a few months, classmates were leaving. My exposure to the Lisle Fellowship, my parents' friends, and my dad—a World War I veteran turned pacifist—had led me to believe in solutions other than war. So in 1942, I registered as a conscientious objector (C.O.). However, my Selective Service committee didn't want to deal with that, so they classified me as 4F (physically unfit) because of my hemophilia. (Nearly a decade later, I was again drafted, this time during the Korean War. By that time, I had become a Quaker. Once more, I requested C.O. status and once again was rejected as 4F.)

For my generation, I believe, World War II was the defining event. Many of my high school and college friends never returned. For the rest of us, it became the opening gambit in nearly every social encounter in ensuing years: "Where did you serve? What outfit were you with?" As a C.O., or even a 4F, I never got over the feeling of missing out on a great shared experience. Some close friends have passed this off with a well-intentioned "You didn't miss much" or "You were better off." But I still wonder how I would have measured up in the armed services.

Strangely, I don't think it has to do with courage or with sacrifice. Later at Yale, while we were still at war, I volunteered for high-altitude aeromedical experiments (actually, I needed the money). I took U.S. Air Force pilots up to acclimate them to high altitudes, including going into sudden descents. This gave most of them the "bends" (severe joint pain because of nitrogen bubbles appearing in the bloodstream). For some reason, I never got them and so participated in many rescue efforts as well.

I also tested high-altitude equipment, once setting a (then) world altitude record of 52,000 feet with a new oxygen mask. And I participated in experiments on oxygen-deprivation—for five dollars an hour and without "informed consent." What this did to my brain, I'm not sure. (On a recent visit to the Holocaust Museum in Washington, I saw photographs of the brains of people whom the Nazis forced to perform similar "brutal experiments.")

Meanwhile, anticipating the end of my Swarthmore days and still on my own financially, my first priority was to earn money. I tried working in a shipyard as a junior engineer, which paid well and amounted to only about six hours of work a day. But it was boring and, strangely, I felt trapped. The work seemed devoid of human contact, and I had an awakening about work. I had always thought my father worked too hard—he seemed to be working with people 18 hours a day. Although I wanted to be different, my shipyard experience made it clear that I too loved working with people. Intending to try my father's path, I applied to Yale Divinity School in the fall of 1943 and was accepted.

At the end of my senior year at Swarthmore, I spent part of the summer in the mountains of Southern California at Trabuco Ranch. This was a center for mystical life and practice created by Alduous Huxley, Christopher Isherwood, and Gerald Heard. During one session, Heard mentioned a French priest in the 13th century who was exiled to a small village in Southern France because of his independent views. Some years later, news crept back to Paris that this priest had become a remarkable healer who meditated six hours a day and ministered to the sick and disabled for the other eighteen. Heard referred to him as a "seer," and I suddenly experienced an intense desire to become like this person.

It seemed clear that whatever else was required to be a seer, nobody had become one much before age 60. Figuring I had almost 40 years at my disposal, I thought I should learn all I could about every aspect of life, starting with my weakest areas: science and the human body. That summer, I wrote all my friends a letter that effectively outlined my plans for the next 20 years. I would spend the next four years learning about the human body, then a similar period learning about the human mind. Next, I wanted to teach. Following those phases, I would do research. In retrospect, it seems strange how closely I have followed that plan.

By the time I entered Yale, I was fairly sophisticated socially, comfortable academically, and making enough money to meet the modest demands of my life. These included dating, travel, an old car (I paid $19 for it), movies, and the theater (60 cents for second-balcony seats at Broadway plays). I found myself enjoying the upper-class Ivy League life that I had spurned four years earlier.

My teachers at Yale were outstanding, too. I had Richard Neibuhr for theology, Robert Calhoun in philosophy, Luther Weigle in Bible, Liston Pope in social ethics, Roland Bainton in church history, and Hugh Hartshorne in psychology. My old love won out over theology, however, and I gradually drifted into courses in the Department of Psychology, where Rollo May was then a young doctoral student.

In 1944, I became terribly infatuated with a psychology grad student, a gorgeous woman of Russian and Japanese origin. She was probably the most exotic-looking woman I have ever known. My intense sensual and spiritual relationship with her reawakened the goal of becoming a seer. It also involved the coming of spring, both for New Haven and for Bud Baldwin.

"Haf You Effer Considered Medicine?"

Soon after, I stumbled into a course at the medical school taught by Leo Simmons, an anthropologist, and Eugen Kahn, the professor of psychiatry (and a former student of Kretschmer). It was probably this country's first formal seminar in medical sociology, and all the concepts fascinated me. At the end of the course, I asked Dr. Kahn, "Where could I learn more about this sort of thing?"

Raising his huge eyebrows, he asked, "Haf you effer considered medicine?"

I hadn't. Although I wanted to learn more about the human body, I had no particular interest in medicine. Nonetheless, his query stimulated me to become a pastoral counseling intern at the Massachusetts General Hospital in the summer of 1944. There, I studied under Rolly Fairbanks, one of the pioneers in pastoral counseling.

I also met some of the truly great physicians then on the Harvard faculty, men such as Fuller Albright, the world-renowned endocrinologist; premier surgeons Reginald Smithwick and Oliver Cope; thyroid expert Joseph Aub; the neurologist Stanley Cobb; and psychiatrists Erich Lindemann and Abe Feinsinger. All of them lavished on me their knowledge and enthusiasm for medicine. I adored the experience and realized I could be helpful to people in need. In preparation for becoming a seer, I decided to study medicine as well as the ministry. Medical school would be my way to learn about the human body.

Having avoided science in college, I now had to make up time. I took a full slate of undergraduate pre-med courses at Yale's Sheffield Scientific School while concurrently attending my second full-time year at the divinity school. The two schedules did not conflict, fortunately, so I was able to complete most of my basic pre-med courses one month before my divinity school exams.

Unfortunately, the divinity school's new dean refused to let me continue such a schedule. This forced me to choose between medical school and divinity school. A concurrent, equally important event also affected my eventual choice of career. Because of his radical ecumenical views and the Lisle Fellowship's interfaith philosophy, my father was sandbagged at the annual conference of the Methodist Board of Missions. Each of two committees apparently was told that the other had decided to drop Dad's work with students. I'd like to think that the committees each reluctantly went

along, thinking it was a *fait accompli*. Even so, he was once more
unemployed.

This was a tremendous blow to him and to my mother because
their pioneering experiential service–learning work at Lisle was
proving very effective and successful. It also affected me greatly. I
cut off the church at that point, and it hasn't been very important to
me ever since. By that time, I had seen too much of the kind of
people and decisions that ran it.

I decided to go with medicine and have never regretted the
choice, although I have often wished that I could have completed
divinity school as well. In the spring of 1945, I was accepted to
medical school, but the way was not yet clear. I still had to complete a few more pre-med courses. The medical school's registrar
kept asking about my transcript for those classes, and I kept claiming ignorance—and stayed out of her sight.

In addition to taking both pre-med and medical school courses,
and managing an extensive extracurricular life, I managed to support myself through graduate and medical school. I went to classes
only when I absolutely had to. Luckily for me, Yale was the only
school in the country that treated students as responsible adults
and allowed them the freedoms of a European system. To maintain
good standing, one only had to pass the examinations of the National Board of Medical Examiners at the end of the second and
fourth years. This meant not having to take course exams during
my first two years, which—because of my double schedule and my
predilection for independence—would have very soon found me
out. Near the end of the second year, I spent three solid months
cramming so I could pass the National Board exams. I recall reading an entire pathology textbook (for the first time) the night before
the exam. It worked!

When I was a 26 year-old junior in medical school, I finally
experienced my first sexual intercourse. I don't suppose I would

have had the courage to try it then if the young woman hadn't made it so easy. My mother had spent years warning me of the dangers of the nonvirginal life, and I was deeply conflicted over sex. For me, sleeping with a woman was tantamount to a declaration of marriage and carried with it tremendous responsibilities. Besides, I was panic-stricken that I would make her pregnant—or someone else would—and I'd be forced to marry her.

For the next ten years, however, I expended a great deal of my energy and resources in search of romance. My quest fueled many of the famous Baldwin sagas that amused my buddies on camping and ski trips in the late 1940s. I dated at all the women's colleges in New England, attending proms, house parties, and Winter Carnivals. This was when I really took up skiing, taking off from New Haven every weekend I could (which was most).

However, with the third year of medical school and clinical work on the pediatric wards, my life changed completely. At last, I had found what I was seeking. The professor was one of the most kindly and humanistic physicians I have ever known, and I felt drawn to the care of children. I loved this work and from then on was sold on medicine.

I followed my adventurous desires throughout much of graduate and medical school. In 1949, that changed when I entered internship and residency training at the University of Minnesota Hospitals in Minneapolis. Not only was there no time (we worked every other night and every other weekend) but my pay was only $15 a month. It was always a gamble whether I'd have enough money to do what I wanted. To earn extra money, sometimes I'd work all day as a resident and then all night as a special nurse, followed by another day on duty—and another night on call. I burned the candle at both ends.

Still, I managed to have a few adventures. During my second year there, I set out in the "Brown Bear" (my Chevy convertible), accompanied by a young English physician who was studying in this country. He wanted to see the country and I wanted to ski. My aim was to experience every ski area in the West (I'd already skied all the ones in the East). I would be on the slopes all day, have a hasty meal, climb back into the car, and drive to the next area. We often arrived on the last day of operation for the year, since this was in April. Since some of these spots were several hundred miles apart, we often drove most of the night and slept only a few hours. It was my time to be a ski bum, and I lived it fully: camping out-doors, eating cheaply (crackers and ketchup were free on tables at ski areas), and skiing all the famous resorts. The month-long trip cost us under $200 each. I succeeded in my goal, but I think my English "friend" was no longer that by the trip's end, although he certainly had an adventure.

After two years at the University of Minnesota, I returned to Yale in 1951 to specialize in child development. Earlier, I had worked at the Child Study Center at Yale with Arnold Gesell. Now I worked under his successor, Milton Senn, and people such as Ernst Kris, Al Solnit, and Sally Provence. The stimulating year introduced me to psychoanalytic theory and inspired me later to enter analysis. Perhaps equally important, I had my own practice of pediatrics, made up of patients in the pioneering Natural Child-birth Program at Yale under Edith Jackson. Again, I loved it. For the first time, I thought seriously about becoming a practicing physician.

In 1952, at the end of my Yale fellowship year, I accepted a job in California as head of pediatrics at the new Walnut Creek Hospital, which was to be the showpiece of Henry Kaiser's Permanente Medical Group. As frosting on the cake, Mr. Kaiser's assistant took me along on a boat trip through the fjords of British Columbia. The June weather, the mountains, the forests, and the snow were gorgeous—and I fell in love with the Northwest. It was my first exposure to the region and to Native American culture. At the trip's end, I told him that I wanted to stay there. He said he would give me 48 hours to make up my mind. By that evening, I had found a job teaching pediatrics at the University of Washington. I didn't intend to teach, but there I was, following my long-forgotten plan.

The Move West

Working in the Department of Pediatrics at the University of Washington, I had five glorious years in Seattle. I don't suppose I've ever been happier. Aside from teaching and practicing pediatrics, I was free, single, and earning good money at last ($6000 per year as a young professor). Every weekend I was free to explore a different place and do a different thing. This meant hiking and skiing in the Cascade mountains, sailing in the waters of British Columbia and Puget Sound, and running the many rivers of the Northwest in my kayak. I lived frugally, but my lifestyle was perfect for me. I wanted nothing more than to live and work in Seattle the rest of my life. It was a wonderful life.

Being able to burn the candle at both ends stood me in good stead when I entered psychoanalysis in 1953. It cost much more than I was making but, with my usual luck, I always found ways to do what I wanted. Several nights a week, I'd work a 12-hour shift as a physician at the city jail. My salary was $20—exactly the amount I needed to pay my analyst when I showed up on his doorstep at 8 o'clock the next morning. After our session, I'd go on to another full day's work at the university.

In the summer of 1955, I suddenly noticed an enlargement of my right testicle. My physician's diagnosis was cancer, and he recommended immediate surgery. It was a shock. All my life, I had struggled against feeling vulnerable because of my hemophilia—

from early unawareness to later compliance, to still later denial and rebellion. Now, in 1955, getting cancer doubled my sense of vulnerability. After the operation came massive, unprotected radiation.

For the first time, I had to come to terms with dying. Much earlier, because of my hemophilia, I had accepted that I probably would not live a long time. I'd bled out several times more since my out-of-body experience at age four, so for me, death itself did not represent anything fearful. At times, I'd even thought of it as a form of surcease from the frequent rat race of my life. Having led a very full and exciting life, I genuinely felt willing to call it quits if necessary.

But I had one last desire. My bargain with God (I still believed in God, apparently, if not the church) was: "I've had a good life, had fun, done almost everything I ever wanted for the first 35 years of my life, but I've never known love or a family. Please let me experience that." I guess my part of the bargain was that I would settle down, give up my playboy existence, and become serious about my life, love, and work. (Interestingly, these were very close to my mother's admonitions.)

That commitment was a watershed for me: from loneliness to togetherness, from work as an end to work as a means, from a broad focus to a narrower one. Until then, a key piece of me had been refusing to be dominated by or revealed to others. That piece has manifested itself in many ways throughout my life, including a memorable experience with Alexander Lowen, the bioenergetic psychoanalyst. Inviting me to work with him, he sat on my chest, pinned my shoulders to the ground, and told me to repeat the words "I won't give up" as I attempted to free myself. I tried this several times and then told him it didn't feel right. The words I wanted to use were "I won't give in." To me, "I won't give up" is a cry of survival; "I won't give in" is a cry of independence, a statement of life and of life force.

Love

By reminding me once again of my vulnerability, the cancer made me more conscious of my isolation, my loneliness. I had sought love for years (perhaps of all my life), running from one woman to another. Certainly, I was filled with romantic notions. I dated widely and intensely and was serially infatuated with a number of wonderful women. Each relationship had seemed totally honest and authentic. Even so, they were not love as I now understand it.

Rather than being a case of "looking for love in all the wrong places," it was as though I had never known what love was and was blind to it. While I could be very caring, I wasn't capable of loving anyone, even—maybe especially—myself. Even now, Michele sometimes makes a loving gesture or statement and I think, "My gosh, she really *loves* me," as if it were somehow unthinkable or impossible. Deeming myself lovable had been a struggle for many years (and still is, to a degree).

I often wish I could apologize to some of the women who were hurt by my inability to love. I always came up against that piece, "I won't give in." I had probably never totally given in to anyone or anything. While appearing to be loving, to conform, to be accommodating, to be kind, I always held back something in myself. Without moving through that feeling, I could not truly surrender myself to my capacity to love, or even to love myself. Recently, I saw the same pattern in the movie *Good Will Hunting*.

Another major block was my intense fear of my own anger—rage, actually. When it erupted, it knew no bounds. Early in life, I learned to curb it so as to get along with people. Although many friends never saw this side of me, I was terribly aware that it was an unpredictable force that I feared I could not control. Intimate relationships represented an arena in which it might be unleashed.

My breakthrough began in 1957 during a party I held in Seattle to introduce Michele to my friends. A Fulbright Scholar from

France studying at the University of Washington, she was my new romantic object, so I hoped she would be impressed with them and they with her. During the party, I couldn't find her. Since I often found her unpredictable (karma for a control freak like me, I guess) and knew she didn't like big parties, I mistakenly concluded that she had walked out on me. Infuriated by this abandonment (the key to my rage, I suspect), I went berserk. Spewing out my anger to a friend, I felt as if I were a dragon breathing flames.

Until then, my fear had always been that if I ever got that angry around people, I would incinerate them. To my amazement, this friend—a wonderfully sensitive and mature neighbor whom I greatly admired and cared for—didn't flinch. She responded in a firm yet supportive way. At that moment, I realized that my anger did not need to be my master. I could control myself, and others could protect themselves.

Somehow that experience lanced the boil of deep anger within me. Slowly, it began to heal. I had later outbursts with Michele, but we got through them. Having someone accept my rage without abandoning me really helped me begin caring for myself. Concurrently, my ability to care for others grew. Freeing my anger somehow also freed me to begin to love.

All the same, I don't think I fell in love with Michele for a long time after that. At first, my feelings about her were a bewildering mix, although I desperately wanted to be in love. The final barrier was surmounted on a desperate, lonely night after she had "abandoned" me again (well, went back to France). While reading the chapter on commitment in Erich Fromm's *The Art of Loving*, I thought, "I guess I've simply got to hold my nose and jump, or I'll never fall in love."

Soon after, I proposed. I had to tell her that I might die of cancer or hemophilia in a few years. Furthermore, my doctors had not shielded me or the other testicle during my heavy radiation treatments, and everyone now advised me to forget about having children. To this day, I don't know why Michele said yes. She was very young—only 20 when I met her (I was 35)—and not ready for children. I wanted them badly, but we agreed that we wouldn't have any until she was ready. (I was great at denial.)

I was a pretty narrow, judgmental guy when we got married on December 27, 1957. After all those years of waiting, somehow, the marriage had to be perfect—and so did Michele. How she ever tolerated it (or me), I'll never know. Our first six months were extremely rocky. If we'd had the money, I'm sure she would have left, and I probably would have been relieved. But I was only making $200 a month, and we both had pride and were stubborn. It would have been difficult for either of us to admit failure, so we stayed together.

We share a basic life experience of early abandonment, and I suspect both of us may have a deep core of depression that has never been—may never be—resolved. We also share that feeling of being "different," strangers, homeless. She, too, had many early childhood moves and never felt like she belonged anywhere.

People sometimes ask us about our relationship. Part of our success has been her tolerating me. Part of it was her incredible ability to make me laugh at myself. (Michele still complains that I misrepresented myself to her as a playboy, leading a fun life. Then, when she married me, I became a serious workaholic.) She has always been able to cut through my pomposity and my rigidity, my judgmental piece, and make me more human. And of course, she is a woman of excitement, charm, beauty, and mystery. Her integrity has been a major part of making our relationship work. I often liken her to a silver bell that always gives off a true note.

I cannot say that life has been always easy for her—or with her. She has been enormously kind and loving, as well as hard and demanding on occasion. It's probably what I needed to balance my life. In many ways, she has been my teacher, and I have learned much from and through her. I'm enormously grateful to her. I still sit in awe of her physical and spiritual beauty, her professional qualities, as well as her sound judgment. We have great respect for each other and a very deep love.

Recovering from the cancer and, despite heavy radiation, later conceiving two children are miracles—of nature, of my life force and, I believe, of putting my anger to rest and learning to love. These experiences also helped put me more in touch with my body— or rather, with the fact that I was and still am often *not* in my body. That I somehow broke through some of my conflicts and was able to know and experience love with Michele may well have played a role in the fitness I have enjoyed since. Of course, we often repeat Ingrid Bergman's famous line: "Happiness consists of good health and a short memory."

New Challenges

In 1956, the new head of pediatrics at the University of Washington began demanding academic research of the faculty. I was primarily a clinician and teacher: I saw patients and taught students. I loved it and had even won a prize for my teaching. But it became clear I wasn't going to survive unless I did research or made myself otherwise indispensable. One way seemed to be to have a unique clinical specialty. Since the university had never been able to recruit a child psychiatrist, and I had always been interested in psychology, I agreed to go to Boston to get such training, with the promise of a joint appointment when I returned.

The period of my psychiatric training was difficult. I had to go back to being a resident (and night call) for four more years, away from my beloved West. My first year was at a Harvard-affiliated state hospital where I was the only resident. Michele and I were newlyweds and going through major adjustments. Yet, as she has ever since, she supported me in taking this job at a substantially reduced income because it was more interesting and challenging.

In 1958, I became Chief Resident in adult psychiatry at the Massachusetts Memorial (now University) Hospital, in Boston. Two years followed in child psychiatry at the Boston City Hospital, where I studied with Eleanor Pavenstedt, one of the world's leading child psychoanalysts. Although the Boston years were hard, once more I had the privilege and opportunity of working with some incredible teachers: psychoanalysts Felix Deutsch (who had been Freud's personal physician), Elvin Semrad, and Greta Bibring.

Deutsch was a marvelously inventive man. He once reported that to get beyond the resistances of an analytic patient, he released odors into the room and found that activated a great deal of work on the part of the patient (the origins of aromatherapy?). His use of patients' drawings later sparked my own interest in research on children's drawings.

Ironically, by the time I finished my training, I gave up going back to my beloved Seattle. Instead, I joined Harvard's faculty as a pediatric researcher in 1961. Shortly after, I received a U.S. Public Health Service Career Development Research Award, which supported me over the next six years.

Four years into our marriage, Michele and I decided to try having a child. Again, every doctor told me that I couldn't. I even decided to get a sperm count, but my wonderfully human oncologist said, "Why don't you just give Mother Nature a chance?" Two or three months later, Michele was pregnant. I count that as a blessing and a miracle as well as further evidence that God was living up to His part of the bargain. I felt so lucky to have a child—and Lisa was a beautiful child. Four years later, we had another beautiful daughter, Mireille. Both are blond. Michele has dark hair, like mine used to be, so when people have wondered about the blond hair, she always says, "I don't know about Bud, but I know I'm the mother!" Blame it on the radiation.

Six months after Lisa was born, Michele got ill. The chief of medicine at Boston University came by to see her a couple of times and said it was probably the flu. But the illness had a bizarre course. One night, I saw her eyes cross and thought, "My God, she's got T.B. meningitis." Having trained at Minnesota, where we still saw tuberculous meningitis, I recognized it and knew it to be a fatal disease or worse.

It was late at night and in dead of winter. Panic stricken, I literally carried her to the emergency room at Massachusetts General Hospital (I couldn't get a taxi or a car to stop for us). My doctor, the oncologist, came in from a dinner party, agreed with my diagnosis, and started treatment, although the diagnosis wasn't fully confirmed for several weeks. Michele's tuberculous meningitis proved to be only the most prominent manifestation of an active tuberculosis throughout her body. She was in coma for several weeks and in the hospital for several months. She lost so much weight she was like a skeleton. Newly invented drugs finally let her begin to recover.

She was not openly contagious, but hospital rules did not allow children to visit. Given my knowledge of child development, however, I wanted to keep the mother–child connection going, so I used to smuggle Lisa into the hospital in the pocket of my winter coat. It paid off when Michele came home from the hospital and Lisa exploded with excitement.

The children have been the joy of my life. I feel completely fulfilled as a parent. They're both joyful and lovely, although three weeks after Lisa was born, we both agreed we should have called her April, because her moods ranged from sunshine to storm—and still do. She has grown to be a powerful and charismatic woman, a lot like Virginia Satir. When she walks into a room, people look to

her to take charge. She and I have talked about this, because charisma is also a burden.

Mireille has been a different story. She too is beautiful and
blond—adorable, shy, almost waiflike when she was young; earthy,
sexy, and complex as she grew up. She has never wanted for
friends—especially boyfriends. In a way, it's been a curse. She's
had difficulty defining her own boundaries but seems to have
established them lately. Of course, she's a Capricorn (like my
mother), and they take time to mature.

Changes

In 1967, my career at Harvard led to an invitation to join the
planning team for a unique combined medical/dental school at the
University of Connecticut. I had always dreamed of building a
learning environment that would produce humanistic, caring,
socially concerned physicians and dentists. I hoped we could recruit
a faculty of like-minded persons and do what no school to date had
been able to do. It was exhilarating.

My first attempt to recruit faculty radically changed my life.
After locating Harry Sloan, a former student I wanted to hire, I
called him on the West Coast. "I'm trying to build a humanistic
school," I said, "I want you on my faculty."

"If you want to talk, you'll have to come out here." he said.

"Where's that?"

"Esalen," he replied. So I went out to Big Sur on the California coast with my button-down shirt, Harvard tie, and gray flannel
suit. It was obvious immediately that I was out of place. By nine
o'clock that evening, however, I realized that I felt at home. I stayed
the weekend and have never been the same.

When I got home, I grabbed Michele and said, "We're going
back." We borrowed the money and went back to Esalen for a whole

week, attending a couples' workshop with Betty Fuller. We worked all day in the group and then stayed up half the night, talking about our relationship. It blew things wide open—to wonderful new places. Our ten-year marriage had been on a plateau for some time, going nowhere. We had closed off many areas of our life, and our relationship had brought out her blaming and my placating. I still couldn't deal effectively with her anger, and I don't think she could, either. Our relationship has since gone through several more plateaus and growth spurts, but our Esalen experience opened the doors to growth and love I couldn't have imagined before.

We returned to Esalen that year for several more fascinating workshops with Fritz Perls, Bob Tannenbaum, George Brown, John Lilly, and Bill Schutz. It was mind blowing, and it would have been easy to become an "Esalen freak." My nature, however, is to apply things, to see if they work in the real world; so I returned to Connecticut and tried to make those things work.

A different kind of experience also occurred in 1968 when the Milbank Foundation sent me to Europe to look at combined medical/dental education. Several countries there believed that dentistry was really a specialty of medicine and trained them together—the very experiment we were trying at Connecticut. I learned a lot, but the experience that stands out was an airline mistake that landed me in East Berlin during the height of the Cold War, when Americans were decidedly not welcome in East Germany. Suddenly behind the Iron Curtain, I went through a harrowing experience with confused and upset officials, an impromptu lecture before a large group of professional students at the Free University of East Berlin, lunch with several professors, a performance of the East Berlin opera, and a midnight getaway to West Berlin.

Far less exotic or adventurous was the way the new Connecticut school developed. It not only failed to realize my original dream for a humanistic learning environment but seemed deliberately to confound it. Fed up with the situation, I left in 1971. The same pattern was playing out at other new schools, unfortunately, and I felt totally disillusioned with medical education. It was the nearest I've ever come to feeling crazy, because when I'd say to my fellow faculty members, "Can't you see what's happening? We're going in the wrong direction," they couldn't seem to see it. I knew I wasn't crazy, but wondered why other people couldn't see what I saw as a destructive path.

I think my capacity to see trends or foresee things goes back to Burma and being the only white kid in my first two schools. In those schoolyards, being safe meant anticipating every experience, every encounter. I developed a finely honed, intuitive ability to read people and situations. In Connecticut, it turned out I was reading the scene correctly. Ten years later, people on that faculty confirmed my impressions.

Meeting Virginia Satir

I grew up with a tendency to go against convention or the crowd (even when I appear to conform). One example was my going to "old" Europe to find an integrated medical/dental education plan for a "new" school in America. While others are focusing on "foreground," I am looking for the gestalt's "background"—as well as the converse. In the cyclical nature of things, I often find I'm thinking differently than others, ahead of the next wave of interest because I started looking for it earlier.

Virginia Satir had that same finely developed ability. Most people need a number of points in a row to say, "That's a line, a trend; that's where things are going." Some people will begin to guess after three points. Virginia and I seemed to have an ability to see patterns emerging as a second point was just beginning to appear. I think that was her genius with clients. I used to watch in fascination while she was working. Lots of times I would note someone's word, gesture, or expression and think, "Go for it!" Next thing I knew, she was working with it. She made me feel confident that my intuitive judgments were on target.

It has taken a long time for me to get to the influence of Virginia Satir on my life and that of my family. Michele met her first in 1969 at a workshop in Portland, Maine. She was so impressed that she telephoned me to come up that weekend and meet this remarkable person. Virginia was all of that, and I was smitten with her charisma and incredible insight. It didn't take long—a workshop in Boston, another in Hartford—before Michele and I were committed to working with her.

At that point, Virginia looked to me like a miracle-maker (a seer, perhaps?). She seemed to reach and elicit the humanness in every person. In all my training and teaching, I had never seen anyone like her. I wanted to learn from her and her wholeness more fully. Or perhaps I sensed I could reach my own wholeness through her.

Thus began one of the most important relationships I, we, and our family have ever known—one that became more and more like "family" through the years and brought her to our home on many occasions. I estimate that before she died, even our children had spent over six months in her presence—at workshops, at family camps, at our home and hers.

The *Reader's Digest* used to carry an occasional feature called "The Most Unforgettable Character I Ever Met." Despite my long and eventful life, I think Virginia fills that role for me. Somehow it seems fitting that my story should appear in *her* book. She was the greatest therapist I have ever known, and I loved to watch her work with a family. Eventually I became convinced that her work was more than magic: it was the extremely meticulous product of a great artist and a diligent laborer. I admired these qualities in her.

At the simplest level, she helped free me from the rigid constraints of my formal psychiatric training and my super-reasonable personality. She showed me—gave me permission—to be more open and active, more authentic, with my patients. She enabled me to bring out their essential humanness through manifesting more of my own. That meant recognizing and accepting more of my own vulnerabilities and finding, as a result, more of my own power and strength. I think she saw and respected that in me.

I often resisted her suggestions—we both were stubborn. We were also both born in the zodiacal sign of Cancer, and she spoke a number of times about our similarities. The last time was about a month before her death, when we were alone at her house and she warned me to be careful how I used myself, saying that we were too much alike.

Over the years, I was caught up in my admiration of Virginia's magnificent energy and her ability to bring forth humanity in people. She inspired me to try to do likewise. I owe her a lot. I am deeply grateful for her gift to me. It was a double gift. It also gave life to my relationship with Michele and to our growing children.

Nevada

Meanwhile, my Connecticut experience so disillusioned me that I seriously considered leaving medicine. I even asked George Brown if I could work with him at the University of California at Santa Barbara, where he was using humanistic learning principles with very young preschool children. Before I could make the decision, however, someone introduced me to the dean of a new medical school that was being planned in Nevada. He was an unusual—and persuasive—man, somewhat unprepossessing at first glance, but an outstanding leader and person who had the rare ability to let the people around him develop their ideas. So I decided to give medical education one last try and accepted a position as a member of his planning group.

The University of Nevada (Reno) program allowed me a lot of scope. First, I was able to get a million dollars from the Robert Wood Johnson Foundation to start a unique interdisciplinary program in the health sciences for all preprofessional and professional students. Then I assembled a special faculty who wanted to use lots of humanistic approaches.

In many ways, I borrowed many ideas from my parents' work at Lisle—such as Hocking's principle of alternation. The Interdisciplinary Health Sciences program also introduced a lot of experiential stuff and a lot of Virginia's ideas into the curriculum. I brought in all kinds of far -out people to teach, such as Ivan Illitch (medical nemesis), Elizabeth Kübler-Ross (death and dying), Alexander Lowen (bioenergetics), Cecily Saunders (hospice), and Frederick Leboyer (*Birth Without Violence*). Others—including Yetta Bernhard, Sam Ferry, and Jack Gibb—came and taught about humanistic psychology. Richard Bandler and John Grinder gave one of their first workshops on neurolinguistic programming. Virginia came several times. One of these workshops resulted in the 1972 videotape, *A Family in Crisis,* one of the first teaching tapes that showed her working with a family.

The next five years involved an incredible experience of freedom and development. Perhaps the happiest I have been in my adult life was in Reno, where the sun shone nearly every day. Waking up on my first morning there, I had the feeling of being home. I never lost that feeling while I was there. I've always liked to live in sunny climes. In Burma, most days dawned sunny, even during the monsoon season. It always seemed to put a happy face on things.

When the University of Nevada medical school changed from a two-year to a four-year school in 1978, I saw the beginning of the end—at least for me. They began to hire big-name clinical professors from the east, and I realized that the school would simply recreate the same old patterns. The medical school part of it began to look more traditional, but the interdisciplinary program was still truly exciting. We built a program that was way ahead of its time— and still is (parts of it are still in place). Our daughter Mireille experienced it a few years ago as a student in social work.

Meanwhile, the agreement to convert the school carried with it the Nevada legislature's original and continuing mandate to do something about rural health. Having been interested in community development ever since my Lisle Fellowship days, I started an Office of Rural Health in 1976. In three years and with half a million dollars, again from the Robert Wood Johnson Foundation, we doubled the number of physicians in rural Nevada. Health services became available to 19 communities for the first time, and we significantly improved services to 22 others. Still going strong, that program was the one for which the National Rural Health Association awarded me the Louis Gorin Award for contributions to rural health in 1991.

East Again

I loved living in Nevada. I like being involved in the creative, conceptual phase of an innovative project. I like planning it, getting it organized, putting it in place, and making sure it's going to survive. Once it's established, however, I'm ready to leave. By 1983, my eyes were on the next horizon. I knew I couldn't change medical education—I had tried that. More and more convinced that fostering broad and humanistic physicians probably required starting during the preprofessional years, I wanted to get back to "real" education, to my early interest in liberal arts and the humanities. When the opportunity came to become president of Earlham College, a fine Quaker liberal arts college, I accepted.

I think Carl Rogers' letter got me the job. I've never seen it, but the head of Earlham's search committee said that it was the most incredible letter she had ever received. Carl thought a lot of me and liked what I was trying to do in medical education. Michele and I had been closely associated with him for some years in the Human Dimensions in Medical Education program in La Jolla, California, and I think he wanted me to have the chance to do something about the ideas we had been talking about.

Like him, however, I was also a maverick. Maybe that's why the Earlham thing didn't work out as I had hoped. Once again, I dreamed of creating the kind of diverse, humanistic learning community my parents and those other idealists had tried to create back in the 1930s. I thought that the chances were excellent at Earlham, whose literature spoke of many of these same ideas. Apparently, however, this was scary to some of the established faculty and the Board. I didn't realize until too late how badly I was being sabotaged. People accused me of being too close to the students and decentralizing decision-making too much. My later attempts to make some changes in administration were rejected, and I resigned.

For the next year, I went through a prolonged grieving process for the "death of the dream." It was also one of the few times I felt I had failed—even if not in my mind, or the eyes of my family and friends, or the students and junior faculty. All the same, I had to accept the feeling of failure. It was difficult.

By then, I was entering the shadow side of my life. I was over 60, and I wondered if I would get another chance to build lasting institutions that exemplified Virginia's and my dream of enabling

people to become more fully human. I am proud that every grant I
ever received (nearly $12 million altogether) resulted in a program
that has made an impact and outlasted my tenure. The people I
have mentored now head their own programs and are doing similar
things.

A driving force in my life has been the idea of gathering a
group of people who have great potential and can accomplish much
more than I can individually. Teamwork, collaboration, interdisciplinary education, and team training have thus been constant
themes in my professional work since 1952. Yet my interest goes
back even farther, having its roots in my early childhood and boarding school experiences, when I probably longed to be part of a
close family. Collaboration also fits in with my interest in family
therapy, co-therapy, groups, and the work of Virginia Satir.

A related piece is the realization that children who are separated from their parents tend to band together and turn to each
other for emotional support and survival. Along this line, I recently
realized the importance to me of Louisa May Alcott's book *Little
Men*. In it, Jo (one of the sisters in *Little Women*) marries the teacher,
Mr. Baer. Since they are childless, they decide to take wayward
and lost boys into their home and provide for them a nurturing
environment. *Little Men* intrigued me profoundly as a boy. Seeming to answer my childhood wishes to be part of a large, caring
family, it reflected the realities of group living that were my boarding school experience. It also provided the dream of caring, kindly,
and firm parents. It became a sort of ideal for me, the kind of thing
I wanted to do with my life.

Unconsciously, I have tried to replicate this concept in a number of ways throughout my personal life and professional career. In
Seattle, I rented a house and over the years took into it a series of
young single men like myself. As a sort of senior landlord, I had
the feeling of providing a home for a group of peers, while at the

same time creating an atmosphere of caring and generativity. Likewise, in my various professional positions, I have worked to develop an environment of acceptance and nurturance for my associates. I built such a group at Connecticut, selecting an outstanding, multi-talented group of fellow professionals whom I felt could bring about needed changes in medical and dental education. At the University of Nevada, it happened again with the faculty of the Health Sciences program. We used to talk about our program as being an island of sanity in the midst of an authoritarian, hierarchical bureaucratic system that was not concerned with individual needs and growth.

On a smaller scale, assembling a small collaborative group generated the accomplishment that gives me the greatest delight—as opposed to pride. In the early 1970s, our family friend Henri Kummermann wanted to develop some land he owned near the newly announced scientific center of Sophia Antipolis in southern France. The French government had promised a considerable subsidy for the right plan, so Henri had contacted both Arthur D. Little and the Bechtel Corporation. I told him I thought I could do as well. Laughing, he told me to have at it. I talked it over briefly with Robert Graeff, a young relative who was an architect. Along with a friend in operations research, we got together on two weekends in September, developed a proposal, and sent it to Henri. It turned out to be the best of three and, with some adaptations, eventually won the French government contract. Without any comparable background, we managed to beat both Arthur D. Little and Bechtel at their own game!

I even recognize this appeal of collaboration in my going to Earlham College. Because of its literature, I thought it would be the kind of environment—a community, a family, if you will—in which I could somehow participate, as well as guide and empower like a parent. Perhaps one source of my difficulty there might have been my attempt to be both a leader and a participant in the kind of community I thought they and I had in mind.

As I was leaving Earlham, I got a call from a friend of mine who had just gone to head up the Education and Science group at the American Medical Association (AMA) in Chicago. He said, "Bud, I need an elder statesman who knows medical education and what the issues are, and who can forecast 'futures' for us: predict what problems we're going to face in the future and design the research and the policies we need."

It came at the right time and launched me—lucky me—on what was probably the best job anyone's ever had, one that fully challenged my ability and imagination. All I had to do was scan the horizon, see those little dots forming, and figure out where the next dots were going to appear. For example, people were beginning to talk about the lack of humanistic qualities in physicians, and I began to look at the learning and working conditions of medical trainees. I came up with the first empirical studies recording their perceptions of significant psychological, physical, and sexual mistreatment and abuse at the hands of their supervisors. In my later studies on residents-in-training, I came up with exactly the same results. This work has shaken up medical education and led to changes. That's part of what drives me.

Because of my peregrinating intellectual background and curiosity, my work incorporates concepts from many disciplines: medicine, psychology, sociology, religion, literature, and others. My greatest joy is when people call me with a question and I start weaving a pattern for their inquiries. (It's interesting that I use the word *weaving*, because that's what Virginia used to say she did.) All told, I've written over 150 scholarly articles. Some express my passions, fighting hard for causes that are close to my heart. They have spanned many fields, including medicine, psychology, microbiology, sociology, anthropology, dentistry, psychiatry, holistic or alternative medicine, philosophy, ethics, and education. Topics have included everything from health care to communication, from moral development to facial appearance, automobile accidents, and children's drawings.

Michele and I both are into a workaholic piece at present. I don't fully understand it, as officially I'm retired. I once thought work would have a definable end, but the research I started over the last decade at the AMA keeps pouring off the assembly line, and somehow I feel I have to get it out so changes can be made. Over the past decade, some 80 of my papers appeared in scholarly journals, and the annual Research in Medical Education meetings have accepted at least one paper each year. Beyond that, new ideas and projects seem to appear constantly. I have material to write about for years. Indeed, as I write this, I've just been rehired to help staff the AMA's new Institute for Ethics. I always thought when I retired, I would get in a car and do a "travels with Charlie" kind of thing—visit all the places I'd ever wanted to go, hopefully with Michele. It hasn't happened.

I didn't start writing until I was over 40, but I've made up for lost time. The other day, I found myself thinking, "I guess I live to write." That's weird, because when I started out in medicine, where it's expected (no, required), I stubbornly insisted that I would never clutter up the literature. Besides, I was a doer—not a writer. Willy-nilly, however, I've become a writer who can't seem to help himself. I must write, and it gives me pleasure. I've been known to spend a week at a ski resort writing instead of enjoying the slopes.

There you have it—dilettante or searcher? (Well, at least *searcher* starts with the same letter as *seer*.) I regret not working more effectively at the broader issues of life, such as poverty, peace, homelessness, illness, and violence, but I have worked consistently and hard for *my* causes, and perhaps those define me.

When I go behind the pleasure (and the obsession) of my writing, I come to the fact that my passions have taken on a different form. Where I used to "do," I now need to "tell," mostly about things I feel are wrong with medicine and conventional medical education. These have an inexorable, homogenizing effect on young doctors that doesn't produce much, if any, flexibility. My recent research shows that medical education actually inhibits the growth of moral reasoning in medical students. We have also made it quite difficult for students and residents to learn about the more human side, the art of medicine. Much of my work lately is about obstacles to developing ways of "being with" rather than "doing to" the patient.

I've been pretty persistent as well as prolific about this, and the establishment has not always been happy with me. I've sometimes had trouble getting my things published. Several key papers have languished on editors' desks for years before seeing print (and by then, readers seem to say, "But, of course"). All the same, many people now associate my name with research into the nature and cause of our deficits in medical training, and policies and educational interventions are now in place to correct some of them.

My Quest

My mother's death a decade ago has colored my thoughts about the end of life. I had gone through life resenting her control and her physical infirmities. She had remarkable stamina but seemed to have a constant succession of debilitating complaints. I resented them, in part because my own body seemed to have inherited some of her weaknesses. For instance, my hemophilia came from her side of the family. At the same time, she bestowed enormous gifts on me in terms of intellectual, aesthetic, and spiritual life. She constantly challenged my thinking, stimulated my use of words and concepts, encouraged me to become more disciplined, taught me about people and the world. But she also was always very critical—judgmental, with a seeming need to comment on everything.

During childhood, I found my father unskilled in many things. He never seemed to be able to tell a joke or story right, and his sermons seemed prosaic. Besides, he seemed never to be around. I can remember only two times when he and I spent any personal time together alone. Both were at my mother's insistence, and both were awkward. Early in life, I allied myself with her against him, finding fault with his performance as a minister, a man, and a father. This was not helpful to me as I grew into manhood.

At age 16, I deliberately sought to identify more with him, minimizing my mother's role and eschewing her control in my life. This shift created not a wall but a space in my relationship with her that persisted until her death. From the age of 25 on, my visits were only occasional, and I seldom if ever wrote. After I married, things were somewhat better. Michele made an effort to be in contact with her, and we did spend a number of holidays together as the children were growing up. But even into her 80s, my mother was a critical and judgmental person for whom the best was never quite good enough.

Her prolonged death was one of the most agonizing experiences of my life. Despite my belief that she would die from her body, she died by her brain—the one thing she had always counted on. We thought she might have Alzheimer's, but an autopsy identified her problem as cerebral arteriosclerosis. She died on a Christmas Eve—alone—within two weeks of her 87th birthday.

I doubt if I will live that long, let alone as long as my father, who lived to within a week of his 95th birthday. What I fear most is following in my mother's path and losing my mind before my time.

I would prefer to die earlier if, by so doing, I would avoid the horrible spectre of declining mental capacity or the even greater shame of becoming incontinent as well as incompetent.

Meanwhile, I like my life and feel at peace with it. I'm not sure I would change it very much if I had the opportunity. I believe I have been a kind, generous and thoughtful person. I've been blessed with a wonderful family that has provided me with the means of working on (if not necessarily working out) my karma. They have helped me develop the necessary discipline and hard work that I did not have as a single person, giving me a richness of relationship as well as a joy of generativity. I have two wonderful daughters and two remarkable grandsons.

I'd still like to explore some parts of the world I haven't seen and to revisit and seek closure with those parts I have. Michele and I also often think of places we'd like to live some day. My picture has always been a place of nature—in the mountains or on the seacoast. For Michele, it is Paris. She loves the vibrancy of the city and of the people. Oh, well, that's what marriage is all about—accepting differences. Virginia put it best: "We get together on the basis of our similarities [in our case, our sense of rootlessness], but we grow on the basis of our differences [and we sure have them]."

I recently had my first Tarot reading, which challenged my apparent abandonment of the seer's path and made me aware of ignoring a number of my life's dimensions. One card that intrigued me related to the presence in my life of a vital life force. I believe it has been the key to my energy, my curiosity, my creativity, and my survival. All my life, I've been drawn to exploring frontiers, the edges of things: in nature, geography, ideas, and myself. In some ways, I feel I've failed in my early life dream of becoming a seer. I got so busy for so many years—making a living, raising a family, and creating a career—that it got lost. The story of Parsifal and the Quest for the Holy Grail has come to have great meaning for me.

Early in his career, the young Parsifal chances upon the Grail and fails to ask the right question of it, dooming him to years of fruitless pursuit of the vision. The right question was "Whom does the Grail serve?" The psychologist Robert Johnson speaks of the common male pattern of an early vision that gets lost in the need to prepare for life in the real world. Sometimes this vision is lost forever. Sometimes it is possible to recapture it—but only after much struggle and travail. Perhaps it is not too late for me.

The world of medicine has been a seductive and exciting world, one to which I have had no trouble devoting myself fully. It has involved another bright, shiny vision—of how people should be with one another and what healing was all about. So far, that life has seemed enough. However, deep in myself, I wonder. For the last year or two, I have again felt the stirrings of my original quest. As I pass my 77th birthday, I feel that I must once again begin to seek my Grail.

Hugh Gratz once said that Margarita Suarez is "the heart of Avanta." No one disagreed, and she was the unanimous choice as the organization's executive director. I remember Virginia appreciating Margarita's sensitivity to injustice. She is also loyal and brave—and funny, too. Her humor and humanity mean she is in great demand as a speaker.

—*Robert S. Spitzer*
Publisher

9

My Connection
with Virginia

by Margarita M. Suarez

For me, it has always been uncomfortable to talk, or to hear other people talk, about a connection with Virginia Satir. At times I felt as if we were siblings competing to see who was Mother's favorite. It is a human aspect of all of us, and maybe I feel this even more keenly, as I come from a large family. Like many others, I wanted to be special to Virginia. I wanted to be someone who brought her something different, and I felt that I was able to do that. Yet, until the end, I felt that she was the teacher, the mentor, the leader.

Many people were in Virginia's life: many whom she influenced, many whom she invited to join Avanta (her professional network), and many who worked with her in various ways. She touched my life, and I think I touched hers. I felt lucky because she saw my work, respected it, and encouraged it. One of her gifts to me was the freedom to do Satir work "à la Margarita." She allowed me to fly and chart my own course.

433

What did I give her? As a coworker and trainer, I gave her of my time, my energy, my creativity. We worked together on the 1980 family research project, and I gave trainings at her Process Community, the annual one-month workshop in Crested Butte, Colorado.

On a few occasions, I even felt like a peer with her. I was very lucky to have the opportunity to do several presentations to groups in which she was more or less a participant. I say "more or less" because she was still the leader of those groups. Sometimes she made comments during my presentation, sometimes she waited until the end to add her understanding. Yet she was respectful of what she felt was my contribution to the understanding of human nature.

At times she allowed me to give her my gift of healing, letting me in some way minister to her. I also brought laughter, teasing, and some kind of lightness to the work we did together. Twice I was able to share with her my storytelling: once when she was alive, and then later at her memorial service.

We Avantans had a birthday celebration for her one year, and I told a story of a gifted gardener. This was a gardener who was able to see what others didn't see, a gardener who transplanted plants, helped with their growth, and who seemed to do the impossible, because of her belief in others. I talked about her magic, her being able to help plants to take risks and move around to find more sun or more water. I said this gardener was a gardener of people; and, of course, at the end of the story, I revealed the name of the gardener: Virginia.

Later on, at one of her memorial services, I told another story. This one was about a little star in the heavens that asked and was given permission to come to the earth to walk with people, to teach, to share, to heal. The story ended with the star returning to the heavens. Then astronomers discover a new bright star and call it Virginia.

While I was telling this story, a bird came and sat on a nearby tree branch, where it started to talk to us with bird noises. It was so loud that I had to stop my storytelling. Looking at the bird, I said something like this: "As I was preparing for this day, I did wonder if or how Virginia would participate. Maybe through this bird is her way to participate." The bird was quiet. I went back to the story, but I slowed down. Later on, someone told me that the bird slowed down, looked at me, and behaved as if it was paying attention. It was quiet, but it was looking at me. After the story ended, it flew away.

I am not saying that the bird was Virginia. I am not saying that the bird was a messenger from Virginia. What I am saying is that this incident was another time when I felt connected to Virginia and her own capacity to bring laughter and lightness—as if, once more, she was there in some way as an active participant.

I see this chapter as another connection with her. While writing it, I have felt her encouragement and her gentle push to move farther on—to work on the book of my own life, which she knew I wanted to do.

Virginia and I enriched each other's lives in different ways and at different moments. As she did with many people, she was able to look into my heart, my soul, and help me grow and develop. I am not sure what she would say I did for her, but I feel our connection was one of mutual relationship: walking together, sharing, laughing, learning from each other.

Who Am I?

The day was August 5, and I was revising this chapter at my office. It was my 50th birthday, and on my desk were several gifts: candy, jewelry, birthday cards, and two drawings from young kids whom I counsel. The older child's drawing is a picture of me with a smiley face, a very bright dress, and a beautiful sun in the corner. This captures a lot of who I am.

These days, I am the executive director of Avanta, a counselor, and also a speaker. Most of my time goes to Avanta. It used to be that I spent more time working with children, couples, families, individuals, and doing grief counseling. Years ago, Lorna T. Wilturner and I started the Northwest Center for Personal and Family Counseling. Like Virginia, Lorna has been one of the mentors who taught me to let go, to be light, not always to take the world so seriously.

On that birthday years ago when I was writing, several messages lay around my desk, waiting to be answered. Jo Chase—who helps me with appointments and workshops, with my English and my books—was on vacation but had left notes all over the place. She'd also sent me a birthday card. Another note thanked me for a memorial service I led for the writer's sister (another aspect of my work). Nearby were evaluations from some workshops I had just given. I really like giving workshops and trainings. Those are times when I feel I can give my gift to many people at one time.

Also on my desk were some Avanta papers. As coordinator of the Learning Center Committee in those days, I had the privilege and the hard job of working with peers, trying to develop a dream inspired by Virginia's dreams. The Avanta family includes too many people to mention by name (and I'm afraid I'd leave somebody out), but they have influenced me tremendously, and I honor them.

So who am I? I am many things and—for all who are aware of Virginia's use of the Parts Party—I can feel all my parts. I invite you to come with me on a metaphorical train trip to visit some of the stations—some of the places and events that have contributed to who I am and what I do.

☆

My Family

Most of us might like to start from the beginning, so the first stop is my family of origin. As we arrive at that station, you notice one thing: a lot of people are at this stop. A big crowd. In my family, we are 14 siblings, many of whom are now married. And we have a bunch of nieces and nephews.

To make it easier, I want to draw a brief Family Map. My parents were born in Cuba and all of us siblings were, too. The years between us are very few. I think the biggest age difference is about two years. There were also two deaths, stillbirths; one twin and, at the end, another boy.

Many people ask me what it was like to live in a large family. What I can say is that it was fun, it was difficult, it was crowded, it was community living. We all had our roles or assignments. Mine, I feel, was to be funny, to bring humor, and also to be stoic and brave. I think I was a good baby, a "normal" child, and that a lot of my difficulties did not start until I was a teenager.

It is hard to describe my family of origin. We have very strong bonding, but also at many times we drift apart. One thing that is both a blessing and a difficulty in my family is a strong belief system. A blessing because sometimes it allows us to go ahead and take charge and become leaders; a difficulty because in many areas it made us judgmental and critical of other people. As I have not followed all of the family beliefs, I have sometimes felt alienated and separate.

Family Life in Cuba

In Cuba, the church was the center of our family life. Being a good Catholic was a very important part of being a human being, and definitely of being a Suarez. Almost every evening, we ended the day by getting together and praying the rosary. In boarding school, we went to mass every day. Even after we left school, we tried to go to mass daily. So the church was central.

From a young age, I remember the importance of being brave, of not crying. I don't know how this was for the rest of my siblings, but it was definitely important for me. One late evening when I was about ten years old, we were playing outside when I fell and broke my arm in two places. The pain was incredible. My father came out and picked me up. He realized what had happened, put the arm in a splint, and said we would go to the doctor the next day. He also said, "Okay, that's enough crying."

The next day we went to the clinic to have the arm set and put in a cast. Dad was with me while Mom was in the waiting room. Someone held the top part of my arm while someone else pulled and then got the bone in place. This was all done without anesthesia and I remember crying because it was so painful. Again, I remember Dad asking me not to cry and to be brave. That was the beginning of the role for me.

The more I deal with other families and family systems nowadays, the more I realize that my family is like others that have possibilities, functional parts, and dysfunctional parts.

Life in the United States

Another tradition of ours is what we call family letters. A lot of this developed after we moved here to the United States. We keep our family connection by writing long or short letters to everybody else. During my father's illness some years ago, several family letters arrived from those who spent time with my parents. Now we stay in touch by e-mail.

To an outsider, it might look as if we deal with a lot of details. For our family, it is a way for us to share what is happening. As I was writing and recollecting ideas for this chapter, I went through some of those letters—some of the ones I had written, some from other siblings. Our letters were an incredible way of keeping the bonding, the stories, the opinions, the judgments, the fun parts.

After we had been in this country for a few years, for instance, one of my brothers entered a contest by sending in a drinking-soda bottle cap. He won second or third prize: a chance for the family to go into a grocery store for about 15 minutes and come away with whatever groceries we could grab.

My father—who was an engineer and someone who knew how to prepare things—went around and talked to several grocery store owners or managers. Eventually, he found someone who agreed to his incredible idea. Instead of going for a certain amount of groceries that our family would need, we could go for what was expensive. The soda company would pay the store for our haul, and then the store would buy back from us all the undamanged goods. In this way, we could go for expensive stuff and end up with cash, which we needed at the time.

When the soda company representative first came to the house, he was a little bit worried. Children, teenagers, and a few adults (I was in my mid 20s) kept coming out from different rooms. He told my father that only family members could participate in this event. My father assured him that we were all his.

Now, my father didn't stop after just finding the perfect store. He told us we needed to practice—yes, *practice.* He talked to the manager and sometimes, about half an hour before the store closed, one of us would come with Dad to practice. He wanted to be sure we knew what it meant to run for 15 minutes. He told us, "You pick up your grocery stuff, you run close to one side of the aisle, and then when you come back, you run on the opposite side." We practiced hard, learning how to run for 15 minutes without getting in each other's way.

My day to practice arrived. Dad had us grab a bag of dog or cat food from the end of one aisle, run to the cashier, and then run back. This way, if we damaged the goods, it was not that expensive—although I don't remember our having a dog or a cat at that time. So there I was, practicing one day, despite a few shoppers who were rushing to buy things before the store closed. A young man saw me running like crazy from one end of the store to the cashier with a bag of dog food. Very nicely, he asked me if he could help. Puffing, I said, "No, thank you. Get out of the way."

I guess he realized that he had better stay out of the way, but when he saw me repeating this several times, he got a bit concerned and followed me. Then he saw my father, timer in hand, urging: "Two more minutes."

This poor fellow couldn't believe his eyes. He went to the manager and said, "I don't think you will believe this."

"What?"

"Well," said the young man, "there is this woman running back and forth with dog food from the pet food aisle to the cashier, back and forth and back and forth, and there is a man—her father, I gather—timing her and encouraging her to hurry up."

The manager smiled and gave what he felt was a very clear explanation: "Oh, don't worry. Those are the Suarezes. They are practicing for their big event."

The big event came a few weeks later, and we were father and mother and about ten of us siblings, I think. We knew our places, and we knew what we needed to do. Once it started, it was absolutely hysterical pandemonium. People were watching us and cheering us. (The store was also running its own contest: whoever guessed the value of the groceries we amassed would get a trip for two to Miami.) Back and forth, back and forth, the 12 of us. I think the soda company people were not enjoying this too much as they filmed us. I don't remember all the details, but I think we got about $11,000 worth of groceries.

I hope this gives you the flavor of my family, the bonding, my father's capacity for seeing many possibilities, the struggle, and the creativity.

Cuba

The next station's sign says CUBA. Looking around, you realize that my life has many events from this place. One of its gifts was living on a beautiful island: water, green trees, fruit. It is hard to tell you about it without also feeling some tears. I have been away from Cuba since 1960. I have heard so many different things about it that I don't think I have an accurate picture of everything that Cuba was and is. So many of my experiences were linked to the Cuban revolution and the Communist takeover that it is hard to look at my other experiences. But I will share a few.

I don't know exactly how we were taught about courage or being brave. I know the idea of not crying when I got hurt came directly from my father. From him, too, came: "To be brave is not to not be afraid, but to do what you need to do even if your knees are shaking." It is one of the things that has stayed with me forever.

The lesson came on several occasions. One event from when I was 15 is vivid in my mind. Baptista was still in control of Cuba, and the newspaper and rumors were full of stories about political assassinations or killings of people who were against him. We lived close to a man-made lake, where several people—usually politically active anti-Baptista men—had been found dead. We were aware of this (or at least that is the way I remember it).

One night I was ready to go to sleep when I heard what I thought was a man running by. After him came other men running, and a car. I knew at some level that this was probably someone running away from the police. A few minutes later, I heard several shots and a scream, followed by dead silence.

The scream got to me. It was piercing, animal-like, and incredibly anguished. I sat on the side of my bed in my pajamas, with two voices inside me. One said, "Out there is a human being dying alone. You should go and be with him." The other said, "But I'm only 15. I'm too young. I'm afraid." The voices went back and forth, over and over.

As they went on and on for what I think was several hours, something else happened inside. I was not a child anymore. I was not a teenager anymore. I felt like an adult. I was growing up. The burden of something that I felt I needed to do but that I was too afraid to do weighed on me like a ton of bricks. "I'm too afraid." "Someone is dying alone."

I was immobilized, sitting on my bed, not feeling good about myself and yet unable to move. It is incredible to me now, looking back, that I did not think of any other alternative, such as waking up Dad or even my sister, who was in the same room. All I remember was the dialogue: "You should go." "I can't." And then this feeling of being old. "You should go. Someone is dying alone. You should go." I sat on the bed and felt, in my heart and soul, that I was being tested and that I was failing the test. At that time, however, I also thought that being brave meant you were not afraid. "You should go." "I cannot move."

Early the next morning, I finally got up. I went into the bathroom, sure that my hair would be gray. Some months earlier, I had read a book about a young woman who was in some kind of war and whose hair had turned gray overnight, out of anguish. I looked in the mirror, and mine was not. The only thing that had changed was deep inside—the realization that I had failed the test, the realization that fear could paralyze me, and the realization that I felt older than 15. As I saw in the mirror that my hair had not changed, I noticed that my eyes had. They were very, very sad.

Later that day, we did hear that a dead man with several gunshot wounds in his body and head had been found, and that somehow he was linked with an anti-Baptista group. I don't remember if anyone mentioned his name. A feeling of change came over me again. Now he was not just a voice. He had been someone real.

I never told this story to anyone in Cuba. In fact, I don't think I ever told it until a few years ago, when I finally remembered its impact. I do recall promising myself that fear would never again control my behavior; that no matter how scared I was, I would try to do what needed to be done. Since then, many other times when I have been afraid, I have told myself, "Fear will not be what conquers me."

Often people ask me if I am not afraid about this or that. Of course I am. But being afraid is not a deterrent for me (although I cannot say that this is 100 percent true). As the years have gone by, I have learned that there is such a thing as "healthy" fear, which is like a light telling me that I need to pay attention to something. Later in my life, unconsciously, this was one of the things that allowed me to go to Vietnam and do some of the things that I did there. "You should go. Someone is dying there." "But I can't. I'm immobilized."

Now that I am older and look back, I know that maybe it was asking too much of the 15-year-old. On some level, I think I have forgiven and embraced her, because after that, fear was no longer a wall prohibiting my action.

Later, when I was 17, I did some work for the underground against Castro. My father had discouraged us from joining, saying something like, "I feel that you will be risking a lot, putting your family and yourself in danger, and maybe the accomplishment will not be so great." Yet I joined up, and some of my sisters did, too.

It was early 1960, and people were just beginning to express their dissatisfaction with Castro. The Cuban underground was not well developed. In fact, we were kind of disorganized. One of my assignments was to mail anti-Castro propaganda: letters telling people things that were going on in the Communist country. I don't know where the envelopes came from, but another woman and I had thousands to mail. None of them had a return address—a sign that they might be propaganda—so the idea was to mail them from different mailboxes. Otherwise, the state-controlled post office might realize what all these unmarked envelopes were about and then destroy them. The danger was that whoever mailed them could get caught and arrested.

This woman and I went around town by bus. At the first mailbox, she threw in a few envelopes, and I threw in a few. At the second mailbox, no problems. At the third mailbox, a young policeman came toward us. I was holding a bag full of letters, and although I was trying to be brave, my knees started to shake. Very wisely, my friend said, "Smile." So I smiled as he approached, hoping that he could not smell the fear in all of me.

"Hi there," he said. "What are you up to?"

I couldn't talk. I was smiling, but I couldn't talk.

My friend said, "Oh, we just left the office early because we have some letters to mail." Looking at him and giving him a very nonchalant smile, she said, "Do you want to help us?" I cannot remember her name, but she was one of the bravest persons I have ever met.

He picked up some of the letters and while I held the mailbox open, he mailed them. My friend thanked him, and we got back on the bus to go to the next place. I was still shaking. When we were a few blocks away, my friend turned to me and said, "All right, Margarita. You can stop smiling now." I realized that my smile was frozen on my face.

Mine was not one of the bravest actions, and not one of the bravest moments in my life, but it was an incredible experience. We made a few more stops and then I said good-bye to my friend. By the time I got home, I was literally exhausted.

I don't know if I told my father what had happened, but at the dinner table I mentioned something about not liking to be afraid. He again said, "Margarita, being brave does not mean that we are not afraid. Being brave means that we do what we need to do, even if our knees are shaking." This continued to cement my belief about courage.

The last event that I want to talk about from Cuba is my departure in August 1960. Sure that God wanted me to go to a convent to be a nun, I had applied to and been accepted at the Convent of the Maryknoll Sisters in Mexico. At 18, I left Cuba under some restrictions: I was allowed to take only my clothes, one suitcase, and five dollars. No matter, I was leaving with the belief that I would come back. After my suitcase was checked at the airport, I was put in another room, where I could see my family, relatives, and friends through a glass partition.

My mother was not there. She was having trouble with her pregnancy, so she had stayed home. But in my purse, I had a gift from her: the part of her diary in which she talked about her pregnancy with me and my birth. That was an incredible gift, and I read it as I was on the plane. She had written about what it was like for her to be pregnant with me. Somehow, it had been a spiritual time for her. Then she talked about the birth. My father was able to get her to the hospital in time, but I was born before they got her into the delivery room. For my father, it was, I think, the first birth he saw. For my mother, it was an easy birth (remember, I was number five.) I was a good baby who, according to what I recall from those pages, "goo-gooed" and laughed and entertained myself.

This gift from my mother later inspired me to tell many parents to write about or record the birth of their children and to share that with them later. For me, even if a lot of painful things happened to me during my life in Cuba, my beginning was a good one. Nowadays, as I work in therapy with people trying to process their first memories, I feel lucky that my beginning was so special.

Life in the Convent

So, filled with this feeling of warmth and a new beginning, I undertook the next part of my journey. It took me up a hill in St. Louis, Missouri, to the Maryknoll Sisters Novitiate, where I was to do my training.

My background from Cuba and from what I call a Spanish Catholicism was very strict, very inflexible. At the novitiate, I was surprised to realize that the rules were no more strict than in my previous boarding school. The novitiate also had humor. Later, in the convent classroom, I learned that different ways existed for looking at God, even within the Catholic Church.

The novitiate also offered me a good beginning in this country. For many Cubans, including my family, immigrating here was a very hard life. By contrast, my beginning was in a very loving place with shelter, food, and people who cared. The combination of that caring and the chance to start seeing God differently was life changing.

The convent was also where I realized the difficulty of the English language. One of the things in the novitiate was that we had assignments, such as housework. Another thing was what is called silence—that is, while doing our assignments, we were supposed to be quiet, either praying or meditating. We could talk during recesses and sometimes at the dinner table, but most of the time we were in silence.

Well, there I was, brand new, smiling, wanting to prove myself. I was assigned to the nun in charge of the kitchen. Asking me what I could do, she soon realized how limited my experience with chores had been. In boarding school, all we really had to do was make our beds; and at our house in Cuba, we had maids who helped with the work.

The same nun was in charge of the grounds: the trees, plants, and flowers. Outside the novitiate building were little trees, just starting to grow but bending under the weight of the snow. I had never seen snow until I arrived in Missouri, and several snow-storms came that winter.

This nun looked at me and said, "Sister, do you see those little trees out there?"

"Yes, I see them."

"Okay, what I would like you to do is, you see how they are bending?"

"Yes."

"I would like you to go outside and brush the snow from the trees with this broom, so that they don't bend. But be careful you don't get frostbite."

So I went outside and my first thought was, "Wow, this is cold." I don't know if it was subzero, but it was really, really cold. I was supposed to pray as I worked, but there was no way I could keep my mind on anything but how cold I was, although I was wearing gloves and boots. I also knew that I had better be careful with this little "frost"—whatever type of animal it was—that could bite me. My thinking was that, if there is such a thing as a frost, there might be some kind of American frog that lives in the winter and goes around biting people. So although I had no idea of how this animal would look, I felt that it was very dangerous, because it could survive that snow.

I went around the building cleaning the little trees but not really praying. All I could remember saying to God at the time was, "I hope I can finish this job before I die, and please, God, don't let any frosts bite me." I decided that I was not going to take a break. I was going to do the whole thing fast. So I went to the left side of the novitiate, brushing off the snow. I went to the front, and I was coming back to the kitchen side. I did feel funny. My fingers felt numb, my toes felt numb, my face felt numb. I was very careful to look for little frosts.

I don't remember how long I was outside, but at one point I started feeling a little bit disoriented. Then a truck delivering oil for the furnace came by, and the driver said, "Sister, you don't look too good. Why don't you go inside and warm up?"

I thought it was good advice, and he helped me with some steps going toward the kitchen. When I got inside the door, the poor nun who was in charge of me got really worried. I was still a bit disoriented. I sat on a chair. It felt so hot inside that room. I remember someone trying to untie my boots and remove them, and two of the other novitiates helped remove my gloves.

The nun looked at me and, very seriously and with concern, said: "Sister, I told you to be careful about frostbite."

I felt like crying, but I couldn't. I think my tear ducts were frozen. With my best English, I replied, "Nothing bit me. I kept looking for the little frosts. Nothing bit me. I'm just cold."

I don't remember all the details after that. On looking back, I can laugh about it, although I don't remember the nun laughing. I think some of the other novitiates did, though.

Life Goes On

So, friends, with this memory of my difficulty with English, let me take you farther down the track. I don't remember too much about the end of my time at the novitiate, but I do know I was not happy. I kept breaking the rules, and somehow my heart and soul did not feel that the convent was the best place for me. The Mother Superior called me to her office once and very charmingly asked me, "Sister, have you thought of serving the Lord in another place?"

In the end, I did decide to leave. My family had come to the United States from Cuba, and we were really experiencing many difficult times. Those were the worst years of my life. We were very poor. Sometimes people say that we learn a lot from difficult events. For me, these included experiencing hunger for the first time, the difficulty of raising or working with a family, and not knowing all the ins and outs of the American way of doing things.

I had a few different jobs and then started a three-year nursing school program. This did not work out. Later, I started in a four-year program. But then I found out that the U.S. Army would pay for my training if I enlisted for three years. Another lucky break: going to school full time and having the incredible experience of training at Walter Reed Army Medical Center. On the other hand, at some point I started having difficulty with some of the military discipline. Yet discipline was part of my upbringing, first at boarding school and then at the novitiate. So it was kind of known territory.

This was in the late 1960s, and a lot of restlessness and grief was happening in our country: the Vietnam War, the Civil Rights movement, the death of Robert Kennedy, the death of Martin Luther King, Jr. For me, in some sense, nursing school brought some security and some stability. The training was superb because Walter Reed is an incredibly big hospital. We learned a lot.

Working in a hospital and becoming a nurse was not just a four-year journey. After the novitiate, one of my early jobs had been as the night receptionist in an emergency room. Again, some of the funny parts had to do with understanding English. Late one evening, a woman came in an ambulance after being in a car accident. She was not hurt badly but had been hit on the head or something like that. As she was explaining to me what had happened and I was taking down some of the information, she fainted.

The doctor and a nurse came over, put her on a stretcher, and took her to another room to check her. A few minutes later, her husband came running in. "I am Mr. So-and-So, and I heard my wife was brought here."

"Yes, you can sit down. She is fine, she just passed away."

He fainted, too.

I thought, "You know, these Americans faint very easily."

Hearing the noise, the doctor came running. "Margarita, what happened?"

"Well, he just did like his wife did. I was telling him that she was okay, that she just passed away. He did the same thing—just passed away."

The doctor looked at me and said, "Maybe someone should explain to you the difference between passing away and passing out." So from then on, I used the word *faint* rather than trying to deal with using the right "passing."

Vietnam

The next stop in this story is Vietnam. It is 1969. According to the President of the United States, the Vietnamese are taking on more and more of the war responsibility, and we are starting to pull out. When I went to Vietnam, I was very idealistic. This was my second chance, I felt—my second chance to fight the Communists, my chance to do what I was not able to do for Cuba.

After a week, I realized that the war was crazy. Since then, the whole Vietnam experience has taken many years of recovery. When I came home, I thought I would never bounce back. Today, as I look again, I realize that a lot of healing has taken place.

In many of my talks and even when I work with clients, I use the metaphor that we all see life through our own video cameras. The lens and the flexibility that our cameras have allow us to see either a lot or just a little. Sometimes growth is like opening the camera, cleaning the lenses or the filters, adding new filters, and keeping some old filters.

For me, Vietnam turned my video camera upside down, let it be opened, cleaned, and changed. For that I am very thankful. My time there allowed me to question, and it allowed me to grow. Some people might feel that these changes were not for the better. For me, they were.

Meanwhile, some of those we tended were prisoners of war. One in particular is still vivid in memory. Lying there, he looks small, skinny, young, and afraid. I'm not saying that he might not have been capable of cruelty to our own men, but I want you to meet him the way I did.

He cannot see. He has been permanently blinded by an exploding mine, so he doesn't know where he is. He's listening to a foreign language. I approach him, trying to speak softly. He jumps, afraid of what it is that I will do to him. He has been told horror stories about us, the Americans. I realize that this man is the enemy, the one I am supposed to hate.

In a nearby bed is another prisoner of war, slightly wounded. Arrogant, he might have been a captain—we don't know. He's not telling us much about himself. He can look back at me. Later, we enter into a dialogue, and he challenges me as to what the whole war is about. Broken English, Vietnamese accent, Cuban accent.

Again, I'm not saying these men are not capable of a lot of cruelty to us. That is evident, simultaneously, in the young American men with no legs, no arms, some also blind. But I start questioning, and I realize that the enemy soldiers, like our men, are the peons of political systems. They are sons, husbands, lovers, partners, children, fathers. The lens of my video camera opens and my camera starts becoming more flexible, able to take in more.

The withdrawal of the U.S. troops is starting, so the hospitals are closing. I go to work at a second facility, which has asked for people to work in a children's hospital attached to the U.S. hospital. I volunteer. In one bed is a nine-year-old girl in a great deal of pain. Interestingly or sadly enough, she had been preparing some kind of booby trap for Americans. It exploded as she worked on it. Now burned over 90 percent of her body, she has no hope.

In another bed is a baby. We have no idea how old he is. Malnourished, he can hardly open his tiny mouth. He is cold, so I pick him up. One of the ways I carry him around is to put him inside my blouse, using it like a pouch, with enough openness for him to breathe. He lies close to my heat, close to my heart. In one of the contradictions of this crazy war, his mother is not allowed to stay with him. We never know when civilians are civilians, so this is the rule: at night, parents have to leave. When the infant dies, I know that his mother will soon be able to come back, so in a few days, all I'm going to hand her back is a dead baby.

Another little boy teaches me a lot. We gather he is about eight, and he has some kind of intestinal tumor. His stomach is really big, swollen. One day he throws a temper tantrum. Children do not always tell me in words what is going on with them, but they tell me with behavior. This time, I miss his meaning. I pick him up, show him the mess he's made on the floor, and—in the universal language of shame—point my finger. I scold: "Look at the mess you have made!"

I pick up the mess and hurry away to other work. A few minutes pass and I feel guilty, realizing that probably something else is going on with him. When I finally have time, I come to his bed. He is semi-comatose, not even able to communicate with me through his behavior. Using another universal language—that of caring—I bathe him with warm water and put on his favorite shirt. Americans have sent us clothes for the children, and he likes this particular colorful one.

I hold him. A few minutes pass, and he starts to die. Someone calls the doctor, who comes in as I am holding the boy. The doctor says, "Margarita, you realize there is nothing we can do." I agree. I hold the child for a few more minutes, gently rocking him, while he goes through his own transition from life to death. After his spirit goes, I put him back on the bed as gently as I can.

I promise myself that I will learn more about this process of dying and more about how children talk to us. This is where a lot of the grief therapist and consultant is born.

Other deaths come—of young American soldiers. I hesitate to talk too much about this. We want to keep a picture of people dying bravely, maybe even saluting the U.S. flag, and this is not my experience. Many of them do not want to die, and many of them die calling to their wives or children or lovers or mothers. We nurses hold them, rock them, touch them—trying to be with them at this time of transition.

Looking back, I see my life as a mixture of deep events but also humor. Even in Vietnam I find humor. At times, we all laugh. We all develop our own humor: in the way we talk, the way we tease each other. But because my experience there is more of an awakening and a change, I am skipping the funny parts. Anyone who watched *M*A*S*H* can see that in the middle of all that, there was also humor.

While in Vietnam, I start wondering a lot about religion and God, and what is sinful and what is not. As do many people who go through tragic experiences, I am wondering a lot about who God is and how this can be happening. For me, it is very important to continue with the belief that even if I do not understand the whole thing, there is still a God.

One of the worst days is when there is a mass casualty. A lot of wounded people arrive in a short time. Some kind of explosion or direct hit has occurred, and we are suddenly getting a bunch of wounded troops, on and on and on. The noise of the helicopters becomes inscribed in my brain as they bring us more and more wounded and dead soldiers.

The work is hard and hot. We have been at it for several hours. Waste of human life, blind, wounded, crazy. Someone brings us big jars of cold lemonade and ice water. A barrel of water stands in the middle of the emergency area, and whenever we get a chance, we dip in our shirts, wring them out, and put them back on.

Because the doctors need to be in the operating room or doing a lot of the life-saving techniques, I end up doing some of the triage: deciding who needs to be in surgery right away, who goes later, and who goes to a corner—no chance. I have been at this for several hours and am feeling like a machine, going and going and going. In the middle of the tension, in the middle of this craziness, somehow I feel someone's presence. He is a chaplain, who I believe definitely understands a lot about God. We are friends. We have done a lot of talking before this.

He goes into the corner where several soldiers have severe head wounds. Soon that corner becomes peaceful and quiet. Don't ask me how or what happens. All I know is that this is what I experience.

The chaplain comes toward me and, at that moment, I see him as representing a confusing and unloving God who allows something like this to happen. He comes to me, looks in my eyes, and says, "Hi, Margarita."

With all the anguish and pain that I felt inside, I say, "Don't come here talking to me about God. I cannot stand this any more."

Very gently, he touches my shoulder, touches my dirty shirt—dirty with blood, sweat, water—and in a clear and gentle voice says, "Margarita, be as angry with God as you want, but don't ever stop the dialogue."

I don't know now where this man is. I don't even remember his name. But this is one of the most incredible gifts of Vietnam.

My last assignment is with drug addiction. Again, this whole experience is another book, too long for this brief journey, so I don't even want to come to a complete stop. I am working in a hospital where a lot of the men come when they do not pass the urine test before leaving Vietnam. I feel strongly that, for political reasons and for the Army's own cover-up, no one understands or pays attention to the depth of drug addiction that is happening here.

I am head nurse of intensive care, caring for addicted men who are having withdrawal symptoms or who are seriously ill. One day I learn something about the power of language. The way we talk in Vietnam leaves a lot to be desired. Everything is "fucking this" and "fucking that" and, of course, all the officers are "motherfuckers" or whatever. People swear at me ten thousand times every day. Others ask, "Margarita, doesn't it bother you when they call you those names?"

"No, if they want to say it, that is their choice. I don't care."

Often some of the soldiers say, "Fuck off."

I say back, "Well, I will, but not right now. This is not the time or place to do it."

One day we have a patient who is from Puerto Rico and he starts using the Spanish "f" word. Once he looks at me and says the Spanish for "You motherfucker."

"Don't you ever, ever, ever call me that."

Startled, he says, "Why not? All the gringos call you that."

"You can do it in English, but you cannot do it in Spanish." Interesting, the power of the words we learn in childhood.

Healing

After I came back, I was learning to be a pediatric nurse, working with babies and families and children. But I had spent so much compassion in Vietnam that I had little left. Here in the States, nothing could compare to the pain that I had seen. Nothing compared to the tragedy of Vietnam. I realized that I was in a lot of trouble, yet I didn't know where to go.

For the nurse practitioner's training, I needed to learn how to do physical exams on newborn babies. Stethoscopes around our necks and nurse practitioner bags in hand, we students went to a nursery and spent our weekends just practicing exams on the infants there. One Saturday, a staff nurse said, "Margarita, we are really busy. We would like it if you had time to feed him." She was referring to a tiny boy who'd been born prematurely. I wish I could remember his name, but I am terrible with names. If I could give him four ounces of formula, they would be very grateful, because it took him so long to eat.

So I picked him up, got the formula ready, and started feeding him. You know how babies eat, as if they are looking at you? As I fed him, he gazed up and his tiny little hands grabbed one of my fingers. And something happened between us at that moment. I started feeling warmth and compassion again. He drank his four ounces.

Four ounces is a very small amount—half a cup. Yet for this baby, it was vital. Afterward, he wet his diaper. This was an important sign, a good sign. Since we kept track of how much these babies took in and excreted, I measured the urine output by weighing the diaper. At that point, the experience for me was that four ounces of formula was very important to this tiny human being. I guess I realized that pain or success is relative to the time and moment.

Also, I felt caring and empathy for this infant in my arms, even if he was not a victim of war nor as bad off as other babies. I don't know exactly how long I stayed with him. All I know is that, for a while, I started paying attention to what four ounces was. I allowed myself to begin healing, understanding that it is the moment and the person in the moment that have value or importance.

Many other people, many experiences passed through this station called *Healing*. I also give myself credit. I don't think healing happens unless we do a lot of the work. At the same time, I also believe that healing happens with other people, by walking together. And because other people and events have been part of my healing, I believe that I can be part of the walking with other people. In counseling, I don't think we counselors do the changing for other people. I do feel that we walk with them, and it is in this interaction that healing happens.

For me, healing continues to be part of my life. I believe it continues to be part of most of us, a station of healing—a place to come in, to return, to stop by when we have to, when we need to, when we want to.

A Question of Identity

As we approach the end of this chapter, I want to visit one more place. Not to analyze too much, not to talk about it too much, but to give it the value it has within all of who I am. It is a struggle that has been with me for a long time, a struggle that has ended in a peaceful acceptance, joy, and celebration of me.

When I was 13 or 14, I was having trouble in school. At that time, my parents—or at least my mother—thought it would be good for me to see a psychiatrist. In one of the first sessions, I spoke about some of my sexual feelings. Ever since my first sexual feelings, my desires had been for women. The way the psychiatrist explained it to me at the time, these were part of a developmental phase, something I should outgrow and not continue having.

As therapy continued and I grew older, my feelings didn't change. They became one of those big, shameful secrets. I don't know if the psychiatrist ever told my parents what was going on. We never talked about that then, and I struggled alone within my old religious beliefs, my own life, and my family.

For me, the novitiate was not a place in which sexuality was expressed. I continued struggling with the Church's saying that homosexuality was sinful, psychiatrists and therapists thinking at the time that it was not normal, and knowing that my family would never approve of it.

It was in Vietnam that some freedom finally came for me. On a day when we had had a lot of wounded soldiers, I remember thinking, "How can they call my sexual feelings sinful if it is done within a caring, loving, adult relationship? And how can they call what we are doing out there okay because it is in the name of justice?"

But I still did not have complete freedom. When I came back to the States, I thought that coming out as a lesbian could be a handicap in my profession (as a pediatric nurse and, later, as a counselor). Another problem would be consequences for all my women friends. That is, because of myths and misconceptions, some people might suspect all my friends, former friends, or former roommates of also being lesbian. When I told friends that I would clearly come out as a lesbian in this chapter, some were concerned about the price I could pay or would pay. I decided to talk about this anyway, although some consequences may arise.

When people ask me how I made the decision to accept my sexual orientation, I say that it has been a struggle. Yet I made my decision not so much because of an event or a process but because of a person. The decision to accept my sexuality came when I fell in love with an incredible, wonderful woman. At that point, I realized it was not a conflict as much as a clear decision about who and how I wanted to be in the world.

I can honestly say now that I have never experienced such peace and calm as when I accepted and embraced and rejoiced in this part of me. No experience, not even Vietnam, compares with the anguish of not being able to be myself. Nothing. The freedom to say, "This is me, this is who I am, this part of me, this is my choice."

In that first relationship, I also learned that one can be a lesbian and pray to God. I feel calm in knowing that God, as I see God, also embraces this part of me. Knowing that I can be a lesbian and still pray and have God as part of my life is a peaceful experience.

I did share my secret with Virginia, and she accepted this part of me. I have no idea what Virginia's own journey was in seeing lesbian or gay relationships as a human possibility. What I do know was that she was very supportive of my being in a relationship that was committed. She gave us a union gift that I still have. Virginia also was there when that first relationship ended. It was painful, difficult, yet it was a relationship that gave me an incredible freedom.

Being in a caring relationship—committed, monogamous, serious, fun, loving—-brings an incredible peace into my life. As some in my family have never accepted this part of me, it has been a source of pain and concern. It also used to be hard in groups and professional gatherings, where others could introduce their spouses or boyfriends or girlfriends, and it was accepted. How difficult it has been for many of us to say, "And this is my partner, my love [life] companion." So I am grateful to those who have helped me, to other lesbians, and to other women who have shared with me their struggles and finally their freedom.

That first relationship lasted seven years. During that time, I experienced the warmth and sense of belonging that come from being part of a lesbian community. Since then, I have learned a lot about myself, about relationships, and about what a loving lesbian relationship can bring into my life. At present, I am single (to use a heterosexual word). Yet I still have the peace that came in accepting myself as I am.

Life Now

Since I first started writing this chapter, a lot has happened and a lot has changed. Both my parents have died: my dad on March 20, 1996; my mother, on March 18, 1998.

I am more "out" to my family regarding my sexual identity. Some family members still have difficulties with my choice; others voice their support of me in our family discussions. I still have struggles, especially as some cannot accept my choice because of their religious beliefs against gays and lesbians. This caused a lot of problems at first and continues to cause conflict at times. On and off, mostly through the family e-mail, we get into a debate about this. I think some of them would prefer that I keep this a secret.

When I first went to a family reunion with a woman partner, it was a big source of conflict. It was on a trip to Florida for my youngest brother Fred's wedding. That event was a mix of everything I am and everything I do. It had started a few months before with organizing and coordinating the wedding reception. I also was trying to support some of my sisters who were going, as well as making arrangements for my partner and me.

It was a tense trip for both my partner, Sandi, and me. It was her first meeting with my family as my partner, her first trip to Miami, and her first time meeting so many new people at once (15 to 20 Suarezes is plenty for anyone). To realize how overwhelming it can be to meet such a large family, all anyone has to do is look at a family picture of us, a calendar of events, or the Family Map.

Sandi and I arrived Thursday afternoon, went to our hotel, and then began the balancing act. I was balancing my successful professional part with the part that was coming back as one of many girls (women for me, but "girls" in this family, in which we often felt that the men are somehow more important than the women). Balancing also applied to our schedule: sandwiching time for all the wedding events, the family times, the Avanta meeting phone calls, and time for ourselves. Another balancing act involved my wanting to stay within my budget but feeling the pull of doing something good and adequate, and also the question of how good to make it. It was a fourth balancing act to know how and to whom in my family I would introduce Sandi.

For everyone, it was a balancing act among different cultures. In a sense, four cultures were mixing in this marriage. The bride Myra's Jewish family, with its culture and traditions, would mix with our Catholic family, its culture, and its traditions. An American family would mix with a Cuban family. (A fifth set of culture and traditions was the Suarez family itself, of course.)

Three different celebrations were on the calendar. The first evening, Thursday, was the rehearsal dinner at the home of my brother Xavier and his wife, Rita. Friday evening was the Catholic wedding with a reception at the hotel, which Sandi and I were hosting. Saturday was the Jewish wedding and reception lunch, put on by Myra's family at a nearby country club.

Overall, we did very well. I went through every feeling while I was in Miami. The first night there, at my brother's house, I felt welcomed by Myra's family, by Rita, and by Olga (Rita's mother). My own family all greeted Sandi and welcomed her nicely, but somehow I felt disconnected from them. I am not sure how much of this was me and how much was them.

I saw my father for the first time since his stroke a few months before. He looked okay, yet it was so sad to see him getting old. I'm not sure he recognized me, and his "Hi" was not as enthusiastic as it had been in the past. The same was true with my mother. One of my brothers told me that their energy was very much in their own recovery and in all that was going on locally. (Southern Florida had suffered Hurricane Andrew just about a month before.) As he suggested, I tried not to take it personally.

The next day, Friday, started with doing Avanta/Learning Center Committee work on the phone. On hearing some good news and some not-so-good news, I realized once more the amount of work it takes me to be involved in an organization, my job, my family, plus my own private life. Balancing was difficult.

The morning was relatively relaxed. Sandi and I checked out things with the hotel about the reception, and then we had a wonderful time outside in the sun by the ocean. Every time I go to the South, and especially Miami, I realize that Cuba is only 90 miles from Key West.

Then came the Cuban Catholic wedding and a lot of feelings: the familiarity of the Catholic Church plus my difficulty with some of the rituals. The exclusivity of the Catholic Church bothered me. Because Myra and her family are Jewish, I guess I was expecting that the prayers and the ceremony would be more inclusive, but they weren't. For me, the ceremony and the priest's talk were very, very painful. Once more, I felt betrayed. I also realized that some organized religions still desperately need their exclusivity.

Yet it was good to be there with the family and Sandi. It was definitely a family affair. Thirteen of us siblings were there—including my brother George and his wife, Gina—plus nieces and nephews. That was good.

As soon as the ceremony was over, Sandi and I left for the hotel to start the Cuban festivities there. At first, things were not smooth. Somehow, another group of people were still in our room (although in only one part of it). So we had to deal with life. Eventually, it all went very well—sparkling cider, punch, coffee, tea, and a delicious big cake.

One of my sisters and her husband had also brought in Cuban cider, which does not look at all like sparkling cider. The hotel concession's owner/manager soon realized that we were having something besides what we ordered from him. My brother-in-law dealt with him very well, but the punchline came when, in the middle of trying to find out what we were doing, the manager realized that my brother Xavier, who was also the mayor of Miami, was putting some of these special bottles on the tables. My admiration for my brother increased, not only because of the way he handled uncomfortable moments like that, but because of his openness, his friendship, and the love that I see flowing to him from the people.

After everyone else arrived, Rita cut the cake, my sisters Rosie and Lala helped serve, and my sister Mary passed things out. The whole family pitched in. My brothers helped. Myra's family helped. So, amid all the English and Spanish being spoken, I was able to relax fully and let go for the first time. In fact, I let my brother make the toast. He was funny, he was political, and he was entertaining. It was good. People from Myra's family joined in the toasting, and Fred and Myra were very happy. They toasted with a special wine glass that my sister Rosie had brought for them with their names on it. So this, the second Cuban celebration, went wonderfully well.

The next morning, I talked again to my colleague Mel about Avanta, heard which proposals had been approved, and got news about some of the things that the Governing Council was still dealing with. Later, as Sandi and I were having breakfast, my father joined us at the hotel. It was a bittersweet time. He was friendly to Sandi, but I recognized what people had told me about and what I had experienced on the telephone: his difficulty with some words. Yet, part of the old spirit was still there. It was amazing how he still wanted to do and be part of things, how alive he seemed.

The Jewish wedding, later that day, was incredibly beautiful. The rabbi was wonderfully inclusive, and I felt a strong connection with God. The whole ceremony was spiritual and wonderful. Then came the reception, the Jewish wedding dance with its lifting of Myra and Fred's chairs, the Cuban conga, and the wedding pictures. The reception lunch and the rest of the afternoon were again a mixture of the two families and their four cultures: Jewish, American, Cuban, Catholic.

It was a very hot night, so Sandi and I went back to the hotel to relax before going to one of my sister's. She had invited another sister and us to dinner. It was a women's kind of gathering. Afterward, we watched videos of Cuba. Once more, I balanced between my Cuban/Spanish culture and my American part with Sandi. Later, my brother-in-law Manuel joined us, and he was really funny.

On Sunday and Monday night, our last two nights there, Sandi and I stayed with Rita's mother. Olga was very generous in inviting us to stay at her apartment, and we felt very comfortable and cared for. Sunday and Monday were days of vacation for Sandi and me, although hurricane damage kept us from going to many places we had wanted to visit. Xavier and Rita were still very involved in some of the relief and organization of the work.

We did go through part of Homestead and Florida City, where we saw some of the incredible devastation. As we went through a place with houses destroyed and military people directing traffic, I flashed back to Vietnam. Florida did not look like war-torn Vietnam—even the hurricane did not do the same kind of devastation—but I felt a similar desolation and despair and anguish as I had then. Once more, I realized how enriched my life has been with so many different experiences, in spite of (and including) the difficult ones, and how lucky I am overall.

Apart from the devastation, Sandi and I got to see some of the pleasures. The state parks and the surroundings are quite different from what we have in Washington state. We saw alligators (which apparently is very easy to do in this part of Florida), and we took a boat trip through part of the Everglades, enjoying new trees, birds, and animals.

We ended our Florida trip with Monday night dinner at Xavier and Rita's house. While we sat visiting, Rita finished cooking. Sandi and I went through stories, and they told us about Xavier's job, Rita's life, and the family. Xavier and I clarified which days we wanted him to join us for an Avanta meeting in Miami that fall.

The next morning, we went to the airport and flew home. I was back to work on Wednesday, catching up with all the business of my own job and my private work, telling stories about the family, and then seeing clients. I came home late and tired, and Sandi and

I had dinner together. She already had the pictures back, and we talked about the visit and all that.

Later, after I was asleep, the night ended with this answering machine message from my mother:

> Margie, It's hard to get in touch with you. It's Mommy. It's half past 11 here, but I know it is early there, and I hoped I was finding you in your home. Whenever you want to call me tomorrow, but not at the siesta time, please. I like to talk to you abut all the things that happened that were good and nice. Okay, dear. God love you.

That's how my week ended. It's not a typical week, but it draws a picture of who I am and how I am.

Back to the Main Station

As I finish work on this chapter, years after its inception, I am also in the middle of writing my own book, an autobiography. It has given me the opportunity for a lot of soul and heart searching. And it has reconnected me to the beginning and to the now.

Since 1993, I have been the executive director of Avanta and have witnessed that organization grow through the disorientation after Virginia's death to the establishment of a new form of governance in its board of directors. I think we—we Avantans—are becoming adults in our own rights. That is, we still carry the mission that Virginia started and at the same time adapt and make changes as needed. I believe Virginia is smiling as she sees our work. For example, Avanta is currently supporting work in North America as well as El Salvador, Honduras, Guatemala, Eastern Europe, and Asia. It also has affiliates in North America, Venezuela, Taiwan, and Hong Kong. Avanta members continue to work the mission in their own lives as well as professionally.

What Avanta has become is due to many people and their work. To honor their support and contributions as members, Virginia started the Living Treasure award in 1983. While we usually pay tribute at funerals, she explained, this was a way to say thank you while the award-winner could really enjoy the honor and be part of the celebration. I feel very lucky to be one of them.

And now we are back where we started, in a way. I am again at my desk in my office. Just as I have revised many of these stories over and over, I find myself again revising and changing the ending over and over. So instead of continuing to search for a perfect ending, let me tell you a story.

Once upon a time a woman went to the forest, looking for wisdom. She said to the animals and to the trees, to the mountains and the lake, "I have been asked to write a chapter of my life, but for now I need to come to an end. And I don't know how to end it."

The lion said, "Why don't you end it with a big roar that shows your strength and your courage?"

The eagle said, "Why don't you end it with a high and long flight, sharing with your readers the capacity to fly and be free?"

And the squirrel said, "Why don't you tell them that there can be no end to the chapter because you are still gathering knowledge and wisdom?"

A big owl said, "Why don't you end with a list of everything that you have learned, sharing the wisdom and knowledge you already have?"

The rabbit said, "Why don't you end with a story about the times you have been afraid, showing them that fear is part of us, part of life?"

And then in front of her were the children with whom she had been during their transition and death. They said, "Why don't you share all you have learned about how to be with children when they are dying?"

Other children appeared with whom she had worked at the time of their pain—whether it was the divorce of their parents, or a struggle in school, or the death of a parent or a sibling. They said, "Why don't you share with them the stories we have told together or the games we have played?"

Some of the other people she had worked with—participants in workshops, clients, and so on—said, "Why don't you end with some of the metaphors that you used for us to show the complexity of life or the complexity of people, or the simplicity of making choices?"

Then she heard laughter, that good belly laughter, and she looked up and saw tree branches moving with the wind. They said, "Why don't you end with one of your funny stories, showing the benefit and the healing of humor and laughter?"

She saw the faces of friends, lovers, peers, and coworkers, who said, "Why don't you end by talking about our capacity to let other people walk with us—the importance of not trying to heal alone or walk alone, and at the same time, the importance of doing our own work?"

Next she saw an incredible baby girl, an infant she had met and held a few weeks before the baby died. And the tiny girl said, "Why don't you end your story by telling about the power of seeing God in others, about the gentleness of your voice when you gave me permission to go if that's what I needed to do?"

The woman thanked the forest and the trees and the wind. She thanked the children, the other people, and the animals. "You have given me so many good ideas, and maybe you all are right—there are so many ways to end or close this chapter, so many ways to stop this journey." Very gently, she said good-bye to them all, closed her eyes, and left the forest.

One of Virginia's equestrian days near
New Orleans, Louisiana

Ever since I met her, Barbara Jo has predicted unabashedly that Virginia's effect on psycho-therapy will last longer than that of Sigmund Freud. While she is the only person I know who feels she was not changed or benefited significantly by Virginia's process of Family Reconstruction, Barbara Jo has devoted her professional life to studying and writing about Virginia.

Her account of Virginia's life is the most com-prehensive biography published to date, thorough and well researched. The book's original editor, Mel Suhd, chose Barbara Jo for just that quality of work. He envisioned a new way of writing and absorbing history: as a kaleidoscopic mosaic of tales by people whose lives influenced each other. In her autobiography, Barbara Jo adds some glimpses of herself as well as of her relationship with Virginia.

—*Robert S. Spitzer*
Publisher

10

Blossoms Along the Trail

by Barbara Jo Brothers

The reader should not consider this chapter an autobiography in the classical sense. It is rather a "bouquet" of persons mixed in with key experiences—a variation on Virginia's model of the Wheel of Influence. Described in *The Satir Model* (Satir et al., 1991), this was one of the information-gathering vehicles she used in preparation for a Family Reconstruction. It "shows every person who supported the Star emotionally or physically during childhood and adolescence" (p. 374). I have adapted the concept for this chapter: here, my wheel of influence includes people I encountered in adulthood—some during the childhood and adolescence of my professional career. The list is nowhere near exhaustive, and the focus is not on my developmental history as such. These people are, as it were, "blossoms along the trail" of my professional development. Virginia was, of course, a whole garden of possibilities at the beginning of my career.

Following this garden motif, I have decorated the chapter with poems. They serve as little stories sprinkled throughout to illustrate a given person or event. This material is as autobiographical as is the content; the poems were written by my father, a published poet. Lately, I have heard it said by experts that meaning is conveyed more accurately by metaphor and symbol than by literal description (e.g., Miller, 1996). This is welcome news to a right-brained introvert who has struggled much of her life to fit into linear contexts. Having been the daughter of this poet and growing up in the country among butterflies and burrows and wild things, I was trained in this style from birth—and find it more illuminating in the end. I think this would be all right with Virginia. According to Sheldon Kramer (1996), she once told him she did not have a left brain.

Speaking somewhat more seriously, I have felt both privileged and burdened to be the "tile" in Virginia Satir's mosaic who wrote her biographical chapter. Doing her justice was my major concern. I very much appreciate Mel Suhd's concept of biography as gestalt, including a team of people writing from different perspectives. I find great comfort in the fact that this book therefore depicts Virginia as seen by more eyes than my own. It takes a whole symphony to play the extraordinary composition we knew as Virginia Satir. Her message: we can find the ways to act in resonance rather than in dissonance; harmony among humanity is a possibility.

My first exposure to Virginia was in graduate school at Tulane University School of Social Work, circa 1964. In the margin of my notes for Social Casework 202, I had written—"satirically"—"Who is afraid of Virginia Satir?" Such double entendres and clowning were part of my way of dealing with the element of boredom that seemed to be an essential ingredient of academia. That same year, I also told my classmates I was going to become a writer "when I grow up," return to those ivy-covered halls, and rewrite all the boring articles we were forced to read. I would translate them all into lively, readable material. In this way, I would spare future students the tedium we were all enduring.

In fact, I am now the editor of a professional publication, *Journal of Couples Therapy,* and was, for ten years, associate editor of *Voices: The Art and Science of Psychotherapy.* Although I have found that my own journal is only as "unboring" as my contributors are willing to make it, I continue to provide the forum, inviting subjective, anecdotal articles as well as more formal studies and reviews of the literature. I have not yet found a feasible way to slip into Howard-Tillotson Library at Tulane and convert the Social Work reading list into lively essays, but at this point I have written over 73 articles published in several different professional journals and in newsletters, monographs, and books.

My current mission is to engender articles, through the *Journal of Couples Therapy,* about Virginia's work. It is important to me that she becomes more widely understood and that I do my part in making sure her work is not lost. The simplicity and clarity of her work tends to hide its complexity and high art. As with little diamonds strewn over a sunny, sandy beach, anybody can see the sparkle, but one must look closely for the points of origin of the brilliance.

Very fortunately for me, Virginia Satir did not remain a joke in the margin of my class notes. In the early 1960s, she made several appearances in the New Orleans area. I first saw her in action in 1965. Three years later, we were introduced to each other after her week-long seminar for the Southern Regional Institute of the National Association of Social Workers at Biloxi, Mississippi.

As a recent graduate employed on the adolescent unit of Southeast Louisiana Hospital, I was suffering all the pangs of the brand-new therapist: knowing I did not know enough, but thinking I was supposed to know by now. I will never forget the feeling of intense relief that week in June as I watched Virginia's work unfolding like Shakespeare's lines: ". . . the quality of mercy is not strain'd; it droppeth as the gentle rain from heaven" (1949, p. 222).

I could sense the organic nature of her process, and something deep in my soul knew it was right. It was all right to not know, to ask questions. Struggling for clarity was actually an important task, and my sense of self-esteem need not—must not—be hooked to knowing "right" answers.

The best thing Virginia did for me was to give me permission early in my career to follow my common-sense instincts about treating people with respect and compassion. She also confirmed that I was correct to be ever suspicious of that which is boring. I was at the perfect point for the encounter: duly credentialed, I was a professional blank slate. She wrote her philosophy across my heart and soul.

This heart-and-soul connection interfaced directly with my mind. I felt almost compelled to study with her—to *know*, to understand intellectually, what was behind this philosophy and how to implement what I had experienced. This yearning brought me to my first month-long seminar, in 1971, at Glenwood Springs, Colorado (organized by Laura Sue Dodson).

Pioneer Stock and PTSD
. . . or Meanwhile,
Back at the Ranch

I grew up on a cattle ranch ten miles from one of Texas's oldest towns, on land my father had been given at birth by his cattle-baron grandfather. At one time, his grandfather ran 20,000 head under his LK brand (Ford, 1936). At the time of my father's birth, our ranch was considered "the far pasture"; altogether, my great-grandfather owned 200,000 acres and leased another 100,000.

My Texas roots are deeper than its ubiquitous mesquite tree, my ancestors having arrived before the oxcarts that rumbled up from Mexico and left their seeds sprouting along the trail. Comanches killed one of my great-great-great-grandfathers, and two others—representing both sides of my family—were what is known in my part of the world as "Texas Heroes"—those who were actively involved in wresting independence from the oppressive Mexican government. One was in the Mier Expedition of 1842, which was part of the ongoing struggle between Texas and Mexico during the period when Texas was still a republic (George Lord, 1842). Texas declared its sovereignty on March 2, 1836 and won the decisive victory in the Battle of San Jacinto, April 21, 1836.* However, Mexico continued refusing to recognize the newly formed nation, so Texans launched the Mier Expedition.

Captured by the Mexican army, those Mier Expedition men's individual fates were determined by each drawing a bean. White, you lived; black, you died. My ancestor lived to write an account of that experience. For years, his portrait hung in the Alamo museum.

The other Texas Hero ancestor missed the Alamo by 48 hours, although he was marching enthusiastically in that direction when he received word that it had already fallen. Part of this same great-great-grandfather's story is that, a few years before, he had been shipwrecked off the Texas coast near Galveston and would have died of thirst had his single shot not felled the crane who showed up on the deserted beach three days later. Drinking the bird's blood, he mobilized enough strength to push inland until he finally came to a settler's house. He, too, lived to write that tale.

And I have survived to write this one, my genes having wound their way through the lives and loins of these hardy souls whose

---

*My great-great-great grandmother Julia Anna was on that battlefield tending the wounded. For her service, she later received a land grant—in her own name. Her bones now rest on that land somewhere, 160-odd years later, under an immense Exxon refinery on Galveston Bay.

tenacity prevailed against all the odds on all the frontiers along the way. They did not talk of Post-Traumatic Stress Disorder (PTSD); in those days, they were still using words such as *liberty* and *justice*. It was guts and guns and grit. And yes, of course, a therapist in the woodwork might well have made note of PTSD springing up here and there like prickly pear. Modern readers associate PTSD with Vietnam or World War II while leaving stories of the frontier in the category of inspiration and entertainment.

My father used to tell me that the real definition of *adventure* was "some poor bastard having a hell of a hard time a long way from home." Imagine for a moment crawling on your belly along a parched beach where your comrades have already died of thirst, where your one and last hope for life is to fell this crane with your muzzle-loader. Imagine spending a year in a Mexican prison circa 1842 and watching your comrades being shot as you hold your lucky and decisive white bean. Imagine picking up your life with ten children and a homestead to tend after you finally find one of your husband's bones out in the pasture—and now you know, three weeks after he disappeared, that he is not coming back.

These experiences flow down through the generations in one form or another. More than simply the genes pass down from forebears to child. In *Scripts People Live*, Claude Steiner (1974) describes the way such a process moves down through families, psychologically speaking. In *Search for the Beloved*, Jean Houston (1987) provides an exercise for tracing the route on a spiritual level. We are immensely influenced by the experiences of our progenitors.

We can read the tales written by many of our forefathers in yellowed copies of centennial issues of old Texas newspapers and archives. Tales of the foremothers occupy less space in the history books. The ancestor who had drawn the white bean married his 17-year-old bride along the trail to California in the Gold Rush of '49. The story is that she was the babysitter going along to tend his two children after his original wife died somewhere along the way. The ancestor who was marching toward the Alamo was marching in the opposite direction from his young wife. She was six months pregnant with their son, my paternal great-grandfather (the one who grew up to amass the 200,000 acres and to leave my father our ranch).

Polly Power, the wife of the man the Comanches killed, found only a bone and a distinctive button which she remembered having recently sewn on his shirt. The Indians had also killed one of her older boys, along with his father, so she was left with ten children. She carried on. The next year, 1840, her brand—P—is on the rolls of the first cattle brands registered in the county, and her name is on the county rolls of the "registered voters."* Two years later, it is said that she lost another son to the Comanches.

Busy ladies. Hard to say whether they took time out to cry. In any case, by the time the tears both shed and unshed got filtered down through the succeeding generations, I know both my parents had very good psychosocial reasons to be the people they were. All that riding, shooting, and dying must surely have left a residue that drifted down along with the genes.

The rural experience is very different from the urban one. Growing up on a working ranch ten miles from the nearest town is not at all the same as growing up in even that small town. We quite literally shook our boots out every morning to empty them of possible scorpions. My aunt, who lived down the road, once found baby rattlesnakes crawling out of her fireplace. My father used to tell me of the time he saw two-year-old me standing in the front

---

*As a property owner, my great-great-great-grandmother's name appeared on the voter rolls and beside her cattle brand in the county's old brand book. Texas was not so advanced in 1839, however, as to have preceded the United States in giving women the vote.

yard with a little coral snake quietly crawling between my bare feet.

None of that happened in the town of Gonzales, Texas, population 5000. Town kids were dudes. I had my own registered cattle brand by the time I was three and my own horse by the time I was six.

Growing up in the country was one of the experiences Virginia and I had in common. Her grandparents were known for having been among the pioneering settler families in the Neillsville area of Wisconsin. They had set out on their ship with the same pioneering spirit as my ancestors had in their prairie schooners. Both she and I were heavily influenced by our relation to the land our ancestors worked so hard to settle.

Living on and via the land builds in a certain level of humility (it is not by chance that the Latin root of *humility* is *humus*: "earth"). One grows up in an atmosphere of knowing one does not control one's environment: if rain does not fall, grass, cotton, and corn all stop growing, and no amount of determination or desperation will pull that rain down from the skies. If the wind does not blow, the windmill does not turn and you do not have water. After a couple of weeks when the cistern is empty, your father goes somewhere and returns with two full wooden barrels. That process repeats until Whatever Forces begin again to move the winds.

"Deep in the West Leaving a Crimson Stain"

I also grew up during the second-worst drouth my section of Texas had ever known. The year that drouth began, my father wrote and published the following poem (R. L. Brothers, 1998).

Southwest

All day the heated sky melted and dripped
In blurred horizons on the arid plain.
The gleaming sun sank to the hilt and ripped
Deep in the west leaving a crimson stain.
A little wind panted over the sand
And bellied down among the gnarled mesquite.
One pale star roosted high above the land,
And a thin moon reposed with claw tipped feet
Hooked on a distant hill. Aloof and proud,
With soft and silver plumage all unfurled,
It preened itself, and sailed behind a cloud,
Flashed out again, and dropped beyond the world.
At dawn the little wind awoke, and prowled
The prairie with a cold, dry nose . . . and howled.

The year before, when I was in the first grade, I had a little red clear plastic raincoat; in the second grade, I got a blue one. That was the last raincoat I had until I was a freshman in high school. For the next seven years, there was no reason to have one. The ground cracked open, big live oaks eventually began to die, and too often my father returned from riding with reports of finding deer starved to death in the pasture.

Our drouth was not, of course, quite as bad as growing up in the dustbowl and Depression days of Virginia's adolescence. At least the rest of the country was enjoying reasonably good post-war prosperity. However, the prolonged rainless years did add their own tension to the family tensions that might have existed in any rural household in our part of the world.

Our Mexican-American tenants left in the fifth or sixth year of the drouth. This, in itself, affected our lives. The boys had served as cowhands and the girls had done our house-cleaning, washing, and baby-sitting. Their father had sharecropped the cotton, corn, and alfalfa. Our lives had been interwoven in the strange intimacy characteristic of that economic arrangement in that day and time. When the drouth drove out the "Mexicans," who left to join the itinerant fruit-pickers, our father sold 300 good bottomland acres of his inherited ranch and we stayed in place.

The year before that catastrophic shift began in the weather patterns, I was taken into town to start school. I was five (my birthday is in late November). I still remember that last late Indian summer afternoon at home. I recall a certain wistfulness mixed in with my anticipation of finally having the chance to learn to read. This would be the last day of freedom—the last day of being in the saddle with my father after he rode home from working cattle late in the afternoon. He always took my sister and me, by turns, into the saddle with him. Handing us the reins, he gave us daily lessons in horse-reining. Tomorrow, my sister would have all the turns . . .

The Scholastic World

School became center stage—as, even then, I knew it would be for the next nearly 20 years. The flavor of my experience is in my father's musing on his daughters' passages (R. L. Brothers, 1998):

Migration
Graduation —1960

> The tender season fades, my birds have flown.
> The nest has served its purpose and must be
> No more circumference and boundary
> Of those whose limits now shall be their own

As each migrates to some uncharted zone
And the full-feather of identity.
Had not the doves of Noah been set free
The olive branch might never have been known.

Let no warped thought turn or ill wind blow
Them backward from the high, uncertain course
To the remembered safety of a nest
That twig by twig is falling with the snow;
Spare them the bitter berries of remorse,
Sustain them in the hunger of the quest.

I left town right after high school. The summer I graduated, I
entered the University of Texas, not waiting for autumn. Down the
hall in my Scottish Rite Dormitory lived Susan Ford from the Texas
Panhandle—so far away from where I grew up that it might as well
have been another state. Susan (who is now Dr. Susan Ford Wilt-
shire, recent chair of the classics department at Vanderbilt) was
too busy studying to be very companionable, but I was enormously
impressed with the radiance of her soul.

Sonnet to Susan

When I first heard my daughter speak of you
And saw your bright reflection in her eyes,
I chose the thought appropriate and drew
A portrait on the parchment of surmise.
Oh, it was lovely, yes, but when I met
The You behind the face and form and name
I knew such quality cannot be set
In lines or limitations of a frame.
My colors are too commonplace; I need
A glint of sunset on a swallow's wing,

The crush of cycles bursting in a seed;
Something superior to remembering,
For memory is album's occupation
With summary, and You are inspiration!

—*Robert Lee Brothers (1998)*

At graduation in 1961, I was pleased that my first job was in Susan's part of the state, that far away Texas Panhandle. Although my new job would be in Amarillo, 125 miles north of her family's home in Lubbock, the miles would be no obstacle to visiting. In those parts of Texas, people drove that far just to go to a movie. The first holiday weekend she was home, I drove my little Volkswagen bug down the flat, windy corridor through the wheat fields and past the grain elevators to see her.

Susan introduced me to her mother, Lucille Davis Ford, who exclaimed, "Brothers! Are you related to the poet, Robert Lee Brothers?"

"Yes ma'am, he is my father."

Mrs. Ford rushed to the bookshelf and drew forth a copy of *Democracy of Dust,* his first book, published in 1947. It had been autographed for her mother (Susan's grandmother). Both women had been among his far-flung fans for years. Thrilled, Mrs. Ford wanted me to arrange a meeting at the first possible opportunity. They became fast friends, as did my father and Susan's father, J. Frank Ford.

My father died on Mother's Day of 1979. It was important to Susan and me—and many others—that his poetry not be buried with him. His first book, *Democracy of Dust,* had drawn glowing praise from the now long-dead Clement Wood, who said it was the best first book of poems he had ever seen, including his own. In 1953, his second book, *Hidden Harp,* won the Texas State Institute of Letters Award. In 1962, he was among the Councilors of the Poetry Society of Texas. With the financial backing of Susan's parents, his friends-become-patrons, my father published his third book, *Threescore and Ten,* ten years after his award-winning second one.

Therein lies the ongoing tale. All these years later, Susan is now a highly respected scholar with a national reputation in classics, who believed in the importance of getting my poet father's work onto university library shelves. She committed herself to the now successful task of pulling together all his poems, getting them into publishable form, and finding a firm willing to publish poetry. This new volume would contain his last unpublished manuscript, *Late Harvest,* as well as his previous three books. In the summer of 1996, Susan arranged their publication by Eakin Press under the title *Prairie Laureate: The Collected Poems of Robert Lee Brothers.* Coming out in 1998, three decades after his first volume, the book was made possible by Susan and her brother, Davis Ford. *Prairie Laureate* appeared 50 years after my father wrote his name in Mrs. Davis' book that April day—while Susan and I were still scampering around on our respective playgrounds 500 miles and a decade away from meeting each other.

On to the
Professional World

Like Virginia, I have a background in child welfare. After two years of ferrying children out of abuse and into protective care, also like Virginia, I had a keen need to learn more about helping people deal with shattered lives.

Requiem for a Foundling

". . . and I named him Victor. . .
even if he dies he ought to have a name . . ."
From the case files of a Child Welfare Worker.

The earth will rock him gently,
Her dust upon his eyes;
The wind will croon above him
Softly where he lies.

The stars will watch him kindly;
While quiet ages pass
His narrow little cradle
With its coverlet of grass.

And he shall wake to Glory
Who never dreamed of shame,
A wisp of The Eternal
Ignited with a name.

—Robert Lee Brothers (1998)

A gap existed between my knowledge base and the weight of the work. Even on the relatively affluent high plains of the Texas Panhandle, the depth of human misery sobered me, as did the ineptitude I felt in response. Having started the job before I even turned 21, I did not like affecting the lives of human beings with what felt like scant educational preparation.

So I enrolled in Tulane School of Social Work, in New Orleans. It offered me a tuition waiver for the first year and a full National Institute of Mental Health stipend for the second. Again like Virginia, I found myself in an uncomfortable position with my first field supervisor. I went to my faculty advisor, telling her that my supervisor trembled visibly during our supervision sessions. I noted that the lady seemed to me to be too threatened by me to be effective.

Fortunately, nobody suggested tossing me out of the program, as happened to Virginia. My advisor, Enolia Archinard, quietly moved me into the unit of Ethyl Van Dyke, the brightest and best supervisor in that particular field placement. And the next year, Mrs. Archinard got me into the best second-year placement.

Mrs. Archinard turned out to be one of the best things that happened in my professional life. Her husband had been from one of the old French families of New Orleans; she was an authentic part of New Orleans society with its traditional Mardi Gras Krewes and balls that date back to the mid 1800s. In one sense, she fit the role well, as she had a certain Southern-lady style of graciousness and elegance. Her presence generated a sense of verandas and gardenias and the hum of bees on leisurely summer afternoons. Glasses of ice tea in gardens. Open books laid face down in rocking chairs.

However, there was more to Enolia Archinard than magnolia blossoms and mint. She was from Missouri, both geographically and, to a great extent, metaphorically and intellectually. Gentle and gracious as she may have been, she was thoroughly laced with hardy pragmatism and sagacity. You would have been quite glad to have her along if you found yourself stuck on a desert island.

She taught the Human Development courses—and, in so doing, she laid a foundation for my assimilation of Virginia's kind of philosophy: the mentality of general mercy toward humankind. Mrs. Archinard managed to combine common sense, wit, wisdom, and a deep appreciation of art and beauty with compassion and intelligence. She was one of the few professors who did not bore us. This, in itself, seemed remarkable at the time.

And she appreciated me. I did not know at the time how rare an experience this is in graduate school. All I knew was that I felt like one of the African violets on her sill, still a little dewy-eyed, fresh and receptive, trusting and fragile—and well tended. Her life was a warm hearth to those of us who passed her way before she died May 7, 1995.

Enolia Introduces Virginia

I might never have become as connected with Virginia as I did had it not been for Enolia Archinard. When Virginia came to the Gulf Coast in 1968 for the Southern Regional Institute, my by-then-ex-professor ferried her back to the New Orleans airport from Biloxi. Thinking I might like to spend that much time with the famous Virginia Satir, she invited me to go along on this two-hour drive. From the back seat, Virginia leaned forward at intervals to feed me chocolates because, she said, she liked to see the expression on my face as she put them in my mouth.

Given my introversion and usual reticence, I might never have been in a position to connect with Virginia otherwise. In this as in other ways, Enolia Bradsher Archinard was my link to full expression of my professional self. She saw the spark, gently blew it toward its small initial flame, then placed the glowing embers within the reach of the great energy source that was Virginia Satir.

War on Poverty

I had graduated from Tulane in 1965. At that point, although my training had all been in the clinical area, I was not functioning as a clinician. I was busy trying to save the world via the anti-poverty program. In those days, the world seemed wiser —understanding that basic, constructive change would have to take place through empowering people on the grass-roots level.

My focus on community organization notwithstanding, I arranged to take time from my job to go watch the eminent Virginia Satir work. This was only a few months after my graduation, and I was already aware of her importance. Tulane School of Social Work had spoken of her in such glowing terms, I knew I needed to go to her presentation at Kingsley House (a local neighborhood settlement house). She would be working with an entire family—something I had not yet seen.

Indeed, she was as remarkable as Max Siporin, our casework professor, had said she was. So taken was I with the work I had just seen her do with the family, I wanted to say something to her, make some contact. Maybe I did walk up to her receiving line. It is likelier that I got in my Volkswagen bug and drove back to work in my inner-city ghetto. In any case, the impact registered. Far removed as family therapy was from my in-the-trenches attempts at organizing the poor on their own behalf, I stored the memory of the wondrous artistry of the work I had just witnessed.

I now see that my community organizing was not all that far from Virginia's work: my community was the city of New Orleans; hers was the world. The first time I looked back at those anti-poverty program days, I was startled to realize that I had that job for only seven months. The experiences had been so vibrant that somehow my mind had made the time into years. Filled with youthful idealism and fresh from the scschool of social work where I had just read Michael Harrington's *The Other America,* I had taken a job with Social Welfare Planning Council. This was the mid 1960s, the Great Society's experiment was launching, and I was part of a team assigned to the section of New Orleans arbitrarily called Central City. I was the only white person on the staff in my section and for blocks and blocks in either direction. In those days, this was far from a usual experience.

I had the extreme good fortune to be on the same team with Oretha Castle Haley. (At that point, she had not yet married Richard Haley. Both angels—the former avenging, the latter delivering. Together they were magnificent.) Oretha and I were contemporaries and peers, both 25, both beginning our careers. Richard, who was twice our age, had quit his job in the music department of some northern university to come down and be the Southern Regional Director of the local CORE (Congress of Racial Equality) office. Both Oretha and Richard were pinnacle, cream-of-the-crop civil rights workers as well as incredibly gifted human beings. I, on the other hand, could hardly have been more of a novice. All the knowledge I had was that "equal rights" was a good idea and I wanted to help bring them to birth.

Oretha looked at me balefully that first day. I later turned out to be one of her very few exceptions: she did not like white folks. After I had walked through the streets of New Orleans with her for a few weeks, I did not like us much either. The first week or so, we had gone to the nearest eating establishment at lunchtime. I was puzzled about why the service was taking so long. Oretha informed me: it was her presence. She was black, and this was the newly— but not quite—integrated South.

This experience of sudden, arbitrary discrimination is hard to describe to those who have not had it. Invariably, we (I more than Oretha, who was more used to it) were caught between growing anger and a wish to stand our ground and, on the other hand, mounting agitation about whether we really wanted to devote our lunch hour and energy to the campaign at that particular time. She and I would discuss it before lunch: did we want to go to the closest place and endure the potential hassle, going through the ambiguity of whether we would be served, or did we want to get on the bus and go to the nearest black neighborhood, where we could just get lunch? The decision generally depended on how many frustrations the day had held so far.

Then there was the time we were out on the streets and needed to make a phone call. It was a black neighborhood, and I started to follow Oretha into a bar, which had the nearest phone. She pushed me back outside, saying she had seen a police car pass as she was opening the door.

"So what?" I asked, again puzzled.

She informed me that New Orleans still had a law on the books prohibiting a black person and a white person from being together on the same premises that served alcohol. And she was not interested in going to jail this particular afternoon. (Oretha liked to choose when she went to jail, and she preferred ample media coverage for the occasion.)

Such jarring episodes stick with you. They bring a visceral meaning to the concept of human rights. And they can be more than merely jarring. People struggling for civil rights risked their lives in those days. One of the guys from CORE was driving what had been James Chaney's Volkswagen—I saw it every day, parked on the street. Chaney, Michael Schwerner, and Andrew Goodman (whose story was told years later in the movie *Mississippi Burning*) were the young men whose bodies had been found buried in a river bank in Mississippi.

Black civil rights workers were very clear as well as very respectful about it: they never pressured or expected any workers to go anywhere or do anything. Everybody was left to make the choice every time: "Is this a day I feel like risking death or not?"

Eventually, I left and went to work at the local state hospital instead. Partly, I thought I might ultimately do more good for the cause if I entered the mental health field and got further training on what makes human beings tick. The other part was that I felt I was too young to die.

The day I left, I told my coworkers that I would never forget them. I will always remember the immediate, spontaneous and impassioned response from Mrs. Stella Jourdan, one of the indigenous workers.

"No!" she urged, her voice filled with concern, "You must forget us!" She said I must go back to my white middle-class life and forget my connections with her and the poor blacks with whom we had all been working. Forget that we had ever met. If I did not forget them, I would have continual trouble. I would be called "nigger-lover." My life would be threatened. It would be as if I were dragging a ball and chain behind me. No, it would be far better for me simply to slip quietly back into the white community and take up the life I had before.

She meant it. This was her loving counsel to me as I left the streets and the projects. My eyes still fill with tears as I remember her entreating me to leave them when I left.

Moscow

My time in the streets and housing projects of New Orleans created the receptor in me that could resonate to Virginia's desire to free all people from the burden of not celebrating personhood and not valuing uniqueness. My postgraduate career having begun with that brief time in community organization, I found Virginia's idea of prevention on a grand scale quite plausible. Virginia envisioned intervention in whole populations. Having come to understand effective therapy to be far more than a set of techniques, she was prepared to apply the universal principles on a universal basis.

In an interview with Sheldon Starr, she spoke on the subject of changing the world (Satir, 1985b):

> Statistically, if 20 percent of the world is into a new place, we've made it . . . that is all it takes to get a new thing going. Twenty percent of the population: 6 percent to start it off, and then another 14 percent to make it go. Those are the movers and shakers in the world. And if we can get that many we'll have it, we can do it . . . it is also one of the other reasons why, for me, any therapeutic transaction that decreases a person's self-esteem, demeans or humiliates them defeats the purpose of making this a better world.

I was very taken with Virginia's statement. Discounting another human being, even in minor ways, is toxic. Awareness is the key; connection—at the points of heart, soul, and spirit—is the formula. And if only one-fifth of the world mobilizes in the human-connectedness direction, we might all burst forth as fields of poppies in the spring—and union and communion can prevail.

Her statement also explained her motivation for going around the world, for tirelessly holding seminar after seminar, and for struggling to be congruent in her own communication. Her extensive clinical observations had revealed the great Pattern of Peace—the way to world harmony: helping 6 percent of the world's population understand the relationship between self-esteem, communication, and system rules would mean being over the hump.

In that interview, Virginia said she had been depressed when she first realized she was not able to connect with the then 4.5 billion people on the face of this earth. However, in good social-worker fashion, she began partializing her problem, pointing out that all abuses—child, spouse, drug, etc.—probably do not represent more than 10 percent of the population. I could resonate with that number. One of my biggest surprises in my anti-poverty program work had been my observation that *poor* by no means equals *criminal.* Regarding the housing project schools buried deep in the "worst" areas, consultants had long known that the problems came from only a handful of students.

When Starr noted that this "small percent" of problem people still amounted to about 20 million, Virginia pointed out that the focus belongs on the process of change itself. She spoke of the importance of cooperation and of moving from the world of concept to the world of action. She added that each person must begin with her- or himself: "We all have to do it. Nobody can do it alone and there is no concept that is going to make it. We have to do it and I think what we have to face is each one of us has to be a part of all this." We who understand this issue have to be part of this shift toward cooperation, and it would take only 20 percent—actually, just 6 percent—to start things rolling.

In my life, this miracle happened. Her "6 percent" observation came true before my very eyes on a grand scale in 1991, when I followed Virginia's trail to the then Soviet Union. My link was Laura Dodson (who had organized the first month-long Satir training I had attended in Glenwood Springs, Colorado). Laura had recruited me into that summer's joint project of the Institute for International Connections (USA) and the Institute for Professional Development (USSR). Both groups had their roots in the trip Virginia had made to the Soviet Union in May 1988, just four months before her death. (Laura writes in her chapter about accompanying Virginia on that trip.)

So it was that in August 1991, I was in Moscow with a motley crew of family therapists, social workers, and their friends and families. Our conference completed, we had all gone home with our Russian friends to visit and play tourist that week. Thus, I had the incredibly good fortune to be on hand for one of the most amazing set of events in human history: the peaceful mobilizing of the people of Moscow to defeat the old guard Communists' coup attempt in August 1991. The day the first democratically elected president, Boris Yeltsin, replaced the last Communist dictator, Mikhail Gorbachev. The day Russia and a cascade of countries proclaimed independence from the Soviet Union, beginning its subsequent swift disintegration. The day the long silent bells began to peal again in Russia.

One week, I was working with Russians who had worked with Virginia. The next, I saw those same people and their students (along with more than 100,000 other Muscovites) mobilize peacefully to defeat the coup's attempt to turn back the clock and calendar. People whose names I knew and whose homes I had been in now stood at bristling barricades—all night, night after night, in the rain. They faced tanks with nothing between their bodies and the steel but their conviction that they had the right to live in dignity.

The Russian defenders of democracy were simply—if courageously—standing up for themselves. The crowds were strangely quiet. No one shouted insults. The violence that took place was entirely accidental. A couple of our Russian friends—Julia Gippenreiter and her husband, Alex Rudachov—witnessed a tank running over a young man and said it was clear the driver did not intend his death. I will never forget Alex's face as he later poured out his story of watching that event. Exciting as the new victory was, the element of tragedy was laced in the heroism.

I will also never forget the funeral procession Moscow held for the three people killed inadvertently. I marched in that body, right behind the official delegation from Lithuania, with the old flag of Lithuania fluttering black and gold before us. The coffins lay on truck beds that moved slowly through the streets. As they passed, people stepped out from the crowds and placed flowers on the coffin lids.

Marching right behind us—like a portrait of the 18th century in motion—were five of the defenders who had been on the front barricades. They wore white headbands. One was wearing an old army greatcoat. He carried the tricolored red, blue, and white flag of old Russia. I felt like I was marching through history, flanked by all who had ever defended liberty in all centuries and lands.

Having the streets of Moscow filled with Russians determined to commit no violence graphically represented Virginia's high hopes for humankind: to create power based on respect for self rather than on dominion over others. Taking "steps on their own behalf"— as Virginia so often encouraged wherever she worked—the people of Moscow ushered "the possible" into reality. It was a living example of her concept of how to bring about change in favor of human beings. As she passed through our world, Virginia brought with her a vision of possibility that we sorely need. Seeing effective family therapy and world peace as one process, she also saw that the essential—as well as eminently practical—starting point was the level of self-worth (Satir, 1986b, tape 1):

> the more you appreciate yourself, the less you will have to depreciate any one else. Put another way, the more you can appreciate yourself, the more you can appreciate others.

Make what you will of her "6 percent" statistics—metaphor or mathematics—the truth of that statement stood in August 1991. Those 100,000 movers and shakers in Moscow numbered far less than 6 percent of that city's population of eight million. Yet they changed world history. (If you think for a moment that is not true, consider what would have happened had they all stayed home and sat on their hands that week.)

Those three days were a rare and potent example of just what Virginia had meant. Link together enough people who have enough self-appreciation to demand respect from others—respectfully— and you have the essential motion of world peace. It swirled in the air that day I joined the Russians to march back and, on Yeltsin's suggestion, to reclaim Red Square.

Among a crowd of several thousand very happy Russians, I watched the red hammer-and-sickle flag move slowly down the flagpole atop the parliament building, feeling chills run down my spine. Yeltsin's voice, from the building's steps, boomed out over the gathered crowd: "People of Moscow, you have just saved the world!"

I could not help but think of Virginia. Part of her dream was to empower people to act definitively on their own behalf, respectful of self and others as they become aware of the uniqueness of each human being. Those 100,000 or so Muscovites had wrestled history to the ground when they surrounded their "white house" to defend the only democratically elected president their country had known.

"Democratically elected" is the operative term. They were not defending Yeltsin; many did not even like him. For them, the *roles* of Yeltsin and Gorbachev were far more important than their names or even their personalities. Our Russian friends were never nearly as taken with either man as the American public was. The people were defending the democratic process—the right to choice.

Among the most touching of my memories is singing "We Shall Overcome" a few days later with a roomful of our Russian colleagues, at their suggestion. Valodya from St. Petersburg had his guitar with him and knew all four verses. When I had been singing with my black friends 25 years earlier, those same words had apparently been echoing half a world away among these Russians on these distant shores.

Having thoroughly fallen in love with Russians, I am still an active board member in the Institute for International Connections that Laura founded in 1989. The IIC has been instrumental in the professional training and success of a growing number of Czech, Russian, Lithuanian, and Latvian psychologists, teachers, organizational development consultants, and now social workers. Since that bright August day when Communism left the stage of history, I have spent several weeks in Russia each year. "From Russia with Soul," my account of the courage of my Russian friends during the first wave of the economic crisis immediately following their independence, was published by *Psychology Today* (January/ February 1993). Elena Ivanov, whose picture appears in the article, and Tanya Antonyan, in whose home I stayed during the 1991 coup attempt, are both significant figures in the wheel of influence of my soul.

A Mystical Thread

Over the years, my connection with Virginia was like a thread that wove between us in a mystical way. Whether or not I willed it, I found myself in connection with her over and over again. I would have an inexplicable impulse to inquire about her welfare, only to learn she had been ill. Or I would interview her for an article, observe something disturbingly puzzling in the process, and make sense of it only years later when it suddenly fell into place with new developments in her life.

Did any of this make me "special" in any way? Only, perhaps, to Virginia's resident angel, who wanted this book written. Certainly Virginia herself was not planning these coincidences of timing and these correlations in backgrounds.

In March 1982, I interview Virginia for the 1983 *Voices* issue called "Steps Toward a History of American Psychotherapy." The following December, I call her office to verify the spelling of "Gyarfas" and "Horab." Her secretaries are evasive—no, she is not there, and maybe she would not know how to spell those names either.

I smell a rat. Virginia Satir not know how to spell her own friends' names?! She could spell my mother's name, and they had never even met, outside of a role play. Come on. What is going on here?

Long silence. "Well, Virginia didn't want us to tell anybody. She's having surgery tomorrow."

"For what?!!"

"A malignancy—she is having a hysterectomy. She is home now, if you want to call her."

Of course, I called her—and the first thing she asked was how had I found out. I explained that her staff had simply been too congruent to be able to hide from me the fact that something was terribly wrong.

At that point, Virginia became as vulnerable as I have ever heard of her becoming. She said, "I know what cancer is about. I know the deep loneliness that it reflects . . .." She spoke of feeling shame and humiliation. I don't remember the rest of the few words she said—there were not many—but I realized she had opened the door to her soul to me, and her soul was in great pain. I wished with all my heart to be able to comfort her—and felt my own helplessness puddle around my feet. Felt a tall wave of sadness, both in resonance with hers and because I knew my ineptness in expression was letting her down. There was nothing I could do about it.

Whatever I said in response felt limp as it left my mouth. I felt, in that moment, like a person on land whose hand will not quite reach the outstretched hand of someone who is drowning. I asked if I could assume she did not want me to talk about her surgery and diagnosis. Correct: she did not want that at all. So I did not say a word about it for the next six years, until the summer of 1988, when I heard about the pancreatic cancer that would take her life.

My last words to Virginia came about through the compassionate concern of another great person who had entered my life years previous to 1988: Jean Houston, noted educator, author, philosopher, and evocator of souls. Another blossom along my trail.

Jean Houston

Long before my Russian experiences and Virginia's illness, Jean Houston had emerged as a figure in the spiritual sector of my wheel of influence. Later, in 1996, she was widely known as advisor to the First Lady, Hillary Clinton. Intelligent people themselves, both Hillary and Bill Clinton both recognized Jean's gifts and made good use of them—until politics intruded.

I recognized the splendor of Jean's soul and the sparkle of her mind years before. It was immediately obvious that she has the most original mind I have encountered since Virginia's. Since our meeting, she has consistently mentored my own creativity. The number of articles I published increased exponentially after her entry into my life. On the one hand, she has generated original ideas; on the other, she consistently promotes my expression of them, delighting in the style in which I write.

I met Jean at the 1982 annual institute and conference of the American Academy of Psychotherapists in Washington, D.C. At that point, I was still editor of *The Newsletter* of that organization and associate editor of their journal, *Voices: the Art and Science of Psychotherapy*. In her afternoon workshop, Jean mentioned her "Southern Baptist agnostic father from Texas." My own father used to describe himself in the exact same words! So, uncharacteristically, I introduced myself afterward, asking from what part of the state her father came.

"Nacogdoches—East Texas. What part of Texas are you from?," Jean asked, politely.

"I grew up ten miles out of Gonzales, Texas."

"Gonzales. Oh, do you know Kent Gardien?"

"Sure I know him! He is my cousin."

"I had my first date with Kent Gardien." Jean added, "Gonzales must be a little hotbed of culture."

Native Texans have looked blank when I said "Gonzales." To have this instant recognition by the eminent Jean Houston and to hear my little home town described as a "hotbed of culture" was startling for me. There are reasons, however, for Jean's observation. Kent was a Harvard graduate and a writer. Gonzales also boasted my poet father and Liz Smith, New York columnist and author of *The Mother Book*. Long, long ago (mid to late 1800s), the town had one of the state's first colleges to enroll women; it was also said to be the first college in the nation to provide a Bachelor of Arts degree for female students (Gonzales County Historical Commission, 1986, p. 121).

In the same conversation, I learned Jean is a direct descendent of Sam Houston. This discovery reveals a bit of "mystical" whimsy: my own paternal great-great-grandfather, David L. Kokernot, had been quite taken with Sam Houston. (David was the same Texas Hero who survived the shipwreck, tried to join the forces at the Alamo, and fathered the son who amassed a vast cattle ranch. At roughly the same time, in the same little frontier settlement in the wilds of Texas, Laura Sue Dodson's great-great-grandfather was founding Baylor University. Laura and Jean are also longtime friends dating back to finding themselves roommates in the Union Graduate School program.) Looks like a multidimensional trail to me!

David engaged with Sam Houston in serious discussion about the upcoming Texas Revolution. From David's memoirs:

as I walked up the street I noticed the finest looking man I ever saw, seated on the steps of Col. Thorn's storehouse. He was dressed in a complete Indian costume made of buckskin and ornamented with a profuse variety of beads, and his massive head was covered with a fine broad beaver hat. When he arose I stopped and looked at him with both surprise and admiration and bid him good morning. He asked me whence I had come. I told him from Galveston Bay, Middle Texas. Then he invited me to sit down and have a chat with him in reference to land matters, which I did for considerable time. Our conversation ended, he invited me into the store to take a glass of wine with him, which I readily accepted . . .

Sam and David discussed the rumors of Santa Anna's military build-up, apparently intended to implement a little "gun control" among the colonists. Naturally, this was not setting at all well with the rough and ready frontiersmen, who were "determined not to surrender our arms . . ." After Sam had suggested, with David's agreement, "The people ought to organize and get ready to meet him," Sam asked, "Who will command the army?"

David replied: "My dear sir, if I had the authority to make the appointment, you are the man; for you are the finest looking man I ever laid eyes on."

Sam Houston promised David Kokernot a commission if he, Sam, got that appointment (later making good the promise). On many a future occasion, David stated: "From that day I loved Sam Houston" (Sharfman, 1977).

This discussion of compelling physical appearance means even more to those who have seen the nearly-six-feet-tall Jean Houston in her beaded buckskin suit, wearing her long white feather war bonnet. Sam, who had spent his later adolescence among the Cherokee, was no doubt the prototype of the unmistakable Houston magnetism, buckskin and all. I had the same response to a Houston's commanding presence 150 years later with his great-great-great-granddaughter.

The whole account felt very parallel. I think of old Sam and David as a sort of primitive personal template, on a metaphysical level. One might even say I, too, began participating in a revolution, though of a very different order. Less literally and on a wider scale, Jean invests most of her energy in turning our world around. Like David with his bold Houston, I have committed myself to helping my own later version. In efforts to help nudge one or other portions of the planet in the right direction, we have collaborated on important wordsmithing projects, eventually combining our energies with Virginia to fight the cancer that was sapping her life. Obviously, we did not experience the specific kind of success for which we had hoped, but the story belongs to my own circle-of-influence account. To date, it remains the most poignant joint project of my life.

Virginia was life-oriented. She had been actively engaged in living almost to the very moment of her dying. Although few can believe that healing cancer is possible, Virginia believed in the power of choice and had more faith in positive possibility than do many of us. Her initial active engagement toward her own healing reflected the essence of her great being. Aware of people whose cancers had gone into remission and vanished, Virginia would have thought that if even one such person had existed, there was no reason why she could not be the second.

She had her own well-thought-out theories about the emotional factors in the etiology of cancer and about cancer as a body metaphor (Brothers, 1987a, 1989a). There are people alive today with whom she had served as therapist; their cancers are still in remission. Sharing Virginia's conviction about the boundless potential for wholeness by harmonizing body, mind, heart, and spirit, Jean's goal was to reinforce Virginia's belief in the possibility of exchanging her cancer cells for healthy cells.

None of the interchange was designed simply to comfort a person with a terminal illness. Jean had enormous respect for

Virginia, although they did not know each other well. Their paths had crossed at various meetings, and they had worked together on at least one committee. Virginia had once entered a room during a lecture by Jean; Jean had stopped mid-lecture to acknowledge Virginia's entrance, saying she would not continue until Virginia was seated (Satir, 1988b).

However respectful, these path-crossings were just that. Jean called me when she learned of Virginia's illness. "I know how much you love her—I just couldn't have that information without being sure you knew about it, too."

The next day, not quite out of shock but at least able to put two thoughts together, I called Jean back. "Is there anything I can do?"

There was. She wanted me to help her think of images that would speak to Virginia—images that would help Virginia turn around her immune system to activate her own healing processes. At that point, Jean was in telephone contact with her twice daily, leading her in healing meditation. So images tailored specifically to Virginia would be quite valuable.

I simply took those rural images I had heard Virginia use to clothe her own concepts and coated them lightly with some thoughts from Jean that seemed to parallel Virginia's. I would have liked Virginia to know of my role, but that posed the risk of diluting the potential healing power of Jean's meditations. Much more than wanting her to know of my presence in this work, I wanted her to become one of that small number who survive malignancy. Doing so would be difficult enough.

After using the first script that I wrote, Jean eagerly requested more images. Virginia had responded deeply and with enthusiasm. I told Jean it was no real wonder. They were Virginia's own words wearing slightly different dresses.

I include much of the text here because it represents a distillation of Virginia's ideas about growth—and about illness as a metaphor for growth thwarted. Through the script, I laced Virginia's own words and concepts (reprinted here in italics), hoping that the robust seeds of her own genius might lift her back to physical wholeness. She believed in the possibility and knew the power in her own work.

This is not your cancer. It is your mother's. She did not know how to let go of it, but you do. She did not know she had another choice. You can make that other choice.

The other choice is to be *open*. To let Love *flow* through. Let your *system* open, really open, to whatever love is there in the moment, in all the moments, the full richness of the moments . . ..

. . . You can *allow yourself to take the next steps*. Let the rest of yourself evolve.

Like light on the cornfields—like the breezes rustling through the husks—the wind blowing the chaff away . . ..

My voice is bearing the Wholing/Loving/Living/Healing Life from the ages. Let my voice shine through all your cells—let that Life sweep away the *wild, uncontrolled growth* . . ..* Receive your next thirty years here on this planet. You are not finished yet. Let the *reconstruction* of your deepest innermost parts take place. Something in you is trying to *grow*. Let the cells that don't need to be there get out of the way, let them be plowed under so they can come back the kind of growth that is *congruent* with who you really are.

Let the matter that is in those cancer cells be transformed into the blaze of loving energy that can sweep you into your new form.

You need the courage to open that deepest door.

Love is struggling for a deeper, fuller birth, stuck in your cells. *Spirit* is trying to be born of flesh . . ..

---

*Virginia spoke of life energy bottled up in the "wild, uncontrolled growth" of cancer cells. For an explanation of her theories about emotional factors in the etiology of cancer as a body metaphor for personal growth stymied, see B. J. Brothers (1987a, 1989a).

Let the trust open those last heavy doors. Let the warmth that is born in *real connecting* melt the membranes so the protein and minerals in all those cancer cells may be released back into the fertile grounding of your lovely body. You need the light and the heat of the energy held in those cells.

Let the warmth of the Spirit that moves across the waiting earth touch the very deepest parts of you. Let the Breath of Life blow away the shadows. Release the fear and be as a little child again, receiving . . . receiving . . ..

Your *wholeness* has packed together into the cancer cells. Like a *seed* waiting for Spring's warm, moist light. Let the Light pour deep into you like the morning sun on a freshly plowed field.* [*Emphases added*]

Virginia made her choice for the sooner date with Eternity. And if the song sang her to sleep instead, at least the lyrics were shadows and shimmers of her own sweet song, sung back to her.

In Closing

This brings to a close my wanderings through my life's garden of some of the people who have brightened my soul as well as my days. What does it all mean?

Conation

Perhaps the paths of snails may be
A wasted effort marked by slime,
But I, too, bear the shell of me
That hinders and protects my climb.
Through cycles of uncertainties

---

*Full text appears in B. J. Brothers (1991a, "Healing Virginia").

We blindly grope and slowly crawl
Up awful cracks in theories
Or fissures in a garden wall.

—*Robert Lee Brothers (1998)*

Most of us who had the blessing of having known Virginia Satir are still out here, each in our respective gardens, doing our best to remember what she said about all the shining selves inside all the blindly groping shells. She so wanted us all simply to remember who we really are—and then to remind the rest of our family—the human race—for whom she had worked very hard.

Sleep well, Virginia. We'll take it from here.

Circle of Influence

by Robert S. Spitzer

"Circle of Influence" is an exercise that Virginia used to prepare the star for a Family Reconstruction.

1. Place a small dot in the middle of a blank page. The dot stands for you.
2. Now place dots for the significant people in your life at a distance from you that represents their relative importance to you. Most people make six to twenty dots for significant people. It is very helpful to represent your relationships visually with yourself as the center.

Virginia would have had to put in thousands of dots. Her deep, continuing connection with so many people is truly remarkable. I was in only one of many four-week-long residential workshops that Virginia led both here and abroad. These were very intense learning and bonding experiences. Afterwards we could continue the connection with each other through IHLRN and Avanta.

The following list is my guess of some of the people in her Circle of Influence. It is just a starter. I know I have omitted hundreds, so if you send us your name, we will add it to the list in Volume Two.

Jesse Adams
Ramona Adams ☆
Teresa Adams
Dorothy Agbor
Paul Alexander
Leslie Asplund
Lynne Azpeitia
DeWitt Baldwin
Michele Baldwin
Anne Banmen
John Banmen ☆
Madonna Beard
Jeanette Benson
Barbara Berendzen
Yetta Bernhard
Jean Anne Berning
Kaye Bishop
James Bitter
Peter Bos
Janice Ann Bradnam
Barbara Jo Brothers
Andrea Brown
Beverly Brown
Moira Lesley Brunner
☆ Doris Bryant
Stephen Buckbee
Mary Jo Bulbrook
Michael Callaghan
Ames Camerson ☆
Jesse Carlock
Carlie Casey
Nonie Casselman-Reed
Catherine Caston
Irene Yue Cheung
Janet Christie-Seely
Noemi Contreras

Priscilla Cooley
Barbara Corneille
Allen Cox
Lois Creighton
William Davis
Cor de Bode
Sofia de Melaasecca
De Rivas, Eliana Lara
Alla Destandau
Lynn Delvaux DeWitte
Jamie Dickey
Carole Dillon
Joe Dillon ☆
Laura Dodson
Bunny Duhl
Fred Duhl
Michael F. Dupont
Pamela M. Elish
Ellen Elmaleh
Todd Embree
Reiko Endo
Paula Englander-Golden
Sharon Faff-Armstrong
Debra Fromm Faria
Rette Farren
Dot Feldman
Sandra Finkelman
Patrick Fleming
Fred Ford
Karl Fossum
Joanne Francisco
Bengt Fredricksson
Miriam Freeman
A. Marie George
Jo Ann M. George
Jane Gerber

Alvin Gervais
Peral Gervais
Mary Ann Gisler
David Golden
Maria Gomori   ☆
Paul Gomori
George Gondron
Julius Gordon
Lori Gordon
Trish Graham
Kay Grask
Chris Gratz
Hugh Gratz
Maureen Graves
Tom Graves
Todd Gravois
Annos Gross
David Gross
Stan Gross
Sara Guevara
Russ Haber
Patricia Hagerty
Diana Hall
Judith L. Harrison
Sally Harwood
Charles Heller
Jean Hermann
Harland Hermann
Joan Herrick-Hanson
Nyra Hill
Olga Holubova   ☆
Catherine Huber
Wendy Huntington
Deborah Huntley
Lucille Hurwitz
Virginia V. Husband

Ann Jones   ☆
Megan Jordan
Bill Kelly
David Kennedy
Linda Kennedy
Renata Kolackova
Jerry Konecki
Sheldon Z. Kramer
Karen Krestensen
Frederic La Belle
Marie Shen Lam
Carmen Lara
Sue Lauber-Fleming
Marlies Lenglachner
Shirley Lennox
Martha Levert
J. Alfred Levertt, II
Judi Loberg
Sharon Loeschen
John Logue
Connie Lundgren
Nancy Macdonald
Susan J. McFeaters
Lynne McGuire   ☆
Jock McKeen
Jean McLendon
Mel MacNeil
Mary Madland
John Madsen-Bibeau
Kathlyne Maki-Banmen
Mabs Mango
Hazel Martin
Amanda Mathis
Annie Meyer
Shelia Meyers
Karen Miller

Ian Leigh Mishkin
Gerd F. Mueller
Gaby Mueller-Moskau
Joyne Munschauer
Evelina Muze ☆
Sandra E. S. Neil
Peter Nemetschek
Nawne Nerin
Susan Newton-Chambers
Chris Kee Ng
Jean C. Noah
Jean C. Novak
Jane Parsons-Fein
Marilyn Peers
Pari Pelonis
Monique Plamondon
Sherry Powers-Clark
Ray Price
Jacqueline Prud'homme
Doris Purdom
Ximena Reedy
Philip Reichline
Lessie Ann Rhodes
Hilda Richards
Marygrace Robinson
Erv Ruhl
Lorraine Sando
Carl Sayles ☆
Judi Schaim
Phyllis Schiff
Gerd Schuning
Johanna Schwab
Jackie Schwartz
Hana Scibranyova
Selena Sermeno
Naomi Serrano

Bob Shapiro
Shannon Sheridan
Robert L. N. Silverberg
Judy Small
Becky Spitzer
Robert S. Spitzer
Anna Stefkova
Edith Stoltzenberg
Jonathan Stolzenberg
Margarita Suarez
Gloria Taylor
Cecilia Tendler ☆
Carrie Thie
John Thie
Lani Tolman
Jana Trepacova ☆
Janet Trever
Nancy Truluck
Meryl Tullis
Gerri H. Tyler
John Vasconcellos
Will Venable
Judith Wagner
Charles Welch
Colene West
Wheelock Whitney
Martha Wigglesworth
Barbara A. Wiley
Ruth Williamson-Kirkland
Judith Wilson
Sonya Wilt
Joan Winter
Ben Wong ☆
Betsy and Bruce Woolport
Steven Young
Walter Zahnd

References and Readings

Adams, T. M. (1987). *Living from the inside out*. New Orleans, LA: Self published.

Aldridge, R. (1994). Interview with B. J. Brothers. (Ron Aldridge is the current director of the Dallas Child Guidance Center.)

Bach, G., and Wyden, P. (1968). *The intimate enemy*. New York: Avon.

Baldwin, D. C. (1992, Mar.). Interview with B. J. Brothers.

Baldwin, D. C. (1996, Jan.). Interview with B. J. Brothers.

Barfield, G. S. (1993). Conversation with D. Dreher.

Basch, R. V. (1980). Videotaped interview with Virginia Satir. Washington, DC: Richard Vennard Basch Studios (2627 Connecticut Avenue, NW, Suite 300; 20008; telephone 202-232-3100).

Bateson, G. (1979). *Mind and nature*. New York: Dutton.

Benton, W. (1943). *This is my beloved*. New York: Knopf.

Berberet, J. (1993). Interview with D. Dreher.

Berne, E. (1964). *Games people play: The psychology of human relationships*. New York: Random House.

Bielenberg, L. T., Gordon, L. H., and Raber, M. (1992). *An exploratory study of PAIRS: An integrative group approach to relationship change*. Unpublished paper, Catholic University of America, Washington, DC.

Blaker, K. (1993). Conversation with D. Dreher.

Boszomenyl, I., and Spark, G. (1984). *Invisible loyalties.* New York: Brunner/Mazel.

Bowen, M. (1989). Personal correspondence with B. J. Brothers.

Branden, N. (1983). *If you could hear what i cannot say.* New York: Bantam.

Briggs, J. (1988). *Fire in the crucible.* New York: St. Martin's Press.

Brothers, B. J. (1983). Virginia Satir: Past to present. *Voices: The Art and Science of Psychotherapy, 18* (Win.):48–56.

Brothers, B. J. (1987a). "Independence" *avoids* intimacy: Avoidance of intimacy kills. *Voices: The Art and Science of Psychotherapy, 23* (Spr.):10–23.

Brothers, B. J. (1987b). "Bless me, father, for I have sinned," or: ". . . Wake me, mother, when you rise . . ." *Voices: The Art and Science of Psychotherapy, 23:* (Fall): 12–20.

Brothers, B. J. (1988a). What is a mystery school? *Voices: The Art and Science of Psychotherapy, 24* (Spr.): 24–33.

Brothers, B. J. (1988b). Tribute to Virginia Satir. *Voices: The Art and Science of Psychotherapy, 24* (Sum.): 14–21.

Brothers, B. J. (1989a). The cancer patient is the self-contained patient. In E. Mark Stern (Ed.), *The self- contained patient* (pp. 227–241). Binghamton, NY: Haworth Press.

Brothers, B. J. (1989b). Remorse and regeneration. In E. Mark Stern (Ed.), *Psychotherapy and the remorseful patient* (pp. 47–62). Binghamton, NY: Haworth Press.

Brothers, B. J. (1989c). The possible therapist: Virginia Satir and congruent communication (letter to Jean Houston). *Voices: The Art and Science of Psychotherapy, 24* (Win.):12–27.

Brothers, B. J. (1990). Self-esteem and congruent communication: Virginia Satir's road to integration. *Advanced Development: A Journal on Adult Giftedness, 2* (Jan.): 23–31.

Brothers, B. J. (Ed.) (1991a). *Virginia Satir: Foundational ideas.* Binghamton, NY: Haworth Press.

Brothers, B. J. (Ed.) (1991b). Ask not for whom the siren wails. In B. J. Brothers (Ed.), *Coupling: What makes permanence* (pp. 14–16). Binghamton, NY: Haworth Press.

Brothers, B. J. (Ed.) (1991c). *Peace, war, and mental health: Couples therapists look at the dynamics.* Binghamton, NY: Haworth Press.

Brothers, B. J. (Ed.) (1992a). *Spirituality and couples: Heart and soul in the therapy process.* Binghamton, NY: Haworth Press.

Brothers, B. J. (Ed.) (1992b). *Couples therapy, multiple perspectives: In search of universal threads.* Binghamton, NY: Haworth Press.

Brothers, B. J. (1996a). Virginia Satir and Lao Tzu: Con-gruence and the tao. In B. J. Brothers (Ed.), *Couples and the tao of congruence* (pp. 3–11). Binghamton, NY: Haworth Press.

Brothers, B. J. (Ed.) (1996b). *Couples and the tao of con-gruence.* Binghamton, NY: Haworth Press.

Brothers, R. L. (1998). *Prairie Laureate: Collected poems of Robert Lee Brothers.* Austin, TX: Eakin Press.

Buber, M. (1958). *I and thou.* New York: Charles Scribner's Sons.

Casriel, D. (1972). *A scream away from happiness.* New York. Grosset & Dunlap.

Coogler, J. (1979). *Structured mediation in separation and divorce.* Lexington, MA: Lexington Books.

Counsell, Mr. and Mrs. David (1992). Interview with B. J. Brothers.

De Beauvoir, S. (1952). *The second sex.* New York: Knopf.

DeMaria, R. M. (1998). *A national survey of married couples who participate in marriage enrichment.* Unpublished doctoral dissertation, Bryn Mawr College, Bryn Mawr, PA.

Dodson, L. S. (1977). *Family counseling: A systems approach.* Muncie, IN: Accelerated Development.

Dodson, L. S. (1980). An archetypal view of world distress. *Inward Light* (Spring), 7–15.

Dodson, L. S. (1983). Combined analytic and system approaches in working with families. *Journal of American Academy of Psychoanalysis* (Spring/Summer).

Dodson, L. S. (1987). Problems and pitfalls at the crossroads of cultural change. *Inward Light* (Spring).

Dodson, L. S. (1991a). The dying process of a conscious woman: Virginia Satir. In B. J. Brothers (Ed.) (1991a). *Virginia Satir: Foundational ideas.* Binghamton, NY: Haworth Press.

Dodson, L. S. (1991b). Possible pitfalls in the process of change. *Urania Journal* (Moscow).

Dodson, L. S. (1991c). Virginia Satir's process of change. In B. J. Brothers (Ed.) (1991a). *Virginia Satir: Founda-tional ideas.* Binghamton, NY: Haworth Press.

Dodson, L. S. (1992). Der proze der veranderung. In G. Moskau and G. Miller, *Wegezum Wachstum* (pp. 13–38). Germany: Junfermann Verlag Paderborn.

Dodson, L. S. (1993). Intertwining Jungian depth psychology and family therapy through use of action techniques. *Journal of Group Psychotherapy, Psychodrama and Sociometry* 35:4 (Winter).

Dodson, L. S., and Gibson, T. (1997). *Psyche and the family.* Chicago: Chiron Press.

Dodson, L. S. (*n.d.*) *Toward a Jungian view of cultural analysis with Zimbabwe, Africa as an example.* Chicago, IL: Archives of Jungian Doctoral Theses, Jungian Institute.

Duhl, B. (1988). Virginia Satir memorial talk. Presented at a meeting of the American Association of Marriage and Family Therapists in New Orleans, LA.

Duhl, F. J. (1974). Videotaped interview of Virginia Satir. Boston, MA: Boston Family Institute (315 Dartmouth Street; 02116).

Durana, C. (1994). The use of bonding and emotional expressiveness in the PAIRS training: A psychoeducational approach for couples. *Journal of Family Psychotherapy, 5* (2), 65–81.

Durana, C. (1995). *Enhancing marital intimacy: A longitudi-nal evaluation of the effectiveness of the PAIRS psychoeducational program.* Unpublished doctoral dissertation, Saybrook Institute, Los Angeles, CA.

Durana, C. (1996a). A longitudinal evaluation of the effectiveness of the PAIRS program for couples. *Family Therapy, 2,* 11–36.

Durana, C. (1996b). Bonding and emotional education for couples in the PAIRS training: Part 1. *The American Journal of Family Therapy, 24* (3), 269–328.

Durana, C. (1997). Enhancing marital intimacy through psychoeducation: The PAIRS program. *The Family Journal, 5* (3), 204–215.

Durana, C. (1999). "Integrated psychoeducational approach," in Carlson, J. and Sperry, L. (Eds.), *The intimate couple.* New York: Brunner/Mazel (Taylor and Francis Group).

Durana, C., and Gordon, L. H. (1999). PAIRS (Practical application of intimate relationship skills). In R. Berger and M. Hanna (Eds.), *Preventive approaches to couples therapy.* New York: Brunner/Mazel (Taylor and Francis Group).

Englander-Golden, P. & Satir, V. (1990). *Say it straight: From compulsions to choices.* Palo Alto, CA: Science and Behavior Books.

Ford, G. L. (1936). *Texas cattle brands.* Dallas, TX: Clyde C. Cockrell Company.

Fromm, E. (1956). *The art of loving.* New York: Bantam.

Fromm, E. (1976). *To have or to be.* New York: Harper & Row.

Gaines, J. (1979). *Fritz Perls here and now.* Millbrae, CA: Celestial Arts.

Gerber, J. (1993). Interview with B. J. Brothers.

George Lord diary memoirs 1842: The Mier expedition. Austin, TX: Archives Division, Texas State Library.

Gibran, K. (1982). *The prophet.* New York: Knopf.

Gonzales County Historical Commission (1986). *The history of Gonzales county.* Dallas, TX: Curtis Media Corpora-tion (9954 Brockbank Drive; 75220).

Gordon, L. H. (1977). *A laundry list of marital mishaps, knots and double binds.* Washington, DC: Family Relations Institute.

Gordon, L. H. (1978). *The PAIRS dialogue guide.* Washington, DC: Family Relations Institute.

Gordon, L. H. (1986). *The PAIRS handbook.* Falls Church, VA: PAIRS Foundation.

Gordon, L. H. (1990). *Love knots: How to untangle those everyday frustrations and arguments that keep you from being with the one you love.* New York: Dell.

Gordon, L. H., with Frandsen, J. (1993). *Passage to intimacy.* New York: Fireside/Simon and Schuster.

Gordon, L. H. (1996). *If you really loved me . . . . : Identifying and untangling love knots in intimate relationships.* Palo Alto, CA: Science & Behavior Books.

Goss, M. D. (1994). *The effects of gender and a marital enrich-ment program on communication responses, individuation, and marital satisfaction among married couples.* Unpublished doctoral dissertation, Howard University, Washington, DC.

Gottman, J., Notarius, C.; Gonso, J; and Markman, H. (1976). *A couples' guide to communication.* Champaign, IL: Research Press.

Goulding, M. M., and Goulding, R. L. (1979). *Changing lives through redecision therapy.* New York: Brunner/Mazel.

Gray, J. (1980). *What you feel, you can heal.* Santa Monica, CA: Heart Publishing.

Hardel, E. (1992). Interview with B. J. Brothers.

Harrington, M. (1962). *The other America: Poverty in the United States.* New York: Macmillan.

Hillman, J. (1995). Pseudologia fantastica: A curious need to falsify, disguise or destroy the story of your life. *Disillusionment. Spring: A Journal of Archetype and Culture, 58* (Fall):83–101.

Houston, J. (1987). *The search for the beloved.* Los Angeles, CA: Jeremy P. Tarcher.

Houston, J. (1996). *A mythic life.* San Francisco, CA: HarperCollins.

Jahr, E. W. *(n.d.).* History of Henrietta Carlotta Ernestina Maria Simon. In *Family history, Wilke-Simon* (unpub-lished manuscript).

Janov, A.(1980). *Prisoners of pain: Unlocking the power of the mind to end suffering.* Garden City, NY: Doubleday.

Kiersey, D., and Bates, M. (1978). *Please understand me: Character and temperament types.* Del Mar, CA: Prometheus Nemesis.

King, L. (1989). *Women of power.* Berkeley, CA: Celestial Arts.

Kramer, Sheldon (1996, Jan.). Telephone conversation with B. J. Brothers.

Ladd, A. (1989). PAIRS: *A psychoeducational approach to marital intervention.* Unpublished master's thesis, Catholic University of America, Washington, DC.

Laign, J. (1988). Healing human spirits, creating joy in living. Interview with Virginia Satir. *Focus on Chemically Dependent Families, 11* (Oct./Nov.):20–21, 28–32.

Liedloff, J. (1977). *The continuum concept.* New York: Warner.

Loeschen, S. (1991). *Magic of Satir: Practical skills for therapists.* Long Beach, CA: Event Horizon Press.

Love, P., and Robinson, J. (1994). *Hot monogamy.* New York: Dutton.

Lynch, J. (1977). *The broken heart.* New York: Basic Books.

Lynch, J. (1985). *The language of the heart.* New York: Basic Books.

MacLean, P. D. (1973). *A triune concept of the brain and behavior.* Toronto, Canada: University of Toronto Press.

McCarthy, B., and McCarthy, E. (1990). *Couple sexual awareness: Building sexual happiness.* New York: Carroll & Graf.

Miller, D. (1996, Jan.). *In the beginning: The soul of creativity and the spirit of creation.* Presented at the Parker Institute for Spirituality, New Orleans, LA.

Miller, S., Wackerman, D., Nunnally, E., and Saline, C. (1982). *Straight talk.* New York: Rawson Associates.

Missildine, W. H. (1988). *Your inner child of the past.* New York: Pocket Books.

Morgan, L. (1996, Win.). Reflections by our mad historian. *Middle Atlantic Division Newsletter of American Associa-tion for Marriage and Family Therapy.*

Mueller, G. & Moskau. G. (1995, Aug.). Interview with B. J. Brothers.

Murphy, B. (1993). Conversation with D. Dreher.

Myers-Pelton, L. (1989). In *Tiospaye Network Newsletter,* Virginia Satir memorial issue (Sum.). Sioux Falls, SD: Tiospaye Network (209 South Spring Avenue; 57104).

Nemetschek, P. (1982). In J. K. Zeig, *Ericksonian approaches to hypnosis and psychotherapy.* New York: Brunner/Mazel.

Pagenkopf, Ray (1992, Jul.). Interview with B. J. Brothers.

Pagenkopf, Russell (1994). Interview with B. J. Brothers.

Pascoe, W. (1997, Apr.). Telephone conversation with B. J. Brothers.

Perls, F. S. (1969). *In and out the garbage pail.* Lafayette, CA: Real People Press.

Podesta, R., Jr. (1993). Interview with D. Dreher.

Progoff, I. (1975). *At a journal workshop.* New York: Dialogue House Library.

Relatives of Virginia Satir (1992). Interview with B. J. Brothers, in Milwaukee, WI.

Rock, L. (1993). Conversation with D. Dreher.

Rosenstein, N. (1990). *The unbroken chain.* New York: CIS Publishers.

Sager, C. J. (1976). *Marriage contracts and couples therapy: Hidden forces in intimate relationships.* New York: Brunner/Mazel.

Saint-Exupery, A. (1943). *The little prince.* New York: Har-court, Brace.

Satir, V. (1950). Letter from Lewis Leftkowitz. Santa Barbara, CA: Virginia Satir Archives, Special Collection, Davison Library, University of California.

Satir, V. (1967). *Conjoint family therapy.* (Published in 1983 in its third edition.) Palo Alto, CA: Science and Beha-vior Books.

Satir, V. (1968). Presentation at a workshop for the National Association of Social Workers, Southern Regional Institute, Biloxi, MI.

Satir, V. (1971). Personal communication with Barbara Jo Brothers.

Satir, V. (1972a). *Peoplemaking.* (Revised in 1988 as *The new peoplemaking.*) Palo Alto, CA: Science and Behavior Books.

Satir, V. (1972b). Presentation at the University of Manitoba. Videotape produced by Carter Irwin. Palo Alto, CA: Science and Behavior Books.

Satir, V. (1972c). Presentation at a seminar on Aruba. (Cassette recording 3.) Falls Church, VA: Lori Gordon, PAIRS Foundation, 3705 South George Mason Drive, #C35, 22041).

Satir, V. (1973). Conversation with B. J. Brothers.

Satir, V. (1974). *Differentiation and integration in families.* Presentation at the Northshore Conference, on Long Island, NY.

Satir, V. (1975). *Self-esteem.* Millbrae, CA: Celestial Arts.

Satir, V. (1976). The five freedoms. In *Making Contact.* Millbrae, CA: Celestial Arts.

Satir, V. (1977a) University for being more human. Draft of letter to sponsors. Santa Barbara, CA: Virginia Satir Archives, Special Collection, Davison Library, University of California.

Satir, V. (1977b). What's in the pot?, 1(Spr.):2. Newsletter of the International Human Learning Resources Network.

Satir, V. (1978). *Your many faces.* Millbrae, CA: Celestial Arts.

Satir, V. (1981). First process community, in Park City, Utah. Unpublished transcript by Mary Jo Bulbrook (413 Waterside Drive, Carboro, NC 27510).

Satir, V. (1983). Presentation at Avanta Process Community III, in Crested Butte, CO.

Satir, V. (1984a). Conversation with B. J. Brothers.

Satir, V. (1984b). *Master series videotapes on intimate relationship skills.* Falls Church, VA: PAIRS Foundation.

Satir, V. (1985a). Foreword in E. McCann & D. Shannon, *The two step*. New York: Grove Press.

Satir, V. (1985b, Mar.). Interview by Sheldon Starr. Santa Barbara, CA: Virginia Satir Archives, Special Collection, Davison Library, University of California.

Satir, V. (1985a). Foreword in E. McCann & D. Shannon, *The two step*. New York: Grove Press.

Satir, V. (1986a). *Families and relationships* (series of seven videotapes). Boulder, CO: NLP Comprehensive (attn.: Steve Andreas, 2897 Valmont Road, 80301).

Satir, V. (1986b). Audiotaped presentations at Avanta Process Community VI, Module I, in Crested Butte, CO. (Blue Moon Cassettes, recordings 1, 12, and 18.) Santa Barbara, CA: Virginia Satir Archives, Special Collec-tion, Davison Library, University of California.

Satir, V. (1987a). The therapist story. In V. Satir & M. Baldwin (Eds.), *The use of self in therapy* (pp. 24–25). Binghamton, NY: Haworth Press.

Satir, V. (1987b). Audiotaped presentations at Avanta Process Community VII, Module I, in Crested Butte, CO. (Blue Moon Cassettes, recordings 1, 7 and 11.) Santa Barbara, CA: Virginia Satir Archives, Special Collection, Davison Library, University of California.

Satir, V. (1987c). Telephone conversation with B. J. Brothers.

Satir, V. (1988a). *The new peoplemaking*. Palo Alto, CA: Science and Behavior Books.

Satir, V. (1988b, Mar.). Conversation with B. J. Brothers.

Satir, V. (1988c, Aug.). Conversation with B. J. Brothers.

Satir, V. (1988d). Letter to Russell Pagenkopf. Excerpted in the *Avanta Network Newsletter*, p. 1.

Satir, V. (1992). Prevention: Changing our whole culture: An interview with Virginia Satir: Part V. In B. J. Brothers (Ed.), *Peace, war, and mental health: Couples therapists look at the dynamics* (pp. 7–12). Binghamton, NY: Haworth Press.

Satir, V., & Baldwin, M. (1983). *Satir step by step.* Palo Alto, CA: Science and Behavior Books.

Satir, V., & Baldwin, M. (Eds.) (1987). The u*se of self in therapy.* Binghamton, NY: Haworth Press.

Satir, V., Bandler, R., & Grinder, J. (1976). *Changing with families.* Palo Alto, CA: Science and Behavior Books.

Satir, V., and Banmen, J. (1983). *Virginia Satir verbatim 1984.* (Transcript of the 1983 Process Community III in Crested Butte, CO). North Delta, BC, Canada: Delta Psychological Services (11213 Canyon Crescent, V4E2R6).

Satir, V., Banmen, J., Gerber, J. & Gomori, M. (1991). *The Satir model: Family therapy and beyond.* Palo Alto, CA: Science and Behavior Books.

Satir, V., & Simon, R. (1989). Reaching out to life. *Family Therapy Networker, 13* (Jan./Feb.).

Satir, V., Stachowiak, J., and Taschman, H. (1975). *Helping families to change.* New York: Jason Aronson.

Saunders, M. (1993). Conversation with Diane Dreher.

Schwab, J., Baldwin, M., Gerber, J., Gomori, M, and Satir, V. (1989). *The Satir approach to communication: A work-shop manual.* Palo Alto, CA: Science and Behavior Books.

Schwariess, S. (1994, Aug.). Interview with B. J. Brothers.

Shakespeare, W. (1949). *Merchant of Venice,* Act IV, Scene I. In *The complete works of William Shakespeare* (p. 222). New York: Books, Inc.

Sharfman, I. H. (1977). Citing the *Gonzales Weekly Inquirer* (Jun. 22, 1878 and Jul. 19, 1923), in *Jews on the frontier.* Chicago, IL: Henry Regnery Company. [That Gonzales weekly ran two installments of an article, "Early Days in Texas," which was a biographical memoir of David Kokernot.]

Smith, L. (1978). *The mother book.* Garden City, NY: Doubleday.

Starr, S. (1985). An interview with Virginia Satir. (Available from Sheldon Starr, Ph.D., 686 Maybell, Palo Alto, CA 94306.)

Starr, S. (1992). Prevention: Changing our whole culture: An interview with Virginia Satir. In B. J. Brothers (Ed.), *Peace, war, and mental health: Couples therapists look at the dynamics* (pp. 7–12). Binghamton, NY: Haworth Press.

Starr, S. (1993, Jun.). Interview with B. J. Brothers.

Steiner, C. (1990). *The scripts people live.* New York: Grove/ Atlantic.

Sweeney, V. (1992). Interview with B. J. Brothers.

Teilhard de Chardin, P. (1962). *Letters from a traveler.* New York: Harper & Row.

Teilhard de Chardin, P. (1963). *Activation of energy.* New York: Harcourt Brace Jovanovich.

Toward an ADEPT California (1992). California State Assembly report.

Turner, L. (1998). *The impact of a psychoeducational group intervention on marital discord, adult interaction style, projective identification and perceptive identification.* Unpublished doctoral dissertation, Catholic University of America, Washington, DC.

Turpin, R. (1994). Interview with B. J. Brothers.

Vasconcellos, J. (1979). *A liberating vision.* San Luis Obispo: Impzct Publishers.

Vasconcellos, J. (1982). New human agenda (newsletter).

Vasconcellos, J. (1985). Notes from a dinner discussion at Flea Street Café.

Vasconcellos, J. (1987). Carl Rogers eulogy.

Vasconcellos, J. (1988). *Farewell, Virginia.* Eulogy for Virginia Satir.

Vasconcellos, J. (1993). Conversation with D. Dreher.

de Waal, Frans (1989). *Peacemaking Among Primates.* Cambridge, MA: Harvard University Press.

Weeks, M. (1974). Interview with Virginia Satir. Cited in Myer-Pelton (1989), *Tiospaye Network Newsletter.* [Marjorie Weeks is the editor of *What's in the Pot?,* the newsletter of the International Human Resources Learning Network.]

Winnipeg Tribune (1972a, Aug. 5). Integrated services urged. Winnipeg, MB, Canada: Winnipeg Free Press Library (1355 Mountain Ave.; R2X 3B6).

Winnipeg Tribune (1972b, Aug. 8). Total-care centres her dream. Winnipeg, MB, Canada: Winnipeg Free Press Library (1355 Mountain Ave.; R2X 3B6).

Index